Beginning theory

D1216387

MANCHESTER
1824

Manchester University Press

Beginnings
Series editors: Peter Barry and John McLeod

'**Beginnings**' is a series of books designed to give practical help to students beginning to tackle recent developments in English, Literary Studies and Cultural Studies. The books in the series

- demonstrate and encourage a questioning engagement with the new;
- give essential information about the context and history of each topic covered;
- show how to develop a practice which is up-to-date and informed by theory.

Each book focuses uncompromisingly upon the needs of its readers, who have the right to expect lucidity and clarity to be the distinctive feature of a book which includes the word 'beginning' in its title.

Each aims to lay a firm foundation of well understood initial principles as a basis for further study and is committed to explaining new aspects of the discipline without over-simplification, but in a manner appropriate to the needs of beginners.

Each book, finally, aims to be both an introduction and a contribution to the topic area it discusses.

Beginning theory

An introduction to literary and cultural theory

Fourth edition

Peter Barry

Manchester University Press

The publisher has no responsibility for the persistence or accuracy of URLs for
any external or third-party internet websites referred to in this book, and does not
guarantee that any content on such websites is, or will remain, accurate or
appropriate.

First edition published 1995, reprinted nine times.
Second edition published 2002, reprinted seven times.
Third edition published 2009, reprinted seven times.

Published by Manchester University Press
Altrincham Street, Manchester M1 7JA, UK

www.manchesteruniversitypress.co.uk

British Library Cataloguing-in-Publication Data is available

ISBN 978 1 5261 2179 0 paperback

This edition first published 2017

20 19 18 17   10 9 8 7 6 5 4 3 2 1

Printed in Great Britain
by Bell & Bain Ltd, Glasgow

Contents

Acknowledgements

You'd better not look down
If you want to keep flying
                        B. B. King

Those words have opened this book from the start, and I haven't the heart to remove them now, when they are more applicable than ever.

I am no less grateful than before to all my friends and colleagues at the institutions I have taught at – East Sussex College of Higher Education, now Brighton University; Avery Hill College, now Greenwich University; LSU College, Southampton; and Aberystwyth University.

I am equally grateful to my students at those places, who taught me how to teach, as good students do, and, more especially, how to teach theory.

Over the years, many students and lecturers have emailed with informative, instructive, corrective, appreciative, and amusing comments about the book, and I hope they will continue to do so: I can be contacted at ptb@aber.ac.uk.

Special thanks are due to my editor, Matthew Frost, at Manchester University Press, and to Andrew Kirk for his expert proofreading of the fourth edition.

The book is for my brother Gerard Barry and family, brother-in-law Terry Walker and family, and in memory of my sister Maureen Walker, sisters-in-law Angela Barry and Anne Taylor, and my parents Frank and May Barry.

And for Marianne and Tom, as always.

                        Peter Barry, Llanbadarn Fawr, Aberystwyth

Preface to the fourth edition

Some years ago I opened a talk on teaching literary theory with this statement: 'There are many ways of teaching literary theory. The problem is that none of them work.'[1] All teachers of literary theory have that feeling from time to time, and all we can do in response is try to think up better explanations and attach better examples to them. A new edition is another chance to fail better at teaching literary theory. It is nearly a quarter of a century since this book first appeared, and my own views on theory have, of course, shifted in that period. I am especially aware of an accelerated shift since the early 2000s. For much of this period I taught a session at the annual Literary Theory Day at Rewley House, Oxford, applying three or four theories to a different short literary text each year. My feelings about theorised readings of literary texts remind me now of watching the pre-millennial eclipse at Southsea in Hampshire with eight-year-old Tom in 1999. I kept thinking that theory often eclipses the text, just as the moon's shadow obscures the sun in an eclipse, so that the text loses its own voice and begins to voice theory. Thus, the text is proved by theory to be riddled with deconstructive cul-de-sacs (see Chapter 3), or an enactment of the Oedipus Complex (Chapter 5), or an embodiment of Althusserian repressive structures (Chapter 8). That's how it was, at least, when theory was at its zenith during the 1980s and 1990s. When the literary text met the cutting edge of theory, it got turned over by the blade, like a ploughed

1 'The "Good Science" Approach to Teaching Literary Theory', *English Association Bulletin*, 174 (autumn/winter 2003), pp. 1–3.

field. The outcome of all these encounters was the same – it was an endless parade of triumphant theoretical mastery.

One of the literary texts I used to show how theory 'tackled textuality', as I called it, was a poem called 'To the Man After the Harrow', by the Irish poet Patrick Kavanagh (1904–67). In the final stanza, the poet urges the ploughman to drive on regardless, ignoring the wildlife which may be harmed by the blade of the plough:

> Forget the worm's opinion too
> Of hooves and pointed harrow-pins,
> For you are driving your horses through
> The mist where Genesis begins.

What I began to emphasise, in talking about theory, was not the macho 'cutting edge' of theory, but the soft-edged mist of uncertainty, which Kavanagh unforgettably calls 'The mist where Genesis begins'. Ideas begin in a mist, in a place where we cannot be sure what we are getting into. The mist is the moment of potential, when we have lost sight of our usual landmarks and the mind is in a receptive state – John Keats called it 'negative capability' – it is the good and fertile state of not quite knowing. So I began saying that when theory meets text, we are not looking for a confident re-shaping of the literary text with the blade of theory, but for a more tentative and patient groping about in the mist – an acceptance, in other words, of how uncertain the outcome usually is when theory meets text. I tried to encapsulate it in a soundbite, and what emerged was 'When the irresistible force of theory meets the immovable object of the text, something has to give.' Sometimes the sophistication of the theory exposes the limitations of the text, and sometimes the sophistication of the text exposes the limitations of the theory. This thought, which took me several years to formulate (to think, even), felt liberating and revolutionary, and after it, everything was different. For me this was where Theory 1.0 became Theory 2.0.

One characteristic of the world of Theory 2.0 is a keen awareness of the particularity of the individual literary text (see Chapter 15 on new aestheticism). The text doesn't have a 'grain', in the sense of lines that all run predictably in the same direction, lines that we have merely to push against with our newly acquired theories. On the contrary, texts often have energies that run in all sorts of directions, crossing and contradicting and arguing with themselves. All that messy, sticky particularity is what makes it literature. It's the same with theories: what makes them interesting is not their magisterial certainty and consistency, but their blind spots, the corners they cut, their blurry edges, and their constant, and often conflicting, reformulations. These are the attributes that make them worth spending time on – reading them, thinking about them, arguing about them, talking back to them, and trying to make them into a practice of some kind. By 'a practice' I mean a way of trying to make things better. What things? Well, the world we live in, the way we think about each other, the way we live both our collective and our individual lives. Increasingly, I value theories and approaches that have open intellectual borders, fewer over-adulated superstars, and ideas which do not have the effect of ironing literary texts into theory–compliant flatness. In this book, that is the kind of approach I recommend and speak for. I believe that theory asks the right questions (a huge achievement), and that, at its most useful, it wants to engage us, not in a conversion, but in a conversation.

Aberystwyth, March 2017

Introduction

About this book

The high-water mark of literary theory occurred in the 1980s. That decade was the 'moment' of theory, when the topic was fashionable and controversial. By the 1990s there was already a steady flow of books and articles with titles like *After Theory* (Thomas Docherty, 1990) or 'Post-Theory' (Nicolas Tredell, in *The Critical Decade*, 1993). As such titles suggest, the 'moment of theory' had probably passed. Twenty years on from then, the publication of 'afters' continues, with Nicholas Birns's *Theory After Theory: An Intellectual History of Literary Theory from 1950 to the Early 21st Century* (Broadview Press, 2010), Jane Elliott and Derek Attridge's edited collection of essays *Theory After Theory* (Routledge, 2011), and Judith Ryan's *The Novel After Theory* (Columbia University Press, 2014). See also the books mentioned later at the start of Chapter 15. So why another updated 'primer' of theory so late in the day?

The simple answer is that after the moment of theory there comes, inevitably, the 'hour' of theory, when it ceases to be the exclusive concern of a dedicated minority and enters the intellectual bloodstream as a taken-for-granted aspect of the curriculum. At this stage the glamour fades, the charisma is 'routinised', and it becomes the day-to-day business of quite a large number of people to learn or teach (or both) this material. There are evident dangers of oversimplifying things and so offering a false reassurance to students facing the difficulties of this topic for the first time. All the same, the main responsibility of anyone attempting a book like this one is to meet the demand for clear explanation and demonstration. If the task were impossible, and the mountain of theory could be climbed only by experts, then the whole enterprise of establishing it on undergraduate courses would have been a mistake.

The emphasis on practice means that this is a 'work-book', not just a 'text-book'. As you read you will find suggested activities, headed 'STOP and THINK', which are designed to give you some 'hands-on' experience of literary theory and its problems. You will not just be reading about it, reducing theory to a kind of spectator sport played only by superstars, but starting to do it for yourself. Becoming a participant in this way will help you to make *some* personal sense of theory, and will, I hope, increase your confidence, even if you suspect that your practical efforts remain fairly rudimentary. It is also hoped that the 'STOP and THINK' activities will provide the basis for initiating seminar discussion if this book is being used in connection with a taught course on critical theory.

All the critical approaches described in this book are a reaction against something which went before, and a prior knowledge of these things cannot be assumed. Hence, I start with an account of the 'liberal humanism' against which all these newer critical approaches, broadly speaking, define themselves.

There is a problem concerning how to label the older ways of doing literary studies that were challenged in the 1970s and 1980s by the arrival on the scene of the theoretical developments described in this book. One solution is to use a generalised phrase like 'older approaches to literary study', or 'traditional ways of discussing literature'. But the vagueness of descriptors like these is troubling, and it is never safe to assume that everyone understands such terms in the same way. Until around 2000 the term 'liberal humanism' was widely current in the UK, and the equivalent term 'formalism' similarly so in the USA. It was, and is, convenient to have a simple 'ism' name to use as a handle, but it is also important to have such a label, because the label's very existence asserts the vital point that no ways of studying literature are 'theory-free', for all of them stem from a set of assumptions, or principles, or foundational assertions, even (and especially) when these are seldom made explicit. So I have continued in this fourth edition to use the term 'liberal humanism', and have formally set out (in the section of Chapter 1 called 'Ten tenets of liberal humanism') what I think are its underlying assumptions. Classes and their tutors will want to challenge or supplement this list, of course, but I would be surprised if many believed that there is any untheorised way of studying literature. That is precisely the point which is made by using an 'ism' label to designate the most traditional approaches.

The currently successful versions of Marxist, feminist, psycho-analytic, and linguistic criticism also all define themselves against earlier versions of each of these, and therefore I try in each case to explain the earlier versions first. I think that many of the current difficulties students have with theory arise from trying to miss out this stage. My approach amounts to throwing you in at the shallow end. Potentially this is more painful than being thrown in at the deep end – the technique used in most other student introductions to literary theory – but it does reduce the risk of drowning.

It should, perhaps, be stressed that most of the other general introductions to theory that are now available are different from this one. They offer an even and comprehensive coverage of the entire field, often with relatively little in the way of sustained practical discussion of applications. I find some of them very useful, but they seem to me to be recapitulations of literary theory, often from a viewpoint more philosophical than literary, rather than introductions to it. The evenness of the coverage means that the pace never varies, so that there is no opportunity to stop and dwell upon an example in a reflective way. By contrast, I haven't tried to be comprehensive, and I do try to provide variation in pace by selecting questions, or examples, or key essays for closer treatment.

At undergraduate level the main problem is to decide how much theory can reasonably be handled by beginners. Time is not unlimited, and there is a need to think about a realistic syllabus rather than an ideal one. Theorists, like novelists, are dauntingly plentiful, and the subject of theory cannot succeed in lecture rooms and seminars unless we fashion it into a student-centred syllabus. We are rightly dismissive these days of the notion of teaching a 'Great Tradition' of key novelists, as advocated by the critic F. R. Leavis. But Leavis's Great Tradition was essentially a syllabus, manageable within a year-long undergraduate course on the novel. It is possible to read and adequately discuss a novel or two by Austen, Eliot, James,

Conrad, and Lawrence within that time. We need to make sure that what is presented as theory today makes sense as a sequence of learning and teaching.

When we are about to move into something new it is sensible to first take stock of what we already have, if only so that the distance travelled can later be measured. So in the first chapter of this book I invite you to look back critically and reflectively on your previous training in literary studies. We then go on to look at the assumptions behind traditional literary criticism, or 'liberal humanism' as theorists usually call it.

The term 'liberal humanism' became current in the 1970s, as a shorthand (and mainly hostile) way of referring to the kind of criticism which held sway before theory. The word 'liberal' in this formulation roughly means not politically radical, and hence generally evasive and non-committal on political issues. 'Humanism' implies something similar; it suggests a range of negative attributes, such as 'non-Marxist' and 'non-feminist', and 'non-theoretical'. There is also the implication that liberal humanists believe in 'human nature' as something fixed and constant which great literature expresses. Liberal humanists did not (and do not, as a rule) use this name of themselves, but, says an influential school of thought, if you practise literary criticism and do not call yourself a Marxist critic, or a structuralist, or a stylistician, or some such, then you are probably a liberal humanist, whether or not you admit or recognise this.

In the course of explaining some of the major critical ideas now current, this book provides summaries or descriptions of a number of important theoretical essays. But I want to stress at the outset that it is important, too, that you read some of the major theorists at first hand. Yet as soon as you begin to turn the pages of Barthes, Butler, Foucault, or Derrida you will encounter writing which looks dauntingly difficult and off-putting. How, then, to cope?

I suggest that it is much better to read *intensely* in theory than to read *widely*. By this I mean that you will gain little from reading chapter after chapter of a book that is making little sense to you. You will gain much more by using the same amount of reading time to read one crucial and frequently mentioned chapter or article several times for yourself. Having a detailed knowledge of what is actually said in the pages of a well-known argument, being aware

of how the argument unfolds and how it is qualified or contextualised, will be far more useful to you than a superficial overall impression gained from commentaries or from desperate skim-reading.
However daunting the material, you have to make your reading
meditative, reflective, and personal. Try to become a slow reader.
Further, some intensive reading of this kind will enable you to quote
lines other than the handful that are cited in all the commentaries. And most importantly, your view of things will be your own,
perhaps quirky and incomplete, but at least not just the echo and
residue of some published commentator's prepacked version. In
a nut-shell, intensive reading is often more useful than extensive
reading. English studies is founded on the notion of close reading, and while there was a period in the late 1970s and early 1980s
when this approach was frequently disparaged, it is undoubtedly
true that nothing of any interest can happen in this subject without
close reading.

I suggest, therefore, that you try out for yourself a useful form
of intensive reading, the technique known as 'SQ3R'. This breaks
down the reading of a difficult chapter or article into five stages, as
designated by the letters 'SQRRR', or 'SQ3R', as is it usually given.
The five stages are:

S – That is, *Survey* the whole chapter or section fairly rapidly,
      skimming through it to get a rough sense of the scope and
      nature of the argument. Remember that information is not
      evenly spread throughout a text. It tends to be concentrated
      in the opening and closing paragraphs (where you often get
      useful summaries of the whole), and the 'hinge points' of the
      argument are often indicated in the opening and closing
      sentences of paragraphs.

Q – Having skimmed the whole, set yourself some *Questions*,
      some things you hope to find out from what you are reading.
      This makes you an 'active' reader rather than a passive one,
      and gives your reading a purpose.

R1 – Now *Read* the whole piece. Use a pencil if the copy is your
      own to underline key points, query difficulties, circle phrases
      worth remembering, and so on. Don't just sit in front of the
      pages. If the book is not your own jot *something* down on
      paper as you read, however minimal.

R2 – Now, close the book and *Recall* what you have read. Jot down
      some summary points. Ask whether your starting questions
      have been answered, or at least clarified. Spell out some of the
      difficulties that remain. In this way, you record some concrete
      outcomes to your reading, so that your time doesn't simply
      evaporate uselessly once the book is closed.

R3 – This final stage is the *Review*. It happens after an interval has
      elapsed since the reading. You can experiment, but initially
      try doing it the following day. Without opening the book
      again, or referring back to your notes, review what you have
      gained from the reading; remind yourself of the question
      you set yourself, the points you jotted down at the *Recall*
      stage, and any important phrases from the essay. If this pro-
      duces very little, then refer back to your notes. If they make
      little sense, then repeat the *Survey* stage, and do an acceler-
      ated *Read*, by reading the first and last paragraphs of the
      essay, and skim-reading the main body assisted by your pen-
      cilled markings.

You may well have evolved a study technique something like this
already. It is really just common sense. But it will help to ensure that
you gain *something* from a theoretical text, no matter how initially
forbidding it might be.

Finally, it will, I hope, go without saying that no comprehensive-
ness is possible in a book such as this. Clearly, also, this book does
not contain all you need to know about theory, and it does not in
itself (without the reading it refers you to) constitute a 'course' in
literary theory. It leaves out a good deal, and it deals fairly briskly
with many topics. It is a starter-pack, intended to give you a sense
of what theory is all about, and suggest how it might affect your
literary studies. Above all, it aims to *interest* you in theory.

Approaching theory

If you are coming to literary theory soon after taking courses in
such subjects as media studies, communications studies, or socio-
linguistics, then the general 'feel' of the newer theoretical approaches
to literature may well seem familiar. You will already be 'tuned in' to
the emphasis on ideas which is one of their characteristics; you will

be undaunted by their use of technical terminology, and unsurprised by their strong social and political interests. If, on the other hand, you took a 'straight' 'A' Level, Higher, 'Access,' or High School literature course with the major emphasis on set books, then much of what is contained in this book will probably be new to you. Initially, you will have the problem of getting on the wave-length of these different ways of looking at literature. As you would expect in studying at degree level, you will encounter problems which do not have generally agreed solutions, and it is inevitable that your understanding of the matters discussed here will remain partial, in both senses of that word, as everybody's does.

But whichever of these two categories you fall into, I want to assure you at the outset that the doubts and uncertainties you will have about this material are probably *not* due to:

1. any supposed mental incapacity of your own, for example, to your not having 'a philosophical mind', or not possessing the kind of X-ray intellect which can penetrate jargon and see the sense beneath, or
2. the fact that your schooling did not include intensive tuition in, say, linguistics or philosophy, or
3. the innate and irreducible difficulty of the material itself (a point we will come back to).

Rather, nearly all the difficulties you will have will be the direct result of the way theory is written, and the way it is written about. For literary theory, it must be emphasised, is not innately difficult. There are very few inherently complex ideas in existence in literary theory. On the contrary, the whole body of work known collectively as 'theory' is based upon some dozen or so ideas, none of which are in themselves difficult. (Some of them are listed on pp. 36–8.) What *is* difficult, however, is the language of theory. Many of the major writers on theory write in French, so that much of what we read is in translation, sometimes of a rather clumsy kind. Being a Romance language, French takes most of its words directly from Latin, and it lacks the reassuring Anglo-Saxon layer of vocabulary which provides us with so many of our brief, familiar, everyday terms. Hence, a close English translation of a French academic text will contain a large number of longer Latinate words, always perceived as a source of difficulty by English-speaking readers. Writing with a high proportion of these characteristics can be off-putting and wearying, and it *is* easy to lose patience.

But the frame of mind I would recommend at the outset is threefold. *Firstly*, we must have some *initial* patience with the difficult surface of the writing. We must avoid the too-ready conclusion that literary theory is just meaningless, pretentious jargon (that is, that the theory is at fault). *Secondly*, on the other hand, we must, for obvious reasons, resist the view that we ourselves are intellectually incapable of coping with it (that is, that we are at fault). *Thirdly*, and crucially, we must not assume that the difficulty of theoretical writing is *always* the dress of profound ideas – only that it *might* sometimes be, which leaves the onus of discrimination on us. To sum up this attitude: we are looking, in literary theory, for something we can use, not something which will use us. We ought not to issue theory with a blank cheque to spend our time for us. (If we do, it will certainly spend more than we can afford.) Do not, then, be *endlessly* patient with theory. Require it to be clear, and expect it, in the longer term, to deliver something solid. Don't be content, as many seem to be, just to see it as 'challenging' conventional practice or 'putting it in question' in some never quite specified way. Challenges are fine, but they have to amount to something in the end.

STOP and THINK: *reviewing your study of literature to date*

Before we go on, into what may well be a new stage in your involvement with literature, it would be sensible to 'take stock' and reflect a little on the nature of our literary education to date. The purpose of doing this is to begin the process of making visible, and hence open to scrutiny, the methods and procedures which have become so familar to you (probably going back to the time when you began secondary school) that they are no longer visible at all as a distinct intellectual practice. But stock-taking is not part of our normal intellectual routine, unfortunately, and it is a difficult and demanding thing to do. Yet please do not skip this section, since theory will never make any sense to you until you feel the need for it yourself. What I would like you to do is to try to become conscious of the nature of your own previous work in English, by recalling:

1. what first made you decide to study English, what you hoped to gain from doing so, and whether that hope was realised;
2. which books and authors were chosen for study and what they had in common;
3. which books and authors now seem conspicuously absent;
4. what, in general terms, your previous study taught you (about 'life', say, or conduct, or about literature itself).

Doing this will help you to begin to obtain a perspective on your experience of literature to date. Spend an hour or so doing it. I carried out a similar exercise myself as part of the process of working on this book, and some of the result is given below. It is intended more as a prompt than a model, and I have not responded in any systematic way to the four questions above. Reproducing it will perhaps help to 'personalise' the voice behind this book, but I leave you to decide whether you want to look at this before or after doing your own.

My own 'stock-taking'

Since literary theory is the topic of this book I will concentrate on detailing the course of my acquaintanceship with it. In fact, I heard nothing at all about literary theory as an undergraduate at London University in the late 1960s. I took a straightforward 'Wulf-to-Woolf' English course (*Beowulf* to Virgina Woolf) with compulsory Old and Middle English papers. Essentially, I now realise, the English course I followed in the late 1960s retained the shape and the outlook of the pioneer English degree courses established at London University more than a century before.

The one innovation in English teaching at London was to recognise the existence of something called American literature and to appoint a lecturer to teach it. The lecturer was Eric Mottram, who died in January 1995.[1] As a result of taking this American course I

1 I wrote in detail about Eric as critic and teacher in Chapter 7 of my book *Poetry Wars: British Poetry of the 1970s and the Battle of Earls Court* (Salt Publishing, 2006).

became an enthusiast for a range of American poets who were part of the 'alternative culture' of the time. At the same time, and for several years afterwards, I was also trying to write poetry of more or less this kind. It quickly became apparent that conventional criticism could make very little of poetry like this. So by the early 1970s I was beginning to look at newer critical approaches than those I had encountered at university. But I wasn't at that time an advocate of literary theory, since 'theory' as such was then a non-existent category in literary studies.

The change of emphasis seems to have happened in my own case around 1973, when the words 'structuralism' and 'semiotics' begin to feature in notes about what I was reading and in the titles of the books and articles I was interested in. Structuralism, we were then learning, was a new kind of literary theory which had recently become prominent in France, and semiotics ('the science of signs') was one of its sub-branches. I was loosely connected with the London Graduate Seminar started by Frank Kermode after he became Professor of English at University College, London. The group debated the work of the structuralist Roland Barthes and caught Kermode's enthusiasm for it. I bought and read everything by Barthes then in print in England, no great undertaking since all that was available was *Writing Degree Zero* and *Elements of Semiology*, probably his least interesting and least accessible books. His much more engaging collection *Mythologies* appeared in English in 1973 in the Paladin imprint. 1973 was also the year when *The Times Literary Supplement* devoted the major part of two issues (5 and 12 October) to a 'Survey of Semiotics', with articles by Umberto Eco, Tzvetan Todorov, and Julia Kristeva, major names in these new kinds of critical theory and encountered then (in my case) for the first time. This interest in theory was consolidated in 1981 when I was asked to devise a course on literary theory as part of the BA programme at my previous college, and, in turn, a decade or so of teaching that course led to this book. So far as I am aware, this course, at LSU College of Higher Education, Southampton, was the first undergraduate literary theory course to be taught in Britain.

1
Theory before 'theory'

The history of English studies

It is difficult to understand the basics of the traditional approach to English studies without knowing something about how English developed as an academic subject. So this is the topic of the next few pages.

STOP and THINK

The multiple choice questions below indicate the scope of what is touched upon in this section. Underline what you think are the right answers before reading further, and then correct your answers, if necessary, as you read on:

1. When do you think English was first taught as a degree subject in England? Was it 1428, 1528, 1628, 1728, 1828, or 1928?
2. At which institution was English first taught as a degree subject in England? Was it Oxford University, Cambridge University, London University, Southampton University, or none of these?
3. Until the nineteenth century you had to be a member of the Anglican (Episcopalian) Church and male to take a degree in England. True or false?
4. Until the nineteenth century lecturers on degree courses in England had to be unmarried Church of England clergy. True or false?

5. Until the nineteenth century women were not allowed to
    take degrees in England. True or false?
6. In the early twentieth century women could take degree
    courses in England, but were not allowed to receive
    degrees. True or false?

To explain the rise of English studies we need to indicate briefly
what higher education was like in England until the first quarter of
the nineteenth century. The short answer is that it was a Church of
England monopoly. There were only two universities, Oxford and
Cambridge. These were divided into small individual colleges which
were run like monastic institutions. Only men could attend them,
of course, and students had to be Anglican communicants and
attend the college chapel. The teachers were ordained ministers,
who had to be unmarried, so that they could live in the college. The
subjects available were the classics (ancient Greek and Latin literature), divinity (which was taken by those seeking ordination) and
mathematics. Anyone who was Catholic, Jewish, Methodist, or atheist was barred from entry, and hence, in effect, barred from the professions and the Civil Service. As far as higher education was
concerned, then, you could say that right up to the 1820s, it had not
changed since the Middle Ages.

Many attempts were made to reform the situation, expand higher
education, and introduce practical subjects into the curriculum, but
they all came up against entrenched conservative forces. The break-
though came in 1826 when a University College was founded in
London with a charter to award degrees to men of all religions or
none. From 1828 English was offered as a subject for study, and they
appointed the first Professor of English in 1829. However, it was not
really as we know it. It was mainly the study of English language,
merely using literature as a source of linguistic examples. English
literature as such was first taught at King's College, London
(another college of what later became London University) beginning in 1831.

Girton College, Cambridge, opened in 1869, and Newnham Hall
(later Newnham College) at the same university in 1875, both for
women. But women (as at Oxford from the late 1870s), though they

could attend lectures and take exams, could not receive actual degrees until 1920 (at Oxford) and, incredible though it now seems, 1948 (at Cambridge), so women at Oxbridge only became full members of their universities in the twentieth century. At London, Bedford College (for women) in Bedford Square was founded in 1849, and women could take degree exams and receive actual degrees from 1879, so London University was ahead of Oxbridge. Edith Morley (1875–1964) was the first female professor in England – she was appointed to a Chair in English Language at Reading University in 1908. The United States was ahead of Britain: the institution now called Wesleyan College, in Georgia, was founded in 1839 as the first college in the world chartered to award bachelor's degrees to women. In 1850 Lucy Sessions, graduating with a literary degree from Oberlin College, Ohio, was the first black woman in the USA to receive a college degree.

In 1840 F. D. Maurice was appointed Professor at King's. He introduced the study of set books, and his inaugural lecture lays down some of the founding principles of literary study; the study of English literature would serve 'to emancipate us … from the notions and habits which are peculiar to our own age', connecting us instead with 'what is fixed and enduring'. Maurice regarded literature as the particular property of the middle class and the expression of their values. For him the middle class represents the essence of Englishness (the aristocracy are part of an international elite, and the poor need to give all their attention to ensuring mere survival) so middle-class education should be specifically English, and therefore should centre on English literature. Maurice was well aware of the political dimension of all this. People so educated would feel that they belonged to England, that they had a country. 'Political agitators' may ask what this can mean 'when his neighbour rides in a carriage and he walks on foot', but 'he will feel his nationality to be a reality, in spite of what they say'. In short, learning English will give people a stake in maintaining the political *status quo* without any redistribution of wealth.

You can see from this that the study of English literature is being seen as a kind of substitute for religion. It was well known that attendance at church below middle-class level was very patchy. The worry was that the lower classes would feel that they had no stake in the country and, having no religion to teach them morality and restraint, they would rebel and something like the French Revolution would take place. The Chartist agitation of the 1830s for the extension of voting rights to all adult males was thought to be the start of this, and the first English courses were put in place at exactly the same time.

The conventional reading of the origins of the subject of English is that this kind of thinking (that is, seeing secular, vernacular culture as a substitute for the socially cohesive effect of religion) begins with Matthew Arnold in the 1850s and reaches its height with the publication of the Newbolt Report on the Teaching of English in England in 1921. It is evident from material like Maurice's inaugural lecture that this was happening much earlier. However, I do not accept the simplistic view that the founders of English were motiviated merely by a desire for ideological control. This was undoubtedly one of their motives, but the reality was much more complicated. There was, behind the teaching of early English, a distinctly Victorian mixture of class guilt about social inequalities, a genuine desire to improve things for everybody, a kind of missionary zeal to spread culture and enlightenment, and a self-interested desire to maintain social stability.

London University degrees were taught by external licence at university colleges in major industrial cities – Liverpool, Birmingham, Manchester, Sheffield, Leeds, and so on, all these places eventually becoming major universities in their own right. Hence the spread of the subject at degree level throughout the country. However, Oxford and Cambridge were suspicious of the new subject of English and held out against it, Oxford until 1894 and Cambridge until 1911.

In the last quarter of the nineteenth century there was vigorous discussion and campaigning to establish a Chair in English at Oxford. In 1887 the first attempt was defeated largely because of a speech in the Convocation by the Professor of History, Edward Freeman. Freeman's speech is another key document: it touches upon several problems in English which are still unresolved. He said:

> We are told that the study of literature 'cultivates the taste, educates the sympathies and enlarges the mind'. These are all excellent things,

> only we cannot examine tastes and sympathies. Examiners must have
> technical and positive information to examine.

This is a problem which has never been entirely solved in English.
What, exactly, is its knowledge component? As a way of attaching
specific and technical information to the study of English, early
supporters had advocated the systematic study of language, but
early advocates of English wanted to separate literature and language study, so that the one could be done without the other. Freeman's famous response was: 'what is meant by distinguishing
literature from language if by literature is meant the study of great
books, and not mere chatter about Shelley?'

Freeman won the argument. Literature had to be studied along
with language, otherwise it would not be an academic subject at all.
So when the English course was finally set up at Oxford in 1894 it
contained a strong element of historical language study – Anglo-
Saxon, Gothic, Letto-Slavonic, Middle English, etc., from which it
has still not managed to free itself (or, at least, distinguish itself)
entirely.

In the United States 'English' became a distinct academic discipline towards the end of the nineteenth century.[1] In the earlier part
of the century the 'Humanities' section of the college curriculum
was based on the study of Latin and Greek, taught by daily 'recitations' in which brief passages were set for study and individual students were called on in class to translate a few sentences and answer
questions about any grammatical difficulties contained in the passage. Courses were taught from a single textbook, and 'classes' and
'recitations' were the whole of it – there were no lectures in which a
broader view of the literature and culture under study might be
offered, and no seminars in which the meaning and significance of
the set texts could be discussed. Graduate study in the mid-century
period was virtually non-existent (there were said to be only eight
graduate students in the whole of the USA in 1850), and the idea of
'majoring' in a discipline did not exist either, so there were no 'elec-
tives' (or options), this being a later Harvard innovation. As Gerald

---

1 I am drawing in this sub-section on Gerald Graff's fascinating and definitive book
   Professing Literature: An Institutional History (University of Chicago Press, 1987).

Graff remarks, when lectures and written examinations were introduced later in the century at Harvard and Cornell, they were
regarded as dangerous innovations, not as the essence of conservative pedagogy which they would be taken as today.

As the century progressed, literature in English was allowed a
peripheral presence on the curriculum, and the method of study
was directly based upon the 'philological' model imported from
German universities, which is to say that it was heavily lan-
guage-based, involving the teasing out of the grammar of the text,
the etymology of the words used in it, the provenance of its images,
and the naming and classification of the literary tropes and devices
employed by the authors. Highly specialist and scholarly though
this kind of thing is, as a teaching routine it is more a protracted
form of aversion therapy to literature than a way of interesting
undergraduates in reading and enjoying major authors. By the
1880s there were annotated editions of major writers – Shakespeare,
Spenser, Bunyan, and so on – to cater for this dreary market. But
there was also the growth of a different approach to literature teaching, one which was based on 'rhetoric' rather than philology. These
courses would be taught from a 'reader' containing extracts of
famous passages from major writers. Students would read them
aloud and be coached in doing so with suitable weight and expression, or would memorise them for public performance. From this
approach evolved the Harvard Composition course, in which students would write their own pieces on the same themes, putting into
practice the lessons learned from the models. This, of course, is useful vocational training for the professions which many of the male
students would later take up, as politicians in local, state, or federal
government, as attorneys, or as ministers of religion. But the 'rhetorical' approach, and the emphasis on public speaking, fell out of
favour as the century progressed, as it was seen as stimulating a
rather vacuous and tricksy style of public speaking, so the Harvard
Composition course lost its oral element in 1873 and became a
course in writing.

The 'rhetorical' (or non-philological) mantle was inherited by
the 'generalists', as Graff calls them, teachers like Henry Wad-
sworth Longfellow, Charles Eliot Norton, and James Russell Lowell
at Harvard, who taught a much more generalised kind of literary

appreciation. Generalists and philologists often co-existed uneasily in the same department (a familiar situation), but the drive towards the professionalisation of the discipline was already well underway, and the generalists, in spite of their often charismatic and popular lecturing style, were seen as too unsystematic in their methods to prevail in the era of the MLA (the Modern Language Association, founded in 1883, which became the discipline's main professional body in the USA). So the balance was finally tipped against philology only after the First World War, when an upsurge of patriotism inaugurated the formal study of American Literature, and the emergent 'New Critics' of the 1920s established for the first time a coherent rationale for the study of literature 'as literature', rather than as language.[2]

A greater sense of direction was given to English in the Cambridge English school in the 1920s. Because Cambridge English was the most recently founded, dating only from 1911, it had the least weight of tradition to fight against, so change was relatively easy. The engineers of this change were a group of people who began teaching at Cambridge in the 1920s: I. A. Richards, William Empson, and F. R. Leavis.

I. A. Richards was the founder of a method of studying English which is still the norm today. Firstly, it made a decisive break between language and literature. Richards pioneered the technique called Practical Criticism (the title of his 1929 book). This made a close study of literature possible by isolating the text from history and context. Instead of having to study, say, the Renaissance period as a distinct historical moment, with its characteristic outlook, social formations, and so on, students could learn the techniques of practical criticism and simply analyse 'the words on the page'. The gain from this was that it was no longer possible to offer a vague, flowery, metaphorical effusion and call it criticism. Richards argued that there should be much more close attention to the precise details of the text.

A second Cambridge pioneer was a pupil of Richards, William Empson, who presented his tutor with the manuscript of the book

---

2 This sub-section is reproduced from Peter Barry, *English in Practice: In Pursuit of English Studies* (Bloomsbury, 2nd edn, 2014).

which was published in 1930 with the title *Seven Types of Ambiguity*. This book took the Richards method of close verbal analysis to what many felt to be an extreme. Empson identified seven different types of verbal difficulty in poetry (which is what he meant by ambiguity) and gave examples of them, with worked analyses. Another Cambridge critic, F. R. Leavis, said in a review that it is a highly disturbing book because it uses intelligence on poetry as seriously as if it were mathematics. Not everybody liked this ultra-close form of reading. T. S. Eliot called it the lemon-squeezer school of criticism, and his own critical writing is always on a much more generalised level.

The last of these Cambridge pioneers was F. R. Leavis, probably the most influential figure in twentieth-century British criticism. In 1929 he met and married Q. D. Roth, subsequently known as Q. D. Leavis. He had written his doctoral thesis on the relationship between journalism and literature. She had written hers on popular fiction. These were revolutionary topics, and a certain excitement and glamour attached to this couple in the 1930s. In 1932 they founded an important journal called *Scrutiny* and produced it together for twenty-one years. As the title implies, it extended the 'close-reading' method beyond poetry to novels and other material.

Leavis's faults as a critic are that his close readings often turn out to contain lengthy quotations on which there is surprisingly little comment. The assumption is that the competent reader will see there what Leavis sees. As has been said of him, he often gives the impression that he is analysing the text when he is really just paraphrasing it. Secondly, his approach to literature is overwhelmingly moral; its purpose is to teach us about life, to transmit humane values. His critical terms are never properly defined. He famously refused the invitation offered by the critic René Wellek in the 1930s that he should 'spell out the principles on which he operated in a more explicit way than hitherto'. The result was one more element of intellectual isolation for literary studies. In the period of its growth just surveyed, it claimed independence from language studies, from historical considerations, and from philosophical questions. The consensus which held the subject together from the 1930s to the 1960s rested upon the acceptance of these demarcations. The 'project' of 'theory' from the 1960s onwards

is in essence to re-establish connections between literary study
and these three academic fields from which it had so resolutely
separated itself.

GOOD

Ten tenets of liberal humanism

My personal 'stock-taking' in the introduction mainly responds to
the second and third of the four questions given there. I'm now
going to expand on the implications of the fourth question, which
asked what it is, exactly, that we learn when we 'do' English in the
traditional way. Of course, we learn things about specific books and
authors, but I mean here the more general values and attitudes
which we absorb from English, and which remain as a kind of distilled essence of the subject when all these specific details have been
forgotten. These are not usually formulated and stated, but they
are, in a sense, all the more real for that, being simultaneously both
pervasive and invisible. They can only be brought to the surface by
a conscious effort of will, of the kind we are now trying to make. So
what follows is a list of some of the elements which seem to constitute this 'distilled essence' of the subject, that is, the corpus of attitudes, assumptions, and ideas which we pick up, probably unawares,
as we do it. These seem to have been what we were learning when we
studied English – these are the values and beliefs which formed the
subject's half-hidden curriculum:

1. The first thing, naturally, is an attitude to literature itself; good
    literature is of timeless significance; it somehow transcends the
    limitations and peculiarities of the age it was written in, and
    thereby speaks to what is constant in human nature. Such
    writing is 'not for an age, but for all time' (as Ben Jonson said
    of Shakespeare): it is 'news which stays news' (Ezra Pound's
    definition of literature).

2. The second point is the logical consequence of the first. The
    literary text contains its own meaning within itself. It doesn't
    require any elaborate process of placing it within a context,
    whether this be:

    (a) *Socio-political* – the context of a particular social 'back-
         ground' or political situation, or

(b)   *Literary-historical* – whereby the work could be seen as the product of the literary influences of other writers, or as shaped by the conventions of particular genres, or

(c)   *Autobiographical* – that is, as determined by the personal details of the author's life and thought.

Of course, as scholars, most academics would assert the value of studying these contexts, but as critics their adherence to the approach which insists upon the primacy and self-sufficiency of the 'words on the page' commits them to the process which has been called 'on-sight close reading'. Essentially, this removes the text from all these contexts and presents it 'unseen' for unaided explication by the trained mind.

3.   To understand the text well it must be detached from these contexts and studied in isolation. What is needed is the close verbal analysis of the text without prior ideological assumptions, or political pre-conditions, or, indeed, specific expectations of any kind, since all these are likely to interfere fatally with what the nineteenth-century critic Matthew Arnold said was the true business of criticism, 'to see the object as in itself it really is'.

4.   Human nature is essentially unchanging. The same passions, emotions, and even situations are seen again and again throughout human history. It follows that continuity in literature is more important and significant than innovation. Thus, a well-known eighteenth-century definition of poetry maintains that it is 'what oft was thought but ne'er so well expressed'. Likewise, Samuel Johnson famously denigrated Sterne's novel *Tristram Shandy* on the grounds of its novelty, that is, its originality.

5.   Individuality is something securely possessed within each of us as our unique 'essence'. This transcends our environmental influences, and though individuality can change and develop (as do characters in novels), it can't be transformed – hence our uneasiness with those scenes (quite common, for instance, in Dickens) which involve a 'change of heart' in a character, so that the whole personality is shifted into a new dimension by force of circumstance – the miser is transformed and changes his ways, or the good man or woman becomes corrupted by wealth. Such scenes imply a malleability in the essence of

character which is at odds with this underlying assumption of English studies. The discipline as a whole believed in what is now called the 'transcendent subject', which is the belief that the individual ('the subject') is antecedent to, or transcends, the forces of society, experience, and language.

6. The purpose of literature is essentially the enhancement of life and the propagation of humane values; but not in a programmatic way: if literature, and criticism, become overtly and directly political they necessarily tend towards propaganda. And as Keats said, 'we distrust literature which has a palpable design upon us', that is, literature which too obviously wants to convert us or influence our views.

7. Form and content in literature must be fused in an organic way, so that the one grows inevitably from the other. Literary form should not be like a decoration which is applied externally to a completed structure. Imagery, for instance, or any other poetic form which is detachable from the substance of the work in this way, rather than being integrated with it, is merely 'fanciful' and not truly 'imaginative' (the distinction made by Coleridge in the *Biographia Literaria*).

8. This point about organic form applies above all to 'sincerity'. Sincerity (comprising truth-to-experience, honesty towards the self, and the capacity for human empathy and compassion) is a quality which resides *within* the language of literature. It isn't a fact or an intention *behind* the work, which could be gleaned by comparing, say, a poet's view of an event with other more 'factual' versions, or from discovering independent, external information about an author's history or conduct. Rather, sincerity is to be discovered within the text in such matters as the avoidance of cliché, or of over-inflated forms of expression; it shows in the use of first-hand, individualistic description, in the understated expression of feeling, whereby (preferably) the emotion is allowed to emerge implicitly from the presentation of an event. Moreover, when the language achieves these qualities, then the truly sincere poet can transcend the sense of distance between language and material, and can make the language seem to 'enact' what it depicts, thus apparently abolishing the necessary distance between words and things.

9. Again, the next idea follows from the previous one. What is valued in literature is the 'silent' showing and demonstrating of something, rather than the explaining, or saying, of it. Hence, ideas as such are worthless in literature until given the concrete embodiment of 'enactment'. Thus, several of the explicit comments and formulations often cited in literary history contain specific denigrations of ideas as such and have a distinct anti-intellectual flavour to them. Here we see the elevation of the characteristic 'Eng Lit' idea of *tactile enactment*, of sensuous immediacy, of the concrete representation of thought, and so on. According to this idea (which is, of course, itself an idea, in spite of the fact that the idea in question is a professed distrust of ideas) words should mime, or demonstrate, or act out, or sound out what they signify, rather than just representing it in an abstract way. This idea is stated with special fervency in the work of F. R. Leavis. (For a critique of the 'enactment' idea see 'The Enactment Fallacy', by the present author, in *Essays in Criticism*, July 1980. For a general discussion see James Gribble's *Literary Education: A Re-evaluation*, Cambridge University Press, 1983, chapter 2.)

10. The job of criticism is to interpret the text, to mediate between it and the reader. A theoretical account of the nature of reading, or of literature in general, isn't useful in criticism, and will simply, if attempted, encumber critics with 'preconceived ideas' which will get between them and the text. Perhaps in this phrase 'preconceived ideas' we get another glimpse into the nature of this pervasive distrust of ideas within liberal humanism, for there seems to be the notion that somehow *all* ideas are 'preconceived', in the sense that they will come between the reader and the text if given half a chance. There is, in fact, the clear mark here of what is called 'English empiricism', which can be defined as a determination to trust only what is made evident to the senses or experienced directly. Ultimately this attitude goes back at least to the philosophy of John Locke (1632–1704), which gives a philosophical expression to it. His book *Essay Concerning Human Understanding* (1690) puts forward the view that ideas are formed when direct sense impressions from the world are imprinted on the mind. The mind

then assembles these, so giving rise to the process of thinking. Locke rejected introspective speculation as a source of valid knowledge and insisted on the need for direct experience and evidence of things. Traditional English studies, we might say, has always been Lockean in this sense.

The above list contains a series of propositions which I think many traditional critics would, on the whole, subscribe to, if they were in the habit of making their assumptions explicit. Together, ideas like these, and the literary practice which went with them, are now often referred to as 'liberal humanism'.

Literary theorising from Aristotle to Leavis – some key moments

So far I have perhaps given the impression that theoretical positions about literature were never explicitly formulated by liberal humanists, at least in Britain, and that everything remained implicit. Yet a widely current body of theoretical work existed from the start within English studies, and references were often made to it in books and essays. The average student or teacher of 'Eng Lit' up to the 1970s would probably have had a fairly limited direct contact with this body of work, since the whole thrust of the subject was away from this kind of generalised position-taking.

What, then, constituted the body of theory about literature that has existed for many centuries as an available under-pinning for the study of literature, even if literary students seldom had any extensive first-hand acquaintance with it? Well, the material goes back to Greek and Latin originals. Critical theory, in fact, long pre-dates the literary criticism of individual works. The earliest work of theory was Aristotle's *Poetics* (4th century BC), which, in spite of its title, is about the nature of literature itself: Aristotle offers famous definitions of tragedy, insists that literature is about character, and that character is revealed through action, and tries to identify the required stages in the progress of a plot. Aristotle was also the first critic to develop a 'reader-centred' approach to literature, since his consideration of drama tried to describe how it affected the audience. Tragedy, he said, should stimulate the emotions of pity and fear, these being, roughly, sympathy for and empathy with the plight of the protagonist. By the combination of these emotions came about the effect Aristotle called 'catharsis', whereby these emotions are exercised, rather than exorcised, as the audience identifies with the plight of the central character.

The first prestigious name in English writing about literature is that of Sir Philip Sidney, who wrote his 'Apology for Poetry' in about 1580. Sidney was intent on expanding the implications of the ancient definition of literature first formulated by the Latin poet Ovid (43 BC–AD 17), who had said that its mission is *'docere delectando'* – to teach by delighting (meaning, approximately, by entertaining). Sidney also quotes Horace (65–8 BC), to the effect that a poem is 'a speaking picture, with this end, to teach and delight'. Thus, the giving of pleasure is here allowed a central position in the reading of literature, unlike, say, philosophy, which is implicitly stigmatised as worthy and uplifting, but not much fun. The notion of literature giving pleasure will now seem an unremarkable sentiment, but Sidney's aim was the revolutionary one of distinguishing literature from other forms of writing, on the grounds that, uniquely, literature has as its primary aim the giving of pleasure to the reader, and any moral or didactic element is necessarily either subordinate to that or, at least, unlikely to succeed without it. In a religious age, deeply suspicious of all forms of fiction, poetry, and representation, and always likely to denounce them as the work of the devil, this was a very great step to take. In English too, then, critical theory came before practical criticism, as Sidney is writing about literature in general, not about individual works or writers.

Literary theory after Sidney was significantly advanced by Samuel Johnson in the eighteenth century. Johnson's *Lives of the Poets* and *Prefaces to Shakespeare* can be seen both as another major step forward in critical theory, and as the start of the English tradition of practical criticism, since he is the first to offer detailed commentary on the work of a single author. Prior to Johnson, the only text which had ever been subjected to this intensive scrutiny was the Bible, and the equivalent sacred books of other religions. The extension of this practice to works other than those thought to be the direct product of divine inspiration marks a significant moment of progress in the development of secular humanism.

After Johnson came a major burgeoning of critical theory in the work of the Romantic poets: Wordsworth, Coleridge, Keats, and Shelley. One of the main texts is Wordsworth's *Preface to Lyrical Ballads*. What Wordsworth wrote in this preface was the product of collaborative discussions between himself and Coleridge. The introduction was added to the second edition of the ballads, published in 1800, after the first, of 1798, had been met with puzzlement. The book blends high literature and popular literature, since it contains literary ballads constructed on the model of the popular oral ballads of ordinary country people. The original readers of *Lyrical Ballads* also disliked the abandonment of the conventions of verbal decorum. These conventions had imposed a high degree of artificiality on poetic language, making it as different as possible from the language of ordinary everyday speech. Thus, a specialised poetic vocabulary had required the avoidance of simple everyday terms for things, and an elaborate system of rhyme and a highly compressed form of grammar had produced a verbal texture of much greater density than that of ordinary language. Suddenly, two ambitious young poets were trying to make their poetic language as much like prose as possible, avoiding the conventions of diction and verbal structure which had held sway for so long. Thus, this book is one of a number of significant critical works in literary theory whose immediate aim is to provide a rationale for the critic's own poetic work, and to educate the audience for it. It also anticipates issues of great interest to contemporary critical theory, such as the relationship between poetic language and 'ordinary' language, and that between 'literature' and other kinds of writing.

A second significant work from the Romantic era was Coleridge's misleadingly titled *Biographia Literaria*. The title might lead us to expect a work like Johnson's *Lives of the Poets*, but in fact much of it directly addresses the ideas contained in Wordsworth's *Preface*, showing by a close consideration of aspects of his work that Wordsworth writes his best poetry when he is furthest away from adherence to his own theories of what poetry should be. Indeed, in the years during which he and Coleridge had drifted apart as friends, they had also taken radically different views about the nature of poetry. Coleridge came to disagree completely with the view that the language of poetry must strive to become more like the language of prose. He saw this as an impoverishment of the poetic effect which must ultimately prove suicidal. The argument dovetails neatly with the works already cited: if literature and other works differ in their aims and effects, as Aristotle and Sidney had maintained, and if poetry, unlike other kinds of writing, aims to teach by entertaining, then the major way in which the entertaining is done must be through the language in which it is written. The language entertains by its 'fictive' qualities – this is the source of the aesthetic effect.

Something like this is also connoted in Shelley's *A Defence of Poetry* (1821), which sees poetry as essentially engaged in what a group of twentieth-century Russian critics later called 'defamiliarisation'. Shelley anticipates this term, since for him poetry 'strips the veil of familiarity from the world … it purges from our inward sight the film of familiarity … It compels us to feel that which we perceive, and to imagine that which we know.' This remarkable critical document also anticipates T. S. Eliot's notion of impersonality (put forward in his 1919 essay 'Tradition and the Individual Talent') whereby there is a distinction between (as we might call it) the author (who is the person behind the work) and the writer (who is, so to speak, the 'person' *in* the work). In Eliot's view, the greater the separation between the two the better, since 'the more perfect the artist, the more completely separate in him will be the man who suffers and the mind which creates', so that poetry is not simply the conscious rendering of personal experience into words. Shelley registers all this a hundred years earlier in his characteristically magisterial prose:

> the mind in creation is as a fading coal, which some invisible influence, like an inconstant wind, awakens to transitory brightness; this power arises from within, like the colour of a flower which fades and changes as it is developed, *and the conscious portions of our natures are unprophetic either of its approach or of its departure.*
>
> (*A Defence*, lines 999–1003, my italics)

There is also an anticipation here of the Freudian notion of the mind as made up of conscious and unconscious elements. Indeed, the idea of the unconscious is an essential one in Romanticism, and implicit in everything written about poetry by another major

Romanticist, John Keats. Keats did not write formal literary theory in the way Wordsworth, Coleridge, and Shelley did, but he did reflect on poetry in a sustained way in his letters. He too formulates a notion of the workings of the unconscious, for instance in a letter to Bailey of 22 November 1817 when he speaks of how 'the simple imaginative Mind may have its rewards in the repetition of its own silent Working coming continually on the Spirit with a fine suddenness'. The 'silent working' of the mind is the unconscious and the 'spirit' into which it erupts is the conscious. Keats's idea of 'negative capability' also amounts to this same privileging of the unconscious, this same desire to allow it scope to work, negative capability being 'when a man is capable of being in uncertainties, mysteries, doubts without any irritable reaching after fact and reason' (letter to his brothers, 21 December 1817). In the critical writings of the Romantics, then, there are many anticipations of the concerns of critical theory today.

After the Romantics the main developments in critical theory were the work of mid and late Victorians, George Eliot, Matthew Arnold, and Henry James. George Eliot's critical work ranges widely over classical and continental writers, and philosophical issues, as did Coleridge's. It is worth emphasising this, since there are two distinct 'tracks' in the development of English criticism. One track leads through Samuel Johnson and Matthew Arnold to T. S. Eliot and F. R. Leavis. This might be called the 'practical criticism' track. It tends to centre upon the close analysis of the work of particular writers, and gives us our familiar tradition of 'close reading'. The other track lies through Sidney, Wordsworth, Coleridge, George Eliot, and Henry James. This track is very much 'ideas-led' rather than 'text-led': it tends to tackle big general issues concerned with literature – How are literary works structured? How do they affect readers or audiences? What is the nature of literary language? How does literature relate to the contemporary and to matters of politics and gender? What can be said about literature from a philosophical point of view? What is the nature of the act of literary composition? These 'track two' preoccupations are very similar to the concerns of the critical theorists who became prominent from the 1960s onwards, and it is important to realise that these concerns are not an exotic imposition upon 'native' Anglo-American approaches to literature but, rather, have been part of it from the beginning.

The insistence upon 'close reading' in the 1920s sprang partly from the work of Matthew Arnold in the previous century. Arnold has remained a key canonical figure in the history of English criticism, partly because F. R. Leavis adopted and adapted several of his ideas and attitudes and gave them twentieth-century currency. Arnold feared that the decline of religion would leave an increasingly divided society with no common system of beliefs, values, and images, with potentially disastrous consequences. He saw literature as a possible replacement for religion in this regard, but believed that the middle classes, on whom the burden and responsibility of democracy largely fell, had been progressively debased by materialism and philistinism. The critic would help such people to recognise 'the best that has been known and thought in the world' and thus enable them to give individual assent to the canon of great works which had emerged through the collective wisdom of the ages.

Arnold's most significant thinking is contained in the essays 'The Function of Criticism at the Present Time' and 'The Study of Poetry'. He stresses the importance for literature of remaining 'disinterested', by which he means politically detached and uncommitted to any specific programme of action. The goal of literary criticism is that of attaining pure, disinterested knowledge, that is, to use another of his favourite phrases, of simply appreciating 'the object as in itself it really is' without wanting to press the insight gained into the service of a specific line of action. Arnold's key literary-critical device is the notion of the Touchstone, which avoids any definitions of desirable literary qualities, and merely suggests using aspects of the literature of the past as a means of measuring and assessing the literature of today. The way the Touchstone works is concisely explained in J. A. Cuddon's *Dictionary of Literary Terms and Literary Theory* (Penguin, 5th edn, 2014):

> A touchstone is … so-called because gold is tried by it. Matthew Arnold used the word in his essay *The Study of Poetry* (1880) in connection with literary criteria and standards:

Arnold advises that we should 'have always in mind lines and expressions of the great masters, and apply them as a Touchstone to other poetry'. He suggests that his Touchstone method should provide the basis for a 'real' rather than an 'historic' or a 'personal' estimate of poetry. (See Cuddon, p. 728.)

In the first half of the twentieth century, the key critical names in Britain were F. R. Leavis, T. S. Eliot, William Empson, and I. A. Richards. All except Eliot were at Cambridge in the 1920s and 1930s, involved in the pioneering English School there which had a powerful influence on the teaching of English worldwide up to the 1970s. Eliot's contribution to the canon of received critical ideas was the greatest, his major critical ideas being:

- the notion of the 'dissociation of sensibility', developed in the course of his review article on Herbert Grierson's edition of *The Metaphysical Poets*,
- the notion of poetic 'impersonality', developed in the course of his two-part essay 'Tradition and the Individual Talent', and
- the notion of the 'objective correlative', developed in his essay on *Hamlet*.

All these ideas have become controversial: the idea that a 'dissociation of sensibility' occurred in the seventeenth century, radically separating thought from feeling, is one for which historical evidence has never been found. Later in his career Eliot denied that he thought the dissociation had been caused by the English Civil War, though he added rather cryptically that he thought it might have been caused by the same factors as those which brought about the Civil War – a nice distinction. The best use of the idea is simply as a way of describing the special qualities of mind and sensibility which we detect in the Metaphysical poets: as a historical generalisation it seems quite without support. The best critique of the idea can be found in Frank Kermode's book *Romantic Image*.

The idea of impersonality was partly Eliot's way of deflecting current thinking about poetry away from ideas of originality and self-expression which derived from Romanticism. Eliot's own personality, and the education he had received at Harvard, made this emphasis on the individual highly distasteful. It was much more congenial to him to see poetry not as a pouring out of personal emotion and personal experience, but as a transcending of the individual by a sense of tradition which spoke through, and is transmitted by, the individual poet. The best parts of a poet's work, he says, are not those which are most original, but those in which the voice of his predecessors can be most clearly heard speaking through him. Hence, there is a large distinction to be drawn between the mind of the individual, experiencing human being, and the voice which speaks in the poetry. This was not an original thought – Shelley, as we saw, had something very like it in his *Defence of Poetry* – but Eliot was the first to make it the cornerstone of a whole poetic aesthetic.

The objective correlative, finally, is really another encapsulation of English empiricist attitudes: it holds that the best way of expressing an emotion in art is to find some vehicle for it in gesture, action, or concrete symbolism, rather than approaching it directly or descriptively. This is undoubtedly true: little is gained in fiction or poetry by having characters (or narrators) say what they feel: it has to be *shown* in some way in words or actions. This is perhaps little more than the ancient distinction (first made by Plato) between *mimesis* and *diegesis*. The former is a *showing* of something, in the character's own words, or in actions which we actually see on the stage, if it is a play, while the latter is *telling* the audience or reader about things they don't see for themselves or experience in the direct speech of the characters. All Eliot's major critical ideas are thus flawed and unsatisfactory, and perhaps their long-standing currency is indicative of the theoretical vacuum into which they were launched.

The most influential British critic prior to the theory movement was F. R. Leavis. Leavis, like Arnold in the previous century, assumed that the study and appreciation of literature is a pre-condition to the health of society. He too distrusted abstract thought and looked for a system of literary appreciation (like Arnold's Touchstones) which by-passed fixed criteria, arguing instead for an openness to the qualities of the text. Like Arnold, finally, he rejected any attempt to politicise either literature or criticism directly.

The two differ, however, in a few notable regards: Arnold, for example, takes the pantheon of past great writers more or less for granted: he does not question the excellence of Dante, for instance, which is why Dante can become a Touchstone. By contrast, Leavis sometimes wrote essays attacking the reputations of major established figures, and, indeed, it was the essence of his method to argue that some reputations would *not* stand up to the kind of close textual scrutiny he constantly recommended. Arnold, in his critical ideas, seems essentially to license and encourage the amateur. You may not have read *everything*, he implies (how could you, since you don't have the unlimited time of the professional critic?), but if you have read the best, and can identify its qualities, then you can be confident in looking at new writing and reaching a true judgement on it. This 'protestant' aesthetic encourages a direct relationship between the individual reader and the literary greats.

F. R. Leavis began as an admirer of Eliot's critical work as well as of his poetry, but later greatly modified his views. He avoided the coining of critical vocabulary, and instead used as critical terms words and phrases which already had established lay senses: 'life', for instance, is used by Leavis almost as a critical term, as is the notion of 'felt experience'. For Leavis the crucial test is whether the work is conducive to 'life' and vitality. Leavis's extreme popularity was partly due to the fact that he was essentially a kind of combined re-birth of Johnson and Arnold, offering again the former's moralism and the latter's social vision and anti-theoretical critical practice. Leavis is still so pervasive an influence that little more need be said about him here.

William Empson and I. A. Richards can perhaps be taken as a pair, though the latter was the tutor of the former in the late 1920s. Empson's book *Seven Types of Ambiguity* (1930) was itself somewhat ambiguous in its effects. On the one hand, its ultra-close readings of texts demonstrated the kind of text-led extreme which might be seen as the logical development of the 'track one' tradition of British criticism described above. The word 'ambiguity' in the book's title can be translated as 'verbal difficulty', and Empson unravels his examples by meticulous textual surgery, rather than references out to a wider context. On the other hand, Empson's basic attitude towards language is that it is really a very slippery medium indeed: when we handle language we need to be aware that the whole thing is likely to explode into meanings we hadn't suspected of being there at all. As we go from ambiguity type one to type seven we seem to be approaching the frontiers of language, where the territory eventually becomes un-mappable, and we seem to end up looking into a void of linguistic indeterminacy. This can be seen as an

anticipation from within the British tradition of post-structuralist
views about the unreliability of language as a medium (see Chapter
3). But the placing of language within *any* context naturally tends to
reduce or eliminate ambiguity. (For instance, the word 'pain', when
you hear it spoken in isolation, is ambiguous, since it sounds the
same as 'pane', but encounter it in the context of any actual situation
of usage and the ambiguity disappears.) Hence the later Empson
drew back from the linguistic void by stressing, in particular, the
autobiographical context in which literary works, in his view, are
grounded.

I. A. Richards, finally, is the pioneer of the decontextualised
approach to literature which became the norm in Britain from the
1930s to the 1970s as 'practical criticism' and in America during
roughly the same period as the 'New Criticism'. Richards's experi-
ments in the 1920s of presenting students and tutors with unanno-
tated, anonymous poems for commentary and analysis gave rise to
the ideal of removing the props of received opinion and knowledge
and fostering a 'true judgement' based on first-hand opinion. It is
easy to see the connection betwen this and Arnold's 'Touchstones'.
What is certain is that this decisive 'Ricardian' moment established
the 'track one' 'practical' tradition of criticism so completely for so
long that a selective amnesia descended on the discipline and it came
to be widely regarded as the *only* tradition that had ever existed.

The subsequent conflict between liberal humanism and 'theory'
is a pretty fundamental one, but it is worth reminding ourselves that
it is actually much older than the 1970s when it broke out with such
force in Britain, America, and elsewhere. Similar debates and arguments took place in the 1930s, for instance between F. R. Leavis,
whom we might regard as the archetypal British liberal humanist,
and the critical theorist René Wellek. Leavis and Wellek debated
the relationship between literary criticism and philosophy in the
pages of Leavis's journal *Scrutiny*. Wellek's point against Leavis was
simply that practical criticism was *not* enough – he ought to spell
out the theoretical assumptions on which his readings, and his procedures generally, were based. In Wellek's view a series of 'close
readings' of Romantic poets in Leavis's book *Revaluations* is offered
to the reader in a theoretical vacuum. As he politely put it, 'I could
wish that you had stated your assumptions more explicitly and

defended them systematically' (*Scrutiny*, March 1937, p. 376). This refusal to accept the liberal humanist method as simply the 'natural' and taken-for-granted way of 'doing' literature is the crux of theory's general response to it. Though less politely than Wellek, theorists make the same demand as he did – spell out what you do, and why, when you read and criticise literature, so that your methods can be evaluated along with others. Implicit in this demand is the view that if these things are made explicit (as we tried to do in the previous section) then the weaknesses of liberal humanist assumptions and procedures will become apparent, and other approaches will have a chance of replacing them.

Examples of the work of all the figures discussed in this section can be found in the collection *English Critical Texts*, ed. D. J. Enright and Ernst de Chickera (Oxford University Press, 1962).

Liberal humanism in practice

It is perhaps unnecessary to supply a full-scale example of liberal humanist practice, since that practice will surely be familiar to anyone reading this book. However, I will sketch out, mainly for comparative purposes, what I would consider to be a characteristic liberal humanist reading of Edgar Allan Poe's tale 'The Oval Portrait' (see Appendix 1) since the tale will be used later to illustrate structuralism in practice, and narratology.

A liberal humanist approach to this tale (or, to be more specific, a Leavisite approach) might focus on the evident conflict of values in the story between 'art' and 'life'. The central point of commentary and interpretation might be the moralist argument that true value lies in the 'lived life' of the unique individual, and that it is disastrous for the artist to fail to recognise a necessary subservience of art to a communal reality. Further, when artists begin to see themselves as Faustian super-heroes, able to cross all boundaries of taste, taboo, and conduct, and even to assume the god-like role of creating and sacrificing life itself, then a hubristic act is committed which ultimately dries up the sources of the life of art itself. Hence, the artist in this tale in his isolated turret, feeding vampire-like on the vital energies of his sitter, is an emblem of a debased and degenerate form of art whose values are of the purely aesthetic 'art for art's sake' kind and have no reference to any wider notion of personal and psychic health.

Two things stand out in this approach: firstly, this kind of reading is driven (ultimately) by its moral convictions (laudable in themselves, of course) rather than by any model of what constitutes a systematic approach to literary criticism. The robust championing of 'life' in the above sketch makes the term 'Leavisite' seem an appropriate one to apply to it. The second notable aspect of it is that it seems to by-pass matters of form, structure, genre, and so on, and launches straight into the discussion of matters of content. If the sketch were filled out, there would doubtless be comments on such characteristics as structure, symbol, and design, but they would probably be *secondary* in nature, intended as concrete support for the *primary* focus of the reading, which is the moral position taken. I am not, of course, dismissing such an approach as worthless: my intention is simply to characterise it and distinguish it from other approaches.

The turn to 'theory'

The growth of critical theory in the post-war period seems to comprise a series of 'waves', each associated with a specific decade, and all aimed against the liberal humanist consensus just illustrated, which had been established between the 1930s and the 1950s. In the 1960s, firstly, there were two older, but still unassimilated, rival new approaches, these being *Marxist criticism*, which had been pioneered in the 1930s and then reborn in the 1960s, and *psychoanalytic criticism*, which was of the same vintage and was similarly renewing itself in the 1960s. At the same time two new approaches were mounting vigorous direct assaults on liberal humanist orthodoxies, namely *linguistic criticism*, which came into being in the early 1960s, and early forms of *feminist criticism*, which started to become a significant factor at the end of the decade.

Then, in the 1970s news spread in literary-critical circles in Britain and the United States of controversial new critical approaches, in particular *structuralism* and *post-structuralism*, both of which originated in France. The effect of these two was so powerful as to produce, by the late 1970s and early 1980s, a situation which was frequently referred to as a 'crisis' or 'civil war' in the discipline of English. The questions these two approaches centred upon concerned matters of language and philosophy, rather than history or context. In the 1980s a shift occurred which is sometimes called the 'turn to history', whereby history, politics, and context were reinstated at the centre of the literary-critical agenda. Thus, in the early 1980s two new forms of political/historical criticism emerged, *new historicism* from the United States and *cultural materialism* from Britain. Both these take what might be called a 'holistic' approach to literature, aiming to integrate literary and historical study while at the same time maintaining some of the insights of the structuralists and post-structuralists of the previous decade.

Finally, in the 1990s a general flight from overarching grand explanations seemed to be taking place, and there was what seemed a decisive drift towards dispersal, eclecticism, and 'special-interest' forms of criticism and theory. Thus, the approach known as *post-colonialism* rejects the idea of a universally applicable Marxist explanation of things and emphasises the separateness or otherness of post-imperial nations and peoples. Likewise, *postmodernism* stresses the uniquely fragmented nature of much contemporary experience. Feminism, too, shows signs of dissolving into a loose federation known as gender studies, with gay and lesbian texts emerging as distinct fields of literature, and hence implying and generating appropriate and distinct critical approaches. Also part of this 1990s federation was black feminist (or 'womanist') criticism. *Womanism* now designates, more generally, social and critical theory with specific reference to women of marginalised groups.

Some recurrent ideas in critical theory[3]

These different approaches each have their separate traditions and histories, but several ideas are recurrent in critical theory and seem to form what might be regarded as its common bedrock. Hence, it makes some sense to speak of 'theory' as if it were a single entity

3 For a very useful detailed discussion of these five recurrent ideas see Brian Russell Graham, 'Resistance to Recurrent Ideas in Critical Theory', *Anglo-Files*, 180 (May 2016), pp. 88–97.

with a set of underlying beliefs, as long as we are aware that doing so is a simplification. Five of these recurrent underlying ideas of theory are listed below.

1.   Many of the notions which we would usually regard as the basic 'givens' of our existence (including our gender identity, our individual selfhood, and the notion of literature itself) are actually fluid and unstable things, rather than fixed and reliable essences. Instead of being solidly 'there' in the real world of fact and experience, they are 'socially constructed', that is, dependent on social and political forces and on shifting ways of seeing and thinking. In philosophical terms, all these are *contingent* categories (denoting a status which is temporary, provisional, 'circumstance-dependent') rather than *absolute* ones (that is, fixed, immutable, etc.). Hence, no overarching fixed 'truths' can ever be established. The results of all forms of intellectual enquiry are provisional only. There is no such thing as a fixed and reliable truth (except for the statement that this is so, presumably). The position on these matters which theory attacks is often referred to, in a kind of shorthand, as *essentialism*, while many of the theories discussed in this book would describe themselves as *anti-essentialist*.

2.   Theorists generally believe that all thinking and investigation is necessarily affected and largely determined by prior ideological commitment. The notion of disinterested enquiry is therefore untenable: none of us, they would argue, is capable of standing back from the scales and weighing things up dispassionately: rather, all investigators have a thumb on one side or other of the scales. Every practical procedure (for instance, in literary criticism) presupposes a theoretical perspective of some kind. To deny this is simply to try to place our own theoretical position beyond scrutiny as something which is 'commonsense' or 'simply given'. This contention is problematical, of course, and is usually only made explicit as a counter to specific arguments put forward by opponents. The problem with this view is that it tends to discredit one's own project along with all the rest, introducing a *relativism* which disables argument and cuts the ground from under any kind of commitment.

3. Language itself conditions, limits, and predetermines what we see. Thus, all reality is constructed through language, so that nothing is simply 'there' in an unproblematical way – everything is a linguistic/textual construct. Language doesn't *record* reality, it shapes and creates it, so that the whole of our universe is textual. Further, for the theorist, meaning is jointly constructed by reader and writer. It isn't just 'there' and waiting before we get to the text but requires the reader's contribution to bring it into being.

   [margin note: Implicit argument for philology]

4. Hence, any claim to offer a definitive reading would be futile. The meanings within a literary work are never fixed and reliable, but always shifting, multi-faceted and ambiguous. In literature, as in all writing, there is never the possibility of establishing fixed and definite meanings: rather, it is characteristic of language to generate infinite webs of meaning, so that all texts are necessarily self-contradictory, as the process of deconstruction will reveal. There is no final court of appeal in these matters, since literary texts, once they exist, are viewed by the theorist as independent linguistic structures whose authors are always 'dead' or 'absent'.

   [margin note: Steven this; NO]

5. Theorists distrust all 'totalising' notions. For instance, the notion of 'great' books as an absolute and self-sustaining category is to be distrusted, as books always arise out of a particular socio-political situation, and this situation should not be suppressed, as tends to happen when they are promoted to 'greatness'. Likewise, the concept of a 'human nature', as a generalised norm which transcends the idea of a particular race, gender, or class, is to be distrusted too, since it is usually in practice *Eurocentric* (that is, based on white European norms) and *androcentric* (that is, based on masculine norms and attitudes). Thus, the appeal to the idea of a generalised, supposedly inclusive, human nature is likely in practice to marginalise, or denigrate, or even deny the humanity of women, or disadvantaged groups.

   [margin note: Highly political; Liberal middle-class guilt]

To sum up these five points: for theory:

   Politics is pervasive,
   Language is constitutive,

> Truth is provisional,
> Meaning is contingent,
> Human nature is a myth.

If, at later points in this book, or later in your study of theory, you begin to find that your grasp of things is slipping, it would be worthwhile coming back to this list to remind yourself of the basic frame of mind which theory embodies. It is very likely that a concept with which you are having difficulty will turn out to be a version of one of these positions.

Selected reading

Books representing the liberal humanist position

Alter, Robert, *The Pleasures of Reading in an Ideogical Age* (Simon and Schuster, 1989; rpt. W. W. Norton, 1997, with a new preface).

Polemical anti-theoretical introduction, 'The disappearance of reading', and final chapter, 'Multiple readings and the bog of indeterminacy'; the chapters in between are on traditional literary critical concepts such as 'Character', 'Style' and 'Perspective'.

Gardner, Helen, *In Defence of the Imagination* (Oxford University Press, 1984).

Based on a course of lectures responding to a book by Frank Kermode (then a champion of theory). A vigorous defence of traditional humanist scholarship and criticism against what she saw as the malign influence of theory.

Gribble, James, *Literary Education: A Re-evaluation* (Cambridge University Press, 1983).

One of several books from the early 1980s which mounted a defence of traditional literary scholarship against theory. See chapter one, 'Literature and truth': chapter four, 'The subjection of criticism to theory': chapter five, 'Literature and the education of the emotions'.

Steiner, George, *Real Presences: Is There Anything in What We Say?* (Faber, 1989; rpt. University of Chicago Press, 1991).

Steiner is a polyglot, polymath humanist whose work has never been anti-theoretical. In the three long essays in this book he grapples with the problem of relating theoretical accounts to the actual experience of responding to literature and the other arts.

Watson, George, *The Certainty of Literature: Essays in Polemic* (Harvester, 1989).

Watson's opposition to contemporary theory is absolute and unqualified, as the title of this book implies.

Books about the rise of English as an academic subject

Baldick, Chris, *The Social Mission of English Studies 1848–1932* (Oxford University Press, 1983).

A clearly argued history of literary criticism in England from Matthew Arnold. Detailed, and with a clear introduction.

Doyle, Brian, 'The hidden history of English Studies' in *Re-Reading English*, ed. Peter Widdowson (Methuen, 1982), pp. 17–31.

Asks 'why and how did English become a major subject in higher education?' An influential account, though the emphasis is slightly different from the one I have offered here.

Eagleton, Terry, 'The rise of English', chapter one in his *Literary Theory: An Introduction* (Wiley-Blackwell, 25th anniversary edn, 2008).

A polemical and very readable account of the growth of 'English', broadly in line with Doyle's.

Graff, Gerald, *Professing Literature: An Institutional History* (University of Chicago Press, 20th anniversary edn, 2007).

A detailed account of the growth of English studies in the United States.

Kearney, Anthony, *The Louse on the Locks of Literature: John Churton Collins* (Scottish Academic Press, 1986).

Collins was a nineteenth-century pioneer of English studies. This enjoyable book includes an account (on which I have drawn in the relevant part of this chapter) of debates in the press and Parliament on the proposed new academic subject of 'English'.

Mulhern, Francis, *The Moment of Scrutiny* (Verso, new edn, 1981).

Scrutiny was the journal founded by F. R. Leavis in 1932, so this widely respected book continues the story of 'English' from where Baldick (above) leaves off.

Palmer, D. J., *The Rise of English Studies* (Oxford University Press, 1965).

A readable account.

Potter, Stephen, *The Muse in Chains: A Study in Education* (Cape, 1937, rpt. Folcroft, 1973).

An early account of early English. The specimen examination papers from the nineteenth century (included in the appendices) are very revealing.

Tillyard, E. M. W., *The Muse Unchained: An Intimate Account of the Revolution in English Studies at Cambridge* (London, Bowes & Bowes, 1958).

Continues the story of English from where Potter (above) leaves off, describing Cambridge in the 1920s and 1930s and the early careers of Richards, Empson, and Leavis.

Palmer, Potter, and Tillyard together provide what might be called liberal humanism's own account of its development, distinctly different from that offered by Baldick, Doyle, Eagleton, and Mulhern.

2
Structuralism

Structuralist chickens and liberal humanist eggs

Structuralism is an intellectual movement which began in France in the 1950s and is first seen in the work of the anthropologist Claude Lévi-Strauss (1908–2009) and the literary critic Roland Barthes (1915–80). It is difficult to boil structuralism down to a single 'bottom-line' proposition, but if forced to do so I would say that its essence is the belief that things cannot be understood in isolation – they have to be seen in the context of the larger structures they are part of (hence the term 'structuralism'). Structuralism was imported into Britain mainly in the 1970s and attained widespread influence, and even notoriety, throughout the 1980s.

The structures in question here are those imposed by our way of perceiving the world and organising experience, rather than objective entities already existing in the external world. It follows from this that meaning or significance isn't a kind of core or essence *inside* things: rather, meaning is always *outside*. Meaning is always an attribute of things, in the literal sense that meanings are *attributed* to the things by the human mind, not contained within them. But let's try to be specific about what it might mean to think primarily in terms of structures when considering literature. Imagine that we are confronted with a poem, Donne's 'Good Morrow', let's say. Our immediate reaction as structuralists would probably be to insist that it can only be understood if we first have a clear notion of the genre which it parodies and subverts. Any single poem is an example of a particular genre, and the genre and the example relate to each other rather as a phrase spoken in English relates to the English language as a structure with all its rules, its conventions, and so on. In the case of Donne's poem the relevant genre is the *alba* or 'dawn song', a poetic form dating from the twelfth century in which lovers lament the approach of daybreak because it means that they must part.

But the *alba*, in turn, can hardly be understood without some notion of the concept of courtly love, and, further, the *alba*, being a poem, presupposes a knowledge of what is entailed in the conventionalised form of utterance known as poetry. These are just some of the cultural structures which Donne's poem is part of. You will see that your structuralist 'approach' to it is actually taking you further and further away from the text, and into large and comparatively abstract questions of genre, history, and philosophy, rather than closer and closer to it, as the Anglo-American tradition demands. Now if we use the crude analogy of chickens and eggs, we can regard the containing structures (the *alba*, courtly love, poetry itself as a cultural practice) as the chicken, and the individual example (Donne's poem in this case) as the egg. For structuralists, determining the precise nature of the chicken is the most important activity, while for the liberal humanists the close analysis of the egg is paramount.

Thus, in the structuralist approach to literature there is a constant movement away from the interpretation of the individual literary work and a parallel drive towards understanding the larger, abstract structures which contain them. These structures, as I suggested at the start of this section, are usually abstract, such as the notion of the literary or the poetic, or the nature of narrative itself, rather than 'mere' concrete specifics like the history of the *alba* or of courtly love, both of which, after all, we could quite easily find out about from conventional literary history. The arrival of structuralism in Britain and the USA in the 1970s caused a great deal of controversy, precisely because literary studies in these countries had traditionally had very little interest in large abstract issues of the kind structuralists wanted to raise. The so-called 'Cambridge revolution' in English studies in the 1920s had promulgated *the opposite* to all this: it enjoined close study of the text in isolation from all wider structures and contexts: it was relentlessly 'text-based' and tended to exclude wider questions, abstract issues, and ideas. Structuralism in that sense turned English studies on its head, and devalued all that it had held dear for around half a century, asking long-repressed questions such as: 'What do we mean by "literary"?' 'How do narratives work?' 'What is a poetic structure?' Traditional critics, in a word, did not welcome the suggestion that they ought to switch their attention from eggs to chickens.

Signs of the fathers – Saussure

Though structuralism proper began, as we said, in the 1950s and 1960s, it has its roots in the thinking of the Swiss linguist Ferdinand de Saussure (1857–1913). Saussure was a key figure in the development of modern approaches to language study. In the nineteenth century linguistic scholars had mainly been interested in historical aspects of language (such as working out the historical development of languages and the connections between them, and speculating about the origins of language itself). Saussure concentrated instead on the patterns and functions of language in use today, with the emphasis on how meanings are maintained and established and on the functions of grammatical structures.

But what exactly did Saussure say about linguistic structures which the structuralists later found so interesting? This can be summarised as three pronouncements in particular. Firstly, he emphasised that the meanings we give to words are purely *arbitrary*, and that these meanings are maintained by convention only. Words, that is to say, are 'unmotivated signs', meaning that there is no inherent connection between a word and what it designates. The word 'hut', for instance, is not in any way 'appropriate' to its meaning, and all linguistic signs are arbitrary like this. (There is the minor exception of a small number of onomatopoeic words like 'cuckoo' and 'hiss', but even these vary between languages.) Insisting that linguistic signs are arbitrary is a fairly obvious point to make, perhaps, and it is not a new thing to say (Plato said it in Ancient Greek times), but it is a new concept to *emphasise* (which is always much more important), and the structuralists were interested in the implication that if language as a sign system is based on arbitrariness of this kind then it follows that language isn't a reflection of the world and of experience, but a system which stands quite separate from it. This point will be further developed later.

Secondly, Saussure emphasised that the meanings of words are (what we might call) *relational*. That is to say, no word can be defined in isolation from other words. The definition of any given word depends upon its relation with other 'adjoining' words. For example, that word 'hut' depends for its precise meaning on its position in a 'paradigmatic chain', that is, a chain of words related in function and meaning each of which could be substituted for any of the others in a given sentence. The paradigmatic chain in this case might include the following:

hovel   shed   hut   house   mansion   palace

The meaning of any one of these words would be altered if any one of the others were removed from the chain. Thus, 'hut' and 'shed' are both small and basic structures, but they are not quite the same thing: one is primarily for shelter (a night-watchman's hut, for instance), while the other is primarily for storage: without the other, each would have to encompass *both* these meanings, and hence would be a different word. Likewise, a mansion can be defined as a dwelling which is bigger and grander than a mere house, but not as big and grand as a palace. Thus, we define 'mansion' by explaining how its meaning relates to that of the two words on either side of it. If we have paired opposites then this mutually defining aspect of words is even more apparent: the terms 'male' and 'female', for example, mainly have meaning in relation to each other: each designates the absence of the characteristics included in the other, so that 'male' can be seen as mainly meaning 'not female', and vice versa. Similarly, we could have no concept of 'day' without the linked concept of 'night', no notion of 'good' without a 'bad' to define it against. This 'relational' aspect of language gave rise to a famous remark of Saussure's: 'In a language there are only differences, without positive terms'. All words, then, exist in 'differencing networks', like these 'dyads', or paired opposites, and like the paradigmatic chain of 'dwelling place' words given earlier.

Saussure used a famous example to explain what he meant by saying that there are no intrinsic fixed meanings in language – the example of the 8.25 Geneva to Paris express train (see the *Course*, pp. 108–9, and Jonathan Culler's discussion of this example in *Structuralist Poetics*, p. 11). What is it that gives this train its identity? It isn't anything material, since each day it will have a different engine and carriages, different drivers and passengers, and so on. If it is late, it won't even leave at 8.25. Does it even have to be a train? I once asked at Southampton station for the Brighton train, and the ticket collector pointed to a bus standing outside the station and said, 'That's it'. It was a Sunday, and because of engineering works on the line a bus service was being used to ferry passengers beyond the sections being worked upon. Sometimes, then, a 'train' *doesn't* have to be a train. Saussure's conclusion is that the only thing which gives this train its identity is its position in a structure of differences: it comes *between* the 7.25 and the 9.25, that is, its identity is purely relational.

Thirdly, for Saussure, language *constitutes* our world, it doesn't just record it or label it. Meaning is always *attributed* to the object or idea by the human mind, and constructed by and expressed through language: it is not already contained within the thing. Well-known examples of this process would be the choice between paired alternatives like 'terrorist' or 'freedom fighter'. There is no neutral or objective way of designating such a person, merely a choice of two terms which 'construct' that person in certain ways. Another example of the same concept is seen in the two ways of referring to the domestic tax imposed in Britain by the Thatcher government: opponents of this tax called it the poll tax, evoking images of the Middle Ages and the Peasants' Revolt. The government itself called the tax the community charge, avoiding the negative word 'tax' and making use of the favoured term 'community'. The term for this tax used by a given individual immediately indicated a political position, and, again, no neutral or 'objective' alternative was available. It has been said that there are three versions of every story, your version, my version, and the truth, but the case here is more complicated than that, since *all* the available terms are purely linguistic – there is no truth about these matters which exists securely outside language.

Wherever we look, we see language constituting the world in this way, not just reflecting it. For instance, the words for colours *make* a reality, they don't just name things which are 'there': the spectrum isn't divided into seven primary colours; all the colours merge into one another. So we might have had fourteen names rather than seven. Another example is the terms we give to the seasons of the year. We have four distinct names ('spring', 'summer', etc.), but actually the year runs continuously without any breaks or decisive changes. It isn't, in reality, divided into four. Why not have six seasons, or eight? Since change is continuous throughout the year the divisions could be made anywhere at all. The seasons, then, are a *way of seeing* the year, not an objective fact of nature. So Saussure's thinking stressed the way language is arbitrary, relational, and constitutive, and this way of thinking about language greatly influenced the structuralists, because it gave them a model of a system which is self-contained, in which individual items relate to other items and thus create larger structures.

One other distinction made by Saussure gave structuralists a way of thinking about the larger structures which were relevant to literature. He used the terms *langue* and *parole* to signify, respectively, language as a system or structure on the one hand, and any given utterance in that language on the other. A particular remark in French (a sample of *parole*) only makes sense to you if you are already in possession of the whole body of rules and conventions governing verbal behaviour which we call 'French' (that is, the *langue*). The individual remark, then, is a discrete item which only makes sense when seen in relation to a wider containing structure, in the classic structuralist manner. Now, structuralists make use of the *langue/parole* distinction by seeing the individual literary work (the novel *Middlemarch*, let's say) as an example of a literary *parole*. It too only makes sense in the context of some wider containing structure. So the *langue* which relates to the *parole Middlemarch* is the notion of the novel as a genre, as a body of literary practice.

STOP and THINK

Consider some of the points made so far in this section about language.

Firstly, can you think of other examples of language constituting reality, rather than merely naming something which is already there? Your examples may be of a similar type to those mentioned above ('freedom fighter', 'poll tax', the seasons). You may also like to consider the significance in this context of those 'speech acts' which are known as 'performatives', that is, the kind of utterance which *is* the reality it designates, such as making a promise ('I promise to tell him') or formally opening some new facility ('I now declare this bridge opened').

Secondly, can you see any flaws in the line of argument about language and reality put forward by Saussure? For instance, does it make sense to posit a category of pure difference? Do you see any force in the counter-view once put forward by the critic Christopher Ricks, that you can't just have difference, you have to have difference *between* things? (See his article 'In Theory' in *London Review of Books,* April 1981, pp. 3–6.) If you accepted Ricks's argument, and agreed that you can only have difference between things, what implications would this have for the Saussurean argument that languages have only differences, without positive terms?

Thirdly, are you convinced by that train? Is its position in the timetable really the *only* thing which gives it its identity? Saussure supplements the example with another one:

> Why can a street be completely rebuilt and still be the same? Because it does not constitute a purely material entity; it is based on certain conditions that are distinct from the materials that fit the conditions, e.g. its location with respect to other streets
>
> (*Course*, pp. 108–9)

A counter-argument might be that the 8.25 has to be train-like before it can be the 8.25: nobody will remark, 'There goes the 8.25 to Paris' if a flock of pigeons emerges from under the station canopy: likewise, it is true to say that a given street has a largely relational identity – you define 'X' Street by saying that it's the one that runs at right angles between 'Y' Street and 'Z' Street. All the same, a piece of string stretched between the two will not be mistaken for the street.

The scope of structuralism

But structualism is not just about language and literature. When Saussure's work was 'co-opted' in the 1950s by the people we now call structuralists, their feeling was that Saussure's model of how language works was 'transferable', and would also explain how all signifying systems work. The anthropologist Claude Lévi-Strauss applied the structuralist outlook to the interpetation of myth. He suggested that the individual tale (the *parole*) from a cycle of myths did not have a separate and inherent meaning but could only be understood by considering its position in the whole cycle (the *langue*) and the similarities and difference between that tale and others in the sequence.

So in interpreting the Oedipus myth, he placed the individual story of Oedipus within the context of the whole cycle of tales connected with the city of Thebes. He then began to see repeated motifs and contrasts, and he used these as the basis of his interpretation. On this method the story and the cycle it is part of are reconstituted in terms of basic oppositions: animal/human, relation/stranger, husband/son and so on. Concrete details from the story are seen in the context of a larger structure, and the larger structure is then seen as an overall network of basic 'dyadic pairs' which have obvious symbolic, thematic, and archetypal resonance (like the contrast between art and life, male and female, town and country, telling and showing, etc., as in the 'worked example' later).

This is the typical structuralist process of moving from the particular to the general, placing the individual work within a wider structural context. The wider structure might also be found in, for instance, the whole corpus of an author's work; or in the genre conventions of writing about that particular topic (for instance, discussing Dickens's novel *Hard Times* in terms of its deviations from novelistic conventions and into those of other more popular genres, like melodrama or the ballad); or in the identification of sets of underlying fundamental 'dyads'. A signifying system in this sense is a very wide concept: it means any organised and structured set of signs which carries cultural meanings. Included in this category would be such diverse phenomena as: works of literature, tribal rituals (a degree ceremony, say, or a rain dance), fashions (in clothing, food, 'life-style', etc.), the styling of cars, or the contents of advertisements. For the structuralist, the culture we are part of can be 'read' like a language, using these principles, since culture is made up of many structural networks which carry significance and can be shown to operate in a systematic way. These networks operate through 'codes' as a system of signs; they can make statements, just as language does, and they can be read or decoded by the structuralist or semiotician.

Fashion, for instance, can be 'read' like a language. Separate items or features are added up into a complete 'outfit' or 'look' with complex grammatical rules of combination: we don't wear an evening dress and carpet slippers: we don't come to lectures in military uniform, etc. Likewise, each component sign derives its meaning from a structural context. Of course, many fashions in clothing depend on breaking such rules in a 'knowing' way, but the 'statement' made by such rule-breaks (for instance, making outer garments which look like undergarments, or cutting expensive fabrics in an apparently rough way) depends upon the prior existence of the 'rule' or convention which is being conspicuously flouted. In the fashion world, for instance, (in late 1994) the combination of such features as exposed seams, crumpled-looking fabrics, and garments which were too big or too small for the wearer signified the fashion known (confusingly, in this context) as deconstruction. Take any one of these features out of the context of all the rest, however, and they will merely signify that you have your jacket on inside out or don't believe in ironing. Again, these individual items have their place in an overall structure, and the structure is of greater significance than the individual item.

The other major figure in the early phase of structuralism was Roland Barthes, who applied the structuralist method to the general field of modern culture. He examined modern France (of the 1950s) from the standpoint of a cultural anthropologist in a little book called *Mythologies* which he published in France in 1957. This looked at a host of items which had never before been subjected to intellectual analysis, such as: the difference between boxing and wrestling; the significance of eating steak and chips; the styling of the Citroën car; the cinema image of Greta Garbo's face; a magazine photograph of an Algerian soldier saluting the French flag. Each of these items he placed within a wider structure of values, beliefs, and symbols as the key to understanding it. Thus, boxing is seen as a sport concerned with repression and endurance, as distinct from wrestling, where pain is flamboyantly displayed. Boxers do not cry out in pain when hit, the rules cannot be disregarded at any point during the bout, and the boxer fights as himself, not in the elaborate guise of a make-believe villain or hero. By contrast, wrestlers grunt and snarl with aggression, stage elaborate displays of agony or triumph, and fight as exaggerated, larger than life villains or super-heroes. Clearly, these two sports have quite different functions within society: boxing enacts the stoical endurance which is sometimes necessary in life, while wrestling dramatises ultimate struggles and conflicts between good and evil. Barthes's approach here, then, is that of the classic structuralist: the individual item is 'structuralised', or 'contextualised by structure', and in the process of doing this layers of sigificance are revealed.

Roland Barthes in these early years also made specific examinations of aspects of literature, and by the 1970s structuralism was attracting widespread attention in Paris and world-wide. A number of English and American academics spent time in Paris in the 1970s, taking courses under the leading structuralist figures (and these included Colin MacCabe), and came back to Britain and the USA fired up to teach similar ideas and approaches here. The key works on structuralism were in French, and these began to be translated in the 1970s and published in English. A number of Anglo–American figures undertook to read material not yet translated and to inter- pret structuralism for English-speaking readers; these important mediators included: the American, Jonathan Culler, whose book *Structuralist Poetics* appeared in 1975; and the English critic Terence Hawkes, whose book *Structuralism and Semiotics* came out in 1977 as the first book in a new series published by Methuen called 'New Accents'. Hawkes was the general editor of the series, and its mission was 'to encourage rather than resist the process of change' in literary studies. Another influential figure was the British critic Frank Kermode, then professor at University College, London, who wrote with enthusiasm about Roland Barthes, and set up graduate seminars to discuss his work (though he later in the 1990s became identified, in retirement, with much more traditional approaches). Finally, there was David Lodge, Professor of English at Birmingham, who tried to combine the ideas of structuralism with more tradi- tional approaches. This attempt is typified by his book *Working with Structuralism* (1980).

What structuralist critics do

1. They analyse (mainly) prose narratives, relating the text to some larger containing structure, such as:
    (a) the conventions of a particular literary genre, or
    (b) a network of intertextual connections, or
    (c) a projected model of an underlying universal narrative structure, or
    (d) a notion of narrative as a complex of recurrent patterns or motifs.
2. They interpret literature in terms of a range of underlying parallels with the structures of language, as described by modern linguistics. For instance, the notion of the 'mytheme', posited by Lévi-Strauss, denoting the minimal unit of narrative 'sense', is formed on the analogy of the morpheme, which, in linguistics, is the smallest unit of grammatical sense. An example of a morpheme is the 'ed' added to a verb to denote the past tense.
3. They apply the concept of systematic patterning and structuring to the whole field of Western culture, and across cultures, treating as 'systems of signs' anything from Ancient Greek myths to brands of soap powder.

Structuralist criticism: examples

I will base these examples on the methods of literary analysis described and demonstrated in Barthes's book *S/Z*, published in 1970. This book, of some two hundred pages, is about Balzac's thirty-page story 'Sarrasine'. Barthes's method of analysis is to divide the story into 561 'lexies', or units of meaning, which he then classifies using five 'codes', seeing these as the basic underlying structures of all narratives. So in terms of our opening statement about structuralism (that it aims to understand the individual item by placing it in the context of the larger structure to which it belongs), the individual item here is this particular story, and the larger structure is the system of codes, which Barthes sees as generating all possible actual narratives, just as the grammatical structures of a language can be seen as generating all possible sentences which can be written or spoken in it. I should add that there is a difficulty in taking as an example of structuralism material from a text by

Barthes published in 1970, since 1970 comes within what is usually considered to be Barthes's post-structuralist phase, always said
to begin (as in this book) with his 1968 essay 'The Death of the
Author'. My reasons for nevertheless regarding S/Z as primarily
a structuralist text are, firstly, to do with precedent and established
custom: it is treated as such, for instance, in many of the best-known
books on structuralism (such as Terence Hawkes's *Structuralism and
Semiotics*, Robert Scholes's *Structuralism in Literature*, and Jonathan
Culler's *Structuralist Poetics*). A second reason is that while S/Z
clearly contains many elements which subvert the confident posi-
tivism of structuralism, it is nevertheless essentially structuralist in
its attempt to reduce the immense complexity and diversity possible
in fiction to the operation of five codes, however tongue-in-cheek
the exercise may be taken to be. The truth, really, is that the book
sits on the fence between structuralism and post-structuralism: the
561 lexies and the five codes are linked in spirit to the 'high' structuralism of Barthes's 1968 essay 'Analysing Narrative Structures',
while the ninety-three interspersed digressions, with their much
more free-wheeling comments on narrative, anticipate the 'full'
post-structuralism of his 1973 book *The Pleasure of the Text*.

The five codes identified by Barthes in S/Z are:

1. *The proairetic code* This code provides indications of actions.
    ('The ship sailed at midnight', 'They began again', etc.)
2. *The hermeneutic code* This code poses questions or enigmas
    which provide narrative suspense. (For instance, the sentence
    'He knocked on a certain door in the neighbourhood of Pell
    Street' makes the reader wonder who lived there, what kind of
    neighbourhood it was, and so on.)
3. *The cultural code* This code contains references out beyond
    the text to what is regarded as common knowledge. (For exam-
    ple, the sentence 'Agent Angelis was the kind of man who some-
    times arrives at work in odd socks' evokes a pre-existing image
    in the reader's mind of the kind of man this is – a stereotype
    of bungling incompetence, perhaps, contrasting with the image
    of brisk efficiency contained in the notion of an 'agent'.)
4. *The semic code* This is also called the connotative code. It
    is linked to theme, and this code (says Scholes in the book

mentioned above), when organised around a particular proper name, constitutes a 'character'. Its operation is demonstrated in the second example, below.

5. *The symbolic code*   This code is also linked to theme, but on a larger scale, so to speak. It consists of contrasts and pairings related to the most basic binary polarities – male and female, night and day, good and evil, life and art, and so on. These are the structures of contrasted elements which structuralists see as fundamental to the human way of perceiving and organising reality.

As the last two codes have generated the greatest difficulty (especially in distinguishing one from the other) I will use each in turn as the basis of an example, beginning with the symbolic code, which I will illustrate in use as the organising principle for the interpretation of an entire tale, the story being 'The Oval Portrait' (reproduced in Appendix 1), by the early nineteenth-century American writer Edgar Allan Poe, an author who has received considerable attention from both structuralists and post-structuralists. In terms of the 'What structuralists do' list of activities above, this is an example of category l.(d), treating narrative structure as a complex of recurrent patterns and motifs.

In discussing it I will enlist your help as a co-writer of this structuralist critique. The points at which your help is requested are indicated by the 'STOP and THINK' heading.

A brief working summary of the plot may be useful. During what appears to be a civil war in an unnamed European country a wounded officer (as we may assume him to be) takes refuge in a recently abandoned chateau. The room he sleeps in contains an extremely lifelike portrait of a young woman, and a written account of this portrait, which he finds in the room, tells how the artist was her husband, who had become so carried away with the creation of the portrait that he failed to notice that as 'life' was kindled in the painting it simultaneously drained away from the sitter. At the end of the tale the placing of the final touch of colour which renders the portrait perfect coincides with the death of the sitter.

The most basic difference between liberal humanist and structuralist reading is that the structuralist's comments on structure, symbol, and design become paramount and are the main focus of the commentary, while the emphasis on any wider moral significance, and indeed on interpretation itself in the broad sense, is very much reduced. So instead of going straight into the content, in the liberal humanist manner, the structuralist presents a series of parallels, echoes, reflections, patterns, and contrasts, so that the narrative becomes highly schematised – is translated, in fact, into what we might call a verbal diagram. What we are looking for, as we attempt a structuralist critique, and where we expect to find it, can be indicated as in the diagram below. We are looking for the factors listed on the left, and we expect to find them in the parts of the tale listed on the right:

Parallels			Plot
Echoes			Structure
Reflections/Repetitions	in		Character/Motive
Contrasts			Situation/Circumstance
Patterns			Language/Imagery

Listing some of the parallels, etc., which might be picked out in Poe's tale is perhaps the best way of illustrating all this. Firstly, then, the tale itself has a binary structure (a structure of paired opposites) made up of two contrasting halves: the first part is a 'framing' narrative, containing the first-person account of the wounded officer, while the second is the story-within-the-story which he reads in the commentary on the painting. There is a very marked difference in narrative pace between these two halves, the first being leisurely, ponderous even, reflecting the down-to-earth, rationalistic mind of the officer, while the second moves with increasingly disjointed rapidity, reflecting the frenzy of artistic creation, and the rapid downward spiral of the victim/sitter's health.

A second contrast within the tale is that the chateau itself performs very different functions in the two halves. In the first half it is a place of refuge and recuperation for the officer, where he finds safety from his enemies and, we may assume, recovers his health. In the second half, by contrast, it is a place of danger and ultimately destruction for the sitter, where she is delivered to the whims of her artist-husband and her life is drained away.

STOP and THINK

Now, look for other contrasts between the two halves. For instance, each half features a relationship between two people (the officer and the valet in the first part and the artist and his wife in the second): how do these two relationships differ? There is an unequal distribution of power within each relationship, but the effects are different. How, exactly? Is there a similarity in what the members of each couple do to and for each other?

The main 'actors' in the two halves are (respectively) the wounded officer and the artist. What contrasts are observable in the mental state of these two?

Both the officer in the first part and the artist in the second are, in a sense, engrossed in a painting, but the role of art in the two halves is very different. What exactly is the contrast?

All these are contrasts, parallels, etc., between the two halves. There are also many more *within* the two halves. Firstly, there is a strongly implied contrast between the husband's self-absorbed artistic frenzy on the one hand, and a more conventional outwardly directed sexual passion of the kind which might be expected in a husband for a new bride. Instead of being fascinated by her, this husband is 'entranced before his work' in auto–erotic contemplation. Indeed, the marriage is in a sense bigamous, since the husband is described as 'having already a bride in his art'. The several weeks he spends alone with his new bride executing the painting are a kind of sustained negative parody of a honeymoon. Locked up together for several weeks, the husband painter 'took a fervid and burning pleasure in his task and wrought day and night', and towards the end 'the painter had grown wild with the ardour of his work'. In fact, he has spent this 'honeymoon' in passionate involvement with the first bride rather than the second.

A third level of contrasts and parallels are those which concern narrative mechanisms such as presentation and language, as well as content. One such, for instance, is the parallel between the narrators of the two halves. Both have a degree of anonymity, and in the second case the anonymity is complete, since we are given no information at all about the identity of the author of the 'vague and quaint words' of the story-within-the-story. (The only named character is Pedro the valet, the least important figure in the tale.) But structuralists are encouraged by Roland Barthes to ask of a text the question *'qui parle?'* – 'Who is speaking?' – and if we ask that question of the second part of the tale, then the answer will involve dislodging the narrator from the position of a neutral spectatorial recorder, for this account must have been written by someone who witnessed these events without attempting any intervention. At the very least, this witness is someone without insight, indistinguishable from those who, having seen the portrait, 'spoke of its resemblance in low words, as of a mighty marvel, and a proof not less of the power of the painter than of his deep love for her whom he depicted so surpassingly well'.

STOP and THINK

The first narrator, too, can be seen as to some degree culpable, and as wilfully blind to the events witnessed. Could we go further? Is there a parallel between the two narrators, such that the first is aligned, through the language used, with the attitudes of the artist-husband?

For instance, what do you make of his prolonged contemplation of the painting? Are there elements in that part of the text which parallel the displaced eroticism of the artist's protracted gazing on his wife as he makes the painting? There are two examples, not just one, of an intense masculine gaze in the story. Look at the distribution of the words 'gaze' and 'glory' (or 'gloriously') in the text. Look at the way the passing of time is depicted in each of these cases. In both cases there is a moment when the gaze is averted: what is the significance of this parallelism?

All these contrasts are of a very particular kind, proper to just this one tale. We may then perform a simplifying move which is rather like finding the lowest common denominator of a set of numbers, for these items might be reduced to a set of more generalised ones: the contrast and conflict between *life* and *art*, *male* and *female*, *light* and *dark* (in the sense of enlightenment and moral benightedness, as well as in purely physical terms), *looking* and *doing*, *reality* and *representation*. The thesis of the structuralist is that narrative structures are founded upon such underlying paired opposites, or dyads, so that contrasts such as these are the skeletal structure on which all narratives are fleshed out. If we had to reduce even this list of dyads, to achieve a single pair, then it would have to be the art/life contrast, since the tale seems most to be about life and art viewed as factors in an overall psychic economy.

The obvious final question is to ask which side of this dichotomy the tale is on. There can surely be little doubt that it is on the side of art, for it is the act of artistic creation, and, to a lesser extent, that of contemplating a work of art, which is most vividly and passionately described in the tale, rather than any sense of the waste of a young life. The frenzy of this 'passionate, wild, and moody man' produces a work of art so lifelike that it seems the product of a divine being. This is no way to champion 'life'. 'Officially' the story is a pious protest at the sacrifice of a young life, but in practice the making of the sacrifice is presented with a kind of loving envy. As D. H. Lawrence didn't quite say, never trust the moral, trust the tale.

So much, then, for the symbolic code. The second example centres on the operation within a text of the *semic code*. This code, as we have said, is linked with the process of characterisation and thematicisation but operates on a smaller scale than the symbolic code. For Hawkes, in the book mentioned earlier, it 'utilises hints or "flickers of meaning"', and given that it operates through the nuances of individual words and phrases, the best way to appreciate it in action is to use a variation of what educationalists call 'cloze procedure', which involves deleting words from a text and having readers fill these gaps by drawing inferences from context and overall structure.

The passage below is the opening of a novel by Mervyn Jones called *Mr Armitage Isn't Back Yet* (Cape, 1971). The central character, Mr Armitage, is presented in the opening scene and his character immediately established. I have left gaps in the text and have listed at the end of the relevant sentences several words which might fill that gap (one of which, in each case, is the word actually used by the author). You will see that the character is decisively altered, according to the word you choose to fill the gap, enabling us to feel the semic code actually at work. The paragraphs have been numbered for ease of reference. In terms of the 'What structuralists do' list, this is an example of 1.(c), that is, of relating the text to a projected model of an underlying universal narrative structure, since the critic would assume that the five Barthesian codes are fundamental to the workings of all narratives. Spend time now selecting a word for each gap before going on to my commentary.

STOP and THINK

1. John Edward Scott Armitage: fifty-five years old, five feet eleven inches tall, weight thirteen stone three _____.
   [*pounds, ounces*]

2. June the eighth: a fine morning, nine-fifteen by the programme change on the car radio, also nine-fifteen exactly as he checked the time on his _____ watch.
   [*multi-function, Swiss, Swatch, Timex, pocket, Mickey Mouse*]

3. Hendon Way, north-bound. Armitage was driving a Jaguar, just run in. Its newness pleased him – the _____ smell of the leather, the neat zeros on the mileage dial. He was among those men whose car is never more than a year old.
   [*rich, sweet, heady, sexy, opulent*]

There is further description, then Armitage slows the car to look at two hitch-hikers. They meet his standards of acceptability, and he offers them a lift, but the response to his offer is a momentary hesitation. The text resumes:

4. The boy still presented his pleasant smile, but did not get into the car. Now he seemed to be considering, not only the directions, but also the car, and even Armitage himself. The hitch-hiker, in fact, was deciding whether to accept the driver instead of the other way round. Armitage was _____. In a few seconds more he might have been indignant. But the girl said: 'This is fine – yes it is – super, really'.
   [*baffled, stumped, gob-smacked*]

5. She spoke eagerly, indeed with some impatience at the boy's hesitation. And she too smiled at Armitage, but more

than pleasantly, _____, he thought. Of course, they were lucky to get a long ride in a new Jaguar. The girl clearly realised this; she seemed, moreover, to be happy to travel with Armitage. As soon as this notion occurred to him Armitage saw that it was absurd. Yet it was an attractive thing for her to give such an impression.

[*happily, cheerfully, invitingly, gleefully*]

6. She _____ into the front seat, and the boy got into the back. Armitage pulled away quickly to get ahead of a removal van. He drove in a thrusting style, seizing every opportunity, overtaking in roaring third gear. He met, and then dismissed, the thought that the girl's presence beside him had made him show off his skill.

[*jumped quickly, plumped heavily, slid seductively, slid easily, squeezed awkwardly, slipped quietly*]

I'll comment briefly on the gaps in each of these paragraphs.

In the first, the word in the published text is 'ounces', the precision of which immediately suggests a man with a very precise and ordered attitude to life. (How many people know their weight to the nearest ounce?)

In the second paragraph the character of Armitage is completely changed if we change his watch. In the text his 'Swiss' watch reinforces the image of the well-ordered, well-to-do life already established in the first few lines of the book. But the semic code's 'flicker of meaning' can instantly change him into an ageing gadget-faddist with a multi-function digital timepiece, or a dedicated follower of fashion with a trendy Swatch Watch, or an old fogey with a pocket watch, or a hearty life-and-soul-of-the-party type with a jokey Mickey Mouse watch.

In the third paragraph the words 'sweet', 'heady', and 'sexy' all come close to turning Armitage into a leather fetishist, while 'rich' has a certain directness and vulgarity which implies that his pleasure in things is in direct proportion to their cost. The text's 'opulent' retains an element of this but seems to imply an appreciation of quality and craftsmanship for its own sake.

In the fourth paragraph (as often in fiction) the kind of word used by the narrating voice reflects the character being described. 'Stumped' suggests an undignified cluelessness, as, even more so, does 'gob-smacked', whereas the text's 'baffled' implies the offended dignity of a man of some standing accustomed to a degree of respect.

In the fifth paragraph Armitage's perception of the nature of the girl's smile is a crucial element in his characterisation. The text has him seeing her as smiling 'cheerfully', indicating that he is pleased to perceive a positive reaction towards himself. If she were smiling, in his view, 'invitingly', then the implication would be that his motives were entirely sexual. 'Gleefully', on the other hand, would make her into a child rather than an adult.

In the final paragraph the missing phrase indicates that, all the same, Armitage finds the girl attractive and is physically aware of her. The text tells us that she 'slid easily' into the front seat, implying a certain slender gracefulness. Armitage's attention is less directed towards the boy, so he simply 'got into' the back. If we reverse these two phrases the implication is that Armitage is more interested in the boy than the girl, thus: 'She got into the front seat, and the boy slid easily into the back'. This has the effect of tending to construct Armitage as homosexual, even though no such explicit statement is made.

This simple 'cloze' exercise, then, indicates something of the small-scale, but none the less crucial, workings of the semic code in the construction of character, while also showing how, in sequence, this code can begin to activate thematic motifs, such as the notion of orderliness and control associated with Armitage.

The operation of two other codes could easily be illustrated from the same passage. The *hermeneutic code*, for instance, is obviously important in it. Right at the beginning of a novel the reader has to be drawn into the process of speculating about possible outcomes, working out enigmas, and predicting the possible patterns of events and motives. Thus, with this example we are immediately involved in answering questions like 'What is going to happen as a result of this meeting?' 'Are the hitch-hikers as innocent as they seem?' 'Will Armitage's confidence be shaken in some way as the novel progresses?' Finally, an example of the *cultural code* is seen in the third paragraph when we are told that Armitage 'was among those men whose car is never more than a year old', where the text appeals to our prior knowledge of this kind of man as a distinct type with a whole range of related characteristics and habits. The last code, the symbolic, would be difficult to detect in such a brief and early extract from a novel, and has already been demonstrated at length in the Poe example.

Selected reading

Barthes, Roland, *The Semiotic Challenge*, trans. Richard Howard (University of California Press, 1994).

Essays by the best-known structuralist critic; see chapter in section three 'Textual analysis of a tale by Edgar Allan Poe', on 'The Facts in the Case of M. Valdemar'.

Barthes, Roland, *A Roland Barthes Reader*, ed. Susan Sontag (Vintage, 1993).

Culler, Jonathan, *Structuralist Poetics* (Routledge, 1975).

A book which immediately established the author's reputation as a 'mediator' of difficult theories. Re-issued in 2002 with a new reflective preface by the author.

Culler, Jonathan, *Barthes* (Fontana, 1983).

Culler, Jonathan, *Barthes: A Very Short Introduction* (Oxford Paperbacks, 2002).

Hawkes, Terence, *Structuralism and Semiotics* (Methuen, 1977; Routledge, 2nd edn, 2002).

A pioneering book in a key series. Equivalent to Culler, but does it better, in my view, because the series format makes for brevity and tightness.

Saussure, Ferdinand de, *Course in General Linguistics* (Bloomsbury Revelations, 2013).

An excellent edition, translated and annotated by the eminent linguist Roy Harris (1931–2015).

Scholes, Robert, *Structuralism in Literature: An Introduction* (Yale University Press, 1974; new edn, 2009).

An admirable book. Don't be put off by its age. You won't find anything to match it.

Sturrock, John, *Structuralism* (Paladin, 1986).

Covers structuralism in a variety of fields (language, social sciences, etc.). Chapter four is a good, succinct account of literary structuralism and its antecedents.

3
Post-structuralism and deconstruction

Some theoretical differences between structuralism and post-structuralism

Is post-structuralism a continuation and development of structuralism or a form of rebellion against it? In one important sense it is the latter, since a very effective way of rebelling is to accuse your predecessors of not having the courage of their convictions. Thus post-structuralists accuse structuralists of not following through the implications of the views about language on which their intellectual system is based. As we saw, one of structuralism's characteristic views is the notion that language doesn't just reflect or record the world: rather, it shapes it, so that *how* we see is *what* we see. The post-structuralist maintains that the consequences of this belief are that we enter a universe of radical uncertainty, since we can have no access to any fixed landmark which is beyond linguistic processing, and hence we have no certain standard by which to measure anything. Without a fixed point of reference against which to measure movement you cannot tell whether or not you are moving at all. You have probably at some time had the experience of sitting in a stationary train with another train between yourself and the far platform. When that train begins to move you may have the sensation that it is *your* train which is moving and only realise this isn't so when the other train has gone and you again see the fixed point of the platform. Post-structuralism says, in effect, that fixed intellectual reference points are permanently removed by properly taking on board what structuralists said about language. Or, to change the analogy, in space,

where there is no gravity, there is no up and down, and these pronouncements about language send us into a gravity-free universe,
without upside down or right way up. This situation, of being without intellectual reference points, is one way of describing what
post-structuralists call the *decentred universe*, one in which, by definition, we cannot know where we are, since all the concepts which
previously defined the centre, and hence also the margins, have been
'deconstructed', or undermined, in the manner described later.

The characteristic concerns of post-structuralism, as hinted at
here, may at first seem pretty remote. Why this constant high anxiety about language, we might ask, when it seems to work perfectly
well most of the time for day-to-day purposes? But on reflection we
may find that it is precisely on this matter of anxiety about language
that we can most easily identify with post-structuralist concerns, for
these anxious feelings seem remarkably pervasive whenever we have
to use language at any level beyond that of casual daily exchange
with people we know very well and whose status is the same as our
own. For instance, think of any slightly less straightforward language situation, like writing to your bank, writing an essay, striking
up a friendship with a stranger at a party, or sending a letter of con-
dolence. In these cases, and many more, there is an almost universally felt anxiety that the language will express things we hadn't
intended, or convey the wrong impression, or betray our ignorance,
callousness, or confusion. Even when we use a phrase like 'If you see
what I mean' or 'In a manner of speaking' there is the same underlying sense that we are not really in control of the linguistic system.
These feelings, writ large, are really the same, or, at least, surely have
the same source, as the radical linguistic scepticism which is so typical of deconstruction. Here, then, is a way into the post-structuralist frame of mind which lies very much within attitudes and anxieties
which most of us experience.

However, perhaps it will be helpful simply to list some differences
and distinctions between structuralism and post-structuralism,
under the four headings below.

1. *Origins*   Structuralism derives ultimately from linguistics. Linguistics is a discipline which has always been inherently confident about the possibility of establishing objective knowledge.
   It believes that if we observe accurately, collect data systematically,

and make logical deductions then we can reach reliable conclusions about language and the world. Structuralism inherits this confidently scientific outlook: it too believes in method, system, and reason as being able to establish reliable truths.

By contrast, post-structuralism derives ultimately from philosophy. Philosophy is a discipline which has always tended to emphasise the difficulty of achieving secure knowledge about things. This point of view is encapsulated in Nietzsche's famous remark 'There are no facts, only interpretations'. Philosophy is, so to speak, sceptical by nature and usually undercuts and questions commonsensical notions and assumptions. Its procedures often begin by calling into question what is usually taken for granted as simply the way things are. Post-structuralism inherits this habit of scepticism, and intensifies it. It regards any confidence in the scientific method as naive, and even derives a certain masochistic intellectual pleasure from knowing for certain that we *can't* know anything for certain, fully conscious of the irony and paradox which doing this entails.

2. *Tone and style*   Structuralist writing tends towards abstraction and generalisation: it aims for a detached, 'scientific coolness' of tone. Given its derivation from linguistic science, this is what we would expect. An essay like Roland Barthes's 1966 piece 'Introduction to the Structural Analysis of Narrative' (reprinted in *Image, Music, Text*, ed. Stephen Heath, Fontana Press, new edn, 1993) is typical of this tone and treatment, with its discrete steps in an orderly exposition, complete with diagrams. The style is neutral and anonymous, as is typical of scientific writing.

Post-structuralist writing, by contrast, tends to be much more emotive. Often the tone is urgent and euphoric, and the style flamboyant and self-consciously showy. Titles may well contain puns and allusions, and often the central line of the argument is based on a pun or a word-play of some kind.

Often deconstructive writing fixes on some 'material' aspect of language, such as a metaphor used by a writer, or the etymology of a word. Overall it seems to aim for an engaged warmth rather than a detached coolness.

3. *Attitude to language*   Structuralists accept that the world is constructed through language, in the sense that we do not have access to reality other than through the linguistic medium. All the same,

it decides to live with that fact and continue to use language to think and perceive with. After all, language is an orderly system, not a chaotic one, so realising our dependence upon it need not induce intellectual despair.

By contrast, post-structuralism is much more fundamentalist in insisting upon the consequences of the view that, in effect, reality itself is textual. Post-structuralism develops what threaten to become terminal anxieties about the possibility of achieving *any* knowledge through language. The verbal sign, in its view, is constantly floating free of the concept it is supposed to designate. Thus, the post-structuralist's way of speaking about language involves a rather obsessive imagery based on liquids – signs float free of what they designate, meanings are fluid, and subject to constant 'slippage' or 'spillage'. This linguistic liquid, slopping about and swilling over unpredictably, defies our attempts to carry signification carefully from 'giver' to 'receiver' in the containers we call words. We are not fully in control of the medium of language, so meanings cannot be planted in set places, like somebody planting a row of potato seeds; they can only be randomly scattered or 'disseminated', like the planter walking along and scattering seed with broad sweeps of the arm, so that much of it lands unpredictably or drifts in the wind.

Likewise, the meanings words have can never be guaranteed 100 per cent pure. Thus, words are always 'contaminated' by their opposites – you can't define *night* without reference to *day*, or *good* without reference to *evil*. Or else they are interfered with by their own history, so that obsolete senses retain a troublesome and ghostly presence within present-day usage, and are likely to materialise just when we thought it was safe to use them. Thus, a seemingly innocent word like 'guest' is etymologically cognate with 'hostis', which means an enemy or a stranger, thereby inadvertently manifesting the always potentially unwelcome status of the guest (see below, p. 73). Likewise, the long-dormant metaphorical bases of words are often reactiviated by their use in philosophy or literature and then interfere with literal sense, or with the stating of single meanings. Linguistic anxiety, then, is a keynote of the post-structuralist outlook.

4. *Project* By 'project' here I mean the fundamental aims of each movement, what it is they want to persuade us of. Structuralism, firstly, questions our way of structuring and categorising reality, and prompts us to break free of habitual modes of perception or categorisation, but it believes that we can thereby attain a more reliable view of things.

    Post-structuralism is much more fundamental: it distrusts the very notion of reason, and the idea of the human being as an independent entity, preferring the notion of the 'dissolved' or 'constructed' subject, whereby what we may think of as the individual is really a product of social and linguistic forces – that is, not an essence at all, merely a 'tissue of textualities'. Thus, its torch of scepticism burns away the intellectual ground on which Western civilisation is built.

Post-structuralism – life on a decentred planet

Post-structuralism emerged in France in the late 1960s. The two figures most closely associated with this emergence are Roland Barthes and Jacques Derrida (1930–2004). Barthes's work around this time began to shift in character and move from a structuralist phase to a post-structuralist phase. The difference can be seen by comparing two different accounts by Barthes of the nature of the narrative, one from each phase, namely the essay 'The Structural Analysis of Narrative' (first published in 1966) and *The Pleasure of the Text* (1973). The former is detailed, methodological, and forbiddingly technical, while the latter is really just a series of random comments on narrative, arranged alphabetically, thereby, of course, emphasising the randomness of the material. Between these two works came the crucial essay 'The Death of the Author' (1968) which is the 'hinge' around which Barthes turns from structuralism to post-structuralism. In that essay he announces the death of the author, which is a rhetorical way of asserting the independence of the literary text and its immunity to the possibility of being unified or limited by any notion of what the author might have intended, or 'crafted' into the work. Instead, the essay makes a declaration of radical textual independence: the work is not determined by intention, or context. Rather, the text is free by its very nature of all such restraints.

Hence, as Barthes says in the essay, the corollary of the death of the author is the birth of the reader. So the difference between the 1966 essay and the 1973 book is a shift of attention from the text seen as something produced by the author to the text seen as something produced by the reader, and, as it were, by language itself, for as Barthes also says, in the absence of an author, the claim to decipher a text becomes futile. Hence, this early phase of post-structuralism seems to license and revel in the endless free play of meanings and the escape from all forms of textual authority. Later there is an inevitable shift from this textual permissiveness to the more disciplined and austere textual republicanism suggested in the quotation (pp. 73–4) from Barbara Johnson. For her, deconstruction is not a hedonistic abandonment of all restraint, but a disciplined identification and dismantling of the sources of textual power.

The second key figure in the development of post-structuralism in the late 1960s is the philosopher Jacques Derrida. Indeed, the starting point of post-structuralism may be taken as his 1966 lecture 'Structure, Sign and Play in the Discourse of the Human Sciences' (variously reprinted, for example in abbreviated form in K. M. Newton's *Twentieth Century Literary Theory: A Reader*, Macmillan, 2nd edn, 1997). In this lecture Derrida sees in modern times a particular intellectual 'event' which constitutes a radical break from past ways of thought, loosely associating this break with the philosophy of Nietzsche and Heidegger and the psychoanalysis of Freud. The event concerns the 'decentring' of our intellectual universe. Prior to this event the existence of a norm or centre in all things was taken for granted: thus 'man', as the Renaissance slogan had it, was the measure of all other things in the universe: white Western norms of dress, behaviour, architecture, intellectual outlook, and so on provided a firm centre against which deviations, aberrations, variations could be detected and identified as 'Other' and marginal. In the twentieth century, however, these centres were destroyed or eroded; sometimes this was caused by historical events – such as the way the First World War destroyed the illusion of steady material progress, or the way the Holocaust destroyed the notion of Europe as the source and centre of human civilisation; sometimes it happened because of scientific discoveries – such as the way the notion of relativity destroyed the ideas of time and space as fixed and central absolutes; and sometimes, finally, it was caused by intellectual or artistic revolutions – such as the way modernism in the arts in the first thirty years of the century rejected such central absolutes as harmony in music, chronological sequence in narrative, and the representation of the visual world in art.

In the resulting universe there are no absolutes or fixed points, so that the universe we live in is 'decentred' or inherently relativistic. Instead of movement or deviation from a known centre, all we have is 'free play' (or 'play' as the title of the essay has it). In the lecture Derrida embraces this decentred universe of free play as liberating, just as Barthes in 'The Death of the Author' celebrates the demise of the author as ushering in an era of joyous freedom. The consequences of this new decentred universe are impossible to predict, but we must endeavour not to be among 'those who ... turn their eyes away in the face of the as yet unnameable which is proclaiming itself' (Newton, p. 154). This powerful, quasi-religious appeal to us not to turn our eyes away from the light is typical of the often apocalyptic tone of post-structuralist writing. If we have the courage, the implication is, we will enter this new Nietzschean universe, where there are no guaranteed facts, only interpretations, none of which has the stamp of authority upon it, since there is no longer any authoritative centre to which to appeal for validation of our intepretations.

Derrida's rise to prominence was confirmed by the publication of three books by him in the following year (translated as *Speech and Phenomena*, *Of Grammatology*, and *Writing and Difference*). All of these books are on philosophical rather than literary topics, but Derrida's method always involves the highly detailed 'deconstructive' reading of selected aspects of other philosophers' works, and these deconstructive methods have been borrowed by literary critics and used in the reading of literary works. Essentially, the deconstructive reading of literary texts tends to make them emblems of the decentred universe we have been discusssing. Texts previously regarded as unified artistic artefacts are shown to be fragmented, self-divided, and centreless. They always turn out to be representative of the 'monstrous births' predicted at the end of 'Structure, Sign, and Play'.

STOP and THINK

A key text in post-structuralism is Derrida's book *Of Gramma-tology* (40th anniversary edn, Johns Hopkins University Press, 2016. All the page numbers given here are to this edition.) The slogan 'There is nothing outside the text' is the most frequently quoted line from this book, but it is usually quoted out of con-text to justify a kind of extreme textualism, whereby it is held that all reality is linguistic, so that there can be no meaning-ful talk of a 'real' world which exists without question outside language.

It became common to deny that such a view is the one actu-ally put forward by Derrida, and while I do not recommend that you attempt to tackle the whole book at this stage, you could put yourself considerably ahead of many commentators and critics by acquiring a detailed knowledge of the section of the book in which this remark occurs, using the intensive reading technique I describe in the Introduction. The section is subheaded 'The Exorbitant. Question of Method' (pp. 171–8).

Derrida is writing in this section about Rousseau's 'Essay on the origin of languages', but he stops to question his own method of interpreting this text, and hence the nature of all interpretation. He debates the concept of the 'supplement', a word which in French can also mean a replacement, in the sense that language replaces or stands in for reality. (This idea is out-lined in the immediately preceding pages of *Of Grammatology*, pp. 153–71.) But what exactly is the nature of this 'standing in', since 'the person writing is inscribed in a determined textual system' (p. 174), which is to say that we all inherit language as a ready-made system, with its own history, philosophy, and so on already 'built in'? In this sense one might argue that we don't express ourselves in words, we merely express some aspect of language:

> The writer writes *in* a language [*langue*] and *in* a logic whose proper systems, laws, and life his discourse by definition cannot dominate absolutely. He uses them by only letting himself, after a fashion and up to a point, be governed by the system. And the reading must always aim at a certain relationship, unperceived by

the writer, between what he commands and what he does not command of the patterns of the language that he uses. This relationship is not a certain quantitative distribution of shadow and light, of weakness or of force, but a signifying structure that critical reading should *produce*.

(Derrida, *Of Grammatology*, p. 172)

Reading and interpretation, then, are not just *reproducing* what the writer thought and expressed in the text. This inadequate notion of interpretation Derrida calls a 'doubling commentary', since it tries to reconstruct a pre-existing, non-textual reality (of what the writer did or thought) to lay alongside the text. Instead, critical reading must *produce* the text, since there is nothing behind it for us to reconstruct. Thus, the reading has to be deconstructive rather than reconstructive in this sense. This is the point where Derrida makes the remark which he later calls 'the axial proposition of this essay, that there is nothing outside the text' (*Of Grammatology*, p. 177):

Reading … cannot legitimately transgress the text toward something other than it … or toward a signified outside the text whose content could take place could have taken place, outside of the language [*langue*], that is to say, in the sense that we give here to that word, outside of writing in general. That is why the methodological considerations that we risk applying here to an example are closely dependent on general propositions that we have elaborated above; as regards the absence of the referent or the transcendental signified. *There is nothing outside of the text* [There is no outside-text; *Il n'y a pas dehors-texte*].

(*Of Grammatology*, p. 172)

He expands this further and reiterates that 'beyond and behind what one believes can be circumscribed as Rousseau's text, there has never been anything but writing; … what opens meaning and language [*langage*] is writing as the disappearance of natural presence' (p. 173).

You will not find these pages of Derrida by any means easy, but they will repay some intensive work, ideally in group discussion. Do they enable you to pin down precisely what Derrida is saying about the relationship between word and world, and are his views as stark and uncompromising as they are often accused of being?

A note on the translation of *Of Grammatology* and on 'reading'

Most English-speaking readers are reliant on the erudite and heroic labours of Professor Gayatri Spivak, who translated Derrida's *Of Grammatology*. Her translation, published in 1976, is so good that it is reprinted largely unchanged in the 40th anniversary edition of 2016. This is an impression – changes are not indicated, and I have not attempted to re-read the whole book with the two versions side-by-side. Those I have noticed seem trivial: thus, in 1976 the second paragraph of 'The Exorbitant. Question of Method' begins 'This brings up the question of the usage of the word "supplement"', which in 2016 reads 'This poses the question of the usage of the word "supplement"' (p. 171). The main noticeable recurrent change is that the translator indicates in square brackets, whenever the English word 'language' is used, whether it is translating the French word *langage* (meaning, in Saussure's usage, language as a vast structure of grammatical and syntactical rules and tightly calibrated, mutually defining semantic distinctions) or the French word *parole* (meaning a specific utterance, statement, or remark which can only be understood within that Saussurean system of rules and differences). Also, there is no new annotation that comments on aspects of Derrida's text which have provoked particular controversy or discussion over the years, so we read the text of 2016 entirely from within the perspective of 1976, that is, in a sealed-off, time-warped, Derridean universe. Judith Butler's clear and informative new introduction is a very welcome addition, because it not only gives a summary of Derrida's overall argument in this book, usefully complementing Spivak's pioneering work of elucidation in her own introduction, but it also places it within the wider trajectory of his work. The other major addition is that, forty years after it was first published, this huge book finally has an index, enabling readers to navigate these turbulent

intellectual waters independently of Derrida's relentless pilot-
age. Self-evidently, any academic book without an index disempowers its readers, delaying what Roland Barthes called the birth
of the reader, and forcing them to follow passively in the writer's
footsteps.

For several years discussions about Derrida's thinking focused
on the meaning of the pronouncement 'There is nothing outside the
text', not unreasonably, since Derrida himself refers to this statement as 'the axial proposition of this essay, that there is nothing
outside the text' (p. 177). However, the usual response from
Derrideans is to claim that Derrida never said that, though that is
how Spivak translates what he said, both in 1976 and 2016. But both
times, on the first occurrence of the sentence she meticulously
places a more literal translation of his words immediately after, and
then the exact French words Derrida used, all in square brackets,
thus: '[there is no outside-text; *il n'y a pas de hors-texte*]'. But 'there
is no outside-text' is not really any translation at all. In English, the
words 'There is no' are usually followed by a noun or a noun phrase
– we can say 'There is no time' or 'There is no wine left', but we
cannot say 'There is no outside-text', since the compound noun
'outside-text' does not exist in English. We can have an outside loo,
or an outside chance, but we can't have an outside text. But if we
search for *hors-texte* in a French–English dictionary we find (puzzlingly) the translation 'inset' (Collins Dictionary), and (bizarrely)
'plate' (in the online 'Reverso'). These are explained (but not
excused) when we find out from elsewhere that the *hors-texte* is a
technical term in traditional book production in France which collectively designates all those parts of a book that are not contained
in the main sequence of page numbers. This category includes such
items as pages deliberately left blank; illustrated plates which are
'tipped in' (that is, pasted in) after all the other pages of the book
have been printed, such extra-numeric pages being listed in the
contents as, for example, 'facing page 47'; title pages; pages setting
out copyright details; prefaces that have their own preliminary
numerical sequence (usually in small roman numerals); and the
contents pages themselves. Only after passing all these do readers
reach the textual departure gate – page one. (You can see some of
these features in the book you are reading now.) Together these

pages comprise the *hors-texte*: they are part of the book, but not part of the text.

Having gone through all this, how can we make up our minds about what Derrida's 'axial proposition' actually means? The *hors-texte* is a transitional or in-between space, a hinterland, which is something like the frame and 'mask' of a picture (the mask being the blank space between the frame and the picture) which are like the preliminary pages deliberately left blank in a printed book. There may also by a lined-out frame on the mask, as we get closer in to the picture, perhaps corresponding to the preface of a book, which is always the innermost part of the front-end *hors-texte*. So very loosely translated, Derrida's proposition seems to be saying that there is nothing which is completely outside of and untouched by textuality in some form. That may be something like imagining a world that is 'bookified', or 'textualised', even if the imagining of it takes the form of denying its existence. When I recommend intensive rather than extensive reading, this kind of labyrinthine, tortuous pursuit of signification is what I have in mind, and it seems to me that this is the best part of theorising. Further, theorising itself is simply what Derrida meant by reading. Thus, in the 2005 film *Derrida* (highly recommended, directed by Kirby Dick and Amy Ziering Kofman, and cheaply available online), there is a moment when the interviewer enters Derrida's study, and there are a number of books on the shelves behind him. He is asked if he has read them all, and replies, after a moment's thought, that he has read five of them, adding 'But I have read those five really, really well.' It is clear that he doesn't mean 'reading' in the ordinary sense, and it would not be true to say that Derrida had only read five of the books in his own library, even though that is what he said. But Derrida sees proper reading as something that is sustained over months of intensive engagement. For him 'reading' means writing back, in close, sustained, and intense dialogue with, and to, the author. It should mean that for us too – that rapt and intensive reading-thinking-writing activity which is theorising – and that is what I am trying to do now. Doubtless, we all have our limitations, and we can only do it at our own level, but we can all accept that reading isn't just a matter of moving the eyes and turning the pages, pages which will be forgotten almost as soon as we stand up again.

Structuralism and post-structuralism – some practical differences

An initial problem here is that post-structuralism often claims that it is more an attitude of mind than a practical method of criticism. This is, in a sense, quite true, but perhaps no more true of post-structuralism than of any other critical orientation. After all, in what sense could, say, Marxist or feminist – or even liberal humanist – criticism be called a method? Only in the loosest way, surely, since none of these provide anything like a step-by-step procedure for analysing literary works. All they offer is an orientation towards a characteristic central issue (that is, towards issues of class, gender, and personal morality, respectively) and a body of work which constitutes a repertoire of examples.

What, then, seem to be the characteristics of post-structuralism as a critical method? The post-structuralist literary critic is engaged in the task of 'deconstructing' the text. This process is given the name 'deconstruction', which can roughly be defined as applied post-structuralism. It is often referred to as 'reading against the grain' or 'reading the text against itself', with the purpose of 'knowing the text as it cannot know itself'. (These are Terry Eagleton's definitions.) A way of describing this would be to say that deconstructive reading uncovers the unconscious rather than the conscious dimension of the text, all the things which its overt textuality glosses over or fails to recognise. This repressed unconscious within language might be sensed, for instance, in the example used earlier when we said that the word 'guest' is cognate with (that is, has the same original root as) the word 'host', which in turn comes from the Latin word *hostis*, meaning an enemy. This hints at the potential double aspect of a guest, as either welcome or unwelcome, or as changing from one to the other. This notion of 'hostility', then, is like the repressed unconscious of the word, and the process of deconstruction, in revealing the unconscious of the text, might draw upon such disciplines as etymology in this way.

Another well-known definition of deconstructive reading is Barbara Johnson's in *The Critical Difference* (Johns Hopkins University Press, 1980):

> Deconstruction is not synonymous with 'destruction'. It is in fact
> much closer to the original meaning of the word 'analysis', which
> etymologically means 'to undo' ... The deconstruction of a text does
> not proceed by random doubt or arbitrary subversion, but by the
> careful teasing out of warring forces of signification within the text.
>
> *(The Critical Difference*, p. 5)

Derrida's own description of deconstructive reading has the same
purport. A deconstructive reading

> must always aim at a certain relationship, unperceived by the writer,
> between what he commands and what he does not command of
> the patterns of language that he uses ... [It] attempts to make the
> not-seen visible.
>
> *(Of Grammatology*, 2016, pp. 172 and 178)

J. A. Cuddon, in his *Dictionary of Literary Terms*, asserts that in
deconstruction:

> a text can be read as saying something quite different from what
> it appears to be saying ... it may be read as carrying a plurality of
> significance or as saying many different things which are fundamen-
> tally at variance with, contradictory to and subversive of what may
> be seen by criticism as a single stable 'meaning'. Thus a text may
> 'betray' itself.
>
> (from the entry on Deconstruction, 5th edn, p. 189)

So the deconstructionist practises what has been called textual
harassment or oppositional reading, reading with the aim of
unmasking internal contradictions or inconsistencies in the text,
aiming to show the disunity which underlies its apparent unity. The
aim of the 'New Critics' of the previous generation, by contrast, had
been precisely the opposite of this, to show the unity beneath apparent disunity. In pursuance of its aims, the deconstructive process
will often fix on a detail of the text which looks incidental – the
presence of a particular metaphor, for instance – and then use it as
the key to the whole text, so that everything is read through it.

In talking about structuralism we discussed how structuralists
look for such features in the text as parallels, echoes, reflections, and
so on (p. 53). The effect of doing this is often to show a unity of
purpose within the text, as if the text knows what it wants to do and

has directed all its means towards this end. By contrast, the decon-structionist aims to show that the text is at war with itself: it is a house divided, and disunified. The deconstructionist looks for evidence of gaps, breaks, fissures and discontinuities of all kinds. So a diagram showing the differences between structuralism and post-structuralism at the practical level might look like this:

The structuralist seeks:	*The post-structuralist seeks:*
Parallels/Echoes	Contradictions/Paradoxes
Balances	Shifts/Breaks in: Tone
	Viewpoint
	Tense
	Time
	Person
	Attitude
Reflections/Repetitions	Conflicts
Symmetry	Absences/Omissions
Contrasts	Linguistic quirks
Patterns	Aporia
Effect: to show textual unity and coherence	*Effect: to show textual disunity*

In presenting the example, I will refer back to this list, and will also suggest a simple three-stage model of the deconstructive process. I will end with some questions to help you to try your own 'worked example'.

What post-structuralist critics do

1. They 'read the text against itself' so as to expose what might be thought of as the 'textual subconscious', where meanings are expressed which may be directly contrary to the surface meaning.
2. They fix upon the surface features of the words – similarities in sound, the root meanings of words, a 'dead' (or dying) metaphor – and bring these to the foreground, so that they become crucial to the overall meaning.
3. They seek to show that the text is characterised by disunity rather than unity.

4. They concentrate on a single passage and analyse it so inten-
    sively that it becomes impossible to sustain a 'univocal' reading
    and the language explodes into 'multiplicities of meaning'.
5. They look for shifts and breaks of various kinds in the text and
    see these as evidence of what is repressed or glossed over or
    passsed over in silence by the text. These discontinuities are
    sometimes called 'fault-lines', a geological metaphor referring
    to the breaks in rock formations which give evidence of previ-
    ous activity and movement.

Deconstruction: an example

I try here to give a clear example of deconstructive practice, showing what is distinctive about it while at the same time suggesting
that it may not constitute a *complete* break with more familiar forms
of criticism.

The three stages of the deconstructive process described here
I have called the *verbal*, the *textual*, and the *linguistic*. They are illustrated using Dylan Thomas's poem 'A Refusal to Mourn the Death,
by Fire, of a Child in London' (Appendix 2).

The verbal stage is very similar to that of more conventional
forms of close reading, as pioneered in the 1920s and 1930s in
Empson's *Seven Types of Ambiguity*, and elsewhere. It involves looking in the text for paradoxes and contradictions, at what might
be called the purely verbal level. For instance, the final line of
Thomas's poem reads 'After the first death there is no other'. This
statement contradicts and refutes itself: if something is called the
first then a sequence is implied of second, third, fourth, and so on.
So, the phrase 'the first death' clearly implies, at the literal level,
that there *will* be others. Internal contradictions of this kind are
indicative, for the deconstructionist, of language's endemic unreliability and slipperiness, of which more will be said later. There are
other examples of this kind in the poem. Please look again at the
poem and see if you can identify others. You might begin by considering the use of the word 'until' in combination with 'never' in the
opening line.

One other facet of post-structuralism relevant here is its tendency
to reverse the polarity of common binary oppositions like *male* and

female, *day* and *night*, *light* and *dark*, and so on, so that the second term, rather than the first, is 'privileged' and regarded as the more desirable. Thus, in the poem it seems to be darkness, rather than light, which is seen as engendering life, as the poet talks of 'the mankind making / Bird beast and flower / Fathering and all humbling darkness'. This paradox reflects the way the world of this poem is simultaneously a recognisable version of the world we live in, and an inversion of that world. For the deconstructionist, again, such moments are symptomatic of the way language doesn't reflect or convey our world but constitutes a world of its own, a kind of parallel universe or virtual reality. Identifying contradictory or paradoxical phrases like these, then, is the first step in going against the grain of the poem, reading it 'against itself', showing the 'signifiers' at war with the 'signified', and revealing its repressed unconscious. This first stage will always turn up useful material for use in the later stages.

The 'textual' stage of the method moves beyond individual phrases and takes a more overall view of the poem. At this second stage the critic is looking for shifts or breaks in the continuity of the poem: these shifts reveal instabilities of attitude, and hence the lack of a fixed and unified position. They can be of various kinds (as listed in the diagram given earlier); they may be shifts in focus, shifts in time, or tone, or point of view, or attitude, or pace, or vocabulary. They may well be indicated in the grammar, for instance, in a shift from first person to third, or past tense to present. Thus, they show paradox and contradiction on a larger scale than is the case with the first stage, taking a broad view of the text as a whole. In the case of 'A Refusal to Mourn', for instance, there are major time shifts and changes in viewpoint, not a smooth chronological progression. Thus, the first two stanzas imagine the passing of geological aeons and the coming of the 'end of the world' – the last light breaks, the sea finally becomes still, the cycle which produces 'Bird beast and flower' comes to an end as 'all humbling darkness' descends. But the third stanza is centred on the present – the actual death of the child, 'The majesty and burning of the child's death'. The final stanza takes a broad vista like the first two, but it seems to centre on the historical progression of the recorded history of London, as witnessed by 'the unmourning water / Of the riding Thames'. Hence, no single wider context is provided to 'frame' and contextualise the death of the child in a defined perspective, and the shifts in Thomas's poem make it very difficult to ground his meaning at all.

Look again at the poem to see if you can detect other examples of this larger-scale 'textual' level of breaks and discontinuities. Note that *omissions* are important here, that is, when a text doesn't tell us things we would expect to be told. You might begin by asking whether the poet tells us why he refuses to mourn, or rather, why the expressed intention of not doing so is not carried out.

The 'linguistic' stage, finally, involves looking for moments in the poem when the adequacy of language itself as a medium of communication is called into question. Such moments occur when, for example, there is implicit or explicit reference to the unreliability or untrustworthiness of language. It may involve, for instance, *saying* that something is unsayable; or saying that it is impossible to utter or describe something and then doing so; or saying that language inflates, or deflates, or misrepresents its object, and then continuing to use it anyway. In 'A Refusal to Mourn', for instance, the whole poem does what it says it *won't* do: the speaker professes his refusal to mourn, but the poem itself constitutes an act of mourning. Then in the third stanza the speaker says that he will not 'murder / The mankind of her going with a grave truth'. This condemns all the accepted ways of speaking about this event, and the poet professes to stand outside the available range of clichéd, elegiac stances or 'discursive practices', as if some 'pure' stance beyond these necessarily compromised forms of utterance were possible. Yet this is followed, not by silence, but by the solemn, quasi-liturgical pronouncements of the final stanza: 'Deep with the first dead lies London's daughter', the speaker proclaims, which sounds very like traditional panegyrical oratory, with the dead person transformed into some larger than life heroic figure, becoming 'London's daughter' (an impossible designation for her in life), 'robed' as for some great procession of the dead of all the ages, and now reunited with Mother Earth in the form of the London clay in which she is now buried.

In this poem, we might say, Thomas identifies the language trap, and then falls into it. Look again at the poem with this 'textual' level in mind. Are there other examples of Thomas's being forced to use the rhetorical strategies he has just exposed? You might start by looking at his use of the words 'mother' and 'daughter' and thinking about the nature of the metaphorical 'family' implied by these words. Other metaphorical constructs to look at are those entailed in the word 'murder' and in the notion of the 'unmourning' Thames.

Once the grain of the poem is opened up, then, it cannot long survive the deconstructive pressures brought to bear upon it, and reveals itself as fractured, contradictory, and symptomatic of a cultural and linguistic malaise. A three-step model like this will lend itself to applications to other material; it gives this approach something distinctive as a critical practice, and lays the strengths and weaknesses of deconstruction open to scrutiny, just as other methods are open. The deconstructive reading, then, aims to produce *dis*-unity, to show that what had looked like unity and coherence actually contains contradictions and conflicts which the text cannot stabilise and contain. We might characterise it as waking up the sleeping dogs of signification and setting them on each other. In contrast, more conventional styles of close reading had the opposite aim: they would take a text which appeared fragmented and disunified and demonstrate an underlying unity, aiming to separate the warring dogs and soothe them back to sleep with suitable blandishments. Yet the two methods, far apart though they would see themselves as being, suffer from exactly the same drawback, which is that both tend to make all poems seem similar. The close reader detects miracles of poised ambiguity alike in Donne's complex metaphysical lyrics, and in simple poems like Robert Frost's 'Stopping by woods on a snowy evening', which receive the full-scale explicatory treatment of the ten- or twenty-page article, so that the experience of reading them loses all its particularity. Similarly, after the deconstructionist treatment all poems tend to emerge as angst-ridden, fissured enactments of linguistic and other forms of indeterminacy.

I'll comment further on some of the characteristics listed on the post-structuralist side of the diagram on page 75, using as an example 'The Castaway' (Appendix 3), a well-known poem by the eighteenth-century poet William Cowper. As all critics recognise, this poem works at two levels: on the 'surface' it is an account of the death of a man washed overboard from a ship, who speaks in the poem in his own voice and laments his fate. At a 'deeper' level the poem is about Cowper's own fear of and isolation within his incipient mental breakdown.

For the deconstructionist, firstly, exposing contradictions or paradoxes might involve showing that the feelings *professed* in a poem can be at odds with those *expressed*. For instance, in 'The Castaway' the speaker *says* that he does not blame his shipmates for his plight, but even saying this raises the possibility that he does. Thus, at one point he says that his friends did all they could to save him, but elsewhere he implies that they desert him and hurry off to save themselves. Look again at the poem to identify the points where these inferences might be drawn.

Secondly, pointing to breaks, gaps, fissures, discontinuities is a way of implying that the text lacks unity and consistency of purpose. There may, for instance, be changes in tone, or perspective, or point of view. In 'The Castaway', for instance, the text sometimes uses 'I' and sometimes 'he' for the man lost overboard: 'such a destin'd wretch as I' but '*His* floating home for ever left' (my italics). Look again at the poem and see if you can identify other examples of this. As I have already indicated, at one level it is an imaginative retelling of the death of a sailor lost overboard during one of the expeditions of the explorer George Anson, based on the account of the incident in Anson's published journals. At another level this is merely a metaphor for the isolation and depression felt by Cowper himself. But the relationship between these two levels is very 'unsettled': for instance, all the specific details about Anson and his expedition distract from the generalised notion of loss, abandonment, and isolation, and we shift erratically from one to the other.

Thirdly, the 'linguistic quirks' which seem relevant include several kinds of linguistic oddity or *non sequitur* of the kind which undermine secure meanings. There are many of these in 'The Castaway'. In the final stanza the poet says that no divine assistance came when '*We* perish'd, each alone' – my italics – but the poem has shown the death of only one person. On the other hand, if the statement is a general one about how we all have to face death alone, then we would expect the present tense rather than the past ('We perish' rather than 'We perish'd').

The term 'aporia', finally, is a popular one in deconstructive criticism. It literally means an *impasse*, and designates a kind of knot in the text which cannot be unravelled or solved because what is said is self-contradictory. It perhaps corresponds, therefore, to what the British critic William Empson, in his book *Seven Types of Ambiguity* (1930), designated as the seventh type of verbal difficulty in litera-ture, namely that which occurs when 'there is an irreconcilable conflict of meaning within the text'. For instance, at the start of the third stanza we are told of the drowned man that 'No poet wept him', but the existence of the poem we are reading contradicts this. There seems to be no way out of this 'bind'. It is often said that Roland Barthes's 1968 essay 'The Death of the Author' marks the transition from structuralism to post-structuralism, and in that essay Barthes says that in the text 'everything must be disentangled, nothing deciphered'. The aporia, though, is a textual knot which resists disentanglement, and several of the elements discussed above as contradictions, paradoxes, or shifts might equally be classified under the more general heading of aporia.

While it is easy to see why this process might be called reading against the grain, it is misleading to suggest that the poem has an obvious 'grain' or overt meaning which the critic has merely to rou-tinely counteract. Reading this poem will also have shown, I hope, that structuralist and post-structuralist reading practices are much at odds with each other: identifying patterns and symmetries in the structuralist manner discovers a unified text which is, so to speak, happy with itself, whereas 'reading the text against itself' produces a sense of disunity, of a text engaged in a civil war with itself.

Selected reading

Barthes, Roland, *The Pleasure of the Text*, trans. R. Miller (Hill & Wang, 1975).

This book represents the 'playful' side of Barthes: it is brief, enigmatic, and entertaining.

Culler, Jonathan, *On Deconstruction: Theory and Criticism After Structuralism* (Routledge, 25th anniversary edn, 2007).

Includes a new preface surveying deconstruction's history since the 1980s and assessing its place within cultural theory today.

Derrida, Jacques, 'The Exorbitant. Question of Method', pp. 171–8 in *Of Grammatology*, trans. Gayatri Chakravorty Spivak (Johns Hopkins Uni-versity Press, 2016).

Derrida, Jacques, 'Structure, sign and play in the discourse of the human sciences', reprinted in abbreviated form in K. M. Newton, *Twentieth Century Literary Theory: A Reader* (Macmillan, 2nd edn, 1997).

Derrida, Jacques, 'The purveyor of truth', pp. 173–212 in *The Purloined Poe: Lacan, Derrida, and Psychoanalytic Reading*, ed. John P. Muller and William J. Richardson (Johns Hopkins University Press, 1988).

This essay is Derrida's response, fully introduced within the volume, to Lacan's reading of Poe's story 'The Purloined Letter'. This and the two previous items constitute suggested initial reading of Derrida.

Derrida, Jacques, *A Derrida Reader*, ed. Peggy Kamuf (Columbia University Press, 1998).

An 'assisted introduction' – a substantial selection of Derrida's essays, each with its individual introduction. A very useful book for sustained engagement with Derrida.

Deutscher, Penelope, *How to Read Derrida* (Granta Books, 2005).

A good place to begin with Derrida, this short book is one of the 'How to Read' series, representative of a recent trend towards ultra-brief introductions.

Jefferson, Ann, and Robey, David, eds, *Modern Literary Theory: A Comparative Introduction* (Batsford, 2nd edn, 1986).

See chapter four, 'Structuralism and post-structuralism'.

Lechte, John, *Fifty Key Contemporary Thinkers* (Routledge, 2nd edn, 2006).

Short introductory essays on 'key thinkers' of the post-war period (not limited to post-structuralism and deconstruction).

Norris, Christopher, *Derrida* (Fontana, 1987).

A brief and helpful guide.

Norris, Christopher, *Deconstruction: Theory and Practice* (Routledge, 2nd edn, 1991).

A standard introductory account.

Royle, Nicholas, ed., *Deconstructions: A User's Guide* (Palgrave, 2000).

A series of well-focused essays by a range of important commentators.

Sarup, Madan, *An Introductory Guide to Post-Structuralism and Postmodernism* (Longman, 2nd edn, 1993).

Expanded and updated in 1993. See the chapter 'Derrida and Deconstruction'.

4
Postmodernism

What is postmodernism? What was modernism?

As with structuralism and post-structuralism, there is a great deal of debate about how exactly modernism and postmodernism differ. The two concepts are of different vintage, 'modernism' being a long-standing category which is of crucial importance in the under-standing of twentieth-century culture, whereas the term 'postmodernism', as is well known, has only become current since the 1980s. 'Modernism' is the name given to the movement which dominated the arts and culture of the first half of the twentieth century. Modernism was that earthquake in the arts which brought down much of the structure of pre-twentieth-century practice in music, painting, literature, and architecture. One of the major epicentres of this earthquake seems to have been Vienna, during the period of 1890–1910, but the effects were felt in France, Germany, Italy and eventually even in Britain, in art movements like Cubism, Dadaism, Surrealism, and Futurism. Its after-shocks are still being felt today, and many of the structures it toppled have never been rebuilt. Without an understanding of modernism, then, it is impossible to understand twentieth-century culture.

In all the arts touched by modernism what had been the most fundamental elements of practice were challenged and rejected: thus, melody and harmony were put aside in music; perspective and direct pictorial representation were abandoned in painting, in favour of degrees of abstraction; in architecture traditional forms and materials (pitched roofs, domes and columns, wood, stone, and bricks) were rejected in favour of plain geometrical forms, often executed in new materials like plate glass and concrete. In literature, finally, there was a rejection of traditional realism (chronological plots, continuous narratives relayed by omniscient narrators, 'closed endings', etc.) in favour of experimental forms of various kinds.

The period of high modernism was the twenty years from 1910 to 1930 and some of the literary 'high priests' of the movement (writing in English) were T. S. Eliot, James Joyce, Ezra Pound, Wyndham Lewis, Virginia Woolf, Wallace Stevens, and Gertrude Stein, and (writing in French or German) Marcel Proust, Stéphane Mallarmé, André Gide, Franz Kafka, and Rainer Maria Rilke. Some of the important characteristics of the literary modernism practised by these writers include the following:

1. A new emphasis on impressionism and subjectivity, that is, on *how* we see rather than *what* we see (a preoccupation evident in the use of the stream-of-consciousness technique).
2. A movement (in novels) away from the apparent objectivity provided by such features as omniscient external narration, fixed narrative points of view, and clear-cut moral positions.
3. A blurring of the distinctions between genres, so that novels tend to become more lyrical and poetic, for instance, and poems more documentary and prose-like.
4. A new liking for fragmented forms, discontinuous narrative, and random-seeming collages of disparate materials.
5. A tendency towards 'reflexivity', so that poems, plays and novels raise issues concerning their own nature, status, and role.

The overall result of these shifts is to produce a literature which seems dedicated to experimentation and innovation. After its high point, modernism seemed to retreat considerably in the 1930s, partly, no doubt, because of the tensions generated in a decade of political and economic crisis, but a resurgence took place in the 1960s (a decade which has interesting points of similarity with the 1920s, when modernism was at its height). However, modernism never regained the pre-eminence it had enjoyed in the earlier period.

This gives us a rough indication of what and when modernism was. Does postmodernism, then, continue it or oppose it? To decide this we need to attempt a working definition of this second term.

As a starting point, we can take a selection of the most readily available descriptions of postmodernism. J. A. Cuddon's entry in his *Dictionary of Literary Terms and Literary Theory* describes postmodernism as characterised by 'an eclectic approach, [by a liking for] aleatory writing, [and for] parody and pastiche' (5th edn, p. 533). So far, this doesn't really put much daylight between modernism and postmodernism, since the word 'eclectic' suggests the use of the fragmented forms which, as we have just said, are characteristic of modernism. (Eliot's *The Waste Land*, for instance, is a collage of juxtaposed, incomplete stories, or fragments of stories.) Also 'aleatory forms', meaning those which incorporate an element of randomness or chance, were important to the Dadaists of 1917, who, for instance, made poems from sentences plucked randomly from newspapers. The use of parody and pastiche, finally, is clearly related to the abandonment of the divine pretensions of authorship implicit in the omniscient narratorial stance, and this too was a vital element in modernism. It could be said, then, that one way of establishing the distinction between modernism and postmodernism is to dissolve the sequential link between them, by retrospectively redefining certain aspects of modernism as postmodernist. According to this view, they are not two successive stages in the history of the arts, but two opposed moods or attitudes, differing as suggested in the next paragraph.

The nature of the distinction between modernism and postmodernism is summarised in the excellent joint entry on the two terms in Jeremy Hawthorn's *Concise Glossary of Contemporary Literary Theory* (Edward Arnold, 1992). Both, he says, give great prominence to fragmentation as a feature of twentieth-century art and culture, but they do so in very different moods. The modernist features it in such a way as to register a deep nostalgia for an earlier age when faith was full and authority intact. Ezra Pound, for instance, calls his major work, *The Cantos*, a 'rag-bag', implying that this is all that is possible in the modern age, but also implying regret about that fact. In his poem 'Hugh Selwyn Mauberley' he speaks of the First World War being fought 'For two gross of broken statues, / For a few thousand battered books', and is evidently pained, in lines from the same poem like 'a tawdry cheapness / Shall outlast our days' and 'We see *to kalon* [beauty] / Decreed in the market place', by the rise of commercialism at the expense of 'eternal verities'. In *The Waste Land*, too, the persona says, as if despairingly of the poem, 'These fragments I have shored against my ruins'. In instances like this there is a tone of lament, pessimism, and despair about the world which finds its appropriate representation in these 'fractured' art forms (the collages of Kurt Schwitters, for example, which mix painted areas of canvas with random clippings from newspapers, timetables, and advertisements). For the postmodernist, by contrast, fragmentation is an exhilarating, liberating phenomenon, symptomatic of our escape from the claustrophobic embrace of fixed systems of belief. In a word, the modernist laments fragmentation while the postmodernist celebrates it.

A second, and related, difference between the two is also a matter of tone or attitude. An important aspect of modernism was a fierce asceticism which found the over-elaborate art forms of the nineteenth century deeply offensive and repulsive. This asceticism has one of its most characteristic and striking manifestations in the pronouncements of modernist architects, such as Adolf Loos's proclamation that 'decoration is a crime', or Miës van der Rohe's that 'less is more', or Le Corbusier's that 'a house is a machine for living in'. These pronouncements resulted in the 'shoe box' and 'carbuncle' buildings which generated such hatred and opposition, particularly through the 1980s, but the high idealism they represent retains its power to move. The same refined asceticism is seen in literature in the minimalism which (for instance) shrinks poems to narrow columns of two-word lines registering rigorously sparse, pared-down observations, or in the drama of Samuel Beckett, in which a play may be reduced to a running time of thirteen minutes, with a single speaker, no set, and language which is sparse in the extreme. By constrast, again, postmodernism rejects the distinction between 'high' and 'popular' art which was important in modernism, and believes in excess, in gaudiness, and in 'bad taste' mixtures of qualities. It disdains the modernist asceticism as elitist and cheerfully mixes, in the same building, bits and pieces from different architectural periods – a mock-Georgian pediment here, a tongue-in-cheek classical portico there. A similar postmodernist 'edifice' in literature would be the 'Martian' poetry of writers like Craig Raine or Christopher Reid, where bizarrely colourful mixtures of imagery, viewpoint, and vocabulary jostle on a surface which seems happy to be nothing *but* surface, without the depths of significance which a literary education trains us to seek out. Nothing could be further in spirit from that austere modernist asceticism.

'Landmarks' in postmodernism – Habermas, Lyotard, and Baudrillard

A major 'moment' in the history of postmodernism is the influential paper 'Modernity – an Unfinished Project' delivered by the contemporary German theorist Jürgen Habermas in 1980. For Habermas, the modern period begins with the Enlightenment, that period of about one hundred years, from the mid-seventeenth to the mid-eighteenth century, when a new faith arose in the power of reason to improve human society. Such ideas are expressed or embodied in the philosophy of Kant in Germany, Voltaire and Diderot in France, and Locke and Hume in Britain. In Britain the term 'The Age of Reason' was used (until recently) to designate the same period. The so-called Enlightenment 'project' is the fostering of this belief that a break with tradition, blind habit, and slavish obedience to religious precepts and prohibitions, coupled with the application of reason and logic by the disinterested individual, can bring about a solution to the problems of society. This outlook is what Habermas means by 'modernity'. The French Revolution can be seen as a first attempt to test this theory in practice. For Habermas, this faith in reason and the possibility of progress survived into the twentieth century, and even survives the catalogue of disasters which makes up that century's history. The cultural movement known as modernism subscribed to this 'project', in the sense that it constituted a lament for a lost sense of purpose, a lost coherence, a lost system of values. For Habermas, the French post-structuralist thinkers of the 1970s, such as Derrida and Foucault, represented a specific repudiation of this kind of Enlightenment 'modernity'. They attacked, in his view, the ideals of reason, clarity, truth, and progress, and as they were thereby detached from the quest for justice, he identified them as 'young conservatives'.

The term 'postmodernism' was used in the 1930s, but its current sense and vogue can be said to have begun with Jean-François

Lyotard's *The Postmodern Condition: A Report on Knowledge* (Manchester University Press, 1979). Lyotard's essay 'Answering the Question: What is Postmodernism?', first published in 1982, added in 1984 as an appendix to *The Postmodern Condition* and included in Brooker's *Modernism/Postmodernism* (1992), takes up this debate about the Enlightenment, mainly targeting Habermas, in a slightly oblique manner. Lyotard opens with a move which effectively turns the debate into a struggle to demonstrate that one's opponents are the real conservatives (a familiar 'bottom line' of polemical writing on culture). 'From every direction', he says, 'we are being urged to put an end to experimentation', and after citing several other instances he writes (obviously of Habermas):

> I have read a thinker of repute who defends modernity against those
> he calls the neo-conservatives. Under the banner of postmodernism,
> the latter would like, he believes, to get rid of the uncompleted proj-
> ect of modernism, that of the Enlightenment.

(Brooker, p. 141)

Habermas's is simply one voice in a chorus which is calling for an end to 'artistic experimentation' and for 'order ... unity, for identity, for security' (Brooker, p. 142). In a word, these voices want 'to liquidate the heritage of the avant-gardes'. For Lyotard, the Enlightenment whose project Habermas wishes to continue is simply one of the would-be authoritative, 'overarching', 'totalising' explanations of things – like Christianity, Marxism, or the myth of scientific progress. These 'metanarratives' ['super-narratives'], which purport to explain and reassure, are really illusions, fostered in order to smother difference, opposition, and plurality. Hence Lyotard's famous definition of postmodernism, that it is, simply, 'incredulity towards metanarratives'. 'Grand Narratives' of progress and human perfectibility, then, are no longer tenable, and the best we can hope for is a series of 'mini-narratives', which are provisional, contingent, temporary, and relative and which provide a basis for the actions of specific groups in particular local circumstances. Postmodernity thus 'deconstructs' the basic aim of the Enlightenment, that is, 'the idea of a unitary end of history and of a subject'.

Another major theorist of postmodernism is the contemporary French writer Jean Baudrillard, whose book *Simulations* (1981, translated 1983) marks his entry into this field. Baudrillard is associated with what is usually known as 'the loss of the real', which is the view that in contemporary life the pervasive influence of images from film, TV, and advertising has led to a loss of the distinction between real and imagined, reality and illusion, surface and depth. The result is a culture of 'hyperreality', in which distinctions between these are eroded. His propositions are worked out in his essay 'Simulacra and Simulations' reprinted in abridged form in Brooker's *Modernism/Postmodernism*. He begins by evoking a past era of 'fullness', when a sign was a surface indication of an underlying depth or reality ('an outward sign of inward grace', to cite the words of the Roman Catholic Catechism). But what, he asks, if a sign is not an index of an underlying reality, but merely of other signs? Then the whole system becomes what he calls a *simulacrum*. He then substitutes for *representation* the notion of *simulation*. The sign reaches its present stage of emptiness in a series of steps, which I will try to illustrate by comparing them to different kinds of paintings.

Firstly, then, the sign represents a basic reality: let's take as an example of this the representations of the industrial city of Salford in the work of the twentieth-century British artist L. S. Lowry. Mid-century life for working people in such a place was hard, and the paintings have an air of monotony and repetitiveness – cowed, stick-like figures fill the streets, colours are muted, and the horizon is filled with grim factory-like buildings. As signs, then, Lowry's paintings seem to represent the basic reality of the place they depict.

The *second* stage for the sign is that it misrepresents or distorts the reality behind it. As an example of this let's take the glamorised representations of cities like Liverpool and Hull in the paintings of the Victorian artist Atkinson Grimshaw. These paintings show the cities at night, wet pavements reflecting the bright lights of dockside shops, the moon emerging from behind clouds, and a forest of ships' masts silhouetted against the sky. Life in these places at that time was presumably grim, too, but the paintings offer a romantic and glamorised image, so the sign can be said to misrepresent what it shows.

The *third* stage for the sign is when the sign disguises the fact that there is no corresponding reality underneath. To illustrate this, take a device used in the work of the surrealist artist René Magritte, where, in the painting, an easel with a painter's canvas on it is shown standing alongside a window: on the canvas in the painting is painted the exterior scene which we can see through the window. But what is shown beyond the window is not reality, against which the painting within the painting can be judged, but simply another sign, another depiction, which has no more authority or reality than the painting within the painting (which is actually a representation of a representation).

The *fourth* and last stage for the sign is that it bears no relation to any reality at all. As an illustration of this stage we have simply to imagine a completely abstract painting, which is not representational at all, like one of the great purple mood canvases of Mark Rothko, for instance. I should emphasise that I'm not suggesting that these four painters are examples of the four stages of the sign, merely that the four stages can be thought of as analogous to the four different ways in which these paintings signify or represent things.

The first two of these stages are fairly clear, the second two perhaps less so. Baudrillard's own example of the third stage (when the sign hides an absence) is Disneyland. In one way, of course, it is a sign of the second type, a mythologised misrepresentation of the United States:

> All its [the USA's] values are exalted here, in miniature and comic-strip form. Embalmed and pacified ... digest of the American way of life, panegyric to American values, idealised transposition of a con-tradictory reality.
>
> (Brooker, *Modernism/Postmodernism*, p. 154)

But Disneyland is actually a 'third-order simulation' (a sign which conceals an absence):

> Disneyland is there to conceal the fact that it is the 'real' country, all of 'real' America, which *is* Disneyland (just as prisons are there to conceal the fact that it is the social in its entirety, in its banal omni-presence, which is carceral). Disneyland is presented as imaginary in order to make us believe that the rest is real
>
> (Brooker, p. 154).

In a word, Disneyland has the effect of 'concealing the fact that the real is no longer real, and thus of saving the reality principle'. Within postmodernism, the distinction between what is real and what is simulated collapses: *everything* is a model or an image, all is surface without depth; this is the *hyperreal,* as Baudrillard calls it.

The grand sweep of this kind of rhetoric has a strong appeal. One might see it as a kind of latter-day Platonism, its devotees enjoying the mystical insight that what is normally taken as a solid and real world is actually just a tissue of dreamlike images. If this second aspect of the postmodern condition, this loss of the real, is accepted as a fact, then it is hard to see a ground for literary theory to occupy, since all methods of literary interpretation – Marxist, feminist, structuralist, and so on – depend upon the making of a distinction between surface and depth, between what is *seen* in the text and some *underlying* meaning. Once we accept that what we see is all we get, then there is, clearly, very little which a literary critic or theorist can claim to be doing.

More generally, for postmodernism there are certain ever-present questions and provisos. In this extreme Baudrillardian form, the 'loss of the real' may *seem* to legitimise a callous indifference to suffering. In a now notorious pronouncement Baudrillard maintained that the Gulf War (of 1990-91) never happened, that what 'really' took place was a kind of televisual virtual reality. (But see the discussion of this matter in Chapter 14.) Likewise, if we accept the 'loss of the real' and the collapsing of reality and simulation into a kind of virtual reality, then what of the Holocaust? Could this, too, be part of the reality 'lost' in the image networks? In other words, without a belief in some of the concepts which postmodernism undercuts – history, reality, and truth, for instance – we may well find ourselves in some pretty repulsive company.

STOP and THINK

The crucial category in Baudrillard's four-stage model is the third one, the sign which conceals an absence, which conceals the fact that the supposedly 'real' which it represents is no longer there, that beyond the play of surfaces there is nothing else.

It is not easy to achieve a precise understanding of this concept. It may help in doing so if you try to think of examples other than Disneyland. The idealised images of masculinity or femininity presented in advertisements, for instance, may be helpful: these also are copies or representations for which no original exists – no actual people are quite like these, though people might strive to become like them. In this way the image tends to become the reality, and the two tend to become indistinguishable.

Further, if we agree that the real has indeed been lost then we need to decide how we react to this fact. If we are to revel in the boundary-free zone which results, we will need to be sure that the 'real' is a concept we can do without. Perhaps recent events suggest otherwise. In the televsion coverage of the first Gulf War we saw computer-image film of high-tech 'smart' weapons homing in on Iraqi targets, while the commentary spoke of 'surgical strikes' which could 'take out' key enemy installations. News bulletins also included footage of pilots who spoke of what they were doing in the same 'unreal' terms, using the terminology of video combat games, for instance. Perhaps these things are symptomatic of what can happen when the category of the real is eroded. Likewise, could we condemn the Holocaust without the category of the real, or campaign against (say) racial discrimination or environmental pollution?

What postmodernist critics do

1. They discover postmodernist themes, tendencies, and attitudes within literary works of the twentieth century and explore their implications.
2. They foreground fiction which might be said to exemplify the notion of the 'disappearance of the real', in which shifting postmodern identities are seen, for example, in the mixing of literary genres (the thriller, the detective story, the myth saga, and the realist psychological novel, etc.).
3. They foreground what might be called 'intertextual elements' in literature, such as parody, pastiche, and allusion, in all of which there is a major degree of reference between one text and another, rather than between the text and a safely external reality.

4. They foreground irony, in the sense described by Umberto Eco, that whereas the modernist tries to destroy the past, the postmodernist realises that the past must be revisited, but 'with irony' (Brooker, *Modernism/Postmodernism*, p. 227).

5. They foreground the element of 'narcissism' in narrative technique, that is, where novels focus on and debate their own ends and processes, and thereby 'de-naturalise' their content.

6. They challenge the distinction between high and low culture, and highlight texts which work as hybrid blends of the two.

Postmodernist criticism: an example

A useful example of postmodernist criticism, which makes a straight-forward application of ideas derived from Lyotard, is Jeffrey Nealon's 'Samuel Beckett and the Postmodern: Language Games, Play, and *Waiting for Godot*' (reprinted in the Macmillan 'New Casebook' on *Waiting for Godot* and *Endgame*, ed. Steven Connor, 1992). This mainly shows the first of the six postmodernist critical activities listed above, but also has elements of the second, in the sense that the notion of language as a self-contained system relates closely to Lyotard's idea of the 'disappearance of the real'. Nealon first explains the notion of 'language games', derived from Wittgenstein, whereby when we claim that something is true we are not measuring it against some external absolute standard, but by internal rules and criteria which operate only within that designated sphere and have no 'transcendent' status beyond that. These have a restricted applicability, just like the rules which govern moves in a game. Thus, *Knight to King's Rook Four* might be a winning move in a chess game, but would carry no weight at all in a game of football, say, or an argument about who should do the washing-up. Likewise, the 'move' in a philosophical discussion which establishes a proposition as true or valid has its validity only within the 'language game' of philosophy. For Nealon, Vladimir and Estragon in Beckett's play, *Waiting for Godot*, engage in 'language games' of this type, but with-out realising their full significance. Actually, such language games, the postmodernists agree, are all we have; there is no transcendent reality behind them and they are actually self-validating, and provide us with the social identity we seek. But Vladimir and Estragon hanker for some deeper or 'transcendent' reality over and above this. Thus, says Nealon, 'it is the play of Vladimir and Estragon's words, not any agreed-upon meaning for them, which constitutes their social bond. Waiting for legitimation of their society in Godot is, from the beginning, unnecessary.'

Vladimir and Estragon, then, have difficulty in accepting this postmodern view that 'gaming' is enough (*Just Gaming* is the title of one of Lyotard's books): they wish to have the security provided by some 'Grand Narrative' of guarantee and absolute validation. This desired comprehensive reassurance is linked in the play with Christian notions of redemption, which 'recuperate' (meaning, roughly, explain and give significance to) the apparently meaningless details and trials of daily life. ('Offer it up', my Catholic teachers would say in response to any minor complaint about unfairness or injustice.) Vladimir and Estragon, then, are trapped at the 'modernist' stage, and hence riven with nostalgia for the lost wholeness of the past. For Nealon, the kind of legitimating discourse which Vladimir and Estragon seek is parodied in Lucky's 'think' near the end of the first act. This is a parody of the 'totalising' 'metadiscourse' of philosophy and religion, a practical demonstration of the 'language game of truth' which is all that is available to us. It is, says Nealon, a narrative that disrupts and deconstructs all notions of universal, ahistorical, consistent metanarrative – *all* Godots. Had Godot turned up, the implication is, what could he have offered but pious and pedantic gibberish of this kind?

Lucky has perceived this, hence his exuberant and joyous parody, but the others resist it, so his speech is met with violence. The modernist, that is, wishes to go on believing in the toppled gods and Godots. Vladimir and Estragon, for Nealon, are, throughout the play, on the verge of a 'deconstructive breakthrough'. When they forget about Godot they are happy and inventive in their language games, revelling, we might say, in the openness and uncertainties of 'the postmodernist condition'. But repeatedly they come back to Godot, and the supposed restraints and imperatives he places upon them. 'Let's go far away from here', Vladimir proposes at one point, to which the response is 'We can't … We have to come back tomorrow … To wait for Godot.' We might characterise this view by saying that Vladimir and Estragon prove themselves in the end to have a modernist attitude to the fragmentation of truths and values which we have seen in the twentieth century. They long for a return to the lost fullness of purpose of the past, so their experience of fragmentation is nostalgic and angst-ridden. At times they seem on the verge of making a transition (or 'breakthrough', as Nealon calls it) to a postmodern attitude, in which fragmentation becomes a condition welcomed and enjoyed, but in the end they fail to do this.

The modernist/postmodernist dichotomy that underpins this reading could be applied to many other works. Are there any which stand out in your mind? Waiting, for instance, seems to be an important activity in twentieth-century drama, notably in the plays of Harold Pinter – *The Dumb Waiter* would be a very obvious example. You might like to consider the value or otherwise of using the ideas of postmodernism in the explication of any of his plays with which you are familiar. Another 'waiting' play on which a very similar reading might be attempted is Anton Chekhov's *The Three Sisters* (1901), in which the sisters of the title, Olga, Masha, and Irina, are stranded in lives of bourgeois respectability in northern Russia, twenty-three hours by train from the next town of any size (see Michael Frayn's introduction to the Methuen edition of Chekhov's plays). The sisters wait in vain – like Vladimir and Estragon – for some external force to enter their provincial lives and transform them, and the ideals for which each pines can be seen as personal 'metanarratives', such as an ideal of social progress, or the notion that their sufferings will in some way contribute to a better human life in the future. Irina, for instance, says near the end of the play that 'A time will come when people will understand what it was all for, what the purpose was of all this suffering, and what was hidden from us will be hidden no more'. For the sisters, too, the actually self-sufficient reality of their condition is provided by the language games they play endlessly, and the image of the capital city of Moscow, a glittering amalgam of memory and desire, which constitutes for them a kind of hyperreality or simulacrum.

Selected reading

Benjamin, Andrew, ed., *The Lyotard Reader* (Blackwell, 1989).
   A very useful source.

Brooker, Peter, ed., *Modernism/Postmodernism* (Longman, 1992).

A general reader on the topic to examine alongside Docherty's and Waugh's. I find the introduction makes heavy going of the modernism/ postmodernism distinction, but this is a compact collection of the key items by Habermas, Lyotard, Baudrillard, Jameson, Eco, Hutcheon, etc., as well as earlier material.

Connor, Steven, *Postmodernist Culture: An Introduction to Theories of the Contemporary* (Blackwell, 2nd edn, 1996).

Connor's has been an important voice in this field, stating issues and dilemmas with clarity and force.

Crome, Keith, and Williams, James, eds, *The Lyotard Reader and Guide* (Columbia University Press, 2017).

Arranged in four sections – Philosophy, Politics, Art and Literature – each with a substantial editorial introduction.

Docherty, Thomas, ed., *Postmodernism: A Reader* (Columbia University Press, 1993).

Monumental. The rival reader to Waugh's. A very useful collection of material, with sub-sections, each with its own introduction, but I prefer Waugh for its overall clarity and convenience.

Habermas, Jürgen, 'Modernity; An Unfinished Project', reprinted in *Habermas and the Unfinished Project of Modernity: Critical Essays on the Philosophical Discourse of Modernity*, ed. Maurizio Passerin d'Entrèves and Seyla Benhabib (MIT Press, 1997).

Sarup, Madan, *An Introductory Guide to Post-Structuralism and Postmodernism* (Longman, 2nd edn, 1993).

A helpful section on postmodernism, including Lyotard and Baudrillard, and considerations of selected postmodernist 'cultural practices' such as video and architecture.

Waugh, Patricia, ed., *Postmodernism: A Reader* (Hodder Arnold, 2009).

A valuable collection of material, which includes relevant American essays (such as Susan Sontag's seminal 'Against Interpretation') which pre-date the general use of the term 'postmodern' – as well as key pieces by Lyotard, Baudrillard, and Habermas: also essays from the Marxist debate on postmodernism between Jameson and Eagleton, where postmodernism is reluctantly accepted as the inevitable 'cultural logic of late capitalism'. Essays too from prominent theorists of postmodernism like Linda Hutcheon and Brian McHale.

Woods, Tim, *Beginning Postmodernism* (Manchester University Press, 2nd edn, 2009).

A comprehensive account of postmodernism presented in a lively and readable way. This is one of the titles in the 'Beginnings' series.

Psychoanalytic criticism

Introduction

Psychoanalytic criticism is a form of literary criticism which uses some of the techniques of psychoanalysis in the interpretation of literature. Psychoanalysis itself is a form of therapy which aims to cure mental disorders 'by investigating the interaction of conscious and unconscious elements in the mind' (as the *Concise Oxford Dictionary* puts it). The classic method of doing this is to get the patient to talk freely, in such a way that the repressed fears and conflicts which are causing the problems are brought into the conscious mind and openly faced, rather than remaining 'buried' in the unconscious. This practice is based upon specific theories of how the mind, the instincts, and sexuality work. These theories were developed by the Austrian Sigmund Freud (1856–1939). There is a growing consensus today that the therapeutic value of the method is limited, and that Freud's life-work is seriously flawed by methodological irregularities. All the same, Freud remains a major cultural force, and his impact on how we think about ourselves has been incalculable.

Freud's major ideas include those italicised in the next three paragraphs. All of Freud's work depends upon the notion of the *unconscious*, which is the part of the mind beyond consciousness which nevertheless has a strong influence upon our actions. Freud was not the discoverer of the unconscious: his uniqueness lies in his attributing to it such a decisive role in our lives. Linked with this is the idea of *repression*, which is the 'forgetting' or ignoring of unresolved conflicts, unadmitted desires, or traumatic past events, so that they are forced out of conscious awareness and into the realm of the unconscious. A similar process is that of *sublimation*, whereby the repressed material is 'promoted' into something grander or is disguised as something 'noble'. For instance, sexual urges may be given sublimated expression in the form of intense religious experiences or longings. Later in his career Freud suggested a three-part, rather than a two-part, model of the psyche, dividing it into the *ego*, the *super-ego*, and the *id*, these three 'levels' of the personality roughly corresponding to, respectively, the consciousness, the conscience, and the unconscious.

Many of Freud's ideas concern aspects of sexuality. *Infantile sexuality*, for instance, is the notion that sexuality begins not at puberty, with physical maturing, but in infancy, especially through the infant's relationship with the mother. Connected with this is the *Oedipus complex*, whereby, says Freud, the male infant conceives the desire to eliminate the father and become the sexual partner of the mother. Many forms of inter-generational conflict are seen by Freudians as having Oedipal overtones, such as professional rivalries, often viewed in Freudian terms as reproducing the competition between siblings for parental favour. (As the very idea of the Oedipal complex would suggest, Freudian theory is often deeply masculinist in bias.) Another key idea is that of the *libido*, which is the energy drive associated with sexual desire. In classic Freudian theory it has three stages of focus, the *oral*, the *anal*, and the *phallic*. The libido in the individual is part of a more generalised drive which the later Freud called *Eros* (the Greek word for 'love'), which roughly means the life instinct, the opposite of which is *Thanatos* (the Greek word for 'death'), which roughly means the death instinct, a controversial notion, of course.

Several key terms concern what might be called psychic processes, such as *transference*, the phenomenon whereby the patient under analysis redirects the emotions recalled in analysis towards the psychoanalyst: thus, the antagonism or resentment felt towards a parental figure in the past might be reactivated, but directed against the analyst. Another such mechanism is *projection*, when aspects of ourselves (usually negative ones) are not recognised as part of ourselves but are perceived in or attributed to another; our own desires or antagonisms, for instance, may be 'disowned' in this way. Both these might be seen as *defence mechanisms*, that is, as psychic procedures for avoiding painful admissions or recognitions. Another such is the *screen memory*, which is a trivial or inconsequential memory whose function is to obliterate a more significant one. A well-known example of these mechanisms is the *Freudian slip*, which Freud himself called the 'parapraxis', whereby repressed material in the unconscious finds an outlet through such everyday phenomena as slips of the tongue, slips of the pen, or unintended actions.

A final example of important Freudian terminology is the *dream work*, the process by which real events or desires are transformed into dream images. These include: *displacement*, whereby one person or event is represented by another which is in some way linked or associated with it, perhaps because of a similar-sounding word, or by some form of symbolic substitution; and *condensation*, whereby a number of people, events, or meanings are combined and represented by a single image in the dream. Thus, characters, motivation, and events are represented in dreams in a very 'literary' way, involving the translation, by the dream work, of abstract ideas or feelings into concrete images. Dreams, just like literature, do not usually make explicit statements. Both tend to communicate obliquely or indirectly, avoiding direct or open statement, and representing meanings through concrete embodiments of time, place, or person.

Should we say 'unconscious' or 'subconscious' when discussing Freudian ideas?

The adjectives 'unconscious' and 'subconscious' (as used in phrases like 'the unconscious mind' and 'the subconscious mind') often seem to be interchangeable in popular usage, as if they were synonyms, but this an error in the context of Freudian discussion. Freud used the term 'subconscious' (which was 'in fairly common use in the late nineteenth century'; see Laplanche and Pontalis, p. 430) only in his early writings, and quickly abandoned it because it seemed wrongly 'calculated to stress the equivalence of what is psychical [that is, within the mind] to what is conscious'.[1] The unconscious, as used by Freud, is described in a two-page entry by

---

1 J. Laplanche and J. B. Pontalis, *The Language of Psycho-Analysis* (Karnac Books and the Institute of Psycho-Analysis, 1988). I am extremely grateful to my colleague Dr Luke Thurston for drawing my attention to this issue.

Laplanche and Pontalis as designating a specific area and process in the 'topography' of the mind as first formulated by Freud, and as indicated in this extract from their summary:

> [T]he term 'unconscious' describes ... the repressed contents which have been denied access to the preconscious-conscious system by the operation of repression ... Its 'contents' are 'representatives' of the instincts [aka drives]. These contents are governed ... especially by condensation and displacement ... It is more especially childhood wishes that become fixated in the unconscious. (p. 474)

The 'operation of repression' is described later in this chapter, as are condensation and displacement. Traumatic material which has been repressed into the unconscious only becomes 'accessible to consciousness once resistances have been overcome' in the course of psychoanalytic treatment (p. 475). Full-scale examples of this are given in Freud's case studies, such as the 'Dora' case, which is discussed in the present chapter. As a primary example of 'resistances' being 'overcome' I use an example which is not based on a childhood trauma, but on an adult anxiety which has been temporarily dismissed from the consciousness into what Freud, in his earlier phase, called the preconscious. This term designates a hinterland or antechamber between the unconscious and the conscious, and it is the mental location of something not in our immediate consciousness, but easily recoverable. For instance, we do not usually walk around thinking consciously of the name of a family pet from early childhood, but we can usually recall this name without difficulty if it is the personal information we are asked for when changing a password. Such material seems to be waiting patiently in the 'preconscious' antechamber in case it is called for. Avoiding the term 'subconscious' is sensible, if only because of the risk of confusion with the preconscious which it sets up. So we should be consistent in our own usage and speak of the 'unconscious', not the 'subconscious' when we are referring to Freudian ideas in the context of literary interpretation.

How Freudian interpretation works

Freudian interpretation is popularly thought to be a matter of attributing sexual connotations to objects, so that towers and ladders, for instance, are seen as phallic symbols. This kind of thing had become a joke even in Freud's own lifetime. In reality, Freudian interpretation is often highly ingenious, rather than highly simplistic. For example, let's imagine how a dream featuring a Roman soldier might be interpreted. Freud believes that a dream is an escape-hatch or safety-valve through which repressed desires, fears, or memories seek an outlet into the conscious mind. The emotion in question is censored by the conscious mind and so has to enter the dream in disguise, like a person barred from a club who gets in by dressing up as somebody else. The Roman soldier might be connected with the real subject of the dream by a chain of associations. Let's say that the dreamer is a young adult still under the thumb of an authoritarian father but wanting to break away from his influence and experience adult life to the full. The Roman soldier might represent the father by a process of *association*: the father is associated with ideas of strictness, authority, and power in the domestic sphere; the Roman soldier is linked to the same things in the political sphere; so the one is substituted for the other. So the soldier in the dream is a symbolic representation of the father.

But several meanings might be condensed into this symbol. Suppose the dreamer is tempted to rebel against the father by entering into a sexual liaison of which the father would certainly disapprove. The Roman soldier might also represent this person, the envisaged lover; perhaps the clichéd phrase 'Latin lover' might have prompted this. Thus, both the feared father and the desired lover are *condensed* into the single dream figure of the Roman soldier.

The purpose of devices like displacement and condensation is two-fold. Firstly, as we said, they disguise the repressed fears and wishes contained in the dream so that they can get past the censor which normally prevents their surfacing into the conscious mind. Secondly, they fashion this material into something which can be represented in a dream, that is, into images, symbols, and metaphors. Material has to be turned into this form for dreams, since dreams don't *say* things, they *show* things. In this sense especially, as we have indicated, they are very like literature. Hence the interest of literary critics in Freudian methods of interpretation.

This should raise questions in your mind about how we decide when a Freudian interpretation is plausible and when not. I want to take one more example, this time from a book by Freud called *The Psychopathology of Everyday Life*. In spite of its title, this is one of Freud's most enjoyable and accessible publications. Its subtitle explains what it's about: 'Forgetting, slips of the tongue, bungled actions, superstitions and errors'. (Bungled actions are when you do things like unwrapping a sweet, putting the paper in your mouth, and throwing away the sweet.) The underlying assumption is that when some wish, fear, memory, or desire is difficult to face we may try to cope with it by repressing it, that is, eliminating it from the conscious mind. But this doesn't make it go away: it remains alive in the unconscious, like radioactive matter buried beneath the ocean, and constantly seeks a way back into the conscious mind, always succeeding eventually. As Freud famously said, 'There is always a return of the repressed'. Slips of the tongue or pen, the forgetting of names, and similar 'accidents' show this repressed material in the act of seeking a way back.

The example is from Freud's own experience and it attributes significance to the forgetting of a word from a quotation. It is worth spending a little time on, since it typifies the quality of complexity and ingenuity which I have suggested is common in Freudian interpretation. Freud explains that while on holiday with his family he met an academic young man who, like Freud, was Jewish and they discussed the anti-semitism which might hinder their careers. The young man voiced strong feelings on this matter, expressing the wish that such wrongs might be put right by a future generation. He made this point with a quotation from the Latin poet Virgil, using words spoken by Dido, Queen of Carthage, when she is abandoned by Aeneas. Her words are *'Exoriare aliquis nostris ex ossibus ultor'*, meaning 'May someone arise from our bones as an avenger', but in quoting the line in Latin the young man accidently leaves out the word 'aliquis' (which means 'someone'). Freud corrects the quotation, and the young man (who has read Freud's books) challenges him to explain the significance of this simple act of forgetting. Freud accepts the challenge, and asks the young man to say 'candidly and uncritically whatever comes into your mind if you direct your attention to the forgotten word without any definite aim'. This produces the following sequence of associations:

Firstly, similar-sounding words like *relics*, *liquefying*, *fluidity*, and *fluid*.

Secondly, St Simon of Trent, whose relics he saw some years ago.

Thirdly, an article in an Italian newspaper called 'What St Augustine says about women'.

Fourthly, St Januarius, whose blood is kept in a phial in a church at Naples and on a particular holy day it miraculously liquefies. He says 'the people get very agitated if it is delayed'.

Freud points out that two of these saints (*Januarius* and *Augustine*) have names which link them closely with the calendar, and he has already worked out why the young man forgot the word 'aliquis'. The young man has been uneasy about a certain event, and if he had said the word 'aliquis' that would have reminded him again of this anxiety: so the unconscious protects him by deleting the word from his conscious memory. Perhaps you can already work out what the event is which the young man is worried about. He breaks off and says in some embarrassment 'I've suddenly thought of a young lady from whom I might easily hear a piece of news that would be very awkward for both of us'. He hesitates, and Freud asks 'That her periods have stopped?' The young man is astonished, and Freud explains how he knew: 'Think of the calendar saints, the blood that starts to flow on a particular day, the disturbance when the event fails to take place.'

STOP and THINK

In its elaborateness, and its use of what literary critics would call 'symbolism', this example is fairly typical of aspects of psychoanalytic interpretation. How convincing do you find it? The logic of Freud's deductive process is impressive, but note that the word 'aliquis' may be forgettable because the quotation seems to make sense without it (as 'May an avenger arise from our bones').

Try to pin-point your own reaction in a specific way. What is your judgement based upon? Do you distrust the example because of its elaborateness? (I am assuming some degree of distrust, since that is what I have encountered whenever I have used it.) Should there be a limit to the number of associative steps allowable between the slip and its interpretation? Without some such limit, could not the chain of associations be made to stretch to almost any interpretative destination? Or is it the nature of the steps, rather than their number, which makes the example finally unconvincing? If so, what is it about them which has this effect?

Note that the example seems to require the unconscious to anticipate the flow of conscious thought, to see that any word suggesting liquid will act as a reminder of the feared pregnancy, and then to eliminate the Latin word 'aliquis', pre-emptively, from the conscious mind.

My own feeling about it is that there is an attractive complexity about this example, far removed from the banalities of interpretations which are popularly called 'Freudian'. The anxiety felt by the young man is shown to suffuse the mind, in what seems to me a very plausible way, rather than being locked away in some specific compartment; hence, it is likely to surface anywhere at all. But perhaps this is simply to say that the elaborateness is what I like about this example.

Freudian interpretation, then, has always been of considerable interest to literary critics. The basic reason, again, is that the unconscious, like the poem, or novel, or play, cannot speak directly and explicitly but does so through images, symbols, emblems, and metaphors. Literature, too, is not involved with making direct explicit statements about life, but with showing and expressing experience through imagery, symbolism, metaphor and so on. However, because the 'statements' made are not explicit there is an inevitable 'judgemental' element involved, and in consequence psychoanalytic interpetations of literature are often controversial.

Freud and evidence

Distrust of Freud has grown strongly since the 1980s, partly as a result of his mainly negative views on women, as seen in the notion that women's sexuality is based upon feelings of narcissism, masochism, and passivity, and the idea that they suffer from an innate form of inferiority complex known as 'penis envy'. Influential work seems to show that these views were maintained by misreading, or even misrepresenting, the evidence presented to him by his patients; for instance by taking accounts of sexual abuse in childhood as fantasies rather than reality. Freud's misreading is seen in the case study usually known simply as 'Dora', but officially entitled 'Fragment of an Analysis of a Case of Hysteria' (volume 8 in the Pelican Freud Library). Feminist critics, and others, have read this case study as a means of psychoanalysing Freud. For instance, a collection of essays on the case appeared in 1985 under the title *In Dora's Case: Freud, Hysteria, and Feminism* (ed. Charles Bernheimer and Claire Kahane, Columbia University Press, 2nd edn, 1990). 'Dora' was brought to Freud for treatment in the autumn of 1900 by her father, as an eighteen-year-old. Her parents had found a note threatening suicide, which was the culmination of a period of withdrawal and difficulty. Dora broke off the treatment before it reached any conclusion, so Freud calls the case *'Fragment* of an Analysis of a Case of Hysteria'. The bulk of the material is Freud's analysis and interpretation of two dreams which she related to him in the course of the treatment, and we'll concentrate on one of these.

The family situation at the time the analysis took place was that Dora's wealthy parents were unhappy in their marriage, but they had formed a close friendship with another couple, Mr and Mrs K. A sexual relationship developed between Dora's father and Mrs K, which went on for several years. Mr K knew of this, and all three adults seemed to have an unspoken agreement that in exchange, as it were, Dora should be made available to Mr K. Mr K made approaches to her on two occasions, the first in his office, when she was fourteen; in a state of obvious excitement he suddenly took hold of her and began to kiss her. She reacted with a violent feeling of disgust and ran out. Freud considered this reaction neurotic: in his view 'this was surely just the situation to call up a distinct feeling of sexual excitement in a girl of fourteen', since Mr K, as he explains in a footnote, was 'still quite young and of prepossessing appearance' (p. 60).

The second occasion happened when Dora was sixteen. She and Mr K were walking together beside a lake, and he 'had the audacity to make a suggestion to her'. She slapped his face and hurried away. Freud is puzzled by the 'brutal form' of her refusal, and again sees her reaction as neurotic. When Dora told her father about what had happened he asked Mr K for an explanation, but Mr K denied that the incident had ever taken place. Her father believed him rather than Dora. Given these circumstances, Freud's view of the situation seems remarkably perverse. The first of the two dreams on which much of the analysis centres was a recurrent one, which first happened when they were staying in a house by the lake where Mr K made his indecent proposal:

> A house was on fire. My father was standing beside my bed and woke me up. I dressed quickly. Mother wanted to stop and save her jewel-case, but father said 'I refuse to let myself and my two children be burnt for the sake of your jewel-case'. We hurried downstairs, and as soon as I was outside I woke up.
>
> (Penguin Freud Library, vol. 8, p. 99)

Freud comments, *firstly*, that the immediate trigger of the dream is that when they arrived at this small wooden house her father said he was afraid of what would happen if there was a fire there. *Secondly*, in the afternoon Dora had woken up from an afternoon nap on the sofa to find Mr K standing over her. In the dream the father and Mr K are transposed. *Thirdly*, some years before she had heard her mother and father having a serious argument about jewels. *Fourthly*, Freud points out that the German word 'jewel-case' is a slang term for the female genitals. According to Freud, therefore, the dream expresses Dora's repressed wish to give Mr K what he wants (that is, her jewel-case): the fire represents her own repressed passion. The figure of Mr K is transposed with that of the father to express the wish that her former Oedipal love for her father will protect her from the temptation to yield to Mr K's advances. Freud sees in Dora's resentment of the relationship between her father and Mrs K a residual trace of this Oedipus complex, a feeling that Mrs K is her successful rival for her father's love. Against the combined male forces of her father, Mr K, and Freud it would seem that Dora has little chance, and the whole case study certainly shows Freud and psychoanalysis at their weakest. (Psychoanalysis in relation to feminism is further discussed in Chapter 6 on feminism.)

What Freudian psychoanalytic critics do

1. They give central importance, in literary interpretation, to the distinction between the conscious and the unconscious mind. They associate the literary work's 'overt' content with the former, and the 'covert' content with the latter, privileging the latter as being what the work is 'really' about, and aiming to disentangle the two.
2. Hence, they pay close attention to unconscious motives and feelings, whether these be (a) those of the author, or (b) those of the characters depicted in the work.
3. They demonstrate the presence in the literary work of classic psychoanalytic symptoms, conditions, or phases, such as the oral, anal, and phallic stages of emotional and sexual development in infants.
4. They make large-scale applications of psychoanalytic concepts to literary history in general; for example, Harold Bloom's book *The Anxiety of Influence* (Oxford University Press, 2nd edn, 1997) sees the struggle for identity by each generation of poets, under the 'threat' of the greatness of its predecessors, as an enactment of the Oedipus complex.
5. They identify a 'psychic' context for the literary work, at the expense of social or historical context, privileging the individual 'psycho-drama' above the 'social drama' of class conflict. The conflict between generations or siblings, or between competing desires within the same individual, looms much larger than conflict between social classes, for instance.

Freudian psychoanalytic criticism: examples

What kind of literary problem can Freudian psychoanalytic theories help with? Let's start with Shakespeare's *Hamlet*, an example which is so well-known that it has become a cliché. The relevant items in the above list of what Freudian critics do are: 1. stressing the distinction between conscious and unconscious, 2. uncovering the unconscious motives of characters, and 3. seeing in the literary work an embodiment of classic psychoanalytic conditions. In the play Hamlet's father is murdered by his own brother, Hamlet's

uncle, who then marries Hamlet's mother. The ghost of Hamlet's
father appears to Hamlet and tells him to avenge the murder by
killing his uncle. There is no obvious difficulty about doing this,
but Hamlet spends most of the play delaying and making excuses.
Why? He is not particularly squeamish, as he kills other people in
the course of the play. Also, what the ghost reveals merely confirms
suspicions Hamlet had independently formed himself, and he gath-
ers other external evidence that the ghost is telling him the truth. So
why the delay? Critics have long debated the question without coming to any generally accepted conclusions. Psychoanalytic criticism
offers a neat and simple solution: Hamlet cannot avenge this crime
because he is guilty of wanting to commit the same crime himself.
He has an Oedipus complex, that is, a repressed sexual desire for his
own mother, and a consequent wish to do away with his father. Thus,
the uncle has merely done what Hamlet himself secretly *wished* to
do: hence the difficulty for him of being the avenger. This view of the
play was first sketched out by Freud in *The Interpretation of Dreams*
(1900). As Freud summarises the matter, Hamlet is unable to

> take vengeance on the man who did away with his father and took
> that father's place with his mother, the man who shows him the
> repressed wishes of his own childhood realized. Thus the loathing
> which should drive him on to revenge is replaced in him by self-re-
> proaches, by scruples of conscience, which remind him that he him-
> self is literally no better than the sinner he is to punish.
>
> (Penguin Freud Library, vol. 4, p. 367)

As evidence for this view of the play, the psychoanalytic critic
points to the bedroom scene in which Hamlet shows an intense and
unusual awareness of his mother's sexuality. Freud links the situation of Hamlet in the play to that of Shakespeare himself ('It can, of
course, only be the poet's own mind which confronts us in *Hamlet*').
He cites the view that it was written immediately after the death of
Shakespeare's own father in 1601 ('while his childhood feelings
about his father had been freshly revived') and he adds, 'It is known,
too, that Shakespeare's own son who died at an early age bore the
name of "Hamnet", which is identical with "Hamlet"' (p. 368). All
the same, it is Hamlet the character in whom the Oedipal conflict is
detected, not Shakespeare the author. Here, then, is a famous

problem in literature, to which psychoanalysis can offer the basis of a solution. The sketch for an interpretation of the play put forward by Freud was later developed by his British colleague Ernest Jones in *Hamlet and Oedipus* (1949). There is a famous sustained literary pastiche of this psychoanalytical-autobiographical view of *Hamlet* in James Joyce's *Ulysses* (1922).

Another example of a puzzling play with which the psychoanalytic critic can offer help is Harold Pinter's *The Homecoming*. This example illustrates the third item in the list of what psychoanalytic critics do, the classic Freudian condition embodied in the play being that of the mother fixation. *The Homecoming* centres on an East End of London all-male household consisting of an autocratic father and two grown-up sons. The mother has been dead for some years but her memory is worshipped by the widower and her sons. There is a third son who has emigrated to America where he is a college professor. He comes back on a visit to his family, bringing his wife (this being the literal homecoming of the title). During the visit the sons and the father have the idea of setting their brother's wife up as a prostitute in a Soho flat, and living off the proceeds. Their brother agrees to this, and the wife accepts it calmly when it is put to her, having first extracted the best possible financial terms, and made it clear that she will be in many ways the boss of this new household. Her husband goes back to America without her, and to their three children (all boys). These events seem so bizarre that the play is often performed as a kind of surreal farce.

But, again, the psychoanalytic critic is able to offer an explanation which makes some sense of them. In her article 'Pinter's Freudian Homecoming' (*Essays in Criticism*, July 1991, pp. 189–207) M. W. Rowe suggests that the underlying explanation is to be found in Freud's essay, 'The most prevalent form of degradation in erotic life'. The all-male family shown in the play suffers from a classic condition known as a mother fixation, in which there is an exaggerated reverence for the mother. Such people are attracted only to women who resemble the mother, but because of this the shadow of the incest taboo makes the expression of sexual feelings towards them difficult or impossible. Hence, their only way out is to seek sexual relationships with women who do not resemble the mother, and whom they therefore despise. So in order to generate sexual excitement such men have to degrade their love objects, since if they are not so degraded they will resemble the mother, and hence, in the man's mind, not be available as a sexual partner. Thus, women are polarised into idealised maternal figures on the one hand and prostitute figures on the other. The exaggerated reverence for the mother is usually much diluted by adolescence, but if the mother has died before the child reached adolescence, as in the household shown in the play, then a damaging, idealised image of her can live on, and eclipse that of all possible sexual partners. Hence, when the brothers propose the prostitute plan the husband accepts this because that is how he himself has thought about or fantasised about his wife in order to make a sexual relationship with her possible. Again, then, the action which we see presented in the play turns out to be an enacting of the suppressed desires of one of the central characters.

Lacan

Jacques Lacan (1901–81) was a French psychoanalyst whose work has had an extraordinary influence upon many aspects of literary theory. Lacan began his career by taking a medical degree and then training in psychiatry in the 1920s. In the 1930s he worked on paranoia, publishing his thesis on his patient Aimée. His famous theory of the 'mirror stage' (explained later) was first presented at a conference in 1936. Subsequently his ideas were influenced by figures who successively dominated Parisian intellectual life, such as the anthropologist Claude Lévi-Strauss (1908–2009), and the linguists Ferdinand de Saussure (1857–1913) and Roman Jakobson (1896–1982). Only in the 1950s did Lacan begin to challenge the orthodoxies of his subject field. In 1955 at a conference in Vienna he called for a new 'back-to-basics' Freudianism. But he meant, not a new attempt to understand the 'conscious personality' (the 'ego') and interpret its behaviour in the light of an understanding of the workings of the unconscious (which many would take to be the whole point of Freudianism), but rather a new emphasis on the unconscious itself, as 'the nucleus of our being'. In 1959 these unorthodox views resulted in his expulsion from the International Psychoanalytic Association (a kind of World Congress of Freudian analysts) and in

1964 in Paris he set up his own breakaway Ecole Freudienne and published a section of his training sessions under the title *Ecrits*. By this time he himself was one of the most prominent Parisian intellectuals.

Lacan's reputation, then, rests on the published 'seminars', the *Ecrits*. A French seminar is not a group discussion but a kind of extended lecture for graduate-level students. The intense atmosphere of these occasions is suggested in an eyewitness account of Lacan's seminars in the 1950s:

> He speaks in a wavering, syncopated or thundering voice, spiced with sighs and hesitations. He notes down in advance what he is going to say, then, before the public, he improvises like an actor from the Royal Shakespeare Company … he fascinates his audience with his impressive language … Lacan does not analyse, he associates. Lacan does not lecture, he produces resonances. At each session of this collective treatment, the pupils have the impression that the master speaks about them and for them in a coded message secretly destined for each one.
>
> (Quoted by John Lechte in *Julia Kristeva*, Routledge, 1990, pp. 36–7)

Note here the emphasis on showmanship, on improvisation, on by-passing the formally structured presentation of ideas usual in lectures, and on the transmission of information in a coded form as part of an initiation process. Lacan says, in the piece discussed below, that the only teaching worthy of the name is teaching you can only come to terms with in its own terms. I emphasise all this to prepare you for the initial strangeness of Lacan's writing, all of which was based on the semi-improvised meditations which occupied the two to three hours of these weekly occasions.

The vast output of Lacan has not all been of equal interest to literary critics. The major interest has been in the following:

1. The essay 'The insistence of the letter in the unconscious', reprinted in David Lodge, ed., *Modern Criticism and Theory* (Longman, 1988), pp. 79–106.
2. The seminar on Edgar Allan Poe's story 'The Purloined Letter', reprinted in *The Purloined Poe: Lacan, Derrida, and Psychoanalytic Reading*, ed. John P. Muller and William J. Richardson

(Johns Hopkins University Press, 1988), pp. 28–54, with extensive editorial commentary and annotations.

3. The seminar on *Hamlet*, 'Desire and the Interpretation of
    Desire in *Hamlet*', reprinted in *Literature and Psychoanalysis:
    the Question of Reading: Otherwise*, ed. Shoshana Felman (Johns
    Hopkins University Press, 1982), pp. 11–52.

Lacan's own explication of his ideas is often intimidatingly obscure.
I would suggest that in reading him you should devote some study
time to reading the same piece several times, rather than reading
through a great deal of his work once only. In grappling with Lacan
I have found the following particularly helpful:

1. David Lodge's pre-summary of the argument of Lacan's 'The
    insistence of the letter in the unconscious', pp. 79–80 in *Modern
    Criticism and Theory*.

2. John Lechte's account of Lacan's thinking, 'The effect of
    the unconscious' in his book *Julia Kristeva*, pp. 13–64. I
    have also drawn upon this for the biographical details given
    above.

3. A summary by Toril Moi in *Sexual/Textual Politics*, pp. 99–101
    (Methuen, 1985).

4. The critique of Lacan, 'The mirror stage – a critical reflection'
    in Raymond Tallis's *Not Saussure: A Critique of Post-Saussurean
    Literary Theory*, pp. 131–63 (Macmillan, 1988).

The most important Lacanian text for literary students is 'The
insistence of the letter', first delivered in 1957 to a 'lay' audience of
philosophy students, rather than to trainee psychiatrists, but using
material from the professional seminars. In what follows I attempt a
summary of the argument, trying to show why these ideas have been
used so intensively by literary critics.

Lacan begins the piece by paying allegiance to the intellectual
dominance of language studies: he asks (rhetorically) 'how could
a psychoanalyst of today not realise that his realm of truth is in fact
the word?' Language, then, is central, and this is so because in
investigating the unconscious the analyst is always both using and
examining language – in effect, Freudian psychiatry is entirely a
verbal science. And the unconscious is not a chaotic mass of

disparate material, as might formerly have been thought, but an orderly network, as complex as the structure of a language: 'what the psychoanalytic experience discovers in the unconscious is the whole structure of language'.

So the unconscious, in Lacan's famous slogan, is structured like a language. But how is a language structured? Modern language studies, he goes on, begin with Saussure, who shows that meaning in language is a matter of contrasts between words and other words, not between words and things. Meaning, that is to say, is a network of differences. There is a perpetual barrier between signifier (the word) and signified (the referent). He demonstrates this built-in separation with a diagram showing two identical lavatory doors, one headed 'Ladies' the other 'Gentlemen'. This purports to show that the same signifier may have different signifieds, so that (Lodge, p. 86) 'only the correlations between signifier and signifier supply the standard for all research into meaning'. Hence, 'we are forced to accept the notion of an incessant sliding of the signified under the signifer' (Lodge, p. 87). That is, words and meanings have a life of their own and constantly override and obscure the supposed simplicities and clarity of external reality. If signifiers relate only to one another, then language is detached from external reality, and becomes an independent realm, a crucial notion in post-structuralist thinking (see Chapter 3, pp. 63–4).

But what evidence is there that the unconscious is 'linguistic' in structure as Lacan alleges? He argues that the two 'dream work' mechanisms identified by Freud, *condensation* and *displacement* (this chapter, pp. 100–1) correspond to the basic poles of language identified by the linguist Roman Jakobson, that is, to *metaphor* and *metonymy*, respectively. The correspondence is that:

1.   In metonymy one thing represents another by means of the part standing for the whole. So twenty sail would mean twenty ships. In Freudian dream interpretation an element in a dream might stand for something else by *displacement*: so, a person might be represented by one of their attributes; for instance, a lover who is Italian might be represented in a dream by, let's say, an Alfa Romeo car. Lacan says this is the same as *metonymy*, the part standing for the whole.

2. In *condensation* several things might be compressed into one
    symbol, just as a *metaphor* like 'the ship ploughed the waves'
    condenses into a single item two different images, the ship cut-
    ting through the sea and the plough cutting through the soil.

The use by the unconscious of these linguistic means of self-expression is part of Lacan's evidence for the claim that the unconscious is structured like a language. He goes on to emphasise the
linguistic aspect of Freud's work: whenever the unconscious is
being discussed the amount of linguistic analysis increases, since
puns, allusions, and other kinds of word play are often the mechanisms which make manifest the content of the unconscious – think
back to the 'aliquis' example, for instance.

The transition section of the essay moves attention again from
the conscious self, which has always been regarded as the primary
self, to the unconscious as 'the kernel of our being'. In Western philosophy the conscious mind has long been regarded as the essence of
selfhood. This view is encapsulated in the proclamation by the
philosopher Descartes, 'I think, therefore I am'. Lacan lays down
a dramatic challenge to this philosophical consensus (remember
that he is addressing an audience of philosophy students) when he
reverses this into 'I am where I think not' (Lodge, p. 97), that is, in
the unconscious, where my true selfhood lies. Lacan insists, then,
that the Freudian discovery of the unconscious be followed through
to its logical conclusion, which is 'the self's radical ex-centricity to
itself' (Lodge, p. 101). And he asks 'who is this other to whom I am
more attached than to myself, since at the heart of my assent to my
own identity it is still he who wags me?' (Lodge, p. 102). Hence, the
self is 'deconstructed', shown to be merely a linguistic effect, not an
essential entity. The unconscious, then, is the 'kernel of our being',
but the unconscious is like a language, and language exists as a
structure before the individual enters into it. Hence, the liberal
humanist notion of unique, individual selfhood is deconstructed.
The argument, then, is extremely ambitious and wide-ranging in its
effects. In a few pages Lacan seeks to alter nothing less than our
deepest notions of what we are.

But why, in particular, is it of such interest to literary critics?
I think the answer to this question is a consequence of the relentless

logic of the views put forward in the essay. Thus, Lacan says that the unconscious is the 'kernel of our being', but since the unconscious is linguistic, and language is a system already complete and in existence before we enter into it, then it follows that the notion of a unique, separate self is deconstructed. If this is so, the idea of 'character', which rests in turn on the notion of a unique separate self, becomes untenable. So a major consequence of accepting the Lacanian position would be to reject the conventional view of characterisation in literature. Since Lacan deconstructs the idea of the subject as a stable amalgam of consciousness, we can hardly accept novelistic characters as people but must hold them in abeyance, as it were, and see them as assemblages of signifiers clustering round a proper name. Hence, a wholly different reading strategy is demanded.

Further, the view of language offered by Lacan sees it as fundamentally detached from any referent in the world. Accepting this view leads to a rejection of literary realism, since in realist novels the underlying assumption is that the text figures forth the real world for us. Hence, adopting the Lacanian outlook would involve valuing instead the modernist or postmodernist experimental, fragmented, allusive text, where, for instance, a novel plays with the devices of the novel, alludes to other novels, and so on, just as, for Saussure, the signifiers which make up a language refer only to one another, and interact with one another, but do not figure forth a world. Hence, a wholly different set of literary preferences is also demanded.

Lacan's foregrounding of the unconscious leads him to speculate about the mechanism whereby we emerge into consciousness. Before the sense of self emerges the young child exists in a realm which Lacan calls the Imaginary, in which there is no distinction between self and Other and there is a kind of idealised identification with the mother. Then, between six months and eighteen months comes what he calls the 'mirror-stage', when the child sees its own reflection in the mirror and begins to conceive of itself as a unified being, separate from the rest of the world. At this stage the child enters into the language system, essentially a system which is concerned with lack and separation – crucial Lacanian concepts – since language names what is not present and substitutes a linguistic sign for it. This stage also marks the beginning of socialisation, with its prohibitions and restraints, associated with the figure of the father. The new order which the child now enters is called by Lacan the Symbolic. This distinction between the Imaginary and the Symbolic has been used extensively in literary studies, for instance, by French feminist critics (see Chapter 6, p. 131). In terms of the literary polarisation between the realist and the anti-realist text, the Symbolic realm would have to be seen as the one found in realist literature, a world of patriarchal order and logic. By contrast, the anti-realist text represents the realm of the Imaginary, a world in which language gestures beyond itself, beyond logic and grammar, rather in the way that poetic language often does. Indeed, the contrast between the Imaginary and the Symbolic might be seen as analogous to that between poetry and prose. In practice the two realms, and the two kinds of language, must always co-exist, and the critical stance which follows from an acceptance of the Lacanian outlook will involve a preference for the kind of literary text in which there are constant irruptions of the Imaginary into the Symbolic, as in the kind of 'metafiction' or 'magic realism' in which the novel undercuts and queries its own realism. A fine example of this kind of work would be that of the British novelist B. S. Johnson, whose constant textual inventiveness takes the form, for instance, of moments when the characters cross-question the author, taking issue with his version of their motives, or his handling of the plots in which they figure. Hence, apparently abstract Lacanian notions, such as the constructedness and instability of the subject (the self), or the subject as a linguistic construct, or language as a self-contained universe of discourse can be seen in action in the texture of the work of fiction.

What Lacanian critics do

1. Like Freudian critics they pay close attention to unconscious motives and feelings, but instead of excavating for those of the author or characters, they search out those of the text itself, uncovering contradictory undercurrents of meaning, which lie like a subconscious beneath the 'conscious' of the text. This is another way of defining the process of 'deconstruction'.
2. They demonstrate the presence in the literary work of Lacanian psychoanalytic symptoms or phases, such as the mirror-stage or the sovereignty of the unconscious.

3. They treat the literary text in terms of a series of broader Lacanian orientations, towards such concepts as lack or desire, for instance.

4. They see the literary text as an enactment or demonstration of Lacanian views about language and the unconscious, particularly the endemic elusiveness of the signified, and the centrality of the unconscious. In practice, this results in favouring the anti-realist text which challenges the conventions of literary representation.

Lacanian criticism: an example

To illustrate some of the concerns of a Lacanian approach to literature we can now look briefly at Lacan's well-known interpretation of Edgar Allan Poe's pioneering detective story 'The Purloined Letter'. (The tale is included in the Penguin *Edgar Allan Poe: Selected Writings*, ed. David Galloway, and also reprinted in *The Purloined Poe*.) Lacan analysed this story in a series of 'seminars', as part of the induction process for trainee analysts. In the 1980s several post-structuralist essays were written in response to the publication of these seminars, and much of the material has usefully been collected and republished in *The Purloined Poe*. Also, Newton's *Theory into Practice* contains an essay on the topic by the Lacanian psychoanalytic critic Shoshana Felman. Since it is by Lacan himself, this example demonstrates the fourth of the Lacanian critical activities listed above, Lacan finding in it evidence of his own views on language, and on the process of psychoanalysis.

Poe's story has about it an archetypal air which lends itself well to psychoanalytic interpretation. There is no in-depth characterisation, the characters being suggestive of chess pieces which are moved about by the author in a ritualistic combat of bluff, counter-bluff, and subterfuge. They are named the Queen, the King, the Minister, the Chief of Police and Dupin, the detective. What happens can be divided into four phases:

1. The Minister is in discussion with the Queen in her apartments when the King enters unexpectedly. He notices that she is anxious the King should not see a letter which is on the desk, but she can't conceal it as this would draw his attention to it. When the attention of both is distracted the Minister removes it,

substituting a letter from his own pocket which has a similar appearance.

2. When she discovers the theft the Queen realises who is respon-sible, and when the Minister is away she gets the Chief of Police and his men to search his apartments. In spite of employing the most thorough and scientific methods they find nothing.

3. In desperation she asks for Dupin's help. He visits the Minister and reasons that carrying the letter on his person would be too great a risk, but its usefulness lies in his being able to produce it at any time, so it can't be hidden outside the house. But if it had been *hidden* inside the house the search would have discovered it, so it must be in the house but not hidden. Sure enough, he sees the letter above the mantelpiece, carelessly pushed in amongst other items of correspondence.

4. He visits again, and having arranged a distraction in the street, substitutes a fake letter for it. The letter is returned to the Queen, and the Minister, unaware that he no longer possesses it, brings about his own downfall. A note inside the fake reveals that this is Dupin's revenge for being duped by the Minister in a love affair in earlier life.

Lacan's account of the tale is lengthy, but of markedly different character from the conventional Freudian criticism of Poe, which is best represented by the work of Freud's 1930s disciple Marie Bonaparte (also extracted in *The Purloined Poe*). In Bonaparte the tale is read, as are all Poe's works, as a symptom of the author's neurotic inner life. Thus, she reads beyond the text to the author, identifying in him a mother fixation and necrophilia on the basis of the content of the tales. Lacan, by contrast, does not talk about the psychology of the individual author, but sees the text as a metaphor which throws light upon aspects of the unconscious, on the nature of psychoanalysis, and on aspects of language. We can summarise these as follows:

1. *The stolen letter is an emblem of the unconscious itself.* In the story we find out nothing about the *content* of the letter: we merely see it affecting the actions of every person in the tale. Likewise, the content of the unconscious is, by definition, unknowable, but everything we do is affected by it: we can guess at the nature

of this content by observing its effects, just as we can deduce the general nature of the letter's contents from the anxiety it generates. Freud's investigations resulted in confident assertions about the precise nature of the content of the unconscious, but Lacan is much more sceptical about the possibility of such certainties. Like the letter, the pieces which might make sense of our inner mental universe have been purloined, and we have to learn to operate without them. We have, that is, to use the code without having the key.

2. *Dupin's investigation of the crime of the stolen letter enacts the process of psychoanalysis.* The analyst in psychoanalysis uses repetition and substitution: in getting the patient to verbalise painful repressed memories, the original event is repeated in verbal form, but the verbal account is then substituted in the conscious mind for the repressed memory in the unconscious. Once it is conscious and verbalised, the memory is disempowered and mental well-being is restored. Likewise, Dupin's investigative process in the story centres on repetition and substitution: his theft of the letter from the Minister is a repetition of the Minister's theft of it from the Queen, and the theft in both cases is achieved by substitution, a false letter being used as a replacement for the real one.

3. *The letter with the unknown content is an embodiment of aspects of the nature of language.* In language there is an endless play of signifiers, but no simple connection with any signified content beyond language. The signified is always lost or purloined. In the same way, we see the significance of the letter throughout the story, but we never find out precisely what is signified within it. It is an example of signification itself, not a sign of some specific thing. Likewise, all words are purloined letters: we can never open them and view their content unambiguously; we have the signifiers, which are the verbal envelopes of concepts, so to speak, but these envelopes cannot be unsealed, so that the signifieds will always remain hidden, just like the content of the purloined letter in Poe's tale.

Comparing the Freudian and Lacanian examples discussed in this chapter will make it immediately apparent that there is an immense gulf between these two approaches, even though – paradoxically – they both stem from the same original body of Freudian theory.

Selected reading

General

Ellmann, Maud, ed., *Psychoanalytic Literary Criticism* (Longman, 1994).
A useful collection, showing the influence of Freud and Lacan on criticism.

Felman, Shoshana, ed., *Literature and Psychoanalysis – The Question of Reading: Otherwise* (Johns Hopkins University Press, 1982).
An important collection of essays. Felman's own 'Turning the screw of interpretation' is about Henry James's story 'The Turn of the Screw', one of the earliest texts to be subjected to psychoanalytic criticism (by the critic Edmund Wilson in 1934).

Jefferson, Ann, and Robey, David, eds, *Modern Literary Theory: A Comparative Introduction* (Batsford, 2nd edn, 1986). Chapter five 'Modern psychoanalytic criticism'.
A useful general account, not restricted to Freud.

Kurzweil, Edith, ed., *Literature and Psychoanalysis* (Columbia University Press, 1983).
A very useful collection with good editorial commentary. The first section is on early psychoanalytic theory, the third on literary applications, including essays on Keats, on Henry James's disturbing ghost story 'The Jolly Corner', on Kafka, and on Lewis Carroll. The final section is on French psychoanalytic theory.

Wise, Inge, and Mills, Maggie, eds, *Psychoanalytic Ideas and Shakespeare* (Karnac Books, 2006).
A book which 'links the bard's universe to psychoanalytic thought and practice'.

Wright, Elizabeth, *Psychoanalytic Criticism: Theory in Practice* (Polity Press, rev. edn, 1998).
Short and wide-ranging, dealing with Freudian and Lacanian approaches, as well as others not discussed here, but not an easy read.

Freud

I have used the Penguin edition of Freud, in 24 volumes, published between 1955 and 1967 and translated by the British psychoanalyst James Strachey (1887–1967). The translation seeks to present Freud primarily as a clinician and a scientist, establishing his standing with a full-scale scholarly Collected Edition of his works, so it tends to prefer 'esoteric neologisms' (like the Ego and the Id) for the ordinary German words that

Freud actually used. When the copyright on Freud's work expired on 1 January 2010 (seventy years after his death), Penguin commissioned a new translation under the General Editorship of Adam Phillips, and these are now available in the Penguin Modern Classics imprint. These volumes seek to present Freud primarily as a literary writer and a Humanist. You may find these a more lively read for volumes 4, 5, and 8 listed below and may prefer the contemporary discussion and contextualisation to Strachey's scholarly apparatus. For example, reading the Dora case from the 2004 *Studies in Hysteria* translated by Nicola Luckhurst, and with an illuminating introduction by Rachel Bowlby, breaks away from the masculinist mind-set and raises the issues most readers today will wish to debate.

The Complete Works in the Strachey translation are also available to download free and legally from many internet sites.

Bernheimer, Charles, and Kahane, Claire, *In Dora's Case: Freud, Hysteria, and Feminism* (Columbia University Press, 2nd edn, 1990).

A critique of Freud's handling of this case, by various commentators, including Jacques Lacan (briefly and incisively), Jacqueline Rose, Toril Moi, and Jane Gallop. This book works beyond the traditional (but now outmoded) antagonism between feminism and psychoanalysis by moving towards Lacanian and post-structuralist re-readings of Freud.

Freud, Sigmund, *The Interpretation of Dreams* (first published in 1900. Volume four in the Penguin Freud).

A key work in the creation of twentieth-century sensibility. Explains the basic dream mechanisms, 'Condensation', VIa; 'Displacement', VIb; also the Oedipus complex and *Hamlet* 363–8.

Freud, Sigmund, *The Psychopathology of Everyday Life* (first published in 1901. Volume five in the Penguin Freud).

Very readable and interesting, in spite of the title. Either this book or the case histories would be the best place to begin with Freud.

Freud, Sigmund, *Case Histories I: 'Dora' and 'Little Hans'* (Volume eight in the Penguin Freud).

Detailed records of Freudian interpretation. The element of ingenuity and complexity emphasised above is very evident in these accounts.

Roudinesco, Elisabeth, *Freud: In His Time and Ours* (Harvard University Press, 2016).

A very interesting new life which throws a great deal of new light on the topic.

Thurschwell, Pamela, *Sigmund Freud* (Routledge, 2000).

A useful title in the 'Critical Thinkers' series, which is similar in introductory scope to the old 'Fontana Modern Masters' series.

Timpanaro, Sebastiano, *The Freudian Slip: Psychoanalysis and Textual Criticism* (Verso Paperback, 1985).

I list this fascinating and readable book by a noted Italian Marxist partly because it is illustrative of the traditional antagonism between Marxism and psychoanalysis. Timpanaro 'deconstructs' many of the slips in Freud's *Psychopathology* on the grounds that they are explicable in terms of incidental verbal similarities. See, for instance, his discussion of the 'aliquis' example, pp. 19–28.

Wolheim, Richard, *Freud* (Fontana Press, 2nd edn, 1991).

Still the best introduction. But read some of Freud himself first.

Lacan

Bailly, Lionel, *Lacan: A Beginner's Guide* (Oneworld Publications, 2009).

Clear and well organised with a very useful glossary.

Homer, Sean, *Jacques Lacan* (Routledge Critical Thinkers, 2005).

A useful title in a useful series.

Lacan, Jacques, 'Desire and the interpretation of desire in *Hamlet*', reprinted in *Literature and Psychoanalysis – The Question of Reading: Otherwise*, ed. Shoshana Felman (Johns Hopkins University Press, 1982), pp. 11–52.

Lacan, Jacques, 'The insistence of the letter in the unconscious', reprinted in *Modern Criticism and Theory*, ed. David Lodge (Longman, 1988), pp. 79–106.

Lacan, Jacques, Seminar on 'The Purloined Letter', reprinted in *The Purloined Poe: Lacan, Derrida, and Psychoanalytic Reading*, ed. John P. Muller and William J. Richardson (Johns Hopkins University Press, 1988), pp. 28–54, with extensive editorial commentary and annotations.

Lacan, Jacques, *Ecrits* (Routledge, 2001).

A very welcome publication in Routledge's excellent 'Classics' series which reprints key critical texts of the twentieth century.

Mitchell, Juliet, and Rose, Jacqueline, eds, *Feminine Sexuality: Jacques Lacan and the Ecole Freudienne* (Macmillan, 1982).

Key Lacanian texts translated and discussed.

Rabaté, Jean-Michel, ed., *The Cambridge Companion to Lacan* (Cambridge Companions to Literature, 2003).

More advanced material for the study of Lacan's ideas.

Roudinesco, Elisabeth, *Jacques Lacan: An Outline of a Life and a History of a System of Thought* (Polity Press, 1999).

Sarup, Madan, *Jacques Lacan* (Harvester, 1992).

A volume in the Modern Cultural Theorists series by an able explainer of difficult material. Begins with an account of Freudian ideas and ends with a discussion of Lacan and feminism.

6
Feminist criticism

Feminism and feminist criticism

[handwritten margin note: Hildegard ? C de Pisan ? Margery ?]

The 'women's movement' of the 1960s was not, of course, the start of feminism. Rather, it was a renewal of an old tradition of thought and action already possessing its classic books which had diagnosed the problem of women's inequality in society, and (in some cases) proposed solutions. These books include Mary Wollstonecraft's *A Vindication of the Rights of Women* (1792), which discusses male writers like Milton, Pope, and Rousseau; Olive Schreiner's *Women and Labour* (1911); Virginia Woolf's *A Room of One's Own* (1929), which vividly portrays the unequal treatment given to women seeking education and alternatives to marriage and motherhood; and Simone de Beauvoir's *The Second Sex* (1949), which has an important section on the portrayal of women in the novels of D. H. Lawrence. Male contributions to this tradition of feminist writing include John Stuart Mill's *The Subjection of Women* (1869), and *The Origin of the Family* (1884) by Friedrich Engels.

The feminist literary criticism of today is the direct product of the 'women's movement' of the 1960s. This movement was, in important ways, literary from the start, in the sense that it realised the significance of the images of women promulgated by literature, and saw it as vital to combat them and question their authority and their coherence. In this sense the women's movement has always been crucially concerned with books and literature, so that feminist criticism should not be seen as an off-shoot or a spin-off from feminism which is remote from the ultimate aims of the movement, but as one of its most practical ways of influencing everyday conduct and attitudes.

The concern with 'conditioning' and 'socialisation' underpins a crucial set of distinctions – that between the terms 'feminist', 'female', and 'feminine'. As Toril Moi explains, the first is 'a political position', the second 'a matter of biology', and the third 'a set of culturally defined characteristics'. Particularly in the distinction between the second and third of these lies much of the force of feminism (see Moi's essay in *The Feminist Reader*, ed. Catherine Belsey and Jane Moore). Other important ideas are explained in the appropriate part of the remainder of this section.

The representation of women in literature, then, was felt to be one of the most important forms of 'socialisation', since it provided the role models which indicated to women, and men, what constituted acceptable versions of the 'feminine' and legitimate feminine goals and aspirations. Feminists pointed out, for example, that in nineteenth-century fiction very few women work for a living, unless they are driven to it by dire necessity. Instead, the focus of interest is on the heroine's choice of marriage partner, which will decide her ultimate social position and exclusively determine her happiness and fulfilment in life, or her lack of these.

Thus, in feminist criticism in the 1970s the major effort went into exposing what might be called the mechanisms of patriarchy, that is, the cultural 'mind-set' in men and women which perpetuated sexual inequality. Critical attention was given to books by male writers in which influential or typical images of women were constructed. Necessarily, the criticism which undertook this work was combative and polemical. Then, in the 1980s, in feminism as in other critical approaches, the mood changed. *Firstly*, feminist criticism became much more *eclectic*, meaning that it began to draw upon the findings and approaches of other kinds of criticism – Marxism, structuralism, linguistics, and so on. *Secondly*, it switched its focus from attacking male versions of the world to exploring the nature of the female world and outlook, and reconstructing the lost or suppressed records of female experience. *Thirdly*, attention was switched to the need to construct a new canon of women's writing by rewriting the history of the novel and of poetry in such a way that neglected women writers were given new prominence.

Such distinct phases of interest and activity seem characteristic of feminist criticism. Elaine Showalter, for instance, described the change in the late 1970s as a shift of attention from 'androtexts' (books by men) to 'gynotexts' (books by women). She coined the term 'gynocritics', meaning the study of gynotexts, but gynocriticism is a broad and varied field, and any generalisations about it should be treated with caution. The subjects of gynocriticism are, she says, 'the history, styles, themes, genres, and structures of writing by women; the psychodynamics of female creativity; the trajectory of the individual or collective female career; and the evolution or laws of a female literary tradition'.

Showalter also detects in the history of women's writing a *feminine phase* (1840–80), in which women writers imitated dominant male artistic norms and aesthetic standards; then a *feminist phase* (1880–1920), in which radical and often separatist positions are maintained; and finally a *female phase* (1920 onwards) which looked particularly at female writing and female experience. The reasons for this liking for 'phasing' are complex: partly, it is the result of the view that feminist criticism required a terminology if it was to attain theoretical respectability. More importantly, there is a great need, in all intellectual disciplines, to establish a sense of progress, enabling early and cruder examples of (in this case) feminist criticism to be given their rightful credit and acknowledgement while at the same time making it clear that the approach they represent is no longer generally regarded as a model for practice.

But feminist criticism since the 1970s has been remarkable for the wide range of positions that exist within it. Debates and disagreements have centred on three particular areas, these being: 1. the role of theory; 2. the nature of language; and 3. the value or otherwise of psychoanalysis. The next three sections will look at each of these in turn.

Feminist criticism and the role of theory

A major division within feminist criticism has concerned disagreements about the amount and type of theory that should feature in it. What is usually called the 'Anglo-American' version of feminism has tended to be more sceptical about recent critical theory, and more cautious in using it, than have the 'French' feminists, who have adopted and adapted a great deal of (mainly) post-structuralist and psychoanalytic criticism as the basis of much of their work. The 'Anglo-Americans' (not all are English or American) maintain a major interest in traditional critical concepts like theme, motif, and characterisation. They seem to accept the conventions of literary realism, and treat literature as a series of representations of women's lives and experience which can be measured and evaluated against reality. They see the close reading and explication of individual literary texts as the major business of feminist criticism. Generally, this kind of feminist criticism has a good deal in common with the procedures and assumptions of the liberal humanist approach to literature, although feminists also place considerable emphasis on the use of historical data and non-literary material (such as diaries, memoirs, social and medical history) in understanding the literary text. The American critic Elaine Showalter is usually taken as the major representative of this approach, but other exemplars would be Sandra Gilbert and Susan Gubar, Patricia Stubbs, and Rachel Brownstein.

However, most of these are in fact American rather than 'Anglo', and this should make us question the usefulness of this widely accepted category. English feminist criticism is, after all, often distinctly different from American: it tends to be 'socialist feminist' in orientation, aligned with cultural materialism or Marxism, so that it is obviously unsatisfactory to try to assimilate it into a 'non-theoretical' category. The existence of this kind of feminism has been rather obscured by the fact that certain popular books summarising feminist criticism (like K. K. Ruthven's *Feminist Literary Studies: An Introduction* and Toril Moi's *Sexual/Textual Politics*) do not discuss it as a distinct category. Examples of this kind of work are: Terry Lovell's *Consuming Fiction* (1987), Julia Swindells's *Victorian Writing and Working Women* (1985), and *Sea Changes: Culture and Feminism* (1986) by Cora Kaplan, an American who worked in Britain for many years. Kaplan was a member of the Marxist Feminist Literature Collective, an important group whose very existence indicates the strong political and theoretical interests of this kind of feminist criticism. A similarly important group was the Literature Teaching Politics Collective, which was also a series of conferences and an associated journal. An important figure associated with this group is Catherine Belsey, whose books (such as *The Subject of Tragedy* (1985), and *John Milton: Language, Gender, Power* (1988)) are part of this same socialist feminist British tradition. While the definitive works in the so-called 'Anglo-American' tradition appeared in the late 1970s, the British 'socialist feminist' tradition produced its key works in the mid-1980s and remains active and influential.

In contrast to the Americans (if not, as we have just argued, to the British), the work of 'French' feminism is more overtly theoretical, taking as its starting point the insights of major post-structuralists, especially Lacan, Foucault, and Derrida. For these feminist critics, the literary text is never primarily a representation of reality, or a reproduction of a personal voice expressing the minutiae of personal experience. Indeed, the French theorists often deal with concerns other than literature: they write about language, representation, and psychology as such and often travel through detailed treatments of major philosophical issues of this kind before coming to the literary text itself. The major figures on this 'French' side of the divide are Julia Kristeva (actually Bulgarian, though regarded abroad – as she has ruefully said – as a kind of embodiment of French intellectualism), Hélène Cixous (Algerian-born), and Luce Irigaray.

All three are best encountered initially in the various feminist readers now available. For instance, Kristeva's 1974 interview 'Woman can never be defined' is in *New French Feminisms* (Marks and de Courtivron), as are sections from 'Sorties' and 'The Laugh of the Medusa' by Cixous, and sections from Irigaray's *The Sex Which is Not One*. Extracts from the same Cixous and Irigaray pieces are also in *Feminisms: A Reader* (Maggie Humm).

A sustained discussion of the differences between 'Anglo-American' and 'French' feminisms (though one which is much on the side of the latter) is Toril Moi's *Sexual/Textual Politics*. For a later account see the chapter 'Imaginary gardens with real frogs in them: feminist euphoria and the Franco-American divide, 1976–1988' by Ann Rosalind Jones in *Changing Subjects: The Making of Feminist Literary Criticism* (Greene and Kahn). These French feminists are particularly concerned with language and psychology, which are considered in the two following sections.

Feminist criticism and language

Another fundamental issue, on which opinion is just as polarised, is the question of whether or not there exists a form of language which is inherently feminine. There is a long-standing tradition of debate on this issue within feminism. For instance, Virginia Woolf (in sections four and five of her extended polemical essay *A Room of One's Own*) suggests that language use is gendered, so that when a woman turns to novel writing she finds that there is 'no common sentence ready for her use'. The great male novelists have written 'a natural prose, swift but not slovenly, expressive but not precious, taking their own tint without ceasing to be common property'. She quotes an example and says 'That is a man's sentence'. She doesn't make its qualities explicit, but the example seems to be characterised by carefully balanced and patterned rhetorical sequences. But 'it was a sentence unsuited for a woman's use', and women writers trying to use it (Charlotte Brontë, George Eliot) fared badly. Jane Austen rejected it and instead 'devised a perfectly natural, shapely sentence proper for her own use', but this is not described or exemplified. Presumably, though, the characteristics of a 'woman's sentence' are that the clauses are linked in looser sequences, rather than carefully balanced and patterned as in male prose.

Generally, then, the female writer is seen as suffering the handicap of having to use a medium (prose writing) which is essentially a male instrument fashioned for male purposes. The thesis that the language is 'masculine' in this sense is developed by Dale Spender in the early 1980s in her book *Man Made Language* (1981), which also argues that language is not a neutral medium but one which contains many features which reflect its role as the instrument through which patriarchy finds expression. (This view that the language is man-made is challenged from within feminism by Sandra Gilbert and Susan Gubar in the essay 'Sexual Linguistics: Gender, Language, Sexuality', reprinted in *The Feminist Reader*, ed. Catherine Belsey and Jane Moore (Macmillan, 1989).) If normative language can be seen as in some way male-oriented, the question arises of whether there might be a form of language which is free from this bias, or even in some way oriented towards the female. French theorists, therefore, have posited the existence of an *écriture féminine* (the term is that of the French theorist Hélène Cixous, from her essay 'The Laugh of the Medusa'), associated with the feminine, and facilitating the free play of meanings within the framework of loosened grammatical structures. The heightened prose of the Cixous essay both demonstrates and explains it:

> It is impossible to define a feminine practice of writing, and this is an impossibility which will remain, for this practice can never be theorized, enclosed, coded ... it will always surpass the discourse that regulates the phallocentric [male-dominated] system; it does and will take place in areas other than those subordinated to philosophico-theoretical domination. It will be conceived of by subjects who are breakers of automatisms, by peripheral figures that no authority can ever subjugate.
>
> (Marks and de Courtivron, *New French Feminisms*, p. 253)

Here the user of *écriture féminine* seems to exist in a realm beyond logic ('this practice can never be theorized ... and will take place in areas other than those subordinated to philosophico-theoretical domination'). The user of such language is seen as a kind of perennial freedom-fighter in an anarchic realm of perpetual opposition ('peripheral figures that no authority can ever subjugate') sniping at the centres of power. For Cixous (though not for other theorists), this kind of writing is somehow uniquely the product of female physiology, which women must celebrate in their writing:

> Women must write through their bodies, they must invent the impregnable language that will wreck partitions, classes, and rhetorics, regulations and codes, they must submerge, cut through, get beyond the ultimate reserve-discourse, including the one that laughs at the very idea of pronouncing the word 'silence' ... Such is the strength of women that, sweeping away syntax, breaking that famous thread (just a tiny little thread, they say) which acts for men as a surrogate umbilical cord.
>
> (Marks and de Courtivron, p. 256)

Ecriture féminine, then, is by its nature transgressive, rule-transcending, intoxicated, but it is clear that the notion as put forward by Cixous raises many problems. The realm of the body, for instance, is seen as somehow immune ('impregnable') to social and gender conditioning ('rhetorics, regulations, codes') and able to issue forth a pure essence of the feminine. Such 'essentialism' is difficult to square with a feminism which emphasises femininity as a social construct, not a given entity which is somehow just mysteriously 'there'. And if femininity is socially constructed then it must follow that it differs from one culture to another, so that such overarching generalisations about it are impossible. Who, we might ask, are these women who 'must' write through their bodies? Who imposes this coercive 'must' upon them, and (above all) why?

Further expression of the notion of *écriture féminine* is found in the writing of Julia Kristeva. Kristeva uses the terms the *symbolic* and the *semiotic* to designate two different aspects of language. In her essay 'The System and the Speaking Subject' the symbolic aspect is associated with authority, order, fathers, repression, and control ('the family, normalcy, normative classico-psychologi-cal-tending discourse, all of which are just so many characteristics of fascist ideology'). This symbolic facet of language maintains the fiction that the self is fixed and unified (what she describes as 'a language with a foreclosed subject or with a transcendental sub-ject-ego'). By contrast, the semiotic aspect of discourse is character-ised not by logic and order, but by 'displacement, slippage, condensation', which suggests, again, a much looser, more randomised way of making connections, one which increases the available range of possibilities. She quotes Plato in the *Timaeus* invoking 'a state of language anterior to the Word ... Plato calls this the *chora*', and, again, it is linked with the maternal rather than the paternal. All this is presented at a fairly generalised level, but Kristeva sees the semi-otic as the language of poetry as opposed to prose, and examines its operation in the work of specific poets. Though it is linked concep-tually with the feminine, the poets who use it are not all female, and in fact Kristeva's major exemplars are male writers.

It should be stressed, though, that the symbolic and the semiotic are not two different *kinds* of language, but two different *aspects* of language, both of which are always present in any given sample. The model, again, is that of the unconscious and the conscious, and the Lacanian re-use of these notions. The symbolic is the orderly sur-face realm of strict distinctions and laid-down structures through which language works: this aspect of language is the side stressed by the structuralists, the Saussurean 'network of differences'. But ever-present is the linguistic 'unconscious', a realm of floating signifiers, random connections, improvisations, approximations, accidents, and 'slippage' – everything, that is, entailed in the post-structuralist view of language. Indeed, one way of characterising the process of deconstruction (whereby contradictory cross-currents of meaning are discovered in texts) is to see it as the 'unconscious' of the text emerging into and disrupting the 'conscious' or 'surface' meaning. These disruptive incursions into rational, previously stable structures are seen, for instance, in dreams, in poetry, and in modernist, experimental writing which distorts the surface of language (for example, the poetry of e. e. cummings). This 'random' element can never be escaped by even the most meticulous and painfully deliberate composer of prose. Clearly, since language is by definition an inventive and improvisatory practice, if cut off from Kristeva's realm of the semiotic it would instantly perish.

For her notion of the basic opposition between the semiotic and the symbolic Kristeva is indebted to Jacques Lacan and his distinction between two realms, the *Imaginary* and the *Symbolic*. The Imaginary realm is that of the young child at the pre-linguistic, pre-Oedipal stage. The self is not yet distinguished from what is other than the self, and the body's sense of being separate from the rest of the world is not yet established. The child lives in an Eden-like realm, free of both desire and deprivation. The semiotic is seen as inherently subversive politically, and always threatens the closed symbolic order embodied in such conventions as governments, received cultural values, and the grammar of standard language.

For some feminists this visionary 'semiotic' female world and language evoked by Cixous and Kristeva is a vital theatre of possibilities, the value of which is to entertain the imagining of alternatives to the world which we now have, and which women in particular now have. For others, it fatally hands over the world of the rational to men and reserves for women a traditionally emotive, intuitive, trans-rational, and 'privatised' arena. Not surprisingly, therefore, the language question is one of the most contentious areas of feminist criticism.

Feminist criticism and psychoanalysis

The story so far of feminism's relationship with psychoanalysis is simple in outline but complex in nuance. The story can be said to begin, like so much else, with Kate Millett's *Sexual Politics* in 1969 which condemns Freud as a prime source of the patriarchal attitudes against which feminists must fight. The influence of this view within feminism is still very strong, but Freud was defended in a series of important books in subsequent years, notably Juliet Mitchell's *Psychoanalysis and Feminism* in 1974. This book defends Freud against Millett by, in effect, using Millett's own terms and concepts, especially the distinction, so crucial to feminism, between sex and gender, the former being a matter of biology, the latter a construct, something learned or acquired, rather than 'natural'. This distinction is what Simone de Beauvoir invokes in the famous first sentence in Part Two of *The Second Sex* (1949) when she writes 'One is not born a woman; rather, one *becomes* a woman'. The project of de Beauvoir's book is one which *Sexual Politics* sees itself as continuing. Mitchell's defence of Freud, then, is to argue that Freud doesn't present the feminine as something simply 'given and natural'. Female sexuality (indeed, heterosexuality in general) isn't just there 'naturally' from the start, but is formed by early experiences and adjustments, and Freud shows the process of its being produced and constructed, particularly in the *Three Essays on the Theory of Sexuality* (in volume seven of the Penguin Freud, entitled *On Sexuality*). It follows that gender roles must be malleable and changeable, not inevitable and unchangeable givens.

Thus, the argument runs, the notion of penis envy need not be taken as simply concerning the male physical organ itself (whatever might have been Freud's intentions), but as concerning that organ as an emblem of social power and the advantages which go with it. (I am reminded of an advertisement – which was banned – showing a photograph of a nude woman with the caption 'What women need to succeed in a man's world'. The woman shown had male sexual organs crudely drawn in over her own.) In the reading discussed in the next section, Sandra Gilbert and Susan Gubar use the idea of 'social castration', which amounts to the same thing, for this term signifies women's lack of social power, this lack being represented, by means of the word 'castration', as a male possession, though not as in any sense a male attribute.

Jane Gallop's 1982 book *Feminism and Psychoanalysis* continues the rehabiliation of psychoanalysis, but by switching from the Freudian to the Lacanian variety, partly on the grounds that what is often implicit in Freud is explicit in Lacan's system, namely that the phallus is not the physical biological object but a symbol of the power which goes with it. While men, of course, come out of Lacan's writings better advantaged than women, none the less Lacan shows men too as powerless, since the fullness of signification, which the phallus also represents in Lacan's work, is not attainable by either men or women. Also, Lacan's way of writing – notoriously abstruse, playful, punning, and 'paralogical' (meaning beyond or above logic) – seems to embody the 'feminine' or 'semiotic' aspect of language, rather than the 'masculine' or 'symbolic' aspect.

Another significant name in the rehabilitation of Freud is the British critic Jacqueline Rose, whose book *The Haunting of Sylvia Plath* is an example of an applied feminist-psychoanalytic approach. Rose's project is to combine the insights of feminism, psychoanalysis and politics. She is joint editor, with Juliet Mitchell, of *Feminine Sexuality: Jacques Lacan and the école freudienne* (1982). The argument in favour of Lacan, and of Freud, is, again, that it shows sexual identity to be a 'cultural construct', gives a detailed series of 'insider' accounts of how the construction takes place, and shows examples of this conditioning being resisted.

The resulting position is (as Isobel Armstrong remarked in an article about Rose in *The Times Higher Education Supplement*, 16 July 1993, p. 15) a very complicated one. In general the defence of Freud and Lacan has been more favourably received by French and British feminists than by Americans (another interesting transgression of the usual Anglo-American versus French dichotomy). Elaine Showalter, for instance, in her essay about Ophelia (reprinted in Newton's *Theory into Practice* – see under General readers in the Further reading section) is dismissive of Lacan's evident disregard of Ophelia – he promises to discuss her in his seminar on *Hamlet*, but somehow never gets round to it. Likewise, Jerry Aline Flieger, an

American contributor to *Changing Subjects: The Making of Feminist Literary Criticism* (Greene and Kahn), sounds a note of scepticism when she writes:

> I was fascinated and troubled by Lacan's characterisation of the phallus as the Signifier of Signifiers, as well as by his infamous statements 'There is no sexual relation', and 'Woman does not exist'. Thus I was relieved and grateful when feminists such as Jacqueline Rose and Jane Gallop, in the late seventies and early eighties, performed ingenious and persuasive readings of Lacan as critic of phallocracy, rather than advocate.
>
> (Greene and Kahn, p. 267)

The effect of this comment is partly to draw attention to the ingenuity *needed* to mount such a defence.

Stephen Heath, in an essay in *Feminist Literary Criticism* (ed. Mary Eagleton), quotes Roland Barthes to the effect that 'The monument of psychoanalysis must be traversed – not bypassed' (p. 214). We might say that feminism began by trying to do the latter, then changed course and did the former. The tendency of American feminists to be unconvinced by the rehabilitation of psychoanalysis can perhaps be explained by the fact that psychoanalysis has been more an accepted part of middle-class life in the USA than it ever became in Europe. Hence, it is more difficult for Americans to see it as still possessed of radical potential, least of all for women. Further, there was a new emphasis in the 1990s on the culturally specific nature of psychoanalysis, and hence a reluctance to claim any kind of universal validity for it. In Rose's own work, as elsewhere, there is a strong and growing interest in listening to the voices of the hitherto excluded 'Other', particularly those of the cultures and races which had no place in the work of Freud or Lacan.

STOP and THINK

General: Within feminism there is a strong emphasis on the 'constructedness' of femininity, that is, on such matters as conditioning and socialisation, and the influence of images and representations of femininity in literature and culture. All these formulations are ways of avoiding 'essentialism', which is the contrary view that there is some natural, given essence of the feminine that is universal and unchangeable.

Anti-essentialism has for some years now been a dominant concept in critical theory, but there is some awareness, too, that it is a notion which leaves us with certain difficulties. For instance, does anti-essentialism, by making it hard to make *any* generalisations about women, also make it difficult to politicise women as a group? Does it tend to reduce identity to the sum of circumstances, perhaps in spite of our 'instinctive' feelings that identity may be deeper than that? Is the fact that we have such feelings admissible as evidence – on either side? And in any case, what would consitute evidence on *either* side of this question?

Specific: In the example discussed below, what are some of the ways in which the critical assumptions and procedures differ from those made in non-feminist approaches to the same work? Compare it with the two essays mentioned at the start of the example, or with the pieces in the Macmillan *Casebook on Wuthering Heights* (ed. Miriam Allott, 1992).

What feminist critics do

1. Rethink the canon, aiming at the rediscovery of texts written by women.
2. Revalue women's experience.
3. Examine representations of women in literature by men and women.
4. Challenge representations of women as 'Other', as 'lack', as part of 'nature'.
5. Examine power relations which obtain in texts and in life, with a view to breaking them down, seeing reading as a political act, and showing the extent of patriarchy.
6. Recognise the role of language in making what is social and constructed seem transparent and 'natural'.
7. Raise the question of whether men and women are 'essentially' different because of biology, or are socially constructed as different.

8.   Explore the question of whether there is a female language, an *écriture féminine*, and whether this is also available to men.

9.   'Re-read' psychoanalysis to further explore the issue of female and male identity.

10. Question the popular notion of the death of the author, asking whether there are only 'subject positions ... constructed in discourse', or whether, on the contrary, the experience (e.g. of a black or lesbian writer) is central.

11. Make clear the ideological base of supposedly 'neutral' or 'mainstream' literary interpretations.

Feminist criticism: an example

As an example of feminist criticism I will take the account of *Wuthering Heights* by Sandra M. Gilbert and Susan Gubar, from their book *The Madwoman in the Attic*. The piece is reprinted in the widely used *Debating Texts* (ed. Rick Rylance). Rylance reprints two other accounts of the same novel, one by Q. D. Leavis, which might be considered as liberal humanist, and one by Frank Kermode, which might be seen as post-structuralist. Comparisons can also be made with Eagleton's Marxist account of the same novel in his book *Myths of Power: A Marxist Study of the Brontës*, to which Gilbert and Gubar refer.

Gilbert and Gubar's strategy with Brontë's novel is to see it as a female version of the male form known as the *Bildungsroman* (this German term means the 'formation' or 'education' novel) in which the hero's growth to manhood is traced, as a process of 'triumphant self-discovery', whereby an identity is discovered and a mission in life conceived and embarked upon – a classic example would be James Joyce's *A Portrait of the Artist as a Young Man*. For the heroine, however, things are different, and an equivalent novel (like *Wuthering Heights*) about the growth to womanhood records a process of 'anxious self-denial', this being the 'ultimate product of a female education'. Gilbert and Gubar say that 'What Catherine, or any girl, must learn is that she does not know her own name, and therefore cannot know either who she is or whom she is destined to be'. The process of denial involved they describe as 'social castration'.

Effectively, Catherine has to leave behind all her instinctive preferences, signified by the Heights, and take on an alien attitude, signified by Thrushcross Grange. The point of the word 'castration' here is that in order to achieve acceptability and femininity, Catherine has to lose the power which men take for granted, namely power over their own destiny. This is symbolised by the phallic guard-dog, 'purple tongue hanging half a foot out of its mouth', which bites Catherine's foot as she enters the Grange, a symbolic castration, they say. She then undergoes the initiation ritual of imprisonment at the Grange, similar to that undergone by traditional heroines like Persephone and Snow White.

The Grange is the home of 'concealment and doubleness'. Here she learns, as Brontë says, 'to adopt a double character without exactly intending to deceive anyone'; that is, say Gilbert and Gubar, she must learn 'to repress her own impulses, must girdle her own energies with the iron stays of "reason"'. This 'education in doubleness' involves 'an actual doubling or fragmentation of her personality', as Heathcliff, 'her rebellious alter-ego' is forcibly excluded from her life. In this spirit of self-denial she agrees to marry Edgar, even though she says of Heathcliff that he is 'more myself than I am'. In this process Heathcliff too is degraded and powerless, and so 'Catherine has learned, correctly, that if it is degrading to be a woman it is even more degrading to be *like* a woman'. Hence, Gilbert and Gubar argue, against the run of *Wuthering Heights* criticism, that Edgar does not represent an image of effeminacy in contrast to the manliness of Heathcliff; on the contrary, in his ruthless employment of his social and sexual power, he is an embodiment of the patriarchal principle. The marriage 'inexorably locks her into a social system which denies her autonomy', so that Heathcliff's return, the 'return of the repressed', as we might call it in Freudian terms, 'represents the return of her true self's desires without the rebirth of her former powers'; hence the inevitable descent into self-rejection (Catherine fails to recognise her own face in the mirror), self-starvation, madness, and death, 'a complex of psycho-neurotic symptoms that is almost classically associated with female feelings of powerlessness and rage'. Thus, the events of the novel are 'strongly' read as emblems of the construction of gender identity.

Selected reading

Readers

Belsey, Catherine, and Moore, Jane, eds, *The Feminist Reader: Essays in Gender and the Politics of Literary Criticism* (Palgrave, 2nd edn, 1997).
Excellent introduction. Manageable size. Important essays on the crucial issues.

Cavallaro, Dani, *French Feminist Theory: An Introduction* (new edn, Continuum, 2006).
The best current collection of key essays in this field.

Eagleton, Mary, ed., *Feminist Literary Criticism* (Routledge, 1991).
Interesting collection, with essays paired to represent opposing views on key issues. Very good editorial commentary.

Eagleton, Mary, ed., *Feminist Literary Theory: A Reader* (Wiley-Blackwell, 3rd edn, 2010).
Includes material on black feminism and the impact of postmodernism on feminism. Short extracts from a wide range of critical material.

Freedman, Estelle B., ed., *The Essential Feminist Reader* (Modern Library Classics, 2007).
A comprehensive collection, including historical classics and creative as well as critical material.

Humm, Maggie, ed., *Feminisms: A Reader* (Routledge, 2013).
An excellent book, wide-ranging and accessible, on feminisms from Woolf to the present day, including black and lesbian feminisms. Subsectioned by category, with a separate introduction for each one.

Marks, Elaine, and de Courtivron, Isabelle, eds, *New French Feminisms* (Harvester, 1981).
The pioneering book in introducing much of this material to English-speaking readers.

Moi, Toril, *French Feminist Thought: A Reader* (Wiley-Blackwell, 1987).

Rooney, Ellen, ed., *The Cambridge Companion to Feminist Literary Theory* (Cambridge Companions to Literature, 2006).
Contains extremely useful updating essays on feminist aesthetics of reading, feminism and novel reading, feminism and psychoanalysis, feminism and postcolonialism, etc.

General

Brownstein, Rachel, *Becoming a Heroine* (Penguin, 1982; rpt. Columbia University Press, 1994).
A readable and thoughtful account of what it takes to become a heroine in a 'classic' novel.

Christian, Barbara, *New Black Feminist Criticism, 1985-2000* (University of Illinois Press, 2007).

A collection by a major practitioner and theorist, edited after her death by Gloria Bowles, M. Giulia Fabi, and Arlene Keizer.

Federico, Annette R., ed., *Gilbert and Gubar's The Madwoman in the Attic After Thirty Years* (University of Missouri Press, 2011).

In-depth discussion from a wide range of scholars on the influence and example of this book.

Gilbert, Sandra, and Gubar, Susan, *No Man's Land: The Place of the Woman Writer in the Twentieth Century* (Yale University Press, 1988).

Much of interest. See chapter seven, 'Women, literature and the Great War', and compare with the example of gay criticism in the next chapter.

Gilbert, Sandra, and Gubar, Susan, *The Madwoman in the Attic: The Woman Writer and the Nineteenth Century Literary Imagination* (Yale University Press, 2nd edn, 2000).

A ground-breaking book with chapters on Austen, the Brontës, George Eliot, etc.

Greene, Gayle, and Kahn, Coppelia, eds, *Making a Difference: Feminist Literary Criticism* (Routledge, 1985).

Greene, Gayle, and Kahn, Coppelia, eds, *Changing Subjects: The Making of Feminist Literary Criticism* (Routledge, 1993).

An interesting collection of essays in intellectual autobiography by leading figures in the field.

Jacobus, Mary, ed., *Women Writing and Writing about Women* (Routledge, 2012).

Chapters on *Villette*, George Eliot, Woolf, Ibsen, etc.

Jacobus, Mary, *Reading Woman: Essays in Feminist Criticism* (Methuen, 1986).

Chapters on *Villette, The Mill on the Floss*, Freud's case studies (see *'Dora* and the Pregnant Madonna', etc.).

Mills, Sara, *et al.*, *Feminist Readings: An Introduction to Feminist Literature* (Prentice Hall, 1996).

Discussions of major varieties of feminism and their application to a range of canonical literary texts. Readable, practical, and informative.

Minogue, Sally, ed., *Problems for Feminist Criticism* (Routledge, 1993).

An interesting book which deals with some topics which have caused real difficulty.

Moi, Toril, *Sexual/Textual Politics* (Routledge, 2nd edn, 2002).

A very influential book, though its view of the main kinds of feminist theory and criticism has been challenged.

Moi, Toril, *What is a Woman?* (Oxford University Press, 2001).

A very interesting fundamental rethink of many aspects of feminism.

Ruthven, K. K., *Feminist Literary Studies: An Introduction* (Cambridge University Press, 1984).

A useful overview with a bias towards 'Anglo–American' variants.

Showalter, Elaine, *The New Feminist Criticism: Essays on Women, Literature, and Theory* (Pantheon, 1985).

Showalter, Elaine, *A Literature of Their Own* (revised and expanded edn, Virago, 1999).

Includes a new opening chapter on the reception of the original edition of this book, and a postscript chapter on the legacy of feminist criticsm.

Stubbs, Patricia, *Women and Fiction: Feminism and the Novel 1880–1920* (Routledge, new edn, 1981).

7

Queer theory

Introduction

Queer theory emerged prominently as a distinct field only by the
1990s – there is nothing about it, for instance, in Terry Eagleton's
Literary Theory: An Introduction (1983), or in the first edition of
Raman Selden's *A Reader's Guide to Contemporary Literary Theory*
(1985). As with women's studies twenty years before, the growing
significance and acceptance of this new field is indicated by the
presence of 'queer theory' sections in many mainstream bookshops
and publishers' academic catalogues, and by the establishment of
relevant undergraduate courses, for which the first course reader,
the *Lesbian and Gay Studies Reader*, was published in 1993. The
designating terminology for this field is fluid and shifting, driven
by a desire to be as inclusive as possible. At present (towards the
end of the second decade of the millennium) the most-used terms
are acronyms like LGBT, denoting Lesbian, Gay, Bisexual, and
Transgender, or LGBTQ, with the added 'Q' denoting either
'Queer' or 'Questioning'. Usually a noun follows, such as 'community' or 'studies' or 'theory'. LGBT studies designates a potentially
huge area of concerns (taking in, for example, medical ethics, international law, civil rights, social history, and the history of religion),
while LGBT theory suggests an emphasis on literary, cultural, and
philosophical matters. In both cases, the primary focus of the field
is on matters relating to sexual orientation and gender identity. In
the UK the pioneering academic presence in queer studies was the
Centre for Sexual Dissidence (known as 'SexDiss') in the English

Department at Sussex University, founded by Alan Sinfield and Jonathan Dollimore in 1990, with its landmark 'Sexual Dissidence' MA course. A special issue of the journal *Textual Practice* (Vol. 30, No. 6, 2016) was devoted to Sinfield's work. Both the Centre and the MA are now (2017) strongly multidisciplinary, crossing into media studies, cultural studies, and sociology, as is the whole field of queer studies. Also in 1990, Greg Woods was appointed lecturer at Nottingham Trent University, teaching courses that included 'Contemporary Lesbian and Gay Cultures', 'Post-War Gay Literature', and 'Queering the Modern'. In 1998 he became Professor of Contemporary Lesbian and Gay Cultures, the first such appointment in the UK, and since 2014 he has been Emeritus Professor of Gay and Lesbian Studies at the same institution. In the USA, a course in gay and lesbian literature was taught at UCLA in 1976, and a key founding text is *Epistemology of the Closet* (1990) by Eve Kosofsky Sedgwick (1950–2009), while, in the same year, Judith Butler published her ground-breaking book *Gender Trouble: Feminism and the Subversion of Gender Identity*. So 1990 was a key foundational year in this field; not its beginning, even within universities, but the beginning of its current disciplinary prominence.

It may be helpful, in defining the nature of this field, to make an initial comparison with feminist criticism. It is obvious that not all literary criticism written by women is feminist; that not all books about women writers are feminist; that feminist writing need not be by women; and that feminist criticism is not directed exclusively at a female readership. Likewise, books about gay writers, or by gay critics, are not necessarily part of lesbian and gay studies, nor are books that are part of this field directed solely at a gay readership or relevant only to gay sexuality.

What, then, is the purpose of lesbian/gay criticism? The *Lesbian and Gay Studies Reader* tells us that 'lesbian/gay studies does for sex and sexuality approximately what women's studies does for gender', this being described a few lines earlier as establishing 'the centrality of gender as a fundamental category of historical analysis and understanding' (p. xv). In lesbian/gay criticism, the defining feature is making sexual orientation 'a fundamental category of analysis and understanding'. Like feminist criticism, then, it has social and political aims, in particular 'an oppositional design' (p. xvi) upon society, for it is 'informed by resistance to homophobia [fear and prejudice against homosexuality] and heterosexism ... [and to] the ideological and institutional practices of heterosexual privilege'.

Queer theory and lesbian feminism

However, queer theory is not a single unified body of work. There were differences of emphasis between lesbian and gay theory, and two major strands of thinking within lesbian theory itself. The first of these is *lesbian feminism*, which is best understood by seeing it initially in the context of its own origins from within feminism, for lesbian studies emerged in the 1980s as a kind of annexe of feminist criticism, before acquiring disciplinary independence. Indeed, one reading of the academic situation in the 1990s would be that feminism had become so successful and so institutionalised that lesbian studies laid claim to the radical ground vacated by feminism. On this reading of the situation, feminism found it difficult to accommodate difference, whether racial, cultural, or sexual, and tended to universalise the experience of white, middle-class, urban heterosexual women. This kind of critique of feminism originated in the work of African-American critics who pointed out that academic feminism had reproduced the structures of patriarchal inequality within itself by excluding the voices and experiences of black women. This case is memorably put, for instance, in *Ain't I a Woman: Black Women and Feminism* (Routledge, new edn, 2015) by bell hooks, first published in 1982. A similar accusation against feminism was made by lesbian critics: feminism assumed, they argued, that there existed an essential female identity which all women had in common irrespective of differences of race, class, or sexual orientation. Bonnie Zimmerman, among others, in a well-known essay 'What has never been: an overview of lesbian feminist criticism' attacked this 'essentialism', pointing out the way 'the perceptual screen of heterosexism' prevented any consideration of lesbian issues in pioneering feminist writing (p. 180 in the reprinting of the essay listed at the end of this chapter). Hence, a feminist literary-critical classic like Sandra Gilbert and Susan Gubar's *The Madwoman in the Attic* contains only a single passing reference to lesbianism.

'Classic' feminism, then, had marginalised or ignored lesbianism. This state of affairs was countered by arguing that, on the contrary, lesbianism should be regarded as the most complete form of feminism. This is argued in another crucial essay in the development of lesbian feminism, 'The woman identified woman', by the Radicalesbian collective, published in *Radical Feminism* (ed. Anne Koedt *et al.*, Quadrangle, 1973). The lesbian feminist position identified in this essay makes lesbianism central to feminism, since lesbianism turns away from various forms of collusion with patriarchal exploitation and instead consists of relationships among women which, by definition, constitute a form of resistance to, and a radical reorganising of, existing forms of social relations.

The conflict between heterosexual feminists and lesbians thus opened up was partly defused in another important essay, by Adrienne Rich, which introduced the notion of the 'lesbian continuum' (in her essay 'Compulsory heterosexuality and lesbian existence', collected in her *Blood, Bread and Poetry: Selected Prose, 1979–1985*, Norton, 1996):

> I mean the term *lesbian continuum* to include a range – through each woman's life and throughout history – of woman-identified experience; not simply the fact that a woman has had or consciously desired genital sexual experience with another woman.
>
> (Quoted by Zimmerman in Greene and
> Kahn, *Making a Difference*, p. 184)

This concept of the lesbian continuum therefore designates a wide variety of female behaviour, running, for instance, from informal mutual help networks set up by women within particular professions or institutions, through supportive female friendships and, finally, to sexual relationships. Zimmerman comments that this definition has the virtue of suggesting interconnections among the various ways in which women bond together. As Paulina Palmer points out, however (see chapter two in her *Contemporary Lesbian Writing*), seeing lesbianism in this way has the curious effect of de-sexualising it, so that it becomes almost wholly a political act, rather than a sexual orientation, and is hence 'sanitised' and transformed into something else. Also, the corollary of the position is a moral condemnation of female heterosexuality as a betrayal of women and their interests, with the implication that women can only achieve integrity through lesbianism.

The two ideas of the 'woman identified woman' and the lesbian continuum overlap a great deal, but as ideas they have a clarity and flexibility which ensure their continued importance as personal and intellectual reference points. They introduce the notion of choice and allegiance into matters of sex and gender, so that sexuality is not seen as something merely 'natural' and unchanging, but rather as a construction and as subject to change.

As a result of these critiques, lesbian approaches separated from mainstream feminism throughout the eighties, but only in the nineties does lesbian criticism also reject the essentialism which had, so to speak, been inherited from feminism. Thus, when in 'Lesbians like this and that: some notes on lesbian criticism for the nineties' Zimmerman again surveys the field of lesbian criticism, ten years on from the earlier piece, what strikes her about her original essay is its assumption that lesbianism is a stable category, a 'transcendental signifier', which is just there as a fact, as a trans-historical constant, rather than (as it is) a late nineteenth-century construct. In the 1990s a second, less essentialist notion of lesbianism had emerged, within the sphere of what is now known as 'queer theory'.

Queer theory and libertarian feminism

So far, then, we have discussed the nature and development of the thinking designated as lesbian feminism. The second kind of lesbian thinking, designated libertarian lesbianism by Paulina Palmer, broke away from feminism and made new allegiances, in particular, with gay men rather than with other women, and this kind of lesbian theory sees itself as part of the field of 'queer theory' or 'queer studies', terms increasingly used by gays, in spite of the homophobic origins of the word 'queer' as an abusive one in this context. These terms date (at least in their institutional acceptance) from the 1990 conference on 'queer theory' at the University of California, Santa Cruz. As we have said, 'queer theory' in this sense, rather than being 'woman-centred' like the lesbian feminism just described, rejects female separatism and instead sees an identity of political and social interests with gay men. The key underlying question, for anyone choosing between these two possible alignments, is whether it is gender or sexuality which is the more fundamental in personal identity. Choosing the latter, of course, emphasises lesbianism as a form of sexuality, rather than a form of female bonding or patriarchal resistance. It tends to endorse 'experimental' forms of sexuality within lesbianism, such as sado-masochistic and butch–femme role play. However, it is sometimes argued that one of the effects of accepting the comprehensive term 'queer theory' is ultimately to perpetuate the patriarchal subservience of women's interests to men's.

How exactly, then, in theoretical terms, does queer theory differ from lesbian feminism? The answer is that, like many other current critical approaches, lesbian/gay studies within this 'queer theory' ambit have drawn particularly on post-structuralist work of the 1980s. One of the main points of post-structuralism was to 'deconstruct' binary oppositions (like that between speech and writing, for instance), showing, firstly, that the distinction between paired opposites is not absolute, since each term in the pairing can only be understood and defined in terms of the other, and, secondly, that it is possible to reverse the hierarchy within such pairs, and so 'privilege' the second term rather than the first (see Chapter 3, pp. 76–7). Hence, in lesbian/gay studies the pair heterosexual/homosexual is deconstructed in this way. The opposition within this pair is seen, firstly, as inherently unstable: as Diana Fuss puts it in the introduction to *Inside/Out: Lesbian Theories, Gay Theories*, much current work in the field aims 'to call into question the stability and ineradicability of the hetero/homo hierarchy' (p. 1). In an essay which we might take as a practical example of how this dichotomy can be deconstructed, Richard Meyer writes, in the same volume, about the film star Rock Hudson, once the screen epitome of attractive heterosexual masculinity. In fact, Hudson was gay, but while initially shocking to some, this is less disturbing of categories than the sense that the very qualities which made his image attractive to women were related to his homosexuality, for 'Hudson promised straight women a place of sexual safety – he would acquiesce to domesticity without insisting on male domination' (Fuss, p. 282).

Likewise, straight male viewers had been relieved 'to find a role-model who did not require the exhaustive work of machismo to "measure up" to its masculinity' (p. 282). Deconstructing the hetero/homo dichotomy in this way has radical implications, since all such distinctions are constructed in the same way, so that to challenge this one is to challenge all the others too.

This anti-essentialism in relation to sexual identity is taken further by other critics. Judith Butler, a prominent contributor to *Inside/Out*, points out in her essay that 'identity categories', like 'gay' and 'straight', 'tend to be instruments of regulatory regimes, whether as the normalizing categories of oppressive structures or as the rallying points for liberatory contestations of that very oppression' (pp. 14–15). Hence it might be argued, she says, that the concept of homosexuality is itself part of homophobic (anti-gay) discourse, and indeed, the term 'homosexual' is a medical-legal one, first used in 1869 in Germany, and preceding the invention of the corresponding term 'heterosexual' by eleven years. In this sense, heterosexuality only comes into being as a consequence of the crystallisation of the notion of homosexuality. Thus, lesbianism, say, is not a stable, essential identity, so that, in Butler's words, 'identity can become a site of contest and revision' (p. 19).

Taking this further, she argues that all identities, including gender identities, are 'a kind of impersonation and approximation ... *a kind of imitation for which there is no original*' (p. 21). This opens the way to a 'postmodernist' notion of identity as a constant switching among a range of different roles and positions, drawn from a kind of limitless data bank of potentialities. Further, what is called into question here is the distinction between the naturally given, normative 'self' of heterosexuality and the rejected 'Other' of homosexuality. The 'Other', in these formulations, is as much something within us as beyond us, and 'self' and 'Other' are always *implicated* in each other, in the root sense of this word, which means to be intertwined or folded into each other. As basic psychology shows, what is identified as the external 'Other' is usually part of the self which is rejected and hence projected outwards.

Another critic who argues the fluidity of identity, including sexual identity, is Eve Kosofsky Sedgwick in her highly influential *Epistemology of the Closet*. Sedgwick considers how coming 'out of the closet' (openly revealing one's gay or lesbian sexual orientation) is not a single absolute act. Gayness may be openly declared to family and friends, not so comprehensively to employers and colleagues, and perhaps not at all to (say) banks or insurance companies. Hence, being 'in' or 'out' is not a simple dichotomy or a once and for all event. Degrees of concealment and openness co-exist in the same lives. Nor will sexual orientation alone usually make a person a complete outsider, and therefore innocent of all patriarchal or exploitative taint. A gay person may be a comfortably tenured academic, very much a privileged insider in the eyes of, say, a factory worker, gay or not, in a small town. Sedgwick's point, then, concerns the way subject identity is necessarily a complex mixture of chosen allegiances, social position, and professional roles, rather than a fixed inner essence.

The consequences of this kind of argument are far-reaching, both for politics and for literary criticism. Let's consider the political consequences first. Drawing upon a post-structuralist reading of Saussure, we show that such apparently elemental categories as heterosexual and homosexual do not designate fixed essences at all – they are merely part of a structure of differences without positive terms, like Saussurean signifiers (see Chapter 2). We construct instead an anti-essentialist, postmodernist concept of identity as a series of masks, roles, and potentialities, a kind of amalgam of everything which is provisional, contingent, and improvisatory. The political consequence is that when we claim that gayness, or blackness, is merely a shifting signifier, not a fixed entity, then it becomes difficult to imagine how an effective political campaign could be mounted on its behalf. For in the name of anti-essentialism we have removed these bottom-line concepts on which all forms of 'identity politics' depend. (By identity politics we mean those which campaign for and by groups disadvantaged by some aspect of their *identity*, such as their gender, their race, or their sexual orientation. The opposite of identity politics would be class politics, where the campaign is on behalf of people disadvantaged by some aspect of their *situation* – by being under-paid mine-workers, for instance.)

The literary-critical consequences of anti-essentialism are twofold. Firstly, there is the obvious difficulty of deciding what a lesbian/gay text is. In the list of possibilities which follow we can take 'lesbian' to mean 'lesbian or gay'. The possibilities are (in a slightly re-worked version of Zimmerman's formulation) that a lesbian/gay text is:

1. One which is written by a lesbian (if so, how do we determine who is a lesbian, especially if we take the anti-essentialist line just outlined?).
2. One written about lesbians (which might be by a heterosexual woman or man, and which would also come up against the problem of deciding what a lesbian/gay person is in non-essentialist terms).
3. One that expresses a lesbian 'vision' (which has yet to be satisfactorily described).

The 1. and 2. categories here seem inadequate as they stand, since merely writing about books by and/or about gays is clearly not enough, since gayness is not being defined as an inherent, essential, unchanging category, but as part of a complex of other factors. A solution may be to adopt an approach which is historically specific. Thus, gayness in a novel or an author of the 1920s is not the same as in the 1980s or 1990s, and part of the critique will involve showing how this is so. On the 3. category, critics need to be aware of wider metaphorical extensions of gayness, for instance the suggested link between lesbianism and a state of being poised on the threshold between categories: 'In general, lesbian critical reading proposes the blurring of boundaries between self and other, subject and object, lover and beloved as the lesbian moment in any text' (Zimmerman, 'Lesbians like this and that', p. 11). Thus lesbianism is theoretically linked with notions of 'liminal' consciousness when existing categories are in process of deconstruction.

Yet this 3. category also has obvious risks, notably that gayness will probably assume too great an emblematic burden, since it will tend to be romanticised and stand as a textual emblem of resistance and disruption of all kinds. Zimmerman quotes examples from recent critical writing of this romanticising/idealising tendency. Lesbianism is a force against 'rigid definitions and polar oppositions', expressed in terms of 'gaps', 'spaces', 'disruption', the 'experimental', 'radical disruption', 'interrogation', and so on. This 'heady romantic stuff' ('Lesbians like this and that', p. 4) represents what we might call super-essentialism, since it tries to make one kind of resistance stand for all resistance, and thus places a political and social burden on sexual orientation which is surely unreasonable.

A final and more specific literary-critical consequence of anti-essentialism is a tendency to devalue literary realism, since it tends to rely upon notions of fixed identities and stable points of view. For instance, a realist novel typically has an omniscient narrator who presents and interprets the events from a fixed moral and intellectual position, a linear time sequence in which events unfold chronologically, and characters who are presented as stable essences with a personality which develops in an orderly and cumulative way. Hence, lesbian/gay criticism of the recent 'queer theory' phase tends to favour (as do most other kinds of current critical theory) texts and genres which subvert this kind of familiar literary realism, like thrillers, comic and parodic fiction, and sexual fantasy. Thus a novel like Jeanette Winterson's *Oranges Are Not the Only Fruit* (1985; Vintage edn, 1991) is of interest to the lesbian/gay critic not just because of its lesbian subject matter, but also because of its many anti-realist elements. In her 1991 introduction the author says that the book is 'an experimental novel: its interests are anti-linear' and answers her own question 'Is *Oranges* an autobiographical novel?' by replying 'No not at all and yes of course'. She says (perhaps a little exaggeratedly) that the book is 'unlike any other novel' in structure, style, and content, and deliberately makes the manner of the telling draw attention to itself by her use of 'a complicated narrative structure ... a very large vocabulary and beguilingly straight-forward syntax'. The theme of a young girl's discovering her sexual identity is undercut with comic elements and details, and the narrative flow is interrupted with mythical and fantasy passages. As Paulina Palmer writes of these passages, 'the interplay of narratives which they create highlights the part which fantasy plays in the construction of the adolescent psyche and gives a more complex and multi-faceted representation than is usual in the Coming out novel' (*Contemporary Lesbian Writing*, p. 101). In a basic way, then, this novel and its critical treatment typify the anti-realist leanings of lesbian/gay criticism.

What queer theorists do

1. Identify and establish a canon of 'classic' lesbian/gay writers whose work constitutes a distinct tradition. These are, in the

main, twentieth-century writers, such as (for lesbian writers in Britain) Virginia Woolf, Vita Sackville-West, Dorothy Richardson, Rosamond Lehmann, and Radclyffe Hall.

2. Identify lesbian/gay episodes in mainstream work and discuss them as such (for example, the relationship between Jane and Helen in *Jane Eyre*), rather than reading same-sex pairings in non-specific ways, for instance as symbolising two aspects of the same character (Zimmerman).

3. Set up an extended, metaphorical sense of 'lesbian/gay' so that it connotes a moment of crossing a boundary, or blurring a set of categories. All such 'liminal' moments mirror the moment of self-identification as lesbian or gay, which is necessarily an act of conscious resistance to established norms and boundaries.

4. Expose the 'homophobia' of mainstream literature and criticism, as seen in ignoring or denigrating the homosexual aspects of the work of major canonical figures, for example by omitting overtly homosexual love lyrics from selections or discussions of the poetry of W. H. Auden (Mark Lilly).

5. Foreground homosexual aspects of mainstream literature which have previously been glossed over, for example the strongly homo-erotic tenderness seen in a good deal of First World War poetry.

6. Foreground literary genres, previously neglected, which significantly influenced ideals of masculinity or femininity, such as the nineteenth-century adventure stories with a British 'Empire' setting (for example those by Rudyard Kipling and Rider Haggard) discussed by Joseph Bristow in *Empire Boys* (Routledge, 1991).

STOP and THINK

General: The example at the end of this section is concerned with the second, fourth and fifth of the activities listed above. It suggests that there is a sharp difference, in terms of the sexual feelings involved, between First and Second World War poetry. How far do you feel this to be justified? Do you agree that the former is often homo-erotic while the latter seldom is? Compare two relevant anthologies in the light of this question, such as Jon Silkin's *Penguin Book of First World War Poetry* and *The Terrible Rain* (see below).

Specific: First World War poets often use the motif of bathing with an erotic charge. Lilly quotes from 'Soldiers Bathing' by R. D. Greenway ('You strong and hairy sergeant / Stretched naked to the skies …'). A more famous poem with the same title, by F. T. Prince, is often said to be the best-known poem of the Second World War. How would you discuss it in terms of the debate on war poetry summarised here? This poem is included in *The Terrible Rain*.

Corpses in First World War poems are often homo-eroticised. A famous corpse poem of the Second World War is Keith Douglas's 'Vergissmeiinnicht' (*The Terrible Rain: The War Poets, 1939–1945*, ed. Brian Gardner, Methuen, 1977). Illustrate and discuss some of the differences between this and 1914–18 material in the terms used in the Lilly section.

Queer theory: an example

As an example of this kind of criticism we can take the chapter 'The love poetry of the First World War' in Mark Lilly's *Gay Men's Literature in the Twentieth Century*. The essay is a straightforward survey of a range of First World War poetry from this viewpoint, drawing on poems anthologised in Martin Taylor's *Lads: Love Poetry of the Trenches*, and on the views put forward in its introduction. The essay begins by commenting on the intense feelings between men evident in war conditions, and the general reluctance to admit the presence of homo–erotic undertones, or more, in such relationships. The difficulty of admitting their existence is compounded by the fact that an army in wartime is the particular expression of the most conventionally masculine aspects of a country ('a collective symbol of the controlled virility and power of the society itself', Taylor, p. 65). Hence 'the resistance amongst heterosexuals to the idea that men *upon whom otherwise they would wish to bestow their deepest admiration* might have enjoyed other men carnally' (p. 65, italics in the original). At the same time, references to armies by their own side tend to emphasise the often extreme youthfulness of those involved – the jingoistic headline of the British *Sun* newspaper during the first Gulf War is quoted – 'Our boys go in'.

As well as the intensity of contact brought about by wartime circumstances, war poetry at the time functioned as a kind of licensed area in which it was possible to express male-to-male feelings in an unusually direct and open way (this had changed by the Second World War). Hence, expressing love for a comrade-in-arms (albeit usually dead) was frequent in First World War poetry, though it is difficult to know exactly what is meant by 'love' in these poems (or exactly what kind of love is meant). Most likely the poems frequently operate on a number of different levels, with the heterosexual reader able to read this 'love' simply as grief for the loss of a friend. This enabled the poems to be printed and very widely circulated at the time without scandal. Very likely the poems operate in this multilayered way for the writers too, since by no means all the poets were self-acknowledged gays. Hence, 'conventions of expression sometimes make brotherly affection, physical tenderness and sexual desire all sound the same' (p. 66). If we imagine something like Rich's 'lesbian continuum' to have a male equivalent, especially in the horrific conditions of war, then we would emphasise that these would not each be distinct and separate states. Lilly makes this point, but in different terms, when he suggests that three commonly used terms have slightly different references, so that generalised feelings of affection and physical tenderness might be described as 'homo-erotic', whereas feelings of specific sexual desire would be called 'homo-sexual' or 'gay'. Naturally, this will open up the field beyond those who were 'certainly (Sassoon) or almost certainly (Owen) gay' (p. 66).

Lilly points out that a frequent motif in these poems is to see 'same-sex love as superior to men's love for women'. One such poem is actually called 'Passing the Love of Women' and was written by army chaplain Studdert Kennedy in the persona of an ordinary soldier:

> Yes, I've sat in the summer twilight,
> Wiv a nice girl 'and in 'and,
> But I've thought even then of the shell 'oles,
> Where the boys of the old Bat. stand.
> I've turned to 'er lips for 'r kisses,
> And I've found them kisses cold,

> Stone cold and pale like a twice-told tale,
> What has gorn all stale and old.

And the poem concludes (referring to women), 'But I knows a stronger love than their's, / And that is the love of men.' It is interesting that these poems often seem unusually explicit at several levels, for instance about physical feelings between men and women, and about the impossibility of any solace being had from religion – we might expect the poem to end (especially, perhaps, as it is written by a parson) with the line 'And that is the love of God', but such references seem rare. This tendency towards the 'multi-transgression' of several boundaries simultaneously lends some weight to the contention in lesbian/gay studies that breaking the sexual norm is always potentially emblematic of norm-breaking in general.

However, the poems cannot be seen as simply celebratory of socially stigmatised forms of love, since the sexual object for whom admiration is expressed in the poems is usually dead (if a named or specific individual). Where a generalised admiration for the male body is expressed, the body in question is usually that of a corpse (often an enemy corpse, it seems to me), so much so that Lilly detects an element of necrophilia in this poetry. Sometimes the open expression of sexual desire is combined with necrophiliac elements, as in Herbert Read's 'My Company (iii)':

> A man of mine
> Lies on the wire;
> And he will rot
> And first his lips
> The worms will eat.
> It is not thus I would have him kissed
> But with the warm passionate lips
> Of his comrade here.
>
> *(Gay Men's Literature in the Twentieth Century*, pp. 78–9)

Hence, in order to express these homosexual feelings, the poet first ensures that there is a barrier to their fulfilment – there is no possibility of actual physical expression of these feelings because the would-be recipient is dead. The exception is that there are many poems in which the man written about is wounded – many of these poems are gory, and Lilly makes a connection with the

homo-erotic poems about wounds and hospitals in the American
Civil War by the nineteenth-century American poet Walt Whitman.
The wound is erotically charged in First World War poetry because it allows tender physical contact between males, the war thus
becoming a 'safe' area in which feelings usually suppressed can
be openly expressed, while at the same time the intensity of the
circumstances means that the feelings evoked and expressed are
different from those felt in more ordinary circumstances. Lilly uses
the parallel example of the football field, where men kiss and embrace each other passionately in public, behaviour for which they
could have been arrested (in pre-war Britain) if it were happening
in the street.

Hence, the poems need to be placed in their context to be properly understood. After all, the army itself exploited these feelings at
the start of the war with the setting up of 'Pals' regiments, in which
large numbers of men from the same district enlisted and served in
units together. The intention was to draw upon networks of trust
and loyalty founded on school friendships, upon feelings of class
solidarity, and on local identities and allegiances. (The experiment
was hurriedly abandoned when whole neighbourhoods were plunged
into mass mourning when an attack or bombardment took place.)
Hence, it could be said (as Lilly suggests) that this kind of poetry had
official sanction, since it was good for morale. Certainly combatants'
poetry had ready access to publication, in newspapers, poetry journals, and school magazines. The continuum of feelings, then,
expressed in this poetry, and the varying degrees of self-knowledge
and self-deceiving with which it seems to be expressed, tends ultimately to 'deconstruct' the notion of gayness as (from the heterosexual point of view) a distinct 'Other' with its own stable and
separate identity.

Selected reading

Abelove, Henry, Barale, Michele Aina, and Halperin, David, eds, *Lesbian
   and Gay Studies Reader* (Routledge, 1993).
   A massive and comprehensive collection. Section I chapter two is an extract from the influential *Epistemology of the Closet*. The main literary
   chapters are in Section VII, 'Between the pages', including Dollimore on

Wilde and Gide. Section XII (pp. 662–5) of the invaluable 'Suggestions for further reading' contains the best bibliography on this field up to August 1992.

Bristow, Joseph, ed., *Sexual Sameness: Textual Difference in Lesbian and Gay Writing* (Routledge, 1992).

Contains chapters on the literary representation of same-sex love in major writers such as E. M. Forster, Walt Whitman, and Sylvia Townsend Warner.

Butler, Judith, *Undoing Gender* (Routledge, 2004).

The book constitutes a reconsideration of her earlier views on gender performativity in *Gender Trouble.*

Dollimore, Jonathan, *Sexual Dissidence: Augustine to Wilde, Freud to Foucault* (Clarendon, 1991).

Part Three, chapters three to five inclusive, debates the issue of essentialism touched upon in the present section.

Elliot, Patricia, *Debates in Transgender, Queer, and Feminist Theory: Contested Sites* (Routledge, 2016).

In the interdisciplinary series 'Queer Interventions' which publishes 'queer work which intersects with other theoretical schools'. The introduction, 'Exploring Rifts in Transgender, Queer, and Feminist Theories', sets out some of the issues.

Fuss, Diana, ed., *Inside/Out: Lesbian Theories, Gay Theories* (Routledge, 1992).

I found the introduction and Section 1 chapter one (by Judith Butler) very useful, but there is otherwise little here about literature as such. Chapter ten, on Radclyffe Hall's lesbian novel *The Well of Loneliness*, is actually about the various covers in which the book has been issued.

Hall, Donald E., *Queer Theories* (Palgrave, 'Transitions' series, 2003).

Hall, Donald E., and Jagose, Annamarie, eds, *The Routledge Queer Studies Reader* (Routledge, 2012).

This is the successor to Abelove *et al.*'s pioneering Routledge *Lesbian and Gay Studies Reader* of 1993, which marked the academic emergence of the field. This one too has a set of major essays divided into seven (new) sections. The book's keynote is the statement in the editors' introduction that 'linearly organised narratives cannot easily capture the sometimes-inchoate energies … that mark the rise of queer studies'. It opens with essays by the foundational figures Sedgwick and Butler, followed by Jay Prosser's essay working against what he sees as 'the erasure of the transgender body' in Butler's *Gender Trouble*. Another landmark collection.

Lilly, Mark, ed. *Lesbian and Gay Writing* (Macmillan, 1990).

> Chapters five, six, and ten are about lesbian and gay poetry, very welcome in a field otherwise dominated (like so much current theory) by writing about prose.

Lilly, Mark, *Gay Men's Literature in the Twentieth Century* (New York University Press, 1993).

> An accessible book which does not presuppose wide theoretical knowledge. The first chapter is a general survey of mainstream criticism of gay writers ('The Homophobic Academy'), and the rest are on major authors, including Byron, Wilde, Forster, First World War poetry, Tennessee Williams, James Baldwin, Joe Orton, and Christopher Isherwood.

Morland, Iain, and Willox, Annabelle, eds, *Queer Theory* (Palgrave, 'Readers in Cultural Criticism' series, 2004).

Munt, Sally, ed., *New Lesbian Criticism: Literary and Cultural Readings* (Harvester, 1992).

> Contains useful general theoretical essays, pieces on major figures like the black lesbian poet and theorist Audre Lorde, and material on lesbian popular culture, lesbian utopian fiction, and lesbian pornography.

Palmer, Paulina, *Contemporary Lesbian Writing: Dreams, Desire, Difference* (Open University Press, 1993).

> Begins with a chapter outlining a range of theoretical perspectives and then has chapters on a variety of relevant genres, including political fiction, the thriller, the comic novel, and fantasy fiction.

Salih, Sara, *Judith Butler* (Routledge Critical Thinkers, 2002).

Sedgwick, Eve Kosovsky, *Between Men: English Literature and Male Homosexual Desire* (Columbia University Press, 1985).

> This and the following book have played an important part in laying the theoretical basis of current queer studies.

Sedgwick, Eve Kosovsky, *Epistemology of the Closet* (University of California Press, 2nd edn, 2008).

Sinfield, Alan, *Cultural Politics – Queer Reading* (Routledge, 2nd edn, 2005).

> A lively and provocative text – a pioneering work in its field when first published.

Sullivan, Nikki, *A Critical Introduction to Queer Theory* (Edinburgh University Press, 2003).

> 'This book does not attempt to define what Queer Theory is but, rather, is concerned with providing an overview of what Queer Theories do ... and what kinds of effects have been produced as a result.'

Taylor, Martin, *Lads: Love Poetry of the Trenches* (Duckworth, new edn, 1998).

An anthology of poetry, with an introduction which 're-positions' this body of work. Compare the selection and its commentary with more conventional ones, such as *The Penguin Book of First World War Poetry*, edited by Jon Silkin.

Wilchins, Riki, *Queer Theory, Gender Theory* (Magnus Books, 2014).

Clear and direct throughout, and can be read at a sitting – good chapters on Derrida, Foucault, and Butler.

Woods, Greg, *A History of Gay Literature: The Male Tradition* (Yale University Press, 1999).

An account of gay male literature, from ancient times to the present.

Zimmerman, Bonnie, 'What has never been: an overview of lesbian feminist criticism', reprinted in Gayle Greene and Coppelia Kahn, eds, *Making a Difference: Feminist Literary Criticism* (Methuen, 1985).

An influential survey of lesbian criticism up to the time of its publication, and a good starting point for beginners in this field.

Zimmerman, Bonnie, 'Lesbians like this and that: some notes on lesbian criticism for the nineties', in Sally Munt (see above).

Another survey of the field, written ten years after the previous article, and considering the issues and options for the nineties.

8
Marxist criticism

Beginnings and basics of Marxism

Karl Marx (1818–83), a German philosopher, and Friedrich Engels (1820–95), a German sociologist (as he would now be called), were the joint founders of this school of thought. Marx was the son of a lawyer but spent most of his life in great poverty as a political exile from Germany living in Britain (he was expelled after the 1848 'year of revolutions'). Engels had left Germany in 1842 to work in Manchester for his father's textile firm. They met after Marx had read an article by Engels in a journal to which they both contributed. They themselves called their economic theories 'Communism' (rather than 'Marxism'), designating their belief in the state ownership of industry, transport, etc., rather than private ownership. Marx and Engels announced the advent of Communism in their jointly written *Communist Manifesto* of 1848.

The aim of Marxism is to bring about a classless society, based on the common ownership of the means of production, distribution, and exchange. Marxism is a *materialist* philosophy: that is, it tries to explain things without assuming the existence of a world, or of forces, beyond the natural world around us, and the society we live in. It looks for concrete, scientific, logical explanations of the world of observable fact. (Its opposite is *idealist* philosophy, which *does* believe in the existence of a spiritual 'world elsewhere' and would offer, for instance, religious explanations of life and conduct.) But whereas other philosophies merely seek to understand the world, Marxism (as Marx famously said) seeks to change it. Marxism sees progress as coming about through the struggle for power between different social classes. This view of history as class struggle (rather than as, for instance, a succession of dynasties, or as a gradual progress towards the attainment of national identity and sovereignty) regards it as 'motored' by the competition for economic, social, and political advantage. The exploitation of one social class by another is seen especially in modern industrial capitalism, particularly in its unrestricted nineteenth-century form. The result of this exploitation is *alienation*, which is the state that comes about when the worker is 'de-skilled' and made to perform fragmented, repetitive tasks in a sequence of whose nature and purpose he or she has no overall grasp. By contrast, in the older 'pre-industrial' or 'cottage industry' system of manufacture, home and workplace were one, the worker completed the whole production process in all its variety, and was in direct contact with those who might buy the product. These alienated workers have undergone the process of *reification*, which is a term used in Marx's major work, *Das Kapital*, but not developed there. It concerns the way, when capitalist goals and questions of profit and loss are paramount, workers are bereft of their full humanity and are thought of as 'hands' or 'the labour force', so that, for instance, the effects of industrial closures are calculated in purely economic terms. People, in a word, become things.

There were various influences on early Marxist thinking in addition to that of the political experiences of its founders, including the work of the eighteenth-century German philosopher Hegel (especially his idea of the *dialectic*, whereby opposing forces or ideas bring about new situations or ideas). Marxism also built upon the socialist thinking which was produced in France at the time of the French Revolution, and it inverted some of the ideas of early economic theory, especially the view that the pursuit of individual economic self-interest would bring economic and social benefits to the whole of society (the belief which was and is the underlying rationale of capitalism).

The simplest Marxist model of society sees it as constituted by a *base* (the material means of production, distribution, and exchange) and a *superstructure*, which is the 'cultural' world of ideas, art, religion, law, and so on. The essential Marxist view is that the latter things are not 'innocent', but are 'determined' (or shaped) by the nature of the economic base. This belief about culture, known as *economic determinism*, is a central part of traditional Marxist thinking.

Marxist literary criticism: general

Marx and Engels themselves did not put forward any comprehensive theory of literature. Their views seem relaxed and undogmatic: good art always has a degree of freedom from prevailing economic circumstances, even if these economic facts are its 'ultimate determinant'. Thus, Engels, writing to the English novelist Margaret Harkness in April 1888, tells her that he is 'far from finding fault with you for not having written a point-blank socialist novel … The more the opinions of the author remain hidden the better the work of art.' As cultured and highly educated Germans, Marx and Engels had that reverence for 'great' art and literature which was typical of their class, and there is an obvious desire in such pronouncements to emphasise the difference between art and propaganda.

All the same, Marxist literary criticism maintains that a writer's social class, and its prevailing 'ideology' (outlook, values, tacit assumptions, half-realised allegiances, etc.), have a major bearing on what is written by a member of that class. So instead of seeing authors as primarily autonomous 'inspired' individuals whose 'genius' and creative imagination enables them to bring forth original and timeless works of art, the Marxist sees them as constantly formed by their social contexts in ways which they themselves would usually not admit. This is true not just of the *content* of their work but even of *formal* aspects of their writing which might at first seem to have no possible political overtones. For instance, the prominent British Marxist critic Terry Eagleton suggests that in language, 'shared definitions and regularities of grammar both reflect and help to constitute, a well-ordered political state' (*William Shakespeare*, 1986, p. 1). Likewise, Catherine Belsey, another prominent British left-wing critic, argues (in Chapter 2, 'Challenges to Expressive Realism', of her highly influential book *Critical Practice*, Routledge, 2nd edn, 2002) that the *form* of the 'Realist' novel contains implicit validation of the existing social structure, because realism, by its very nature, leaves conventional ways of seeing intact, and hence tends to discourage critical scrutiny of reality. By 'form' here is included all the conventional features of the novel – chronological time-schemes, formal beginnings and endings, in-depth psychological characterisation, intricate plotting, and fixed narratorial points of view. Similarly, the 'fragmented', 'absurdist' forms of drama and fiction used by twentieth-century writers like Beckett and Kafka are seen as a response to the contradictions and divisions inherent in late capitalist society.

However, it is probably true to say (as Ken Newton does in *Theory into Practice*, p. 244) that traditional Marxist criticism tends to deal with history in a fairly generalised way. It talks about conflicts between social classes, and clashes of large historical forces, but, contrary to popular belief, it rarely discusses the detail of a specific historical situation and relates it closely to the interpretation of a particular literary text. As Newton implies, this suggests one of the main differences between the Marxist criticism of the 1960s and 1970s and the cultural materialist and new historicist criticism (Chapter 9) which came to the fore in the 1980s, since the latter very often dealt closely with specific historical documents, attempting, in an almost archaeological spirit, to recreate the 'state of mind' of a particular moment in history.

'Leninist' Marxist criticism

A much harder line about literature than Marx and Engels themselves would have approved of was generally pursued by officially sanctioned Marxists, at least until the 1960s. In the 1920s, during the early years after the revolution in Russia, the official Soviet attitude to literature and the arts was very enlightened and 'experimental', and characteristically modern forms of art were encouraged. The 1930s saw reaction throughout the whole of Soviet society, and the state began to exert direct control over literature and the arts as well as everything else. At the first Soviet Writers' Congress in 1934 liberal views were outlawed and a new orthodoxy imposed, based on the writings of Lenin rather than those of Marx or Engels. Lenin had argued in 1905 that literature must become an instrument of the Party. 'Literature', he said, 'must become Party literature … Literature must become part of the organized, methodical, and unified labours of the social-democratic party.' Experimentation was effectively banned: writers like Proust and Joyce were stigmatised as exemplars of 'bourgeois decadence' (Joyce's *Ulysses* was denounced at the 1934 Congress as 'a heap of dung crawling with worms'), and straight realism was imposed (known as 'Socialist Realism'). In George Steiner's words, these conditions made literature impossible above the level of, say, *Uncle Tom's Cabin*. Steiner calls the two main streams of Marxist criticism the 'Engelsian' kind, which stresses the necessary freedom of art from direct political determinism, and the 'Leninist', which insists on the need for art to be explicitly committed to the political cause of the Left. (The above discussion of the views of Engels and Lenin draws on George Steiner's chapter 'Marxism and the literary critic', pp. 271–90 in his book *Language and Silence*.)

Those abroad who were sympathetic to the ideas of Communism tried to follow the 'Moscow line' on matters where an official Party policy existed, hence the international influence of the 'Leninist' views which crystallised at the 1934 Congress. Thus, in what came to be called the 'Vulgar Marxism' of the 1930s, a direct cause–effect relationship between literature and economics was assumed, with all writers seen as irrevocably trapped within the intellectual limits of their social-class position. A much-cited example of this rigid kind of Marxist literary criticism is Christopher Caudwell's *Illusion and Reality* (written in the 1930s and published in 1946). Caudwell's writing is both very generalised, in the sense that there is little detailed textual reference to the works under discussion, and very specific, in the sense that every facet of a writer is linked to some aspect of her or his social status. Thus, in Caudwell's discussion of Victorian poets (extracted in Newton's *Twentieth Century Literary Theory*) we read that '[Browning's] vocabulary has a foggy verbalism which is a reflection of his intellectual dishonesty in dealing with real contemporary problems'. Thus, a particular kind of vocabulary is the direct product of the middle-class writer's evasiveness on sensitive social issues. All poets have their own form of escape from modern reality: Tennyson lapses into a Keatsian dreamworld, Browning writes constantly on Italian medieval themes:

> To Tennyson the Keatsian world of romance, to Browning the Italian springtime; both are revolting backwards, trying to escape from the contradiction of the class for whom they speak.
>
> (Newton, p. 87).

The overall result is to provide little more than 'sound-bites' on literature for use in political argument.

'Engelsian' Marxist criticism

From the 1930s, however, a rich variety of what Steiner calls 'Engelsian' Marxist criticism flourished, either in exile, or in suppressed or underground form. The group now called the Russian Formalists had flourished in the 1920s, until disbanded by the Party, and should be mentioned here, even though their work is not strictly Marxist in spirit. The most prominent members of the group were Victor Shklovsky, Boris Tomashevsky, and Boris Eichenbaum, whose work can be sampled in *Russian Formalist Criticism: Four Essays*, edited by Lee T. Lemon and Marion J. Reis (University of Nebraska Press, 2nd edn, 2012). Their ideas included the need for close formal analysis of literature (hence the name), the belief that the language of literature has its own characteristic procedures and effects, and is not just a version of ordinary language, and Shklovsky's idea of 'defamiliarisation' or 'making strange' (expounded in the essay 'Art as Technique', which Lemon and Reis reprint), which claims that one of the chief effects of literary language is that of making the familiar world appear new to us, as if we were seeing it for the first time, and thus laying it open to reappraisal. Another key Formalist idea is Tomashevsky's distinction (again expounded in the essay reprinted in Lemon and Reis) between story (Russian *fabula*) and plot (Russian *sjuzhet*), the former being an actual sequence of (perhaps imaginary) events as they would have occurred, while the latter is the artistic presentation of these events, which might involve reorderings, juxtapositions, repetitions, and so on, in order to heighten their effect in a work of literature. As with the concept of defamiliarisation, there is a careful distinction here between reality itself and its verbal representation in a work of literature, so that we are steered away from any notion that literature simply mirrors reality in a documentary way. Later, in the early 1950s and 1960s, these Formalist ideas were of great interest to the early structuralists, partly because of their emphasis on the distinction between language and reality, and on literature as a set of systematic procedures and structures.

Some of those associated with Formalism, like Mikhail Bakhtin, remained in Russia, but others went into exile and continued their work abroad, thus sowing the seeds of the new forms of Marxist criticism which emerged in the 1960s. One such exile was the linguist Roman Jakobson (1896–1982), who continued his work in Prague, founding the Prague Linguistic Circle, the members of which included René Wellek. Wellek, like Jakobson, went to America shortly before the start of the Second World War, and was influential in the movement known as 'New Criticism' which built upon a number of these Russian Formalist ideas, especially those concerning the need for close verbal analysis of literary texts and the special recognition of literary language as a medium with its own characteristics that set it aside from day-to-day language.

The suppressed Russian Formalists also had an influence in Germany, on the Frankfurt School of Marxist aesthetics. The school was founded in 1923, as a political research institute attached to the University of Frankfurt. They practised a form of criticism which tried to combine Freud and Marx, as well as aspects of Formalism. The best-known figures here are Walter Benjamin, who committed suicide while fleeing from the Nazis in 1940, Herbert Marcuse, a major influence on the radical thinking of the 1960s, and Theodor Adorno. Also forced to flee from Germany was the playwright Bertolt Brecht, another opponent of the simplicities of the doctrine of Socialist Realism. His notion of the 'alienation effect' in drama involves devices which draw the attention of the audience to the fact that what they see on the stage is a constructed literary image, not a natural reality. For example, a 'director' figure might sit at the side of the stage throughout a play, following the script in a book (as in Brecht's play *Galileo*). Such a device is closely linked to the Formalists' idea of defamiliarisation, since, again, it emphasises a boundary or 'shift' between literature and life.

The influence of Althusser

Much recent Marxist thinking on literature has been influenced by the work of the French Marxist theoretician Louis Althusser (1918–90), and his contribution will become clear if we outline some of the key terms and concepts he introduced. One such is the notion of *overdeterminism*, a word borrowed from Freud, which designates an effect which arises from a variety of causes, that is, from several causes acting together, rather than from a single (in this case, economic) factor. This concept of linked and interacting causes is intended to undercut simplistic notions of a one-to-one correspondence between base and superstructure. A related term is the notion of *relative autonomy*, which is the view that in spite of the connections between culture and economics, art has a degree of independence from economic forces. This concept too is a way of attacking simplistic views of a superstructure entirely determined by the nature of the economic base.

Ideology is a key term for Althusser, as for all Marxists. It is a broad concept variously defined within Marxism. Althusser's definition (quoted by Goldstein) is as follows:

> Ideology is a system (possessing its logic and proper rigour) of representations (images, myths, ideas or concepts according to the case) endowed with an existence and an historical role at the heart of a given society.
>
> (Philip Goldstein, *The Politics of Literary Theory: An Introduction to Marxist Criticism*, p. 23)

We can pare this to 'a system of representations at the heart of a given society' to give a concise definition which makes culture (including literature) a crucial vehicle of the values which underpin the status quo in any society. These values and assumptions are usually implicit, often unrecognised, but suffuse all the artefacts and all the culture of a given time. So this definition, too, departs from the crudity of the base/superstructure model, in which the former determines the nature of the latter. Now, says Goldstein, 'the economic infrastructure still influences ideological practices, but only in the "last instance"' (Goldstein, p. 23).

Decentring is a key term in Althusser to indicate structures which have no essence, or focus, or centre. Again, this is partly a way of avoiding the view that the economic base is the essence of society and the superstructure merely a secondary reflection. The notion of decentring implies that there is no overall unity: art has a relative autonomy and is determined by the economic level only 'in the last instance'. These 'Engelsian' pronouncements do not cancel out the

Marxist tendency to imprison art within economics, but they do release literature on bail, so to speak, and allow it a high degree of day-to-day freedom.

Althusser makes a useful distinction between what we might call state power and state control. State power is maintained by what Althusser terms *repressive structures*, which are institutions like the law courts, prisons, the police force, and the army, which operate, in the last analysis, by external force. But the power of the state is also maintained more subtly, by seeming to secure the internal consent of its citizens, using what Althusser calls *ideological structures* or *state ideological apparatuses*. These are such groupings as political parties, schools, the media, churches, the family, and art (including literature) which foster an ideology – a set of ideas and attitudes – which is sympathetic to the aims of the state and the political status quo. Thus, each of us feels that we are freely choosing what is in fact being imposed upon us.

This Althusserian distinction is closely related to the notion of *hegemony*, which was given prominence by the Italian Marxist Antonio Gramsci (1891–1934). Gramsci contrasts *rule*, which is direct political control which uses force when necessary, and *hegemony*, which is (as defined by the British Marxist critic Raymond Williams (1921–88)) 'the whole lived social process as practically organized by specific and dominant meanings, values and beliefs of a kind which can be abstracted as a "world-view" or "class outlook"' (Williams, *Marxism and Literature*, Oxford University Press, 1977, p. 101). Williams relates hegemony to culture in general and to ideology in particular. Hegemony is like an internalised form of social control which makes certain views seem 'natural' or invisible so that they hardly seem like views at all, just 'the way things are'.

The 'trick' whereby we are made to feel that we are choosing when really we have no choice is called by Althusser *interpellation*. Capitalism, says Althusser, thrives on this trick: it makes us *feel* like free agents ('You can have any colour you like…') while actually imposing things upon us ('… as long as it's black'). Thus, democracy makes us feel that we are choosing the kind of government we have, but in practice the differences between political parties, once in power, are far fewer than the rhetorical gulfs between them. Interpellation is Althusser's term for the way the individual

is encouraged to see herself or himself as an entity free and independent of social forces. It accounts for the operation of control
structures not maintained by physical force, and hence for the perpetuation of a social set-up which concentrates wealth and power in
the hands of the few.

The general purport of these Althusserian ideas is to enable a
much more subtle view of how society works than that provided
by traditional Marxism. Instead of force crudely applied from a
single source, as from a lever, there is assent secured in many different and complex ways, and ideological power is shown to be of
ultimately greater significance than material power. Thus, literature is shown to be of crucial importance in its own right, not just
a helpless and passive reflector of the economic base where the real
business of society goes on. Hence, the attraction of Althusser to
recent Marxist critics is that he offers ways of by-passing the crude
base/superstructure model without giving up the Marxist perspective altogether. Althusser's views represent what we might call re-
visionist Marxism, which is to say that they rethink and repackage
the basic concepts in a form which is more subtle and more flexible.
This is not to say that Althusser was a flexible thinker generally: on
the contrary, he was a particularly dogmatic one, much attacked on
the left for his promotion of 'theory' as a separate realm which is
above experience, practice, or activism (see especially *The Poverty
of Theory* by the British Marxist historian E. P. Thompson). But
he did provide terms and formulae when they were needed, in the
liberalising 1960s, which loosened the monolithic fabric of Marxist
thinking and therefore made it acceptable to the radicals of that period. Without these 'loosening' moves Marxism might have been
widely rejected as just one more form of rigid traditional thinking
which the 'counter-culture' of that time needed to reject.

Since the death of Raymond Williams, the best-known British
Marxist critic has been Terry Eagleton, whose work has reflected
a wide range of influences, including for a time that of Althusser.
Marxist criticism seems to conflict in its basic assumptions with
those of post-structuralism and postmodernism, and the most significant Marxist writing in the 1980s and 1990s involved a process
of intricate interaction with these movements. Marxist criticism
has also traditionally been opposed to psychoanalytic explanations

of conduct, on the grounds that psychoanalysis falsely isolates individuals from the social structures in which they exist. All the same, the American Marxist critic Fredric Jameson (in *The Political Unconscious: Narrative as a Socially Symbolic Act*, 1981) has tried to reconcile the two. Essentially, Jameson offers political extensions of basic psychoanalytic terms like 'the unconscious' and 'repression'. Literature, in his view, often tries to *repress* historical truth, but analysis can reveal its underlying ideology (that is, its unconscious). A basic starting point on Eagleton, Jameson, and this whole area of debate would be to read Jameson's essay 'The politics of theory: Ideological positions in the postmodernism debate' and Eagleton's 'Capitalism, modernism, and postmodernism', which are reprinted as items 22 and 23 in David Lodge's *Modern Criticism and Theory: A Reader.*

STOP and THINK

General: The main tenet of Marxist criticism – that the nature of literature is influenced by the social and political circumstances in which it is produced – might well be immediately accepted as self-evidently true.

The difficulty and controversy lie entirely in deciding how close the influence is. Are you going to adopt a 'determinist' position, and argue that literature is the passive product of socio-economic forces, or do you take a more 'liberal' line and see the socio-economic influence as much more distant and subtle?

Your main difficulty will be to show the operation of these economic forces (no matter whether you take the 'strong' or the 'weak' model) in a given literary work. What exactly do directly operating or indirectly operating socio-economic forces look like in a literary work?

Specific: These are difficult questions to cope with in the abstract, and you will find it helpful to think about them in the context of a specific example. In the example below, therefore, is a 'determinist' or a 'liberal' line being taken, and how is this indicated? Is the socio-economic influence seen by the critic in the plot content of the play, in the characterisation, or in the literary form itself, and if so how?

What Marxist critics do

1. They make a division between the 'overt' (manifest or surface) and 'covert' (latent or hidden) content of a literary work (much as psychoanalytic critics do) and then relate the *covert* subject matter of the literary work to basic Marxist themes, for example, class struggle or the progression of society through various historical stages, such as the transition from feudalism to industrial capitalism. Thus, the conflicts in *King Lear* might be read as being 'really' about the conflict of class interest between the rising class (the bourgeoisie) and the falling class (the feudal overlords).

2. Another method used by Marxist critics is to relate the context of a work to the social-class status of the author. In such cases an assumption is made (which again is similar to those made by psychoanalytic critics) that the author is unaware of precisely what he or she is saying or revealing in the text.

3. A third Marxist method is to explain the nature of a whole literary genre in terms of the social period which 'produced' it. For instance, *The Rise of the Novel*, by Ian Watt, relates the growth of the novel in the eighteenth century to the expansion of the middle classes during that period. The novel 'speaks' for this social class, just as, for instance, tragedy 'speaks for' the monarchy and the nobility, and the ballad 'speaks for' the rural and semi-urban 'working class'.

4. A fourth Marxist practice is to relate the literary work to the social assumptions of the time in which it is 'consumed', a strategy which is used particularly in the later variant of Marxist criticism known as cultural materialism (see Chapter 9, pp. 184–9).

5. A fifth Marxist practice is the 'politicisation of literary form', that is, the claim that literary forms are themselves determined by political circumstance. For instance, in the view

of some critics, literary realism carries with it an implicit validation of conservative social structures; for others, the formal and metrical intricacies of the sonnet and the iambic pentameter are a counterpart of social stability, decorum, and order.

Marxist criticism: an example

As an example of Marxist criticism we will take chapter five, on *Twelfth Night*, in Elliot Krieger's *A Marxist Study of Shakespeare's Comedies* (1979). As it is discussed here, the example mainly shows the first of the five Marxist critical activities just listed. The play centres on the love between the Duke Orsino and the Lady Olivia. His love is extravagantly and persistently expressed, but she at first rejects him, having dedicated herself to a period of protracted mourning for her dead father. Subsequently she falls in love with Viola, a young noblewoman who is temporarily disguised as a man and acting as Orsino's servant and go-between (under the name Cesario). Olivia is also loved by her steward, the strict and punctilious Malvolio, who is tricked by her uncle, Sir Toby Belch, into believing that his love for her is returned.

The essay begins by citing the dominant critical view of the play, which is that it presents various extremes of self-indulgence (such as Orsino's wallowing in fantasies of romantic love and Toby Belch's self-abandonment to physical appetites) and contrasts these with an extreme puritanism and resistance to pleasure, as seen in Malvolio. The play is seen as recommending a balance and decorum in which these extremes are avoided and proper human fulfilment becomes possible. Krieger points out that this ignores the question of class in the play: when 'order' is restored at the end, the aristocratic characters suffer no particular ill effects, while Malvolio's fate is much more severe; yet Malvolio's self-interest differs from the obviously narcissistic preoccupations of Orsino and Olivia and the egoistic revelry of Sir Toby *only* because decorum forbids one of his rank to 'surfeit on himself' (p. 99). Thus 'only a privileged social class has access to the morality of indulgence'. Indeed, by definition, 'the members of the ruling class find their identities through excessive indulgence in appetite' (p. 100).

Each of the members of the aristocratic class, he continues, has a private 'secondary world'. For Sir Toby it is the unfettered world he reaches by drink, for he 'forces everyone to care for him while using the enforced incompetence of drunkenness and the willed oblivion of time in order to protect himself from the possibility of caring for others' (p. 102). Likewise, Olivia protects herself from the needs of others by retreating into a private world of bereavement, and Orsino removes himself into a wholly subjective world of love obsession in which everything becomes 'an adjunct of, and accompaniment to, the Duke's psychological condition' (p. 104). In these 'privatised' 'secondary worlds', each becomes, not part of a community, but 'one self king' (p. 103). Viola, too, attempts to retreat into one of these secondary worlds, but though she is actually aristocratic, the disguise she adopts enables her to choose a temporary non-aristocratic status ('I'll serve this duke'), and she thus becomes 'an object within the secondary worlds of Orsino, Olivia and Sir Toby' (p. 107), someone they assume is available for their use or manipulation.

Within the world of the servants in the play, there is much emphasis on 'aspiration': the new servant Cesario/Viola displaces Valentine and Curio from their positions of privileged access to Duke Orsino, and in Olivia's household there is a constant struggle for prime position between Maria (another of the servants) and Malvolio. Both, in fact, aim to marry into the family, which Maria eventually achieves by marrying Sir Toby as a reward for her decisive humiliation of Malvolio. Krieger therefore sees her as a significant element in the play:

> Maria is hardly a proto-bourgeoise, in that her aspiration supports and confirms rather than challenges the continued validity of aristocratic privilege, but with her abilities to separate self from vocation, to express self apart from imposed duty, and to earn by her actions advancement in social degree, only Maria in *Twelfth Night* indicates the bourgeois and Puritan emphasis on independence, competition, and the association of stature with merit. (p. 121)

In contrast, Malvolio is much less of a representative of any kind of change in the social order, since he has an extreme reverence for all the trappings of aristocracy, and attributes the circumstances which, he thinks, have made possible his own elevation to the aristocracy to 'fortune' and his 'stars'. Thus, fortune in the play is a force, like 'nature', which is often a defence or a rationalisation of inherited aristocratic privilege. For the Marxist critic, then, the play demonstrates the gulf which exists between masters and servants and manifests something of the state of mind that is characteristic of each class. The Marxist feature of this essay is the way it introduces the notion of social class into interpretations of the play: this is its special 'intervention' into the large body of critical writing on the play, in which the topic is never raised. Very little indeed is said in the essay about the specifics of the precise historical moment in which it was written: rather, a subtle and original reading is woven round the generalised notions of social–class conflict, class privilege, and aspirations towards what would now be called upward social mobility.

Selected reading

Dowling, William C., *Jameson, Althusser, Marx: An Introduction to The Political Unconscious* (Routledge, 2016).
   A 'contextualising introduction' to Jameson's *The Political Unconscious*. Excellent and brief, and really the best place to begin in studying the recent concerns of Marxist thinking and its transforming engagements with Derrida, Lacan, and postmodernism.
Eagleton, Terry, *Marxism and Literary Criticism* (Routledge Classics, 2002).
   A brief yet thorough introduction to this field.
Eagleton, Terry, *Ideology: An Introduction* (Verso, 2nd edn, 2007).
   Representative of Eagleton's more recent concerns.
Goldstein, Philip, *The Politics of Literary Theory: An Introduction to Marxist Criticism* (Florida State University Press, 1990).
   Useful on specific areas, such as: The Frankfurt School, pp. 17–21; post-structuralist Marxism, pp. 22–8; Terry Eagleton, pp. 59–65; Althusser, Derrida, and Foucault, pp. 164–74.
Goldstein, Philip, *Post-Marxist Theory: An Introduction* (State University of New York Press, 2005).
   Useful on recent developments, such as chapter 4, on 'The Feminist Post-Marxism of Judith Butler'.

Howard, Jean E., and Shershow, Scott Cutler, *Marxist Shakespeares* (Routledge, 2000).

A very useful book in the 'Accents on Shakespeare' series, edited by Terence Hawkes, which takes up the mission of Methuen's 'New Accents' series of bringing literary theory to literary text.

Jameson, Frederic, *The Political Unconscious: Narrative as a Socially Symbolic Act* (Cornell University Press, 1981).

The key text for Jameson, but undoubtedly difficult reading. It would be helpful to read William C. Dowling (above) first.

Krieger, Elliott, *A Marxist Study of Shakespeare's Comedies* (Macmillan, 1979).

'Applied' Marxist criticism.

Mulhern, Francis, ed., *Contemporary Marxist Literary Criticism* (Longman, 1992).

A thoughtful and wide-ranging introduction and some key documents.

Prawer, S. S., *Karl Marx and World Literature* (Verso, 2nd edn, 2011).

A detailed presentation and discussion of 'what Marx said about literature at various times in his life'.

'Ruis', *Marx for Beginners* (Pantheon Books, 2003).

A 'documentary comic book' which summarises Marx's ideas in comic strip form. A good place to begin if you have not encountered Marx's ideas before.

Williams, Raymond, *Marxism and Literature* (Oxford University Press, 1977).

Useful on basic Marxist concepts, and Williams's adaptations of them. See 1.4 Ideology, 2.1 Base and Superstructure, 2.6 Hegemony, 2.8 Dominant, Residual, and Emergent, 2.9 Structures of feeling.

9

New historicism and cultural materialism

New historicism

The term 'new historicism' was coined by the American critic Stephen Greenblatt, whose book *Renaissance Self-Fashioning: from More to Shakespeare* (1980) is usually regarded as its beginning. However, similar tendencies can be identified in work by various critics published during the 1970s, a good example being J. W. Lever's *The Tragedy of State: A Study of Jacobean Drama* (published by Methuen in 1971, and re-issued in 1987 with an introduction by Jonathan Dollimore). This brief and epoch-making book challenged conservative critical views about Jacobean theatre, and linked the plays much more closely with the political events of their era than previous critics had done.

A simple definition of the new historicism is that it is a method based on the *parallel* reading of literary and non-literary texts, usually of the same historical period. That is to say, new historicism refuses (at least ostensibly) to 'privilege' the literary text: instead of a literary 'foreground' and a historical 'background', it envisages and practises a mode of study in which literary and non-literary texts are given equal weight and constantly inform or interrogate each other. This 'equal weighting' is suggested in the definition of new historicism offered by the American critic Louis Montrose: he defines it as a combined interest in 'the textuality of history, the historicity of texts'. It involves (in Greenblatt's words) 'an intensified willingness to read *all* of the textual traces of the past with the attention traditionally conferred only on literary texts'. So new historicism (as indeed the name implies) embodies a paradox (and, for some, a scandal); it is an approach to literature in which there is no privileging of the literary (though we will see later that this statement requires some qualification).

Typically, a new historical essay will place the literary text within the 'frame' of a non-literary text. Thus, Greenblatt's main innovation, from the viewpoint of literary study, was to juxtapose the plays of the Renaissance period with 'the horrifying colonialist policies pursued by all the major European powers of the era' (Hugh Grady, in *The Modernist Shakespeare*). He draws attention to 'the marginalization and dehumanizing of suppressed Others' (Grady), usually by starting an essay with an analysis of a contemporary historical document which overlaps in some way with the subject matter of the play. Greenblatt himself refers to the appropriated historical document as the 'anecdote', and the typical new historicist essay omits the customary academic preliminaries about previously published interpretations of the play in question, and begins with a powerful and dramatic anecdote, as signalled, for instance, by Louis Montrose, in the first sentence of the essay discussed later: 'I would like to recount an Elizabethan dream – not Shakespeare's *A Midsummer Night's Dream* but one dreamt by Simon Forman on 23 January 1597'. These dramatic openings often cite date and place and have all the force of the documentary, eyewitness account, strongly evoking the quality of lived experience rather than 'history'. Since these historical documents are not subordinated as contexts, but are ana-lysed in their own right, we should perhaps call them 'co-texts' rather than 'contexts'. The text and co-text used will be seen as expressions of the same historical 'moment', and interpreted accordingly. This process is well described by Richard Wilson and Richard Dutton in the introduction to their collection of essays *New Historicism and Renaissance Drama*:

> Where [earlier] criticism had mystified Shakespeare as an incarnation of spoken English, it [new historicism] found the plays embedded in other *written texts*, such as penal, medical and colonial documents. Read within this archival continuum, what they represented was not harmony but the violence of the Puritan attack on carnival, the impo-

sition of slavery, the rise of patriarchy, the hounding of deviance, and the crashing of prison gates during what Foucault called 'the Age of Confinement, at the dawn of carceral society' ['carceral' comes from the Latin word *carcer*, meaning a prison].

(Wilson and Dutton, p. 8)

This succinctly conveys the tone and ambitions of new historicism, and the phrase about reading literature 'within the archival continuum' is a vivid encapsulation of the method.

New and old historicisms – some differences

When we say that new historicism involves the parallel study of literary and non-literary texts, the word 'parallel' encapsulates the essential difference between this and earlier approaches to literature which had made some use of historical data. These earlier approaches made a hierarchical separation between the literary text, which was the object of value, the jewel, as it were, and the historical 'background', which was merely the setting, and by definition of lesser worth.

The practice of giving 'equal weighting' to literary and non-literary material is the first and major difference between the 'new' and the 'old' historicism. As representative of the 'old' historicism we could cite E. M. W. Tillyard's *The Elizabethan World Picture* (1943) and *Shakespeare's History Plays* (1944), books against which new historicism frequently defines itself. These books described the set of conservative mental attitudes (to society, to the deity, to the created universe, etc.) which Tillyard saw as typifying the Elizabethan outlook and as reflected in Shakespeare's plays. The 'traditional' approach to Shakespeare (through to the 1970s) was characterised by the combination of this historical framework with the practice of 'close reading' and the analysis of 'patterns of imagery'.

A second important difference between old and new historicisms is encapsulated in the word 'archival' in the phrase 'the archival continuum' quoted earlier, for that word indicates that new historicism is indeed a historic*ist* rather than a historic*al* movement. That is, it is interested in history as represented and recorded in written documents, in history-as-text. Historical events as such, it would argue, are irrecoverably lost. This emphasis bears the influence of the long-familiar view in literary studies that the actual thoughts, or feelings, or intentions of a writer can never be recovered or reconstructed, so that the real living individual is now entirely superseded by the literary text which has come down to us. As it were, the word of the past replaces the world of the past. Since, for the new historicist, the events and attitudes of the past now exist solely as writing, it makes sense to subject that writing to the kind of close analysis formerly reserved for literary texts.

Incorporated into this preference for the textual record of the past is the influence of deconstruction. New historicism accepts Derrida's view that there is nothing outside the text, in the special sense that everything about the past is only available to us in textualised form: it is 'thrice-processed', first through the ideology, or outlook, or discursive practices of its own time, then through those of ours, and finally through the distorting web of language itself. Whatever is represented in a text is thereby remade. New historicist essays always themselves constitute another remaking, another permutation of the past, as the play or poem under discussion is juxtaposed with a chosen document, so that a new entity is formed. In this sense the objection that the documents selected may not really be 'relevant' to the play is disarmed, for the aim is not to represent the past as it really was, but to present a new reality by re-situating it.

New historicism and Foucault

New historicism is resolutely anti-establishment, always implicitly on the side of liberal ideals of personal freedom and accepting and celebrating all forms of difference and 'deviance'. At the same time, though, it seems simultaneously to despair of the survival of these in the face of the power of the repressive state, which it constantly reveals as able to penetrate and taint the most intimate areas of personal life. This notion of the state as all-powerful and all-seeing stems from the post-structuralist cultural historian Michel Foucault whose pervasive image of the state is that of 'panoptic' (meaning 'all-seeing') surveillance. The Panopticon was a design for a circular prison conceived by the eighteenth-century utilitarian Jeremy Bentham: the design consisted of tiered ranks of cells which could all be surveyed by a single warder positioned at the centre of the circle. The panoptic state, however, maintains its surveillance not by physical force and intimidation, but by the power of its 'discursive practices' (to use Foucault's terminology – 'discursive' is the adjective derived from the noun 'discourse') – which circulates its ideology throughout the body politic.

Discourse is not just a way of speaking or writing, but the whole 'mental set' and ideology which encloses the thinking of all members of a given society. It is not singular and monolithic – there is always a multiplicity of discourses – so that the operation of power structures is as significant a factor in (say) the family as in layers of government. Hence, contesting them may involve, for example, the struggle to change sexual politics just as much as party politics. Thus, the personal sphere becomes a possible sphere of political action in ways which might well interest a feminist critic. Here, then, we might see grounds for political optimism. On the other hand, when political power operates in and suffuses so many spheres, the possibility of fundamental change and transformation may come to seem very remote.

On the whole, new historicism seems to emphasise the extent of this kind of 'thought control', with the implication that 'deviant' thinking may become literally 'unthinkable' (or *only* thinkable), so that the state is seen as a monolithic structure and change becomes almost impossible. Foucault's work looks at the institutions which enable this power to be maintained, such as state punishment, prisons, the medical profession, and legislation about sexuality. Foucault makes a less rigid distinction than is found in Althusser between 'repressive structures' and 'ideological structures' (see Chapter 8). All the same, there is a clear affinity between Gramsci's 'hegemony' (see Chapter 8), Althusser's 'interpellation' (see Chapter 8), and Foucault's 'discursive practices', since all of these concern the way power is internalised by those whom it disempowers, so that it does not have to be constantly enforced externally.

It should be added that new historicism, in spite of its foregrounding of the word 'historicism', really represents a significant extension of the empire of literary studies, for it entails intensive 'close reading', in the literary-critical manner, of non-literary texts. Documents are seldom offered entire: instead an extract is made which is then subjected to intensive scrutiny. (Contextualisation of the document is usually minimal, partly as a writerly ploy to increase its impact.) Further, little attention is paid to previous writing about the same text, as if the advent of new historicism has wiped the academic slate clean. Hence, this is a true 'words on the page' approach in which context is dispensed with and the material then studied like the decontextualised, isolated poems which I. A. Richards offered for criticism in the 1920s. Thus, a single historical text is sometimes the sole witness, for, say, a claimed change in attitude towards some aspect of sexuality. The interpretative weight thus placed upon a single document is often very great. So we should not expect to find the methods of new historicism greatly valued or admired by historians. It is, on the contrary, a way of 'doing' history which has a strong appeal for non-historians.

Advantages and disadvantages of new historicism

However, the appeal of new historicism is undoubtedly great, for a variety of reasons. *Firstly*, although it is founded upon post-structuralist thinking, it is written in a far more accessible way, for the most part avoiding post-structuralism's characteristically dense style and vocabulary. It presents its data and draws its conclusions, and if it is sometimes easy to challenge the way the data is interpreted, this is partly because (as in the case of Freud's theories) the empirical foundation on which the interpretation rests is made openly available for scrutiny. *Secondly*, the material itself is often fascinating and is wholly distinctive in the context of literary studies. These essays look and feel different from those produced by any other critical approach and immediately give the literary student the feeling that new territory is being entered. Particularly, the 'uncluttered', 'pared-down' feel of the essays, which results from not citing previous discussions of the literary work, gives them a stark and dramatic air. *Thirdly*, the political edge of new historicist writing is always sharp, but at the same time it avoids the problems frequently encountered in 'straight' Marxist criticism: it seems less overtly polemical and more willing to allow the historical evidence its own voice.

STOP and THINK

'Doing' new historicism essentially involves the juxtaposition of literary material with contemporary non-literary texts. But how would you attempt to set about doing this yourself, rather than just reading published essays which use this formula?

For instance, if you wished to use the new historicist method for an essay about, say, a Shakespeare comedy where would you look for suitable historical material? Then, having found the material, what would be the format of the essay itself?

I wouldn't want to gloss over the difficulties involved, but here is a suggestion: Shakespeare's comedies are 'domestic' in theme, and concern sexual mores, courtship, relations between men and women, and inter-generational conflict. Hence, we would be looking for material on social and family history.

A well-known relevant book would be Lawrence Stone's *The Family, Sex, and Marriage in England, 1500–1800* (Penguin, 1979). Chapter five, 'The Reinforcement of Patriarchy', has useful material, such as Section three, 'Husband and Wife', sub-sectioned into 'The Subordination of Wives' and 'The Education of Women'. Chapters seven and eight are on 'Marriage and Courtship', and Part five is on 'Sex'.

Less well-known, but containing data similar to that used by the major new historicists, is Roger Thompson, *Sex in Middlesex: Popular Mores in a Massachusetts County, 1649–1699* (University of Massachusetts Press, 1986). See Section one, 'Adolescent Mores' and Section two, 'Married Mores'.

Published historical data and social history of this kind should provide an accessible source of 'co-texts' for the new historical approach. Without by-passing the problems associated with the method, you would in this way at least be able to gain 'hands-on' experience of new historicism as a practical approach to criticism.

What new historicists do

1. They juxtapose literary and non–literary texts, reading the former in the light of the latter.

2.   They try thereby to 'defamiliarise' the canonical literary text, detaching it from the accumulated weight of previous literary scholarship and seeing it as if new.

3.   They focus attention (within both text and co-text) on issues of state power and how it is maintained, on patriarchal structures and their perpetuation, and on the process of colonisation, with its accompanying 'mind-set'.

4.   They make use, in doing so, of aspects of the post-structuralist outlook, especially Derrida's notion that every facet of reality is textualised, and Foucault's idea of social structures as determined by dominant 'discursive practices'.

New historicism: an example

As an example of new historicism in practice let us take a closer look at an essay, not by Greenblatt, but by Louis Montrose. His essay 'A Midsummer Night's Dream and the Shaping Fantasies of Elizabethan Culture: Gender, Power, Form' appeared originally in the American journal *Representations*, the 'house magazine' of the new historicism, and is reprinted in Wilson and Dutton. Montrose's famous definition of new historicism is that it centres upon the historicity of the text and the textuality of history, and the essay might be seen as an embodiment of that pronouncement. His overall thesis is that the play 'creates the culture by which it is created, shapes the fantasies by which it is shaped' (p. 130). Thus, the cult of the Virgin Queen is both fostered by literature like Spenser's *The Faerie Queene* and a whole range of court masks and pageants, and at the same time generates such literature: life and literature stimulate and play upon each other. Elizabeth can project herself as the Queen whose virginity has mystical and magical potency because such images are given currency in court masques, in comedies, and in pastoral epic poetry. Conversely, the figure of Elizabeth stimulates the production and promotion of such work and imagery. Hence, in this sense, history is textualised and texts are historicised. A simple modern parallel would be the way images of masculinity and femininity in film pervade our lives and offer us ways of representing ourselves: they give us 'role models' which we can become trapped inside, so that real life mimics the filmic representation of life.

Montrose's essay also represents the eclecticism of new historicism, for it draws upon psychoanalysis, especially Freudian dream analysis, and feminism. It opens with an account of Simon Forman's dream, already mentioned, in which Forman describes an erotic encounter with the Queen, then an elderly woman: the dream turns on the pun of 'wait upon' the Queen and 'weight upon her'. Her dress is trailing in the mud and he offers to solve the problem by causing her belly to lift ('I mean to wait upon you not under you'). In the dream Forman has just saved the Queen from being pestered by 'a weaver, a tall man with a reddish beard', and Montrose interprets this as an Oedipal triangle. He links this to the Queen's projection of herself as mother of the nation, but also as a virgin who is openly flirtatious and provocative – Montrose quotes the French ambassador's accounts of her extremely revealing style of dress ('She kept the front of her dress open, and one could see the whole of her bosom' ... p. 111). He then relates all this to the tensions generated by the peculiar situation that a highly patriarchal society in which all power was vested in men was nevertheless ruled by a woman who therefore had absolute powers of life over all her subjects, men and women, and the power to advance or end the careers of her male courtiers. In Shakespeare's play, there are several instances of a queen who is 'mastered', and thereby feminised – Hippolyta, the Amazonian queen, has been defeated by Theseus, whom she must now submit to and marry: Titania, queen of the fairies, has defied her husband Oberon in her attachment to the changeling boy and hence is humiliated by him in having Puck administer the magic potion which makes her fall in love with the first being she sees on waking. Throughout the play, there is much about the rights of fathers over daughters and husbands over wives, and the precondition of male desire is female subjection. The 'happy' ending depends upon the reinforcement of patriarchy:

> The festive conclusion of *A Midsummer Night's Dream*, its celebration of romantic and generative heterosexual union, depends upon the success of a process whereby the female pride and power manifested in misanthropic warriors, possessive mothers, unruly wives, and wilful daughters are brought under the control of husbands and lords. (p. 120)

Hence, it is suggested, the play might be seen as implicitly trea-
sonous, since:

> When a virgin ruler is ostensibly the virgin mother of her subjects,
> then the themes of male procreative power, autogeny, and mastery of
> women acquire a seditious resonance. In royal pageantry, the queen
> is always the cynosure; her virginity is the source of magical potency.
> In *A Midsummer Night's Dream*, however, such magical powers are
> invested in the king. (p. 127)

Hence, 'Shakespeare's comedy symbolically neutralises the royal
power to which it ostensibly pays homage' (p. 127). In practice, patriarchy is maintained in spite of the presence of a woman at the
pinnacle of power, by constantly insisting on Elizabeth's difference
from other women. This is a familiar strategy even today, for having
a female leader did not lead the Tory Party to revise its ideas about
the role of women in society – on the contrary, under the rule of the
'iron lady' (an interesting locution in this context) reactionary ideas
were reinforced and strengthened. Thus, 'Elizabeth's rule was not
intended to undermine the male hegemony of her culture. Indeed,
the emphasis upon her difference from other women may have
helped to reinforce it' (p. 124). If the pageants and the encomiums
constantly proclaimed her simultaneously 'Maiden, Matron and
Mother' then she becomes, not a real woman, but a religious mystery.
Throughout the essay, then, the account of the play entwines it with
male attempts to come to terms with the simultaneous existence of
a female monarch and a rigorous patriarchal structure. For male
courtiers, there might seem to be a certain 'unmanning' involved in
being chaste servants of the Virgin Queen, while those who sought
advancement from her seemed like children seeking the favours of
the nation's mother. (Montrose describes an extravagant and protracted entertainment in which Raleigh and Greville acted out this
metaphor.) All this demonstrates what is meant in practice by insisting upon the historicity of the text and the textuality of history.

Cultural materialism

The British critic Graham Holderness describes cultural materialism as 'a politicised form of historiography'. We can explain this

as meaning the study of historical material (which includes literary texts) within a politicised framework, this framework including the present which those literary texts have in some way helped to shape. The term 'cultural materialism' was made current in 1985 when it was used by Jonathan Dollimore and Alan Sinfield (the best-known of the cultural materialists) as the subtitle of their edited collection of essays *Political Shakespeare*. They define the term in a foreword as designating a critical method which has four characteristics: it combines an attention to:

1. historical context,
2. theoretical method,
3. political commitment, and
4. textual analysis.

To comment briefly on each of these: *firstly*, the emphasis on *historical context* 'undermines the transcendent significance traditionally accorded to the literary text'. Here the word 'transcendent' roughly means 'timeless'. The position taken, of course, needs to face the obvious objection that if we are today still studying and reading Shakespeare then his plays have indeed proved themselves 'timeless' in the simple sense that they are clearly not limited by the historical circumstances in which they were produced. But this is a matter of degree: the aim of this aspect of cultural materialism is to allow the literary text to 'recover its histories' which previous kinds of study have often ignored. The kind of history recovered would involve relating the plays to such phenomena as 'enclosures and the oppression of the rural poor, state power and resistance to it ... witchcraft, the challenge and containment of the carnivalesque' (Dollimore and Sinfield, p. 3). *Secondly*, the emphasis on *theoretical method* signifies a break with liberal humanism and absorbing the lessons of structuralism, post-structuralism, and other approaches which have become prominent since the 1970s. *Thirdly*, the emphasis on *political commitment* signifies the influence of Marxist and feminist perspectives and breaks from the conservative-Christian framework which hitherto dominated Shakespeare criticism. *Finally*, the stress on *textual analysis* 'locates the critique of traditional approaches where it cannot be ignored'. In other words, there is a commitment not just to making theory of an abstract kind, but to practising it on (mainly) canonical texts which continue to be the focus of massive amounts of academic and professional attention, and which are prominent national and cultural icons.

The two words in the term 'cultural materialism' are further defined: 'culture' will include *all* forms of culture ('forms like television and popular music and fiction'). That is, this approach does not limit itself to 'high' cultural forms like the Shakespeare play. 'Materialism' signifies the opposite of 'idealism': an 'idealist' belief would be that high culture represents the free and independent play of the talented individual mind; the contrary 'materialist' belief is that culture cannot 'transcend the material forces and relations of production. Culture is not simply a reflection of the economic and political system, but nor can it be independent of it.' These comments on materialism represent the standard beliefs of Marxist criticism, and they do perhaps point to the difficulty of making a useful distinction between a 'straight' Marxist criticism and cultural materialism. However, it is added that the relevant history is not just that of four hundred years ago, but that of the times (including our own) in which Shakespeare is produced and reproduced. Thus, in cultural materialism there is an emphasis on the functioning of the institutions through which Shakespeare is now brought to us – the Royal Shakespeare Company, the film industry, the publishers who produce textbooks for school and college, and the National Curriculum, which lays down the requirement that specific Shakespeare plays be studied by all school pupils.

Cultural materialism takes a good deal of its outlook (and its name) from the British left-wing critic Raymond Williams. Instead of Foucault's notion of 'discourse', Williams invented the term 'structures of feeling': these are concerned with 'meanings and values as they are lived and felt'. Structures of feeling are often antagonistic both to explicit systems of values and beliefs, and to the dominant ideologies within a society. They are characteristically found in literature, and they *oppose* the status quo (as the values in Dickens, the Brontës, etc., represent human structures of feeling which are at variance with Victorian commercial and materialist values). The result is that cultural materialism is much more optimistic about the possibility of change and is willing at times to see literature as a source of oppositional values. Cultural materialism particularly involves using the past to 'read' the present, revealing the politics of our own society by what we choose to emphasise or suppress of the past. A great deal of the British work has been about undermining what it sees as the fetishistic role of Shakespeare as a conservative icon within British culture. This form of cultural materialism can be conveniently sampled in three 'New Accents' books: *The Shakespeare Myth* by Graham Holderness; *Alternative Shakespeares*, edited by John Drakakis; and *That Shakespeherian Rag* by Terence Hawkes. (This quaint title is derived from an allusion by T. S. Eliot in *The Waste Land*.) A correspondence in response to a review of the first of these in 1988 ran for over a year in the *London Review of Books*, under the heading 'Bardolatry'.

How is cultural materialism different from new historicism?

Cultural materialism is often linked in discussion with new historicism, its American counterpart. Though the two movements belong to the same family, there is an ongoing family quarrel between them. *Political Shakespeare* includes new historicist essays, and the introduction explains some of the differences between the two movements.

Firstly, in a neat distinction Dollimore and Sinfield quote Marx to the effect that 'men and women make their own history but not in conditions of their own choosing' (p. 3): cultural materialists, they say, tend to concentrate on the interventions whereby men and women make their own history, whereas new historicists tend to focus on the less than ideal circumstances in which they do so, that is, on the 'power of social and ideological structures' which restrain them. The result is a contrast between political optimism and political pessimism.

Secondly, cultural materialists see new historicists as cutting themselves off from effective political positions by their acceptance of a particular version of post-structuralism, with its radical scepticism about the possibility of attaining secure knowledge. The rise of post-structuralism problematises knowledge, language, truth, etc., and this perspective is absorbed into new historicism and becomes an important part of it. The new historicist defence against this charge would be that being aware of the in-built uncertainty of all knowledge doesn't mean that we give up trying to establish truths, it simply means that we do so conscious of the dangers and limitations involved, thus giving their own intellectual enquiries a special authority. This is rather like sailing into dangerous waters knowingly, with all sensible precautions taken, rather than blithely unaware of the dangers and with all lights blazing. Thus, when new historicists claim (in Peter Widdowson's words) that Foucault gives them entry into 'a non-truth-oriented form of historicist study of texts' (p. 161), this doesn't mean that they do not believe that what they say is true, but rather that they know the risks and dangers involved in claiming to establish truths.

A third important difference between new historicism and cultural materialism is that where the former's co-texts are documents contemporary with Shakespeare, the latter's may be programme notes for a current Royal Shakespeare Company production, quotations of Shakespeare by a pilot in the Gulf War of 1990–91, or pronouncements on education by a government minister. To put this another way: the new historicist situates the literary text in the political situation of its own day, while the cultural materialist situates it within that of ours. This is really to restate the difference in political emphasis between the two approaches. Indeed, it could be said that all three of the differences just described have this political difference as their common denominator.

STOP and THINK

The fact that we have spent time spelling out the differences between cultural materialism and new historicism indicates that there is a considerable overlap between them. Are they just two national varieties of essentially the same thing, or are the radical differences (emphasised especially by the British cultural materialists) as deep as is claimed?

Perhaps the question can only be properly answered by reading and comparing essays of each type. Allegedly, the differences lie mainly in two aspects: firstly, in political outlook, and secondly, in the degree of emphasis on the post-structuralist perspective.

In thinking about the question, start by comparing the attitudes evident in the examples of each included in this book, in so far as you are able to judge from the brief accounts given. Then read and compare two further pieces (drawing on the reading suggested at the end of this section).

Of course, the differences between these two approaches are partly the result of their different intellectual frameworks. New historicism was much influenced by Foucault, who sees 'discursive practices' as frequently a reinforcement of dominant ideology. Cultural materialism, on the other hand, owes much to Raymond Williams, who sees 'structures of feeling' as containing the seeds from which grows resistance to the dominant ideology. A sceptic about both approaches suggested that it must be hard for the new historicists to explain how the English Civil War ever got started (since they seem to envisage a pervasive state power which would make resistance virtually impossible) while for the cultural materialists it must be difficult to explain how it ever ended (since their 'structures of feeling' constantly throw up new ideas which would seem to make stasis impossible). In practice, however, the frequently evoked political difference between the two approaches is surely less uniform and predictable than such stark dichotomies would imply.

What cultural materialist critics do

1. They read the literary text (very often a Renaissance play) in such a way as to enable us to 'recover its histories', that is, the context of exploitation from which it emerged.

2. At the same time, they foreground those elements in the work's present transmission and contextualising which caused those histories to be lost in the first place (for example, the 'heritage' industry's packaging of Shakespeare in terms of history-as-pageant, national bard, cultural icon, and so on).

3. They use a combination of Marxist and feminist approaches to the text, especially in order to do the first of these (above), and in order to fracture the previous dominance of conservative

social, political, and religious assumptions in Shakespeare criticism in particular.

4. They use the technique of close textual analysis, but often em-
    ploy structuralist and post-structuralist techniques, especially
    to mark a break with the inherited tradition of close textual
    analysis within the framework of conservative cultural and so-
    cial assumptions.

5. At the same time, they work mainly within traditional notions
    of the canon, on the grounds that writing about more obscure
    texts hardly ever constitutes an effective political intervention
    (for instance, in debates about the school curriculum or na-
    tional identity).

Cultural materialism: an example

An example of an informal variant of this approach is Terence
Hawkes's essay 'Telmah' (in his book *That Shakespeherian Rag*).
This is the fourth piece in the book, each one being centred on the
work of one of the major Shakespearian critics of the early part of
the century, within an overall strategy of looking at how Shakespeare
is mediated and processed to us. In this chapter the critic is John
Dover Wilson, best known for his 1930s book *What Happens in
Hamlet?* The opening section considers aspects of *Hamlet*, emphasising cyclical and symmetrical elements of the play, such as how
the beginning echoes the end, how the same situation occurs several
times in it (like the several father-son parallels) and considering how
indefinite the start and end of any performance are, since the play
is already culturally situated in some way in people's minds before
they see it. A repeated motif of looking backwards in the play (to a
past which was better than the present) leads Hawkes to imagine a
'reversed' *Hamlet* which shadows the actual play, the 'Telmah' of
his title.

The second section is entitled 'To the Sunderland Station', allud-
ing to the title of a well-known history of the Russian Revolution
called *To the Finland Station*. An account is given of John Dover
Wilson on the train to Sunderland in 1917, sent by the government
to sort out labour problems in a munitions factory, and reading
W. W. Greg's article on *Hamlet* which argues that the king's failure

to react openly to the dumb show indicates that he is a figure of some complexity, not just a story-book villain. If he is this then he begins to claim some of our attention, and distract us from the exclusive focus on Hamlet himself which had been the traditional way of responding to the play, at least from the time of the Romantics. Wilson's excited outrage at this notion is related to a fanatical desire for order manifested in his published writings about Russia, which see it as a picturesque 'organic' feudal state, which, in turn, looks like a version of the England which his social class regards with nostalgia and fears might be lost. Dover Wilson's rushing to the defence of Hamlet, the threatened cultural icon, in his reply to Greg, and later in his *Hamlet* book, are seen as symptomatic of this too. Shortly after the First World War Wilson was a member of the Newbolt Committee which reported on the teaching of English, and saw it as providing a form of social cohesion which might save the country from the fate which overtook Russia. Hawkes also quotes a letter from Neville Chamberlain praising *What Happens in Hamlet?*, and thus creates a pattern of appeasing and containing difference. Hence, a way of interpreting the play is placed among several co-texts from twentieth-century life, and thus the play itself is culturally transformed. Hawkes's final reading of the end of the play involves inserting an extra stage direction, and his model for a criticism of this kind is that of the jazz musician who doesn't transmit a received text, but *trans*forms what he *per*forms. That might be taken as the characteristic feature of this variant of cultural materialist criticism.

It is difficult to know how to 'place' writing of this kind. It is lively and interesting, personal and engaged in tone, and most of the formalities of academic writing are dispensed with. Openings are dramatic, transitions abrupt: suspense is maintained by holding back key details about identity or situation till the moment of maximum impact. The structure is a series of seemingly unrelated incidents or situations which turn out to be intimately intertwined. All these features are novelistic, and there is clearly a sense in which this is 'creative writing' which would not accept any absolute distinction between literature and criticism. As in new historicism, literature and history are intertwined, but the perspective and the historicising are much more those of our own day than would be the case with new historicism itself.

Selected reading

Chase, Cynthia, ed., *Romanticism* (Longman Critical Readers, 1993).

Contains three examples of new historicist approaches to the period, namely, the chapters by Karen Swann on Coleridge's *Christabel*, by Marjorie Levinson on Keats, and by Jerome Christensen on Byron's *Sardanapalus*.

Dollimore, Jonathan, and Sinfield, Alan, eds, *Political Shakespeare: New Essays in Cultural Materialism* (Manchester University Press, 2nd edn, 1994).

The introduction gives a useful account of new historicism and explains how it differs from cultural materialism. The book reprints Greenblatt's essay 'Invisible Bullets'.

Drakakis, John, ed., *Alternative Shakespeares* (rev. edn, Routledge, 2002).

The term 'cultural materialism' is not used of these essays, but they are generally representative of this approach; they seek 'to accelerate the break with established canons of Shakespeare criticism', exemplifying 'explorations of the ways in which historically specific readings are generated'.

Gallagher, Catherine, and Greenblatt, Stephen, *Practicing the New Historicism* (University of Chicago Press, 2000).

'In lucid and jargon-free prose, Catherine Gallagher and Stephen Greenblatt focus on five central aspects of new historicism: recurrent use of anecdotes, preoccupation with the nature of representations, fascination with the history of the body, sharp focus on neglected details, and skeptical analysis of ideology.' (Publisher's blurb.)

Grady, Hugh, *The Modernist Shakespeare* (Oxford University Press, new edn, 1994).

Pages 225–35 are on the new historicism. An excellent book, always sharp and readable. Chapter four on Tillyard (the 'old historicism') is very useful. Chapter five discusses the application of contemporary critical trends to Shakespeare.

Greenblatt, Stephen, *Shakespearian Negotiations: The Circulation of Social Energy in Renaissance England* (California University Press, 1991).

The essay 'Fiction and Friction', on cross-dressing in Shakespearian comedies, is a good starting point on new historicism. The essay 'Invisible Bullets' is the best-known piece in the book.

Hawkes, Terence, *That Shakespeherian Rag* (Methuen, 1986).

Examples of cultural materialism in practice. The whole book is a lively read which makes some startling juxtapositions of Shakespeare and the circumstances in which we encounter him.

Holderness, Graham, *The Shakespeare Myth* (Manchester University Press, 1988).

Studies of the 'culturally-produced and historically-determined Shakespeare myth', along with 'interviews with prominent mediators of Shakespeare in education, theatre, the press, and television'.

Levinson, Marjorie, ed., *Rethinking Historicism: Critical Readings in Romantic History* (Wiley-Blackwell, 1989).

New historicism applied to Romanticism.

Sinfield, Alan, *Shakespeare, Authority, Sexuality: Unfinished Business in Cultural Materialism* (Routledge, 'Accents on Shakespeare' series, 2006).

See especially chapters 1 and 11 ('Unfinished Business: Problems in Cultural Materialism' and 'Unfinished Business II') in this exciting book by one of the pioneers of cultural materialism.

Veeser, H. Aram, ed., *The New Historicism* (Routledge, 1989).

A useful and valuable source.

Veeser, H. Aram, *The New Historicism Reader* (Routledge, 1994).

Covers a range of British and American literature, not just the Renaissance.

Wilson, Richard, and Dutton, Richard, eds, *New Historicism and Renaissance Drama* (Routledge, 1992).

A useful collection of key articles, well introduced.

10

Postcolonial criticism

Background

Postcolonial criticism emerged as a distinct category only in the 1990s. It is not mentioned, for instance, in the first edition of Selden's *A Reader's Guide to Contemporary Literary Theory* (1985) or Jeremy Hawthorn's *A Concise Glossary of Contemporary Literary Theory* (1992). It gained currency through the influence of such books as *In Other Worlds* (Gayatri Spivak, 1987); *The Empire Writes Back* (Bill Ashcroft, 1989); *Nation and Narration* (Homi Bhabha, 1990) and *Culture and Imperialism* (Edward Said, 1993). An important collection of relevant essays (though it does not use the term 'postcolonialism') is *'Race', Writing and Difference* (1986), reprinted from two issues of the journal *Critical Inquiry* and edited by Henry Louis Gates, Jr, one of the best-known American figures in this field.

One significant effect of postcolonial criticism is to further undermine the universalist claims once made on behalf of literature by liberal humanist critics. If we claim that great literature has a timeless and universal significance we thereby demote or disregard cultural, social, regional, and national differences in experience and outlook, preferring instead to judge all literature by a single, supposedly 'universal', standard. Thus, for instance, a routine claim about the 'Wessex' setting of Hardy's novels is that it is really a canvas on which Hardy depicts and examines fundamental, universal aspects of the human condition. Thus, Hardy's books are not thought of as primarily regional or historical or masculine or white or working-class novels – they are just novels, and built into this attitude is the assumption that this way of writing and representing reality is the unquestioned norm, so that the situations depicted can stand for all possible forms of human interaction. This universalism is rejected by postcolonial criticism; whenever a universal signification is claimed for a work, then, white, Eurocentric norms and practices are being promoted by a sleight of hand to this elevated status, and all others correspondingly relegated to subsidiary, marginalised roles.

The ancestry of postcolonial criticism can be traced to Frantz Fanon's *The Wretched of the Earth*, published in French in 1961, and voicing what might be called 'cultural resistance' to France's African empire. Fanon (a psychiatrist from Martinique) argued that the first step for 'colonialised' people in finding a voice and an identity is to reclaim their own past. For centuries the European colonising power will have devalued the nation's past, seeing its precolonial era as a pre-civilised limbo, or even as a historical void. Children, both black and white, will have been taught to see history, culture and progress as beginning with the arrival of the Europeans. If the first step towards a postcolonial perspective is to reclaim one's own past, then the second is to begin to erode the colonialist ideology by which that past had been devalued.

Hence, another major book, which can be said to inaugurate postcolonial criticism proper, is Edward Said's *Orientalism* (1978), which is a specific exposé of the Eurocentric universalism which takes for granted both the superiority of what is European or Western, and the inferiority of what is not. Said identifies a European cultural tradition of 'Orientalism', which is a particular and long-standing way of identifying the East as 'Other' and inferior to the West. The Orient, he says, features in the Western mind 'as a sort of surrogate and even underground self' (*Literature in the Modern World*, ed. Dennis Walder, p. 236). This means, in effect, that the East becomes the repository or projection of those aspects of themselves which Westerners do not choose to acknowledge (cruelty, sensuality, decadence, laziness, and so on). At the same time, and paradoxically, the East is seen as a fascinating realm of the exotic, the mystical and the seductive. It also tends to be seen as homogeneous, the people there being anonymous masses rather than individuals, their actions determined by instinctive emotions (lust, terror, fury, etc.) rather than by conscious choices or decisions. Their emotions and reactions are always determined by racial considerations (they are like this because they are asiatics or blacks or orientals) rather than by aspects of individual status or circumstance (for instance, because they happen to be a sister, or an uncle, or a collector of antique pottery). As Said says, after quoting the example of a colonial administrator's 1907 account of life in Damascus, 'In such statements as these we note immediately that "the Arab" or "Arabs" have an aura of apartness, definiteness, and *collective self-consistency* [my italics] such as to wipe out any traces of individual Arabs with narratable life Histories'.

Postcolonial reading

Reading literature with the perspective of 'Orientalism' in mind would make us, for instance, critically aware of how Yeats in his two 'Byzantium' poems ('Sailing to Byzantium', 1927, and 'Byzantium', 1932) provides an image of Istanbul, the Eastern capital of the former Roman Empire, which is identified with torpor, sensuality, and exotic mysticism. At such moments Yeats adopts an ethnocentric or Eurocentric perspective, seeing the East as an exotic 'Other' which becomes the contrasting foil to his own pursuits and concerns, all of which the poem presents as normative. Interestingly, Edward Said has written an essay on Yeats which reads him in the context of postcolonialism (reprinted in Said's *Culture and Imperialism*). Said views the desire, frequently expressed in Yeats's work, to regain contact with an earlier, mythical, nationalistic Ireland as typical of writers whose own position is postcolonial, and this is closely related to Fanon's idea of the need to reclaim the past. Characteristically, postcolonial writers evoke or create a precolonial version of their own nation, rejecting the modern and the contemporary, which is tainted with the colonial status of their countries. Here, then, is the first characteristic of postcolonial criticism – an awareness of representations of the non-European as exotic or immoral 'Other'.

For Yeats, as often with the postcolonial writer, an uneasy attitude to the colonial language is evident: his injunction to Irish poets, that they should learn their craft, implies the need to serve a humble apprenticeship. This 'humble' attitude to language may remind us

of Stephen Dedalus's thoughts about the English language in James
Joyce's *A Portrait of the Artist as a Young Man* (published in serial
form in 1914–1915), especially the early scene in which Stephen
is patronised by an English priest because of his use of a local di-
alect word. Stephen tells himself 'the language in which we are
speaking is his before it is mine ... My soul frets in the shadow of
his language' (*Portrait*, chapter five). More recently, the Irish poet
Seamus Heaney, in a poem entitled 'The Ministry of Fear', recalled
his childhood unease and self-consciousness about his pronunciation of English ('Those hobnailed boots from beyond the mountain
/ Were walking, by God, all over the fine / Lawns of elocution')
and remarks that 'Ulster was British, but with no rights on / The
English lyric' (see the collection *North*, 1975). This linguistic def-
erence amounts to a sense that the linguistic furniture belongs to
somebody else, and therefore shouldn't be moved around without
permission. Some postcolonial writers have concluded that the
colonisers' language is permanently tainted, and that to write in
it involves a crucial acquiescence in colonial structures. Language
itself, then, is a second area of concern in postcolonial criticism.
(For an essay on poetic language from this postcolonial perspective
see Stan Smith's 'Darkening English: Post-imperial contestations
in the language of Seamus Heaney and Derek Walcott', *English*,
Spring 1994.)

As this implies, Yeats, being a member of the Protestant ruling
class in Ireland, has a double identity as both coloniser and colonised, and it is the recognition of such double identities which is
one of the strengths of the postcolonialist view. Thus, the Nigerian
novelist Chinua Achebe, publishing his first novel, *Things Fall Apart*,
in 1958, was criticised by an early reviewer for affecting to identify
with African villagers when actually his university education and
his broadcasting job in the capital city of Lagos should make him
identify, it was implied, with the values of 'civilisation', supposedly
brought to Africa by Europeans. (See Achebe's paper 'Colonialist
Criticism', in *Literature in the Modern World*, ed. Walder.) This emphasis on identity as doubled, or hybrid, or unstable is a third characteristic of the postcolonial approach.

At one level Achebe's use of a village Africa corresponds to
Yeats's evocation of a precolonial, mythological Ireland of heroes

and heroines. At another level, the double or hybrid identity is precisely what the postcolonial situation brings into being. The shift in attitudes in the 1980s and 1990s was towards postcolonial writers seeing themselves as using primarily African or Asian forms, supplemented with European-derived influences, rather than as working primarily within European genres like the novel and merely adding to them a degree of exotic Africanisation. All postcolonial literatures, it might be said, seem to make this transition. They begin with an unquestioning acceptance of the authority of European models (especially in the novel) and with the ambition of writing works that will be masterpieces entirely in this tradition. This can be called the '*Adopt*' phase of colonial literature, since the writer's ambition is to adopt the form as it stands, the assumption being that it has universal validity. The second stage can be called the '*Adapt*' phase, since it aims to adapt the European form to African subject matter, thus assuming partial rights of intervention in the genre. In the final phase there is, so to speak, a declaration of cultural independence whereby African writers remake the form to their own specification, without reference to European norms. This might be called the '*Adept*' phase, since its characteristic is the assumption that the colonial writer is an independent 'adept' in the form, not a humble apprentice, as in the first phase, or a mere licensee, as in the second. This stress on 'cross-cultural' interactions is a fourth characteristic of postcolonialist criticism.

This notion of the double, or divided, or fluid identity which is characteristic of the postcolonial writer explains the great attraction which post-structuralism and deconstruction have proved to be for the postcolonial critic. Post-structuralism is centrally concerned to show the fluid and unstable nature of personal and gender identity, the shifting, 'polyvalent', contradictory currents of signification within texts, and the way literature itself is a site on which ideological struggles are acted out. This mind-set is admirably suited to expressing the numerous contradictions and multiple allegiances of which the postcolonial writer and critic is constantly aware. This post-structuralist perspective is seen in the work of such representative figures as Henry Louis Gates Jr, Gayatri Spivak, and Homi Bhabha. In all three of these a complex Derridean–Foucauldian notion of textuality and fields of discourse is immediately apparent.

Similarly in all three, the surface of the writing is difficult and the route through to any consequent political action (or stance, even) is necessarily indirect. This kind of postcolonial criticism roughly corresponds, then, to the theoreticised 'French' feminist criticism associated with figures like Julia Kristeva or Hélène Cixous. The example of postcolonial criticism offered later is from the work of Edward Said, who is less overtly theoretical, seems to accept some of the premises of liberal humanism, and has a more 'up-front' political affiliation (his identification with the Palestinian Arab cause). His work is in this regard reminiscent of the 'Anglo-American' variety of feminist criticism, which likewise seems (to me) more overtly political and certainly more immediately accessible.

If the three stages mentioned earlier (Adopt, Adapt, and Adept) provide a way of seeing postcolonial literature, then a way of seeing the stages of postcolonial criticism would be to suggest, as we have just been doing, that they closely parallel the developmental stages of feminist criticism. In its earliest phase, which is to say before it was known as such, postcolonial criticism took as its main subject matter white representations of colonial countries and criticised these for their limitations and their bias: thus, critics would discuss the representation of Africa in Joseph Conrad's *Heart of Darkness*, or of India in E. M. Forster's *A Passage to India*, or of Algeria in Albert Camus's *The Outsider*. This corresponds to the early 1970s phase of feminist criticism when the subject matter was the representation of women by male novelists like D. H. Lawrence or Henry Miller – the classic instance is Kate Millett's *Sexual Politics*. The *second* phase of postcolonial criticism involved a turn towards explorations of themselves and their society by postcolonial writers. At this stage the celebration and exploration of diversity, hybridity, and difference become central. This is the stage when, in the title of the well-known pioneering work in this field, 'the empire writes back'. This corresponds to the 'gynotext' phase of feminist criticism, when there is a turn towards the exploration of female experience and identities in books by women. The analogy between these two types of criticism might be pushed a little further, so that a parallel might also be perceived with the split in feminist criticism between 'theoretical' and 'empirical' versions, as suggested above. Thus, in postcolonial criticism we might see a split between variants very directly influenced by deconstruction and post-structuralism – such as the work of Homi Bhabha – and work like Said's which accepts a good deal from liberal humanism, is written in a more accessible way, and seems perhaps to lend itself more directly to political engagement.

STOP and THINK

Postcolonial criticism draws attention to issues of cultural difference in literary texts and is one of several critical approaches we have considered which focus on specific issues, including issues of gender (feminist criticism), of class (Marxist criticism), and of sexual orientation (queer theory).

This raises the possibility of a kind of 'super-reader' able to respond equally and adequately to a text in all these ways. In practice, for most readers one of these issues tends to eclipse all the rest.

For instance, the example of feminist criticism, from Gilbert and Gubar's *The Madwoman in the Attic* (Chapter 6), doesn't comment on aspects of *Wuthering Heights* which would interest postcolonial critics, such as Heathcliff's being described by Emily Brontë in terms of a racial 'Other' (a gipsy, 'a little Lascar, or an American or Spanish castaway'). He is described by Gilbert and Gubar as Catherine's 'alter-ego or Id', and contrasted in his darkness with the blond Edgar who presides over the Grange, which is presented, however ironically, as 'heaven', 'society', and 'reason'. This is a conflating of racial Otherness with the irrational forces of the id or the subconscious which might be thought insensitive.

Should we, in general, try to become super-readers, with multiple layers of sympathy and awareness, or will trying to do so merely produce blandness and superficiality?

Obviously, it is impossible for anybody to answer this question for anybody else. My own feeling is that while an even spread of awareness across all these issues is theoretically possible, in practice *aiming* for this, merely in the interests of political correctness, is almost bound to produce superficiality. A genuine interest in one of these issues can really only arise from aspects of your own circumstances. These perspectives cannot be put on and off like a suit – they have to emerge and declare themselves with some urgency.

What postcolonial critics do

1. They reject the claims to universalism made on behalf of canonical Western literature and seek to show its limitations of outlook, especially its general inability to empathise across boundaries of cultural and ethnic difference.

2. They examine the representation of other cultures in literature as a way of achieving this end.

3. They show how such literature is often evasively and crucially silent on matters concerned with colonisation and imperialism (see, for instance, the discussion of Jane Austen's *Mansfield Park* in the example described below).

4. They foreground questions of cultural difference and diversity and examine their treatment in relevant literary works.

5. They celebrate hybridity and 'cultural polyvalency', that is, the situation whereby individuals and groups belong simultaneously to more than one culture (for instance, that of the coloniser, through a colonial school system, and that of the colonised, through local and oral traditions).

6. They develop a perspective, not just applicable to postcolonial literatures, whereby states of marginality, plurality and perceived 'Otherness' are seen as sources of energy and potential change.

Postcolonial criticism: an example

Let us take the essay by Edward Said on Jane Austen's *Mansfield Park*, an essay which has achieved something of a definitive status and is available in Mulhern's *Contemporary Marxist Criticism*, in Newton's *Theory into Practice*, in Eagleton's *Raymond Williams: Critical Perspectives* and in Said's own *Culture and Imperialism*. Under the title 'Jane Austen and the Empire' Said carefully 'foregrounds the background' of Austen's novel, which is the estate in Antigua which Sir Thomas Bertram owns, and through which the estate of

Mansfield Park is maintained. The central irony, then, is that the estate in England which represents an ideal of order and civilisation is sustained by another estate a world away, so that Mansfield Park would 'not have been possible without the slave trade, sugar, and the colonial planter class' (Mulhern, p. 111), for as Said remarks, 'Sir Thomas's property in the Caribbean would have had to be a sugar plantation maintained by slave labour (not abolished until the 1830s)' (p. 106). Said thus makes central the 'moral geography' of the novel, and sees Austen as the start of a line in fiction which leads to Conrad and Kipling in which the processes of colonialisation are examined. As Mulhern puts it in his introductory note, the consequence is that the 'dating of British culture's imperial phase must be revised back-wards from the beginning of formal Empire into the eighteenth century' (p. 97). Thus, Sir Thomas, returning home and rapidly re-establishing order, without ever the thought that his views and instincts could be narrow or mistaken, is the quintessential colonialising figure who takes himself as the norm of civilisation. He is, says Said, 'a Crusoe setting things in order'. Nothing prevents our assuming, he says, that he 'does exactly the same things – on a larger scale – in Antigua ... to hold and rule Mansfield Park is to hold and rule an imperial estate in association with it' (p. 104).

This reading involves 'concretising' a dimension of the novel which is largely left implicit: it involves, not necessarily arguing that all these things are 'there' in the novel, but that this is the right way to read it. All the same, Said insists, precisely, that these things *are* there: 'all these things having to do with the outside brought in, seem to me unmistakably *there* in the suggestiveness of her allusive and abstract language'. So Said invokes the processes of close reading in his support, for the most part convincingly, but in the end his appeal seems to be to the *conscience* of the (especially) white and middle-class reader:

> We cannot easily say that since *Mansfield Park* is a novel, its affiliations with a particularly sordid history are irrelevant or transcended, not only because it is irresponsible to say that, but because we know too much to say so without bad faith. (p. 112)

There is, I think, no doubt about the effect of reading Said's essay. Any 'innocence' we might have had about this aspect of the novel goes: it is impossible henceforth to read it without a constant awareness of that absentee settler-planter who is at the centre of everything, in one sense, and yet constantly withdrawn and marginal in another. Said's reading likewise locates the centre of the book in an absence, in things unsaid and unspecified. In this sense it is a form of Marxist criticism influenced by post-structuralist views, contrasting with Krieger's much 'straighter' Marxism. It also, like new historicism, comes closer to actually naming the details of a specific social/colonial situation (the absentee planter-landlord class of eighteenth-century Antigua) rather than just evoking a generalised notion of colonial exploitation.

Selected reading

Ashcroft, Bill, and Ahluwalia, Pal, *Edward Said* (Routledge, 2nd edn, 2008).
A useful book in the 'Routledge Critical Thinkers' series.
Ashcroft, Bill, *et al.*, *The Empire Writes Back: Theory and Practice in Post-colonial Literature* (Routledge, 2nd edn, 2002).
A readable and comprehensive book which provides an excellent start on this topic.
Ashcroft, Bill, *et al.*, *The Post-Colonial Studies Reader* (Routledge, 2nd edn, 2005). Covers a vast range of material.
Ashcroft, Bill, *et al.*, *Post-Colonial Studies: The Key Concepts* (Routledge, 3rd edn, 2013).
An A to Z guide by the *Empire Writes Back* team.
Bhabha, Homi K., ed., *Nation and Narration* (Routledge, 1990).
A definitive early collection in this field, with pieces by several of the major figures.
Bhabha, Homi K., *The Location of Culture* (Routledge, 1994).
Examines 'the cultural and political boundaries which exist in between the spheres of gender, race, class and sexuality'. Discusses Morrison, Gordimer, and Rushdie. Not an easy writer, but (says Toni Morrison) 'any serious discussion of post-colonial/postmodern scholarship is inconceivable without referencing Mr Bhabha'.
Césaire, Aimé, *Return to My Native Land* (Penguin Poets, 1969).
This and the next title are early founding texts of postcolonialism, their status corresponding to that of 'classics' like *The Female Eunuch* or *The Feminine Mystique* within feminism.
Fanon, Frantz, *The Wretched of the Earth* (Penguin, 1961).

Gates, Henry Louis, Jr, ed., *'Race', Writing and Difference* (University of Chicago Press, 1987).

Loomba, Ania, *Colonialism/Post-Colonialism* (Routledge, New Critical Idiom series, 3rd edn, 2015).

Another good introduction.

McLeod, John, *Beginning Postcolonialism* (Manchester University Press, 2nd edn, 2009).

An excellent and readable book in the 'Beginnings' series.

McLeod, John, ed., *The Routledge Companion to Postcolonial Studies* (Routledge, 2007).

Wide-ranging and authoritative.

Said, Edward, *Culture and Imperialism* (Vintage, new edn, 1994).

A broad account of the 'roots of imperialism' in European culture.

Said, Edward, *Orientalism* (Penguin, new edn, with new preface, 2003).

Said's work has been a major influence in this field, and he is a useful entry-point since his writing has an immediate accessibility and clarity of impact. This re-issue has a substantial new 'Afterword'.

Spivak, Gayatri Chakravorty, *In Other Worlds: Essays in Cultural Politics* (Routledge Classics, with a new introduction by the author, 2006).

Spivak is another major figure, but her close involvement with post-structuralism makes her writing quite demanding. A starting point might be her essay 'Draupadi' (on a Bengali short story, which she translates and reprints) in Newton's *Theory into Practice*.

Walder, Dennis, ed., *Literature in the Modern World* (Oxford University Press, 2004).

Contains Chinua Achebe's paper 'Colonialist Criticism', and other useful material in the relevant section.

Zabus, Chantal, ed., *The Future of Postcolonial Studies* (Routledge, 2015).

A very impressive book, with sections on religion (hitherto a postcolonial no-go area), ecology, queer theory, and utopianism.

11
Stylistics

Stylistics: a theory or a practice?

Stylistics is a critical approach which uses the methods and findings of the science of linguistics in the analysis of literary texts. By 'linguistics' here is meant the scientific study of language and its structures, rather than the learning of individual languages. Stylistics developed in the twentieth century and its aim is to show how the technical linguistic features of a literary work, such as the grammatical structure of its sentences, contribute to its overall meanings and effects.

The account given below will put a good deal of emphasis on critical practice rather than critical theory, and we should ask at the outset whether stylistics is really a form of critical theory at all. The compilers of most currently available guides to literary theory assume that it is not, since they say nothing about it. But the grounds for this assumption are difficult to see. It is certainly an approach to literature which has yielded a large amount of practical work distinctly different in tone and method from what we are accustomed to. This body of practice is the product of very specific theories about literary language and how it works, and these theories are usually taught alongside the practice.

The grounds for excluding stylistics, therefore, probably lie in the nature of the theoretical outlook behind the discipline, for liberal humanism and stylistics have a good deal in common. *Firstly*, both have a strong empirical bias, that is, a bias towards detailed verbal analysis of specific canonical literary texts, rather than a commitment to establishing generalised theoretical positions. *Secondly*, both have kept aloof from the eclecticism which has led to so much cross-fertilisation between Marxist, feminist, structuralist, and post-structuralist approaches. And *thirdly*, both have generally refused to take on board the notion of the 'floating signifier' (that is, the idea that the meanings established through language are innately fluid, indeterminate, and shifting).

These similarities might lead us to expect the two to be natural allies, but in fact stylistics and liberal humanism fought with each other very bitterly in the 1960s, at least a decade before the outbreak of hostilities between liberal humanism and theory in general. However, stylistics also has its differences from other forms of critical theory, for it has resisted the 'relativism' which permeates most other kinds of theoretical discourse. Everywhere outside stylistics indeterminacy rules: all critics scrupulously avoid 'totalising claims' and acknowledge that there can be no overviews, only viewpoints, each of which is partial. Stylistics, by contrast, remains positivist in outlook; that is, it maintains its faith in the accumulation of knowledge by empirical investigation of external phenomena carried out by disinterested enquirers. There are good reasons, then, for regarding stylistics as different, but none, in my view, for regarding it as untheoretical. Its advantage, too, for those who are just beginning theory is that it does offer a wide range of new practical methods for explicating literature, many of which can be enjoyable to practise, especially when working in class in groups.

Stylistics, it should be added, is not confined to the analysis of literature: it can be applied equally to expository prose, political speeches, advertisements, and so on. It thus assumes that the language of literature is not a 'special case': on the contrary, literary language can be analysed just like any other kind to reveal precisely how effects are created. Hence, stylistics concedes no special mysterious qualities to literary language: it is not seen as sacred or revered; it is simply the data on which the method can be put to use. It is true, of course, that very few literary critics of any persuasion today would make semi-mystical claims that poetry is inspired, or ineffable, or operates beyond reason in a realm which analysis can never fully penetrate. But on the other hand, neither do many of them proclaim the contrary – that literary language never has any transcendent dimension which lifts it above the everyday.

A brief historical account: from rhetoric, to philology, to linguistics, to stylistics, to new stylistics

Stylistics is, in a sense, the modern version of the ancient discipline known as 'rhetoric', which taught its students how to structure an argument, how to make effective use of figures of speech, and generally how to pattern and vary a speech or a piece of writing so as to produce the maximum impact. Rhetoric in medieval times played an important part in training people for the Church, the legal profession, and political or diplomatic life, but once divorced from this vocational purpose it degenerated into a rather arid and mechanical study of the mere surface features of language which involved, for instance, identifying and classifying figures of speech. The pedantic outlook of its practitioners (for instance, their love of impressive-sounding labels) is frequently satirised by Chaucer, Shakespeare and others. Traces of this degenerate form of the discipline survived in school teaching until quite recently.

Throughout the nineteenth century, rhetoric in this medieval sense was gradually absorbed into linguistics. At this time linguistics was usually known as 'philology', and was almost entirely historical in emphasis. It involved studying the evolution of languages, and the interconnections between them, and speculating about the origins of language itself. In the twentieth century there was a movement away from this historical emphasis and a new concentration on how language as a system is structured, looking at such aspects as the way meanings are established and maintained, and the options available (and their consequences) in structuring sentences. This is where a kind of born-again form of rhetoric emerged, shortly before the First World War, with a new interest in literary style and its effects, an interest seen also in the work of the Russian Formalists (Chapter 8, pp. 164–5) in the 1920s, and in the work of the Russian linguist Roman Jakobson, leader of the Prague Linguistic Circle (Chapter 8, p. 165), who lived in America after the Second World War. A famous 'Conference on Style' was held at Indiana

University in 1958, and the proceedings published in 1960 as *Style in Language*, edited by Thomas Sebeok (Technology Press of the Massachusetts Institute of Technology and John Wiley & Sons, New York). The conference was notable, among other things, for Jakobson's 'Closing Statement', which seemed to announce a take-over bid for literature on the part of linguistics:

> Poetics deals with problems of verbal structure: Since linguistics is the global science of verbal structure, poetics may be regarded as an integral part of linguistics ['poetics' here means the study of litera-ture in general, not just poetry].

The gist of the Sebeok collection of material is to claim that linguis-tics offers a more objective way of studying literature, and the book tends to set up 'a confrontation of camps' (Roger Fowler's phrase) between literary and language studies. Fowler responded to what he saw as this unhelpful polarisation by editing a collection called *Essays on Style and Language: Linguistic and Critical Approaches to Literary Studies* (1966), which tried to mend the damage done by what Fowler regarded as 'an unnecessary schism between "language" and "literature"'. But the result, if anything, was to widen the gap: Fowler's collection was reviewed by Helen Vendler in the journal *Essays in Criticism*, 1966, pp. 457–63. She suggested that while lin-guistic study had great potential, at present linguists are 'simply under-educated in the reading of poetry' and are taking on 'docu-ments whose primary sense and value they are not equipped to ab-sorb' (p. 460). This stung Fowler into a riposte which inaugurated a much-cited debate between himself and F. W. Bateson, the journal's editor (see *Essays in Criticism*, 1967, pp. 332–47, and 1968, pp. 164–82). The outcome of this was, again, to solidify the language–literature polarisation.

But the period up to the 1980s saw the development of what Vendler had said was lacking in linguistics, namely a form of 'dis-course analysis' which would enable linguistics to comment on and analyse the structure of complete pieces of writing, rather than just the isolated phrases and sentences to which it had previously been restricted. This meant that non-linguists began to take some in-terest in the findings of linguistic essays, while, at the same time, linguists writing such material realised the need to consult and incorporate non-linguistic material. Allegedly, this resulted, during the 1980s, in what came to be called the 'new stylistics', which had a limited degree of eclecticism (in that it drew on the findings of other new kinds of criticism – feminist, structuralist, post-structuralist, and so on) and was less likely to claim that it alone studied literature in an objective way.

In fact, however, the superiority claims from both sides continued. Fowler, for instance, in his 1986 book *Linguistic Criticism* charac-ter-ises linguistic criticism as 'objective description of texts' (p. 4), while conventional criticism, by contrast, uses 'random descriptive jargon' (p. 3) and is merely 'amateur commentary' using only quasi-grammatical terms. Also, his 1980s writing repeated very similar arguments to those he had used in the 1960s against Bateson. Thus, opponents, he says in 1986, speak as if linguistics were a single en-tity, whereas actually there are many different techniques in use within it, some appropriate for literary study and some not. This is exactly the same point as he had made in the 1960s: 'there is no one linguistics ... bland undefined accounts of "linguistics" lead nowhere' (*Essays in Criticism*, 1967, p. 325). Likewise, not all stylis-tics in the 1960s made uncompromisingly exclusive claims for the discipline, so the more liberal attitude said to be distinctive of the new stylistics is not something which appears only in the 1980s. Thus, Fowler, again, in the Bateson dispute, stressed that just being a linguist isn't a qualification for dealing adequately with poetry. On the contrary, 'although literature is language, and therefore open to ordinary formal linguistic investigation ... it has, like other formally distinctive texts, essentially distinctive contexts which the linguist no less than the critic must study' (*Essays in Criticism*, 1967, p. 325).

Hence, the grounds for setting up a sequence in which stylistics gives way to new stylistics are slender. Combative 'old' stylistics attitudes remained common and were explicit in much work in the field. For instance, Nigel Fabb and Alan Durant, describing the dif-ference between stylistics and literary criticism in the mid-1980s, said that in the latter, critical comment is 'often made without any accompanying systematic, or even explicit, scrutiny of its own meth-ods or assumptions' (*The Linguistics of Writing: Arguments between Language and Literature*, Manchester University Press, 1987, p. 228).

Thus, while it is true to say that stylistics today tends to be more open than before to input from those working in other areas of intellectual enquiry, it would be exaggerating to imply the kind of clean break with the hard-line past implied by the term 'new stylistics'. The ideal of co-operation across the language/literature divide is represented by the 'Interface' series from Routledge (series editor Ronald Carter), which aims to 'build bridges between the traditionally divided disciplines of language studies and literary studies'. It should be added that doubtless the old hard-line attitudes against stylistics still exist too, but for many years structuralism and post-structuralism, rather than stylistics, were usually seen as the major threat to traditional values in criticism, with the consequence that most liberal humanist polemical writing was directed at these targets.

How does stylistics differ from standard close reading?

Stylistic analysis attempts to provide a commentary which is objective and scientific, based on concrete quantifiable data, and applied in a systematic way. In contrast, as we have seen, conventional 'close reading' is often seen by the stylistician (to a greater or lesser extent) as impressionistic, intuitive, and randomised. All the same, the differences between the two approaches might well seem superficial to a casual observer, so it is worth trying to define them. The specific differences between conventional close reading and stylistics include the following:

1. Close reading emphasises *differences* between literary language and that of the general speech community; it tends to isolate the literary text and see it as a purely aesthetic art object, or 'verbal icon', whose language operates according to rules of its own. Stylistics, by contrast, emphasises *connections* between literary language and everyday language. This difference of view about literary language is actually a continuation of a very old dispute. For instance, the critical break between Wordsworth and Coleridge lay in the fact that Wordsworth believed that poetic language when most effective was at its plainest and most prose-like, that is, when it is as close as possible to the language actually used by

'men'. In contrast, Coleridge believed that poetic language depended for its effect on the poet's heightening or intensifying of it (through patterning, compression, repetition, and so on), thus making it more specialised and taking it further away from the patterns of everyday speech.

2. Stylistics uses specialised technical terms and concepts which derive from the science of linguistics, terms like 'transitivity', 'under-lexicalisation', 'collocation', and 'cohesion' (all of which are explained in the final section of this chapter). Terms like these are part of the technical vocabulary of a particular field of intellectual enquiry and they do not have any currency outside this field. Unless you were 'talking shop' with fellow students you could not introduce these terms into casual conversation without explaining what they meant and (more importantly) what they were for. In contrast, close reading (typically) uses lay-person's terms and concepts which may have a slightly 'bookish' air, but are nevertheless part of ordinary everyday language; terms, for instance, like 'verbal nuance', 'irony', 'ambiguity', 'paradox', and 'ambivalence'. If you started to explain the meaning of these terms in the same casual conversation, you would probably seem rather patronising, even though the use of these terms in criticism might be considered slightly specialised, and each of them has its own resonance and associations within the discipline. The point is, though, that these terms are clearly not 'technical' in the way that 'under-lexicalisation' is.

3. Stylistics makes greater claims to scientific objectivity than does close reading, stressing that its methods and procedures can be learned and applied by all. Hence, its aim is partly the 'demystification' of both literature and criticism. Thus, in relation to literature it aims to show, as we saw above, the continuity between literary language and other forms of written communication. In the case of criticism, it aims to provide a set of procedures which are openly accessible to all, in contrast to the tendency within close reading to stress the need for the critic to develop 'tact' and 'sensitivity' towards the literary text and avoid spelling out a method or procedure to be followed. Hence, for instance, the notorious reluctance of F. R. Leavis to describe or set out in detail his critical methods. Likewise, readers often

express the feeling that the language of literature achieves its effects in ways which may prove inherently inaccessible to analysis, so that at the core of literature is a kind of mysterious impenetrable essence. If, as many believe, the sentiments expressed in a poem are uniquely embodied in the form of words chosen by the poet, then it must follow that there are strict limits to what can be added by critical enquiry.

The ambitions of stylistics

1. *Stylisticians try to provide 'hard' data to support existing 'intuitions' about a literary work.* Stylistics is not always just about the interpreting of individual literary works, but when it is engaged in straight textual interpretation it often tries to back up the (as they would see them) impressionistic hunches of common readers with hard linguistic data. Thus, we might, in reading a Hemingway short story, register an impression something like 'Hemingway has a plain style which is very distinctive'. Stylisticians would try to be much more specific: their question might be 'what do we mean, exactly, by "plain"?' Well, perhaps we need no linguistic training to realise that Hemingway generally avoids descriptive words like adverbs and adjectives: where another writer might say something like 'Smith ran purposefully through the heavy rain' Hemingway would omit the adverb 'purposefully' and the adjective 'heavy'. He would want these things to emerge implicitly, which would actually, in his view, given them greater impact. So the sentence would be, simply, 'Smith ran through the rain'. The stylistician might calculate Hemingway's usage in a given tale, in a statement like 'seventy-three per cent of the nouns and verbs used by Hemingway in ... are without adjectival or adverbial qualification'. There might be a comparision with work by other writers generally perceived as having a less plain style, perhaps resulting in the claim that these writers have only thirty per cent of nouns and verbs unqualified. Of course, the calculating would be applied to a section of the work only, perhaps to a tale by each of the writers concerned which would be intuitively felt to be typical of each. The result is not to give us new information, exactly,

about Hemingway, since every reader realises very quickly that his sparse, plain style is one of his most distinctive qualities. But it will have told us a good deal about precisely how, in linguistic terms, the plainness is achieved and maintained.

2. *Stylisticians suggest new interpretations of literary works based on linguistic evidence.* Stylistics brings a special expertise to bear on the linguistic features of a text, and therefore sees a dimension of the material which the ordinary reader would be unaware of. This dimension may well contain material which could alter our interpretation of the work. For instance, Colin MacCabe argues in an essay on stylistics that Falstaff in Shakespeare's history plays has an element of sexual ambiguity. He frequently refers, for example, to his large stomach, and how it makes bravery very difficult, but the word he uses is not 'stomach' but 'womb' ('My womb, my womb, my womb undoes me'). At the time the play was written, says MacCabe, the word 'womb' was in a state of semantic transition. That is to say, its meaning was gradually changing from an older sense to a newer one: in its old sense it was a general word for 'stomach' and was used interchangeably of both men and women. But it was also then acquiring its more specialised modern meaning, where it is gender-specific and designates a particular part of female anatomy. Since both senses of the word were possible while it was in the transition stage from one sense to the other, Falstaff's use of the word suggests a corresponding sexual ambivalence in himself. Only the reader in possession of this specialised knowledge about semantic change would realise this: other readers would at first be puzzled by the word, would then perhaps look it up in a glossary, and would finally conclude that the word is simply being used in an obsolete sense, and hence had no bearing upon questions of characterisation or interpretation. There are, I think, problems in accepting MacCabe's account of this example: he assumes that words which are in process of semantic change have traces of both meanings present in every usage, but it seems more likely that in these cases a word can have either meaning, but not *both*. For example, the word 'disinterested' today is in process of semantic change, but every given usage signifies either 'impartial' or else 'not interested',

and never a combination of these meanings. A more general problem is to decide the status of evidence which is below the threshold of perception of all readers except professional linguists. How, for instance, did such meanings get into the text? Deliberately planted by the author? Presumably not. And in what sense are they 'there' at all if normally perceptible only to a group of readers whose existence, except in the case of present-day texts, could not have been predicted? All the same, the general point is clear: linguists use their specialised knowledge not just to support existing readings but to establish new ones.

3. *Stylisticians attempt to establish general points about how literary meanings are made.* The point here is that, like all the other new approaches to literature, stylistics is interested not just in the individual literary work, but also in much more general questions about how literature works. For instance, linguists argue that a literary effect is created simultaneously in terms of both form and content. In Hardy's *Tess of the D'Urbervilles*, Tess's subjection to the social and physical superiority of Alec is expressed both in terms of what is said, and in terms of the grammatical structure of the 'seduction' (or 'rape' scene), for his having power is reinforced subliminally by Alec (or some attribute of him) frequently being the subject of sentences, while Tess's lack of power is reinforced by her frequently being the grammatical object: thus sentences have patterns like: *he* [subject] *touched her* [object]; *his fingers* [subject] *sank into her* [object], and so on. This kind of argument, if accepted, has implications about how literary effects are created and how they operate. The implication is that the powerful literary effect is 'overdetermined', that is, it comes from different factors combining, so that content is subtly reinforced by grammatical structure, overall 'discourse structure', word choice, imagery, and so on. Literary meaning, this suggests, goes down to the very roots of language and is reflected at the level of grammar and sentence structure. Hence, no aspect of language is neutral; the patterns of grammar and syntax, morphemes, and phonemes are all implicated in literary meaning. Again, I think there are difficulties with this as a general argument: for instance, it

seems to make authors into intuitive genius figures who instinctively 'know' the content of modern linguistics. All the same,
the main point is clear: stylistics tries to establish things which
are generally true about the way literature works.

STOP and THINK

The linguistic terminology used in stylistics may seem daunting
if you have never been taught any formal grammar, but it is
probably unwise to try to learn formal grammar as a prelude to
sampling stylistics. A better way is to make use of a few basic
reference tools and have these by you for consultation as you
read some of the items listed at the end of this section. I would
suggest you use Katie Wales, *A Dictionary of Stylistics* (Routledge, 3rd edn, 2011) and a good up-to-date compendium of
English grammar. I have found the kind intended for advanced
learners of English more useful than others. A good example is
Michael Swan's *Practical English Usage* (Oxford University Press,
4th edn, 2016).

A problem to focus on as you begin your involvement with
this topic is the one highlighted by Stanley Fish in his essay
'What is Stylistics and Why are they Saying such Terrible Things
About It?' Fish says that there is always a gap between the
linguistic features identified in the text and the interpretation
of them offered by the stylistician. We might call this problem
the hermeneutic gap ('hermeneutic' means concerned with the
act of interpretation).

For instance, it may be said that an utterance uses a large
number of passive verbs – those patterned 'I have been informed that ...': this is the linguistic feature. These passives, we
may then be told, indicate a degree of evasiveness in the text:
this is the interpretation.

The difficulty is knowing how we can be sure that there is a
link between the use of the passive and evasiveness. Can we be
sure that the user of the passive is usually being evasive in some
way, for instance, trying to conceal the identity of the informant,
and, so to speak, to conceal that concealment? (Was I being

evasive when I used passives in the previous paragraph?) If the passive is only sometimes evasive, what are the circumstances which make it so?

In your reading of the following examples, then, and of some of the items listed at the end of the section, try to identify the moment when the critic passes from describing linguistic data to interpreting it – the moment when the 'hermeneutic gap' opens up – and consider how convincingly, or otherwise, it is bridged.

What stylistic critics do

1. They describe technical aspects of the language of a text – such as grammatical structures – and then use this data in interpretation.
2. The purpose of doing this is sometimes simply to provide objective linguistic data to support existing readings or intuitions about a literary work.
3. At other times the purpose is to establish a new reading, which may be based only, or mainly, on this linguistic data, and may challenge or counter existing readings.
4. These technical accounts of how meanings are made in literature are part of an overall project which involves showing that literature has no ineffable, mystical core which is beyond analysis: rather, it is part of a common 'universe of discourse' and uses the same techniques and resources as other kinds of language.
5. To this end, stylistics does not confine itself to the analysis of literature and often juxtaposes literary and other kinds of discourse, for instance, comparing the linguistic devices used in poetry with those of advertising.
6. Stylistics moves beyond 'sentence grammar' to 'text grammar', considering how the text works as a whole to achieve (or not) its purposes (for instance, to amuse, to create suspense, or to persuade) and examining the linguistic features which contribute to these ends.

Stylistics: examples

Rather than considering a single example in detail, I will refer more briefly to three, each of which uses some technical aspect of language in critical interpretation. The first makes use of the linguistic terms 'transitivity' and 'under-lexicalisation'. What do these mean? The former refers to the different sentence patterns in which verbs can occur. Traditionally a verb is said to be transitive when the action it designates has a stated 'goal' or 'recipient' or 'object'. Thus, in the sentence 'She shut the door' the action of shutting is 'received' or 'suffered' by the door. Hence the verb 'shut' is said to be 'transitive', which roughly means 'passing through', in the sense that the action 'passes through' to the door. 'Door' is said to be the object of this verb in the sentence just cited. By contrast, in the sentence 'She vanished' the verb is said to be 'intransitive', since the action does not 'pass through' to any stated object – it just happens, and is, so to speak, self-sufficient. These two examples, then, represent different transitivity patterns, and while the grammatical categories 'transitive' and 'intransitive' are derived from traditional grammar, as originally devised to describe the structures of the Latin language, the abstract notion of 'transitivity', designating the range of patterns possible for verbs, derives from the work of the linguist M. A. K. Halliday in the 1960s and 1970s. Halliday made use of the concept in analysing fiction, and Roger Fowler follows him in this.

'Under-lexicalisation' is a term invented by Fowler: it refers to cases where there is a 'lack of an adequate set of words to express specific concepts' (Katie Wales). Thus, we might not know the word for a particular implement and instead call it a 'thingy' or a 'wotsit'; or we might forget the word for a particular object (the word 'handle', say) and use a vague descriptive substitute instead (such as 'the holding thing'). These would be examples of slightly different types of under-lexicalisation.

Let's now look at how a critic uses these terms in discussing the opening of William Faulkner's novel *The Sound and the Fury* (in the essay by Roger Fowler from the collection *Essays on Style and Language*, 1966, already referred to). The opening is narrated from

the point of view of Benjy, who is a thirty-three-year-old man with
the mind of a young child. Benjy is watching a game of golf:

> Through the fence, between the curling flower spaces, I could see
> them hitting. They were coming towards where the flag was and I
> went along the fence. Luster was hunting in the grass by the flower
> tree. They took the flag out, and they were hitting. Then they
> put the flag back and they went to the table, and he hit and the
> other hit.

Fowler writes:

> There is a consistent oddity in transitivity: there are almost no tran-
> sitive verbs with objects, a preponderance of intransitives ('coming',
> 'went', 'hunting', etc.) and one transitive ('hit') used repeatedly
> without an object, ungrammatically.

This constitutes the linguistic data. Fowler now takes the step from
description to interpretation: this 'oddity of transitivity' (such as
using the word 'hit' without saying what was hit) implies that 'Benjy
has little sense of actions and their effects on objects'. This is, I think,
a little over-specific, but clearly we notice, as we read, that there is
something strange about Benjy's language and we register this as
indicating that there is something strange about his mind. The
'something strange' about the language concerns the transitivity
pattern. Implicitly, Fowler's point is that the author's choosing this
linguistic feature to disturb is significant, for, of course, a disturbed
state of mind could, in theory, be conveyed by disrupting *any* language
feature at all. Secondly, Benjy's under-lexicalisation is seen in the
way he often uses descriptive circumlocutions rather than the right
words for things: thus, he never uses the word 'golf' for what he is
watching, and he calls a bush a 'flower tree'. This, again, is the data.
Interpreting it involves the suggestion that doing this indicates the
character's inability to perceive the world in socially acceptable
ways, as most other people do. Thus, the stylistician explains the
extent of the character's isolation by a stylistic analysis of aspects of
the language associated with him.

Another example of the kind of linguistic data used by stylisticians
is seen in Ronald Carter's analysis of W. H. Auden's poem 'Capital' in
Carter and Burton, eds, *Literary Text and Language Study* (Edward

Arnold, 1982). Carter makes use of the notion of 'collocation', a term which 'refers to the habitual or expected co-occurrence of words' (Katie Wales). This is a reference to the fact that words frequently occur in groupings which have a degree of predictability, even when they fall short of being set phrases which invariably have the same pattern. (This aspect of language used to be exploited in the British TV game show 'Blankety-Blank'.) To demonstrate what I mean, let me ask you to complete each of the following phrases with a single word (a different word in each case, and in each case putting in the word which first occurs to you):

A box of . . . A black . . . An uninvited . . .

The note at the end of this chapter indicates the words I think you are likely to have used to fill these gaps. These phrases are not fixed clichés (like 'He went as white as a sheet'), but simply a product of the way each word in an utterance progressively narrows down the range of possibilities for the words which succeed it. Thus, if I say 'It's a fine . . .' you can predict that the next word will be 'day' or 'afternoon', or some such. The sentence *could* be completed with the words 'way to calculate the height of a steeple', but it is very unlikely that any given occurrence of the opening 'It's a fine . . .' would be completed in this way. Now, a common feature of poetry is to break habitual collocation patterns, so that words not usually seen together suddenly occur. Poets divorce words from their usual partners and provide unlikely new partnerships between words which we would never have imagined getting together. Thus Carter shows how Auden, at one point in the poem, avoids an expected collocation like saying that people are 'waiting patiently', and instead says of the idle rich in big cities that they are 'waiting *expensively* for miracles to happen' (my italics). Auden also mentions a part of the city in which political exiles live (and where they meet to plan their eventual return to power in their own countries) as a 'malicious village'. A more usual collocation for 'village' would combine it with approving adjectives to give phrases like 'friendly village' or 'picturesque village' or 'sleepy village'. Carter's overall point is that 'collocational breaks' of this kind signal parts of the poem which are 'thematically-charged' and will hence repay further investigation.

A final kind of linguistic data used by the stylistician concerns 'cohesion'. Cohesion is about 'lexical items' (words) which cross the boundaries between sentences, binding them into a single continuous utterance, even though they are *grammatically* separate sentences. Without cohesion a text has the awkward start-stop quality of a child's old-fashioned early reader, like this:

> This is Mandy. Mandy is my friend. Mandy and I go to the pictures together.

The stop–start quality can be removed and cohesion achieved by what linguists call 'pronominalisation' (using pronouns), thus:

> This is Mandy. *She* is my friend. *We* go to the pictures together.

Notice that although these are still grammatically separate sentences they now flow as a single connected utterance, since the pronouns 'She' and 'We' refer back to people already named. Modern writers have been interested in the effects of distorting patterns of cohesion, and an awareness of this concept helps to appreciate what is going on in something like the following, which is the start of a short story by the American writer Donald Barthelme:

> Edward looked at his red beard in the table-knife. Then Edward and Pia [not 'he and Pia] went to Sweden, to the farm. In the mailbox Pia found a cheque for Willie from the government of Sweden. It was for twenty three hundred crowns and had a rained-on look. Pia [not 'she'] put the cheque in the pocket of her brown coat. Pia [not 'She'] was pregnant. In London she had been sick everyday.

There are many other linguistic effects here apart from the distortions in the expected cohesion pattern which I have indicated. Partly, the effect comes from the sense of incongruity which arises when a grammatically continuous discourse frames content which is logically, conceptually, and emotionally distorted and fragmented. Also, the simple language and short sentences give the tone of a child's reader, again, but the subject matter is very incongruous with this tone, being particularly adult and traumatic. Through a particular way of using language, then, a certain literary effect is created, and in these circumstance we can legitimately use linguistic techniques in our exploration.

Note

I have used these same examples several times with classes to demonstrate the principle of collocation. The phrases have to be completed without conferring and without prolonged deliberation. Most people write 'A box of chocolates' or 'A box of matches'. A few write 'A box of hankies' or 'A box of tricks'. These four usually account for all the choices made by a group of twenty. 'A black' is usually completed by 'cat' or 'box'. 'An uninvited' is always completed by 'guest'. It is an absolute certainty that these phrases will never be completed in anything like twenty different ways by twenty different people.

Selected reading

Birch, David, *Language, Literature, and Critical Practice: Ways of Analysing Text* (Routledge, 1989).

Bradford, Richard, *Stylistics* (Routledge, New Critical Idiom series, 1997).
A very useful and reliable account.

Butler, Lance St John, *Registering the Difference: Reading Literature Through Register* (Manchester University Press, 1999).
A lively and user-friendly linguistics-based approach to literature from slightly outside the mainstream.

Carter, Ronald, ed., *Language and Literature: An Introductory Reader in Stylistics* (Allen & Unwin, 1982).
Chapter five is on Hemingway's 'Cat in the Rain'.

Carter, Ronald, and Simpson, Paul, eds, *Language, Discourse and Literature: An Introductory Reader in Discourse Stylistics* (Routledge, 1988).

Carter, Ronald, and Burton, Deirdre, eds, *Literary Text and Language Study* (Edward Arnold, 1982).
Chapter two, 'Responses to language in poetry'.

Carter, Ronald, and Stockwell, Peter, eds, *The Language and Literature Reader* (Routledge, 2008).
A great resource containing accessible essays by all the major figures in the field.

Chapman, Raymond, *Linguistics and Literature: An Introduction to Literary Stylistics* (Edward Arnold, 1974).
Basic and short.

Fabb, Nigel, *et al.*, eds, *The Linguistics of Writing: Arguments Between Language and Literature* (Manchester University Press, 1987).

Useful material. See especially the introduction, and the chapters by Marie Louise Pratt, Maurice Halle, and Henry Widdowson.

Fish, Stanley, *Is There a Text in This Class?* (Harvard University Press, 1980).

See chapters two and ten, the two parts of the famous essay called 'What is Stylistics and Why are they Saying Such Terrible Things About it?'

Fowler, Roger, *Linguistic Criticism* (Oxford Paperbacks, new edn, 1996).

A good general introduction.

Jeffries, Lesley, and McIntyre, Dan, *Stylistics* (Cambridge University Press, 2010).

An excellent texbook, showing the full range and scope of current linguistics.

McRae, John, *The Language of Poetry* (Routledge, 1998).

A brief and very helpful book in the 'Intertext' series.

Tambling, Jeremy, *What is Literary Language?* (Open University Press, 1988).

Has a useful appendix on 'Critical and rhetorical terms'.

Toolan, Michael, *Language in Literature* (Arnold, 1998).

A very useful introduction and workbook in stylistics.

Toolan, Michael, ed., *Language, Text and Context: Essays in Stylistics* (Routledge, 1992).

An interesting collection representative of developments in stylistics, particularly the strong emphasis on context. For an essay which questions the adequacy of this contextualising see Sara Mills's chapter 'Knowing your place: a Marxist feminist stylistic analysis'.

Toolan, Michael, *Narrative: A Critical Linguistic Introduction* (Routledge, 2nd edn, 2001).

Covers literary and non-literary texts, including film, internet, and TV.

Widdowson, H. G., *Stylistics and the Teaching of Literature* (Longman, 1975).

A brief and simple guide.

12
Narratology

Telling stories

This chapter is about narratology, which is the study of narrative structures. Narratology is a branch of structuralism, but it has achieved a certain independence from its parent, and this justifies it being given a chapter of its own. Also, because it takes much of its character and some of its terminology from linguistic theory, it seems logically to belong immediately after the chapter on stylistics. And because narratology is about stories, I will begin with one of my own.

Some years ago I was in a restaurant called 'Berties'. The menu featured those highly coloured, almost poetic descriptions of the meals on offer – it didn't offer 'cod and chips', for instance, but 'Fresh-caught, succulent North Sea cod, coated in a layer of light golden batter and served with a generous portion of delicious French fries' – you know the kind of thing. In the catering trade these descriptions are called 'narratives' – an interesting fact in itself. But they worry, in the trade, that customers may take them literally and hence complain that the batter isn't golden at all, but sort of brownish – perhaps leaving the restaurant vulnerable to charges of false description of goods or services. So at the bottom of the menu there is a footnote which reads: 'The narratives are guidelines only, and are not to be taken literally.'

This set me thinking about narratives and narrative theory, and about *narratology*, which we can define more closely as the study of how narratives make meaning, and what the basic mechanisms and procedures are which are common to all acts of story-telling.

Narratology, then, is not the reading and interpretation of *individual* stories, but the attempt to study the nature of 'story' itself, as a concept and as a cultural practice. Indeed, that distinction between the *actual* meal – cod and chips – and the *narrative account* of it – the 'succulent, fresh-caught cod' – is much the same as the narratologist's basic distinction between 'story' and 'plot'. The 'story' is the actual sequence of events as they happen, whereas the 'plot' is those events as they are edited, ordered, packaged, and presented in what we recognise as a narrative. This is a crucial distinction; the 'story', being the events as they happen, *has to* begin at the beginning, of course, and then move chronologically, with nothing left out. The 'plot', on the other hand, may well begin somewhere in the middle of a chain of events, and may then backtrack, providing us with a 'flashback' which fills us in on things that happened earlier. The plot may also have elements which flash forward, hinting at events which will happen later. So the 'plot' is a version of the story which should not be taken literally, just like those menu descriptions.

The distinction between 'story' and 'plot' is fundamental to narratology, but the story of narratology itself is that there are many competing groups, each tending to prefer its own terminology; hence, you will find the same distinction made with different terms. For instance, in his well-known essay 'Analysis and interpretation of the realist text' (in his book *Working with Structuralism*, RKP, 1980), David Lodge prefers the Russian Formalist terms *fabula*, instead of 'story', and *sjuzhet* (pronounced 'soojay') for 'plot', though I don't myself see any advantage now in using these terms. Most current North American writing on narratology uses 'story', but instead of 'plot' the term 'discourse' is often preferred. This, I think, is sensible, because it isn't just 'plot' in the narrow sense which is at issue, but style, viewpoint, pace, and so on, which is to say, the whole 'packaging' of the narrative which creates the overall effect. Gérard Genette (see below, pp. 231–40) uses yet another set of equivalent terms, these being *histoire*, which has the same meaning as 'story' or *fabula*, and *recit*, which means the same as 'plot' or *sjuzhet*.

Aristotle

A second story relevant to narratology is the story of narratology itself. A truncated 'history' of narratology follows, centred on three main characters, the first of whom is Aristotle. In his *Poetics*, as we saw in Chapter 1 (pp. 23–4), Aristotle identifies 'character' and 'action' as the essential elements in a story, and says that character must be revealed through action, which is to say through aspects of the plot. He identifies three key elements in a plot, these being (using Aristotle's Greek words, which are here simply Anglicised, but not translated):

1. the *hamartia*
2. the *anagnorisis*
3. the *peripeteia*

The *hamartia* means a 'sin' or 'fault' (which in tragic drama is often the product of the fatal character-defect which came to be known as the 'tragic flaw'). The *anagnorisis* means 'recognition' or 'reali-sation', this being a moment in the narrative when the truth of the situation is recognised by the protagonist – often it's a moment of *self*-recognition. The *peripeteia* means a 'turn-round' or a 'reversal' of fortune. In classical tragedy this is usually a fall from high to low estate, as the hero falls from greatness. In identifying his three key moments, Aristotle did what all narratologists do, which is to look at a number of different stories (Greek stage tragedies in his case) ask-ing what elements they have in common. This is similar to the way a chemist would look at different forms of matter (mountains, lakes, volcanoes, etc.) and realise that they are all made from the same finite set of chemical elements. In both cases the skill lies in the trained ability to see the similarities and consistencies which underlie difference.

We can see traces of these Aristotelian elements in even the most rudimentary of narrative material, such as the cartoon diagram op-posite, which is a very simple complete story, taken from a packet of 'Brekkies' (a British brand of cat food). Aristotle, I should empha-sise, saw all three elements as centred on the 'protagonist' (the 'hero' or 'heroine' of the drama), but in what follows I distribute the three elements among the figures involved in the story, partly because I believe that in using literary theory we don't have to follow the maker's instructions slavishly, and partly in anticipation of the methods of Vladimir Propp, the next figure I will consider. So, the 'hamartia' (or fault) is the cat's leaving dirty paw-prints over the table-cloth, an act which brings reproof and condemnation ('Oh,

Bob, don't'), and involves a 'peripeteia', or fall from grace, so that the cat is out of favour. The fall is marked by the cat's literal descent from the table to the floor. But during the tea, the visiting aunt notices with pleasure that the cloth now on the table is the one she gave her niece as a present. Of course, *she* doesn't know that this cloth was not her niece's first choice, but *we* know this from our privileged overview position as witnesses of the whole sequence of events. Indeed, we might say that the key to story-telling is not the imparting, but the withholding of information – readers often know things that characters don't, and vice-versa, and narrators keep things back from both. The central mechanism in stories is delay, to be specific, delay in imparting this information – the Victorian novelist Wilkie Collins famously said that the formula for writing a successful novel is 'Make them laugh, make them cry – make them wait'.

The 'anagnorisis' in the cartoon is the cat-owner's guilty (offstage) realisation that she has missed an opportunity to show gratitude and proper feeling by using the guest's present when the guest comes to tea. This brings about a further peripeteia, which is the restoration of the cat to favour, not a fall from high to low, but a restoration from low to high. The restoration is marked by the thought bubble ('Thanks, Bob'), by the cat's expression of smirking self-satisfaction, and by its literal raising up now to the favoured position on the niece's lap.

Aristotle's three categories are essentially to do with the underlying themes and moral purposes of stories, being very much about

what might be called 'deep content', since in an important sense
they all concern 'inner events' (a moral defect, the *recognition* of its
existence, and the *consequences* of its existence). The presence of
these three is easy to discern beneath many narratives, acting as the
generative force of their moral impact. They are often the psychic
'raw materials' or 'ingredients' which are 'cooked' and transformed
to make up a specific narrative 'dish', a specific 'plot'. All the same, in
practice a great variety of plots is possible in stories, and to describe
these we seem to need a different kind of system to Aristotle's, one
which would give us a greater variety of possible actions and which
would operate closer to the narrative surface, so to speak. Something
like this was provided by the next of our three historical-marker
figures.

Vladimir Propp

As we would expect, then, later narratologists have developed more
wide-ranging lists and repertoires of the constants which can be
detected beneath the almost infinitely varied surface of narratives.
A second important figure is Vladimir Propp (1895–1970), a Russian
Formalist critic who worked on Russian folk tales, identifying recurrent structures and situations in such tales, and publishing his
findings in his book *The Morphology of the Folktale*, first published
in Russia in 1928. As Propp says in the Foreword, the word 'morphology' means 'the study of forms', so the book is about the structures and plot formations of these tales, and there is nothing in the
book about their history or social significance. Already, by 1928, the
tide in Soviet Russia was turning against this kind of 'Formalist'
study, and the book disappeared from view until the 1950s, when
it was re-discovered by the structuralists, especially the anthropologist Claude Lévi-Strauss, who used Propp's ideas in his own studies
of myth. *The Morphology* was first published in English in 1958
(by the University of Texas Press), translated by Laurence Scott,
with a second edition in 1968.

Propp's work is based on a study of his 'corpus' of a hundred
tales, and he concluded that all these tales are constructed by selecting items from a basic repertoire of thirty-one 'functions' (that is,
possible actions). No tale contains all the items in his list, but all are

constructed by selecting items from it. The complete list of 'functions' given in the book is as follows:

1. One of the members of a family absents himself from home.
2. An interdiction [that is, a prohibition] is addressed to the hero.
3. The interdiction is violated.
4. The villain makes an attempt at reconnaissance.
5. The villain receives information about his victim.
6. The villain attempts to deceive his victim in order to take possession of him or his belongings.
7. The victim submits to deception and thereby unwittingly helps his enemy.
8. The villain causes harm or injury to a member of a family/or, 8a. One member of a family either lacks something or desires to have something.
9. Misfortune or lack is made known; the hero is approached with a request or command; he is allowed to go or he is dispatched.
10. The seeker [that is, the hero in 'questor' mode] agrees to or decides upon counteraction.
11. The hero leaves home.
12. The hero is tested, interrogated, attacked, etc., which prepares the way for his receiving either a magical agent or helper.
13. The hero reacts to the actions of the future donor.
14. The hero acquires the use of a magical agent [that is, an object, an animal, etc.].
15. The hero is transferred, delivered, or led to the whereabouts of an object of search.
16. The hero and the villain join in direct combat.
17. The hero is branded.
18. The villain is defeated.
19. The initial misfortune or lack is liquidated.
20. The hero returns.
21. The hero is pursued.
22. Rescue of the hero from pursuit.
23. The hero, unrecognised, arrives home or in another country.
24. A false hero presents unfounded claims.
25. A difficult task is proposed to the hero.

26. The task is resolved.
27. The hero is recognised.
28. The false hero or villain is exposed.
29. The hero is given a new appearance.
30. The villain is punished.
31. The hero is married and ascends the throne.

These are the basic building blocks of the collection of tales ana-
lysed by Propp. To make the plot of any given individual tale, you
put together a selection of items from this list. No single tale has all
thirty-one functions, of course; each one has a *selection* of them, and
furthermore, the functions always occur in the order listed: for example, a tale may consist of functions 5, 7, 14, 18, 30 and 31: thus,
the villain receives information about the hero/victim (5), and
deceives him (7), but the hero receives help from an animal with
magical powers (14), defeats the villain (18), has him punished (30),
then marries and becomes king (31). But no tale could have a formula
in which the component numbers are out of sequence, say, with 30
coming before 18, for (in this instance) the villain cannot be punished before he has been defeated. The order of the functions is
fixed, partly because, as Propp says, events tend to have a due order
(witnesses may disagree on what they saw, but not usually on the
order in which they saw it – a house cannot be burgled before it has
been broken into). The method of analysis of the tales aims to show
that beneath their 'amazing multiformity' lies a 'no less striking uni-
formity' (Propp, p. 21) – to revert to the metaphor used earlier, they
are different dishes all cooked from the same range of ingredients.

Clearly, we are talking here about stories viewed in a more (literally) 'superficial' way than was the case with Aristotle, but since the
variety of possible surface events is greater than that of the possible
underlying motives, Propp has more variables in play than Aristotle.
All the same, some of the problems thrown up by Propp's system
will be evident after even a very brief study of the basic list of functions: 6 and 7, for instance, are *two* functions concerning deception
of the victim/hero by the villain, but clearly, only *one* action is involved – the deceiver deceives and the deceived *is* deceived, for
an act of deception requires two parties. These two events, then,
are really the same event looked at from different points of view.

Likewise, in 10 and 11, there are not really two distinct events, since in 10 the hero decides to do something, and in 11 he does it.[1]

The description of the thirty-one functions, and their sub-variants, takes up by far the longest chapter in the book, nearly fifty pages, which is getting on for half the main text. By contrast, the possible character types in the tales are much more briefly described (in the four pages of chapter six), the characters being for Propp mainly just the mechanism for distributing the functions around the story. To this end, he notes that the thirty-one functions seem to group naturally into 'spheres' (for example, pursuit, capture, and punishment have a natural grouping). Hence, it makes more sense to see the seven 'spheres of action' as *roles* rather than *characters*, as this reflects the subordination of character to action (a subordination which is also a feature of Aristotle's narratology, for Aristotle says that in narrative character is only expressed in action). Propp's seven 'spheres of action' are:

1. The villain
2. The donor (provider)
3. The helper
4. The princess (a sought-for-person) and her father
5. The dispatcher
6. The hero (seeker or victim)
7. The false hero

Using the list of thirty-one 'functions' and the seven 'spheres of action', we can generate the plot of any individual folk tale in the entire Russian corpus, just as, armed with the grammar, syntax, and vocabulary of English (the *langue*, in Saussure's terms) we can generate any possible utterance in English (the *parole*). Folk tales are relatively simple, of course, but the versatility of a schema like this is much increased by what Robert Scholes reminds us of in his book *Structuralism in Literature* (Yale University Press, 1974, and

1 A number of the major structuralists pointed out some of these limitations and suggested refinements: see Claude Lévi-Strauss, *Structural Anthropology*, vol. 2 (Allen Lane, 1977), chapter eight, 'Structure and form: reflections on a work by Vladimir Propp'; and Tzvetan Todorov, *The Poetics of Prose* (Basil Blackwell, 1977), chapter fourteen, 'Narrative transformations'.

new edition, 2009), that 'One character may play more than one of these roles in any given tale (e.g. the villain may also be the false hero, the donor may also be the dispatcher, etc.); or one role may employ several characters (multiple villains, for instance); but these are all the roles that this sort of narrative requires, and they are basic to much fiction which is far removed from fairy tales in other respects' (p. 65). This potential duplication, then, opens up the Proppian methods used to analyse relatively simple material, and begins to hint at the complexities of characterisation and motivation which form the basis of psychological, realist fiction. In realist fiction, the subordination of character to action is reversed, and roles cannot be simply demarcated as 'hero' and 'villain'. Henry James, the supreme psychological novelist, once said that he wrote not about good and evil, but about 'good-and-evil'. Hence, in a Henry James story, a would-be helper may inadvertently be a hinderer, or may even be unsure which they 'truly' are.[2] So the Proppian approach seems to hint at the way simple archetypes from much more basic narrative material can provide the shadowy deep foundations of complex realist fictions – the way, for instance, the Cinderella archetype (a tale found in some form in cultures worldwide) lies beneath novels like *Mansfield Park* and *Jane Eyre*. However, what Propp's system lacks is anything about the way the narrative is *presented*, such as the viewpoint or the style. These are the areas focused upon by the third of our 'marker' figures, and they need to be treated in a little more detail.

Gérard Genette

One of the most prominent narratologists since Roland Barthes has been Gérard Genette, whose work has as its focus, not the tale itself, so to speak, but how it is told, which is to say, the process of telling itself. What is meant by this distinction will become apparent if we consider six particular areas which Genette discusses (in his book *Narrative Discourse: An Essay in Method*, Cornell University Press,

2 I examine a group of James's tales using an adapted Proppian method in *Orbis Litterarum*, 46(1), (spring 1991), pp. 87–104, 'Embarrassments and predicaments: patterns of interaction in James's writer tales'.

1983). In what follows I ask six basic questions about the act of narration, and sketch under each the range of possibilities identified by Genette, with some supplementary categories of my own.

1. Is the basic narrative mode 'mimetic' or 'diegetic'?

Genette discusses this matter in chapter four, 'Mood'. 'Mimesis' means 'showing' or 'dramatising'. The parts of a narrative which are presented in a mimetic manner are 'dramatised', which is to say that they are represented in a 'scenic' way, with a specified setting, and making use of dialogue which contains direct speech. 'Mimesis' is 'slow telling', in which what is done and said is 'staged' for the reader, creating the illusion that we are 'seeing' and 'hearing' things for ourselves. By contrast, 'diegesis' means 'telling' or 'relating'. The parts of a narrative which are presented in this way are given in a more 'rapid' or 'panoramic' or 'summarising' way. The aim is to give us essential or linking information as efficiently as possible, without trying to create the illusion that the events are taking place before our eyes – the narrator just *says* what happens, without trying to show it *as* it happens.[3]

In practice, of course, writers use the two modes in tandem, moving from mimetic to diegetic, and back again, for strategic reasons. This is partly because an entirely mimetic novel would tend to be infinitely long, and an entirely diegetic one could hardly be more than a couple of pages, and would read like a plot summary. Of course, there are 'single-scene' short stories which are written almost entirely in mimetic mode – for example, many by Ernest Hemingway, such as 'Hills like White Elephants', which is a 'single take' account of an American couple waiting for a train at a remote Spanish railway station. Their thoughts, words, and actions as they wait reveal the crisis in their relationship. We see what they do and hear what they say, and that is all.[4] But the longer structure of a novel usually requires a *blending* of the mimetic and the diegetic,

3 As Genette points out (p. 162), the distinction between mimesis and diegesis was originally made by Plato in Book III of *The Republic*. So, as with Aristotle, contemporary narratology has roots in classical Greek philosophy.
4 In Ernest Hemingway, *The First Forty-Nine Stories* (Arrow Books, 1993).

and the following brief passage illustrates the 'glide' between the two modes:

> For five years Mario took the same route to work every morning, but he never saw Thelma again. Then one morning something very strange happened as he came out of the tube station and began to walk up Charing Cross Road. It was a bright, sunny day, and …

The first sentence is diegesis – a rapid summary of a long sequence of events, but all taking place 'off-stage', as it were. Clearly, it would be impossible to move a plot along efficiently without passages of this kind. The remainder of the passage is mimesis. Having 'fast-forwarded', the writer slows down again at the next crucial 'scene' and begins to construct it for us, telling us about the weather that day, and the exact location, so that we 'see' the scene in our mind's eye. Mimesis and diegesis need each other, and often work together so that the join between them can be difficult to discern exactly, but it is easy to see how fundamental they are as the building blocks of narrative.

2. How is the narrative focalised?

Focalisation (discussed on pages 189–94 of *Narrative Discourse*) means 'viewpoint' or 'perspective', which is to say the point-of-view from which the story is told. There are many possibilities: for example, in 'external' focalisation the viewpoint is *outside* the character depicted, so that we are told only things which are external or observable – that is, what the characters *say* and *do*, these being things you would hear and see for yourself if you were present at the scene depicted. In the opposite, 'internal focalisation', the focus is on what the characters *think* and *feel*, these being things which would be inaccessible to you even if you had been present. Thus, the sentence 'Thelma stood up and called out to Mario' is an externally focalised representation of this moment, for you would see and hear these things if you were present when they happened. By contrast, consider the sentence 'Thelma suddenly felt anxious that Mario was not going to see her and would walk by oblivious on the other side of Charing Cross Road.' This is an internally focalised representation of her; it reveals her unspoken thoughts and feelings, which you would be completely unaware of even if you were standing next to her. If the story is told throughout mainly with this internal focalisation on Thelma, then she can be called the 'focaliser' of the tale (or the 'reflector', in another tradition of narratological terms). Though she is not telling her own tale in the first person, readers are being given the events from her 'point-of-view' – thus, for instance, Elizabeth Bennet is the focaliser (or reflector) of *Pride and Prejudice*. Sometimes a novelist will freely enter the minds and emotions of more than one of the characters, as if privy to the thoughts and feelings of all of them. This kind of narrative can be said to have 'zero focalisation'; this occurs 'when no systematic conceptual or perceptual constraint governs what may be presented', as Gerald Prince elegantly puts it in his *A Dictionary of Narratology* (University of Nebraska Press, rev. edn, 2003). Prince says that zero focalisation is characteristic of 'traditional' or 'classical' narration. Its more familiar name is 'omniscient narration'.

3. Who is telling the story?

Of course, the author is, but not necessarily in his or her own voice or persona. One kind of narrator (the kind that often goes with a zero-focalised narrative) is not identified at all as a distinct character with a name and a personal history, and remains just a voice or a tone, which we may register simply as an intelligent, recording consciousness, a mere 'telling medium' which strives for neutrality and transparency. Such narrators may be called 'covert', 'effaced', 'non-intrusive', or 'non-dramatised'. We may impatiently insist that it is simply the author speaking to us directly, but it is worth remembering that this is not in any sense the author's 'true' voice, since he or she only uses this precise tone, pace, degree of detail, and so on, when narrating a work of fiction. If we met the author at a party or in a bar we wouldn't be able to tolerate this narrative style for more than a couple of minutes. Hence, it makes sense to think of this kind of disembodied narrator as an 'authorial persona', rather than as the author in person.

The other kind of narrator is the kind who is identified as a distinct, named character, with a personal history, gender, a social-class position, distinct likes and dislikes, and so on. These narrators have witnessed, or learned about, or even participated in the events they tell. They can be called 'overt' or 'dramatised' or 'intrusive' narrators, examples being such tellers as Mr Lockwood in Emily Brontë's

Wuthering Heights, Marlow in Joseph Conrad's *Heart of Darkness*, and Nick Carraway in Scott Fitzgerald's *The Great Gatsby*. These dramatised narrators can be of various kinds: the 'heterodiegetic' narrator is one who is not a character in the story he or she narrates, but an outsider to it, as Mr Lockwood is, for example ('heterodiegetic' means roughly 'other telling', since the story being told is that of somebody else). By contrast, the 'homodiegetic' narrator 'is present as a character in the story he tells' (Genette, p. 245) – as Jane Eyre is, for instance ('homodiegetic' means roughly 'same telling', since the story being told is the narrator's own). Notice that first-person narrators may be either heterodiegetic or homodiegetic, since they may be telling someone else's story, rather than their own. Omniscient narrators are necessarily heterodiegetic. The above concerns are discussed in Genette's chapter five, 'Voice', under the sub-heading 'Person'.

4. How is time handled in the story?

Narratives often contain references back and references forward, so that the order of telling does not correspond to the order of happening. Sometimes the story will 'flash back' to relate an event which happened in the past, and such parts of the narrative can be called 'analeptic' (from 'analepsis', which literally means a 'back-take'). Likewise, the narrative may 'flash forward' to narrate, or refer to, or anticipate an event which happens later: such parts of the narrative can be called 'proleptic' (from 'prolepsis', which literally means a 'fore-take'). For instance, in D. H. Lawrence's short story 'The Prussian Officer' a bottle of wine is spilt as a meal is served, and this gestures towards or hints at the bloodshed which will end the tale. Charles Dickens has a similar anticipating moment at the start of *A Tale of Two Cities*, when a barrel of red wine spilt in the street anticipates the bloodshed which will be caused by the revolution. These are 'proleptic' details, and they indicate in a slightly crude way how analepsis and prolepsis are often important in establishing and foregrounding 'themes' in a story. Typically, writers make strategic use of both analepsis and prolepsis in telling a story, for the beginning is seldom the best place to begin – stories tend to begin in the middle (*in medias res*, as the theorists of classical times said), with analeptic material sketching out what went before, and proleptic devices hinting at what the outcome will be, and thereby engaging the reader and generating the basic narrative momentum. These matters are discussed in Genette's first chapter, 'Order', under the sub-heading 'Narrative Time'.

5. How is the story 'packaged'?

Stories are not always presented 'straight'. Often writers make use of 'frame narratives' (also called 'primary narratives'), which contain within them 'embedded narratives' (also called 'secondary narratives'). For instance, the main story in Henry James's *The Turn of the Screw* is embedded within a frame narrative of a group of people telling ghost stories round the fire in a country house at Christmas. One of the stories told by one of the guests in these circumstances is the one which forms the substance of James's tale. Notice that here 'primary narrative' really just means the narrative which comes first, rather than the *main* narrative, which in fact it usually isn't. The 'secondary narrative' is the one which comes second and is embedded into the primary narrative. The secondary narrative is usually the main story. Thus, in James's tale, we first of all hear about the group assembled for the country-house Christmas, then we hear (in a far longer narrative) the story which was told in those circumstances. Likewise, the main story in Conrad's *Heart of Darkness* is embedded within the frame narrative of a group of former deep-sea sailors telling 'yarns' as they wait for the tide to turn. Genette calls the embedded narratives 'meta-narratives' (he says, 'the *meta-narrative* is a narrative within the narrative', footnote 41, p. 228) – so, for instance, the individual tales of Chaucer's *The Canterbury Tales*, which are embedded within the frame narrative of the pilgrimage to Canterbury, are meta-narratives, that is, tales within a tale.

It is possible, too, to go a little further and sub-classify frame narratives as 'single-ended', 'double-ended', or 'intrusive'. A 'single-ended' frame narrative is one in which the frame situation is not returned to when the embedded tale is complete. This is the case with *The Turn of the Screw*: when the story of the governess and the children has been told, we do not return to the frame situation (the Christmas ghost story setting) to hear the reaction of the listeners. Clearly, the frame is single-ended in this case because if we went back to the fireside group, many of the crucial ambiguities which are the essence of the tale would have to be explained or debated.

So the frame is single-ended for very good strategic reasons. By contrast, the frame narrative in *Heart of Darkness* is double-ended, meaning that the frame situation is re-introduced at the end of the embedded tale. Thus, when the tale is over we return briefly to the group of listeners to whom Marlow, the dramatised narrator, has been telling the tale of his experiences in the Congo. Of course, Conrad doesn't attempt to 'solve' or elucidate the enormous moral dilemmas which have been the substance of the tale – he merely re-introduces some of the imagery (of half-light and surrounding darkness) which has been prominent throughout, so that the double frame is used to give a kind of reinforcement to the thematics of the tale.

Frames, finally, can also be what we might call 'intrusive', meaning that the embedded tale is occasionally interrupted to revert to the frame situation. This too happens in *Heart of Darkness*, when Marlow interrupts his own telling for a moment and makes the famous remark 'Of course ... you fellows see more than I could see then. You see me, whom you know...' This reminds us of the limitations of viewpoint to which all story-telling is subject, and shows Conrad's distaste for the traditional narrating stance of zero focalisation ('omniscient narration'). He has deliberately chosen a narrator whose outlook has distinct limitations, and the 'intrusive' passage goes on to stress the darkness and isolation of the listeners ('it had become so pitch dark that we listeners could hardly see one another'). The unnamed recorder, who will later write down Marlow's story, voices the moral unease which the tale provokes, and seems to speak for us as readers, reminding us of the kind of alertness and guardedness which readers need ('I listened, I listened on the watch for the sentence, for the word, that would give me the clue to the faint uneasiness inspired by this narrative that seemed to shape itself without human lips in the heavy night-air of the river' (Penguin edition, ed. Robert Hampson, p. 50)). Again, then, it is clear that the author uses an 'intrusive' frame for strategic reasons, seeming to insert at this point a kind of 'alienation device' which deliberately breaks the spell of the narrative, reminding us of its moral complexities, so that we do not simply become uncritically engrossed in reading it as an adventure story which happens to have a colonial setting.

6. How are speech and thought represented?

Genette discusses this matter in his 'Mood' chapter under the sub-heading 'Narrative of Words'. Various options in this area are open to the writer. The easiest option is to present speech which is 'direct and tagged', like this:

'What's your name?' Mario asked her. 'It's Thelma', she replied.

This is direct speech, because the actual spoken words are given (inside the inverted commas), and 'tagging' is the name for the attached phrases which indicate who the speaker is (as in 'Mario asked her' and 'she replied'). The speech can also be presented 'direct and untagged', like this:

'What's your name?'
'Thelma.'

Clearly, this option might become confusing if more than two characters are engaged in conversation, or if the exchange is not simply a sequence of questions and answers, so the preferred option might be 'direct and selectively tagged', like this:

'What's your name?' asked Mario.
'Thelma.'

Here the tagging is 'selective' because the first utterance is tagged (with 'asked Mario'), but not the second (there is no 'she replied', or equivalent). The differences may at first seem slight, but each inserted tag is a reminder of the presence of a narrator, and therefore tends to blunt the edge of the mimesis, edging the 'showing' back towards 'telling'. Another option is that of 'tagged indirect speech', like this:

He asked her what her name was, and she told him it was Thelma.

Here the speech is in 'reported' form, so that we are not given the actual spoken words (for instance, he actually said 'What *is your* name?' He didn't say 'What *was her* name?'). Also, the tagging is 'integral', so to speak (in other words, 'He asked her' and 'she told him' are not separated from the utterances but run into them). This way of reporting speech seems to introduce an element of formal distancing between the reader and the depicted events. The distancing effect is perhaps slightly reduced by the final option, which is the use of 'free indirect speech', like this:

> What was her name? It was Thelma.

Again, the speech is reported or indirect, which is indicated by the switching of verbs from the present tense to the past tense (so that 'is' becomes 'was', etc.). The effect of this style is quite subtle, and one of its advantages to the writer is that it seems to suit an internally focalised narrative, since it seems natural to 'glide' from it into recording the thoughts and feelings of the speaker, like this:

> What was her name? It was Thelma. Thelma, was it? Not the kind of name to launch a thousand ships. More of a suburban, lace-curtain sort of name, really.

Here the musings on the name are clearly those of the male who has asked the question, rather than the overview of an omniscient narrator, but the narrative can also move easily from free indirect speech in the other direction, giving external indications of actions and reactions. Hence, it can be a usefully flexible tool for the writer.

Genette's terms for representations of speech in a narrative are actually slightly more generalised than those just described, envisaging three layers, which get progressively further away from the actual words spoken, as follows:

1. 'I have to go', I said to her. (Mimetic speech)
2. I told her I had to go. (Transposed speech)
3. I informed her that it was necessary for me to leave. (Narratised speech)

As Genette says (p. 172), transposed speech isn't quite the same as free indirect speech: to be precise, it's indirect, but it isn't free (since it has the declarative verb 'I told', which is a form of tagging). The essential difference between transposed and narratised speech is that the former allows us to deduce the actual form of words used ('I have to go'), whereas the latter conveys the *substance* of what was said, but not the actual verbal formula (which could have been 'I've got to go', 'I am obliged to go', 'I have no option but to go', etc.). Effectively, this converts living speech into narrated event, and interposes the maximum distance between the reader and the direct impact and tone of the spoken words.

'Joined-up' narratology

The material discussed in this chapter gives you a kind of basic narratological tool kit. Firstly, we have the crucial distinction between story and plot, which alerts us to questions of how the narrative is designed, and, indeed, what designs it might have upon us. Secondly, Aristotle's categories tune us in to some of the deep-lying, psychic fundamentals of narrative: thirdly, Propp's system provides data for considering some of the surface specifics of plots, and fourthly, Genette's material directs our attention towards how the story is told, how it sets about achieving its designs. We might add, finally, that the five 'codes' of Roland Barthes which we considered earlier in the book (pp. 51–60) can be used as a supplement to all these, for if Aristotle is mainly focused on theme, Propp on plot, and Genette on narration, then Barthes can be said to focus on the reader, for it is the reader's 'de-coding' which makes sense of all of the factors that narratives bring into play. Taken together, in a kind of strategic blending, all these can provide a 'joined-up' form of narratology, in which the aspects of narrative which may be glossed over in one system can receive their due attention from one of the others.

STOP and THINK

One of the most striking aspects of narratology is the way it tends to provide several different terms for the same phenomenon, each one the creation of a different 'school' (see, for instance, 'zero focalisation' and its equivalent term 'omniscient narration'). We might say that this is of little significance, since the English language has always had a 'layered' vocabulary, with several different available words for the same concept. Thus, the Old English word 'blessing' has an Anglo-Norman synonym 'benison', and the Latinate equivalent 'benediction'. The three words each have their own 'flavour' – 'blessing' is plain, 'benison' a bit showy and archaic, and 'benediction' distinctly 'churchy'. Likewise, the terms currently most in vogue in narratology have a distinctly academic tone, being drawn from layers of the vocabulary which derive from Greek and Latin (like 'mimesis' and 'diegesis', for example), rather than from the more reassuring Old English strata. It is very noticeable that writers themselves, who began to discuss the theory of writing from the nineteenth century onwards, tended to prefer very plain terms – George Eliot and Henry James, for instance, spoke of 'showing' and 'saying', rather than 'mimesis' and 'diegesis', and E. M. Forster, in his book *Aspects of the Novel,* first published in 1927, liked to use homely terms which seem to declare their meanings very openly (such as his 'flat' and 'rounded' characters), without any attempt to impress us with their technicality or learnedness. Is it possible to offer a convincing defence of the narratologists' liking for learned-sounding terms?

This is, of course, a personal matter, and you should try to frame your own response to this question. Here is mine: I think the learnedness reflects the narratologists' greater distance from the actual telling of stories, and that it is ultimately due to the fact that they are not usually creative writers themselves. This is in line with the fact that the language used by practitioners about an art or craft tends to be very down-to-earth, for practitioners display their everyday familiarity with the craft by *not* using technical language. Thus, a musician may be described by outsiders as a violinist in an orchestra, but may tell you in conversation that they play the fiddle in a band. In other words, the learned tone of narratological terminology is to be expected, since it reflects a certain distance from the craft itself. But it hardly ever seems just an empty attempt to impress, and there is an attractive concision and precision about these terms, especially in contrast to the much looser way terminology is used within post-structuralism.

What narratologists do

1. They look at individual narratives, seeking out the recurrent structures which are found within all narratives.

2. They switch much of their critical attention away from the mere 'content' of the tale, often focusing instead on the teller and the telling.
3. They take categories derived mainly from the analysis of short narratives and expand and refine them so that they are able to account for the complexities of novel-length narratives.
4. They counteract the tendency of conventional criticism to fore-ground character and motive by foregrounding instead action and structure.
5. They derive much of their reading pleasure and interest from the affinities between all narratives, rather than from the uniqueness and originality of a small number of highly regarded examples.

Narratology: an example

We will use Edgar Allan Poe's tale 'The Oval Portrait' again (Appendix 1) and try to give an impression of how the 'joined-up' narratology just mentioned might look in practice. The four basic areas outlined will be considered (the plot/story distinction, Aristotle, Propp, and Genette), but in an integrated way, rather than in sequence, and with no attempt to use all the categories we have discussed – effective use of literary theory is nearly always selective rather than comprehensive. We will omit Barthes's codes, since these were looked at in Chapter 2.

The distinction between plot and story is immediately apparent in the way the events in the tale are related to us in two 'blocks' which are presented in reverse chronological order: in the plot, we first hear of the civil war, the narrator's wound, his taking refuge in the castle, and his discovery of the portrait. Subsequently we are given the story of the life of the woman in the portrait, which must actually have happened many years before. Had the events been told in chronological order, the effect would have been very different, and the transition would be more difficult to manage than here (where the officer's picking up the book provides a natural-seeming link).

These two 'blocks' of the story are, of course, the 'primary' or 'frame' narrative (the part concerning the wounded officer) and the 'secondary' or 'embedded' narrative (the part concerning the circumstances of the portrait). We now have these more technical terms to describe what was mentioned more straightforwardly in Chapter 1 as the 'story-within-the-story'. It is notable that frame and meta-narrative are unusually balanced – usually the frame is tiny in comparison with the embedded narrative. Emotionally, too, there is a kind of implied equivalence between them, so that the narrator's wound and the denotation of his processes of perception seem to have an almost equal weighting to the tragic story of the squandering of a young life. Perhaps there is the implication in the first part that the setting is a whole country which has been ravaged in the mistaken pursuit of some ideal – a kind of large-scale equivalent of what we see in the embedded narrative.

This raises the issue of what the frame is actually *for*, and answers by saying that it is a way of giving resonance and wider applicability to the themes of the embedded narrative. But the frame is a delaying device, the role of which is to evoke a certain mood or atmosphere (like the overture played before an opera). If the story had been a folk tale or a fairy tale, generic conventions would have dispensed with the frame, and the story would begin 'There was once a young and talented artist …' Again, the effect would be very different. The frame, we can also add here, is open-ended – we don't go back to the officer and valet at the end, so that the story ends with the climactic moment of the artist realising that his wife is dead. Clearly, a double-ended frame would risk dissipating the dramatic impact of this, and in any case, the narrator would have to make some kind of moralising comment, perhaps along the lines that sometimes the human price of great art can be too high, the effect of which would surely be bathetic.

The Proppian material is surprisingly fruitful in the case of this example, a way into it being to suggest that the pathos of the embedded story lies in the way it conflates two archetypal fairy tale motifs, the first being the tale in which a princess is captured by an ogre or villain, imprisoned in a tower, and perhaps incapacitated, paralysed, or put to sleep by some magical agent. Subsequently she is discovered and rescued by a hero who then marries her. The other motif this tale seems to play with is the Bluebeard myth of the suitor who is actually a serial monogamist and a serial killer, with the bodies of previous brides stored in his dungeon. So in Poe's tale too, the bridegroom is already married ('having already a bride in his Art') and is about to kill his bride. So with the kind of conflating of roles mentioned by Robert Scholes, hero and villain are the same figure, and the magical agency of art – the hero's artistic talent – which should enhance life, instead becomes its destroyer. Notice here that we are freely adapting Propp's function 14 ('The hero acquires the use of a magical agent') to the rather different focus of Poe's tale.

Turning to Genette's categories, we can say, firstly, that both primary and embedded narratives are mainly mimetic, but it is clear that there are *degrees* of mimesis. The opening, as far as the words 'a remote turret of the building', retains a degree of generality: for instance, when the valet 'ventured to make forcible entrance' to the chateau, the phrase has an element of the generalising touch usually found in telling rather than showing; the phrase is slightly 'narratised' (that useful term of Genette's), that is, packaged into 'narrator-speak', so that we don't actually 'see' what is happening – did the valet smash the lock with an axe, or shoulder the door repeatedly till it gave way, or run at it using a broken sundial as an improvised battering ram? Or did he just break a ground-floor window with the butt of his rifle and climb in? Clearly, all these phrases would give 'full mimesis', as we might call it, so that we would 'see' what is happening, whereas 'making forcible entrance' is a phrase which gives only a 'partial mimesis', leaving the actual method still a secret of the narrator's.

The description of the room (from 'Its decorations') moves closer towards full mimesis: the decorations are 'rich, yet tattered and antique', but what exactly, when we stop to think about it, are 'decorations'? What precisely are the 'manifold and multiform armorial trophies'? Are they shields, swords, helmets, suits of armour, or what? How many are there of each, and where exactly are they positioned? Well, this kind of 'mid-mimesis' (let's call it) doesn't precisely say, for its job is not to pan slowly round the room like a camcorder, but just to give us a series of vivid impressions of the nature and atmosphere of the room. Full mimesis is reached with the paragraph beginning 'But the action produced', where the pace of the telling is slowed further, and matched to the sequence of the officer's impressions. So we get very precise stage directions which place us exactly in the officer's position, so that we see *with* him, so to speak, and have the illusion that the events are happening before our eyes. The story then remains in full mimesis until the officer picks up the book and the embedded narrative begins, and that too goes through the same stages, from partial, to mid, to full mimesis.

The focalisation of the two narratives is also of interest: the frame narrative is first-person homodiegetic, told to us by an overt or 'dramatised' narrator who has a distinct personality and life history, which we can deduce from the details of the story, even though we do not know his name – he is educated (he knows the eighteenth-century Gothic novels of Ann Radcliffe, is aware of painterly techniques like '*vignetting*', and seems to have a strong interest in the processes and stages of the act of perception) and he is obviously well-to-do (he has a valet, for instance). The narrator of the embedded narrative is more problematical: the 'small volume' found on the pillow which 'purported to criticise and describe' the 'unusually great number' of paintings in the room suggests that he is what would now be called an art critic or connoisseur, but we know nothing else about him. He is, we presume, a heterodiegetic narrator, not part of the tale he tells, but the source of his information after the period when 'there were admitted none into the turret' is difficult to guess – either he is an omniscient narrator who assumes the privilege of entering and constructing the mind of his subject, or else he has some deeper intimacy with the painter. Perhaps he *is* the painter; certainly, we can assume that the 'unusually great number of spirited modern paintings' on the walls are all painted by the same artist, since they are all evidently in the same style, and perhaps each of them was produced in similar circumstances, each costing the life of the sitter, in a compulsively repeated 'primal scene' in which art and life struggle together for supremacy. Interestingly, then, these at first technical speculations about the nature of the narrator seem to lead quickly to the deepest levels of content.

This brings us to that underlying Aristotelian level: the hamartia (the sin or fault which motors the whole story) is of course the moral blindness of the talented artist, who elevates himself to god-like status, taking on the role of *creating* life, but being able to do so only at the *expense* of life. He lacks both *in*sight (knowledge of himself) and *fore*sight, being unable to see the inevitable outcome of his creative obsessions. Curiously for an artist, he also lacks empathy and imagination, and so cannot reproduce the real thing, only a simulacrum, a kind of spooky hologram from which the essence of the person is quite absent. The moment of self-recognition, or anagnorisis, comes too late, since he never has the thought 'she is dying', only the belated perception 'she is dead'. The peripeteia, or switch in fortune, is perhaps relevant to both characters, for the male figure changes from being an artist of 'high renown' and becomes a vampiric murderer, while the woman is at first a kind of embodiment of the energies of the life force itself, and then becomes the meekly yielding victim whose erotic appeal consists of listlessly allowing her life to be drained away (the fate of most of the women in Poe's tales).

So, approaching the story through these mainly technical narratological categories does seem to open up new avenues which do indeed suggest how meanings are constructed in narratives, at the same time as having the spin-off bonus of giving us new ideas about this particular tale and its well-worn thematic territory of the conflict and contrast between the claims of life and the claims of art.

Selected reading

Bal, Mieke, *Narratology: Introduction to the Theory of Narrative* (University of Toronto Press, 3rd edn, 2009).
    Originally written in Dutch, and first published in English in 1985, this book quickly became a standard text: it has the precision, concision, and clarity which typify narratology at its best – like all the important works in the field, this is not a massive tome. Can be read through with pleasure, or used as a concise encyclopaedia of narratology.
Cohan, Steven, and Shires, Linda M., *Telling Stories: A Theoretical Analysis of Narrative Fiction* (Routledge, 1988).
    Covers narrative across the whole range of contemporary culture (film, advertising, and so on). Plenty of useful material, though rather austerely written.
Genette, Gérard, *Narrative Discourse* (Cornell University Press, 1983).
    Genette's five chapters on 'Order', 'Duration', 'Frequency', 'Mood', and 'Voice' are the source of much contemporary thinking in narratology. It would help if the many sub-headings were printed in the rather minimalist list of contents, but the excellent index makes up for the deficiency,

facilitating the kind of 'encyclopaedic' use which is important in this field.

Herman, David, ed., *The Cambridge Companion to Narrative* (Cambridge University Press, 2007).

Useful chapters on story, plot and narration; time and space; character; dialogue; focalisation, etc., in a collection which aims to cater for 'readers coming to the field of narrative studies for the first time'.

Onega, Susana, and Angel, José, eds, *Narratology* (Routledge, 1996).

An excellent collection. It stresses the mutual influences of narratology and deconstruction, feminism, psychoanalysis, and film and media studies.

Prince, Gerald, *A Dictionary of Narratology* (University of Nebraska Press, rev. edn, 2003).

Contains the briefest and most pithy definitions – this little book is strikingly catholic in its representation of the various narratological sects. Whatever I want to know in narratology, this is usually my first port of call.

Propp, Vladimir, *Morphology of the Folktale* (University of Texas Press, 2nd rev. edn, 1968).

Puckett, Kent, *Narrative Theory: A Critical Introduction* (Cambridge University Press, 2016).

Excellent in its clarity, range, and expertise.

Rimmon-Kenan, Shlomith, *Narrative Fiction* (Routledge, 2nd edn, 2002).

Can seem a little daunting, but this pioneering work, originally published in 1983, is extremely wide-ranging, in spite of its brevity.

13
Ecocriticism

Ecocriticism or green studies?

'Simply defined, ecocriticism is the study of the relationship between literature and the physical environment' (Cheryll Glotfelty). But should we call it 'ecocriticism' or 'green studies'? Both terms are used to denote a critical approach which began in the USA in the late 1980s, and in the UK in the early 1990s, and it is worth briefly setting out its institutional history to date. In the USA the acknowledged founder is Cheryll Glotfelty, co-editor with Harold Fromm of a key collection of helpful and definitive essays entitled *The Ecocriticism Reader: Landmarks in Literary Ecology* (University of Georgia Press, 1996). In 1992 she was also the co-founder of ASLE (pronounced 'Az-lee', the Association for the Study of Literature and Environment). ASLE has its own 'house journal', called *ISLE (Interdisciplinary Studies in Literature and Environment)*, which started in 1993, so American ecocriticism was already a burgeoning academic movement by the early 1990s, beginning to establish its professional infrastructure of designated journals and an official corporate body. Another prominent ASLE figure is Ursula K. Heise, Chair in Literary Studies at the Department of English, and the Institute of the Environment and Sustainability at UCLA, and co-editor of the *Routledge Companion to the Environmental Humanities* (2016). Since ecocriticism in the USA seems to be strongest in the universities of the West – that is, away from the largest cities, and from the major academic power-centres of the East and West coasts – we might expect it to embody 'decentrist' ideals rather than having a 'core' of key terms and procedures.

Ecocriticism as a concept first arose in the late 1970s, at meetings of the WLA (the Western Literature Association, a body whose field of interest is the literature of the American West). In his intro-duction to a series of brief position papers (all entitled 'What is ecocriticism?'), Michael P. Branch traces the word 'ecocriticism' back to William Rueckert's 1978 essay 'Literature and ecology: an experiment in ecocriticism'.[1] A claim for first usage in literary criti-cism of the related term 'ecological' is made by prominent US eco-critic Karl Kroeber, whose article '"Home at Grasmere": ecological holiness', appeared in the journal *PMLA*, 89, 1974, pp. 132–41. Both terms ('ecocriticism' and 'ecological') apparently lay dormant in the critical vocabulary (says Branch) until the 1989 WLA conference (in Coeur d'Alene, USA), when Cheryll Glotfelty (at the time a graduate student at Cornell University, subsequently Professor of Literature and the Environment at the University of Nevada, Reno) not only revived the term 'ecocriticism', but urged its adoption to refer to the diffuse critical field that had previously been known as 'the study of nature writing'.

Ecocriticism, as it now exists in the USA, takes its literary bear-ings from three major nineteenth-century American writers whose work celebrates nature, the life force, and the wilderness as mani-fested in America, these being Ralph Waldo Emerson (1803–82), Margaret Fuller (1810–50), and Henry David Thoreau (1817–62). All three were 'members' of the group of New England writers, essayists, and philosophers known collectively as the transcendentalists, the first major literary movement in America to achieve 'cultural inde-pendence' from European models. Emerson's first, short book *Nature*, first published anonymously in 1836 (included in *Ralph Waldo Emerson: Nature and Selected Essays*, ed. Larzer Ziff, Pen-guin, 2003) is a reflective (rather than philosophical) essay on the impact upon him of the natural world, often voiced in words of powerfully dramatic directness:

1 Branch's introduction, and the sixteen short pieces presented at a 1994 sympo-sium on ecocriticism, can all be accessed in the ASLE website in the section 'Explore Our Field' under the sub-heading 'Definitions of Ecocriticism Archive'. The document is entitled 'Defining Ecocritical Theory and Practice'.

> Crossing a bare common, in snow puddles, at twilight, under a
> clouded sky, without having in my thoughts any occurrence of special
> good fortune, I have enjoyed a perfect exhilaration. I am glad to the
> brink of fear. (Chapter 1, p. 38)

Fuller's first book was *Summer on the Lakes, During 1843* (included
in *The Portable Margaret Fuller*, Viking/Penguin, 1994), which is a
powerfully written journal of her encounter with the American landscape at large, after a period as the first woman student at Harvard.
At Niagara, for instance, she writes:

> For here there is no escape from the weight of a perpetual creation;
> all other forms and motions come and go, the tide rises and recedes,
> the wind, at its mightiest, moves in gales and gusts, but here is really
> an incessant, an indefatigable motion. Awake or asleep, there is
> no escape, still this rushing round you and through you. It is in this
> way I have most felt the grandeur – somewhat eternal, if not infinite.
> (p. 71)

Thoreau's *Walden* (Oxford University Press, World's Classics, 1999)
is an account of his two-year stay, from 1845, in a hut he had built
on the shore of Walden Pond, a couple of miles from his home
town of Concord, Massachusetts. It is, perhaps, *the* classic account
of dropping out of modern life and seeking to renew the self by a
'return to nature' – this is certainly a book which has always exerted
a strong effect on the attitudes of its readers. These three books can
be seen as the foundational works of American 'ecocentred' writing.

By contrast, the UK version of ecocriticism, or green studies,
takes its bearings from the British Romanticism of the 1790s rather
than the American transcendentalism of the 1840s. The founding
figure on the British side is the critic Jonathan Bate, author of *Romantic Ecology: Wordsworth and the Environmental Tradition* (Routledge, 1991). British ecocritics also make the point that many of
their concerns are evident (before the term 'ecocriticism' existed)
in Raymond Williams's book *The Country and the City* (Chatto &
Windus, 1973). The infrastructure of ecocriticism in the UK is less
developed than in the USA (there are as yet no indigenous journals
or formal bodies for ecocritics to join, though there is a UK and
Ireland branch of ASLE designated ASLE-UKI, with its house
journal *Green Letters*), but the provision of relevant course options

on undergraduate degree programmes is becoming more wide-spread, especially in new universities and colleges of higher education. Of course, institutional affiliations change, but at the time of writing, apart from Bate himself (who teaches at the University of Oxford), most of the active British proponents of ecocriticism were based at these institutions, such as Laurence Coupe at Manchester Metropolitan University, Richard Kerridge and Greg Garrard both at Bath Spa University, and Terry Gifford, Visiting Scholar, Centre for Writing and Environment, also at Bath Spa. Garrard, editor of *The Oxford Handbook of Ecocriticism* (2014), has now moved to the University of British Columbia as Associate Professor, and Harriet Tarlo, editor of the influential anthology of environmental poetry *The Ground Aslant: An Anthology of Radical Landscape Poetry* (Shearsman Press, 2011), is a poet and Reader in Creative Writing at Sheffield Hallam University. The earliest definitive UK collection of essays (having equivalent status in the UK to that of Glotfelty and Fromm in the USA) is Laurence Coupe's *The Green Studies Reader: From Romanticism to Ecocriticism* (Routledge, 2000).

The existence of two distinct national variants of the ecological approach suggests a situation similar to the one described in Chapter 9, in which we saw how 'British' cultural materialism and 'American' new historicism are clearly linked in their approaches and aims, but differ in emphasis and 'ancestry'. Generally, the pre-ferred American term was 'ecocriticism', whereas 'green studies' was frequently used in the UK, and there was perhaps a tendency for the American writing to be 'celebratory' in tone whereas the British variant tended to be more 'minatory', that is, it sought to warn us of environmental threats emanating from governmental, in-dustrial, commercial, and neo-colonial forces. For instance, Bate's later book, *The Song of the Earth* (Picador, 2000), argued that colo-nialism and deforestation have frequently gone together.[2] However, during the past fifteen years there has been considerable conver-gence of practice and theory between American and British ecocriticism.

2 He writes: 'As Robert Pogue Harrison has demonstrated in his remarkable book *Forests: The Shadow of Civilization*, imperialism has always brought with it defor-estation and the consuming of natural resources' (p. 87).

Culture and nature

What attitudes, then, are characteristic of ecocriticism, irrespective of which national variant is in question? This sub-section indicates the scope of some of the debates within ecocriticism concerning the crucial matter of the relationship between culture and nature. Perhaps the most fundamental point to make here is that ecocritics reject the notion (common to most of the other theories considered in this book) that everything is socially and/or linguistically constructed (which is the first item in the list of five recurrent ideas in critical theory given in Chapter 1). For the ecocritic, nature really exists, out there beyond ourselves, not needing to be ironised as a concept by enclosure within knowing inverted commas, but actually present as an entity which affects us, and which we can affect, perhaps fatally, if we mistreat it. Nature, then, isn't reducible to a concept which we conceive as part of our cultural practice (as we might conceive a deity, for instance, and project it out on to the universe). Theory in general tends to see our external world as socially and linguistically constructed, as 'always already' textualised into 'discourse', but ecocriticism calls this long-standing theoretical orthodoxy into question, sometimes rather impatiently, as in Kate Soper's frequently quoted remark (in her seminal book *What is Nature?*, p. 151) that 'It isn't language which has a hole in its ozone layer.' Ecocriticism, then, repudiates the foundational belief in 'constructedness' which is such an important aspect of literary theory. Of course, that belief in the universality of social constructedness was always vulnerable to the objection that if true it would necessarily be unknowable (since 'everything' would include the idea itself that 'everything is socially and linguistically constructed'). In the recent past, social-construction gangs seemed to be everywhere, digging up and replacing the academic sidewalks, and for the most part their work is still in place, constituting the main academic thoroughfare in the humanities. So the difficulty of either verifying or falsifying the view that everything is socially or linguistically constructed has not diminished its grip on day-to-day debate about literary theory. Nevertheless, the essence of ecocriticism's intervention in theory has been to challenge it.

This crucial point, however, should not be taken as implying that ecocritics hold a naïve 'pre-theoretical' notion of nature. There have been set-piece confrontations on this issue which will repay study and are equivalent in importance to the key debates over the fundamentals of theory mentioned elsewhere in this book, such as the exchanges between F. R. Leavis and René Wellek in the 1930s over the principles of literary criticism (see Chapter 1), and the dialogue between F. W. Bateson and Roger Fowler over linguistics and literary criticism in the 1960s (see Chapter 11). In the case of ecocriticism, some of the most heated exchanges have been between the American Wordsworth critic Alan Liu and various ecocritics, including Jonathan Bate (in *Romantic Ecology*), Karl Kroeber (in *Ecological Literary Criticism*), and Terry Gifford (originally in *ISLE* in 1996, and reprinted in Coupe's *The Green Studies Reader*, pp. 173–6). The key feature of Liu's position is the view that calling something 'nature', and seeing it as 'simply given', is usually a way of avoiding the politics which has made it that way. Of course, it *can* be so: for instance, the well-known nineteenth-century children's hymn by C. F. Alexander, 'All things bright and beautiful' originally contained the notorious lines (long omitted from most editions):

> The rich man in his castle,
> The poor man at his gate;
> He made them high and lowly
> And ordered their estate.

It is obvious here that social inequality is being 'naturalised', that is, literally, disguised as nature, and viewed as a situation which is 'God-given' and inescapable, when actually it is the product of a specific politics and power structure. (Perhaps Karl Marx had such sentiments in mind when he said, in his 'Critique of the *Hegelian Philosophy of Right*', in 1844, that religion is the opium of the people.) The Left's long-standing assumption is that *any* invocation of nature will have the side-effect of disguising politics and so legitimating inequalities and injustices. Hence, for Liu (in Bate's paraphrase of his position) '*There is no nature* ... in other words, "nature" is nothing more than an anthropomorphic construct created by Wordsworth and the rest for their own purposes' (Coupe, p. 171). Liu's now notorious remark is a frequent target in ecocritical writing and has been, paradoxically, a valuable stimulus to the definition and crystallisation of ecocritical positions (see for instance the chapter 'Surprised by nature: ecology and Cold War criticism' in Kroeber's book, listed below). Gifford quotes Liu directly to the effect that 'Nature is the name under which we use the nonhuman to validate the human, to interpose a mediation able to make humanity more easy with itself' (Coupe, p. 175). Gifford's response is to say that 'while Liu is right to identify the word *nature* as "a mediation", he is wrong to deny the general physical presence that is one side of that mediation' (p. 175). Indeed, the meaning of the word 'nature' is a key 'site of struggle' for nearly all the theories discussed in this book, and it is the word with one of the longest entries in Raymond Williams's influential book *Keywords*, which is a glossary of key terms and concepts from cultural history.[3]

Perhaps it is appropriate in a late chapter of a book of this kind to say that this issue of the social and linguistic constructedness of reality (sometimes called 'the problem of the real') has been one of the areas on which the teaching of theory has tended to generate confusion. Of course, attitudes to nature vary, and some of the variations are culturally determined, but the fact that a phenomenon is regarded differently in different cultures doesn't call its 'reality' into question. Like Terry Gifford (Coupe, p. 176), I can point to my own bald head as evidence of the overarching grand narrative of nature which contains us all in the cycle of growth, maturity, and decay. I may have plenty of Lyotardian 'incredulity' towards this narrative, but it won't make any difference. Yet 'ageing', both as a fact and as a concept, features differently in different cultures. Some cultures regard it as almost a shameful thing, so that the elderly affect youthful styles of speech, dress, tastes, and behaviour. Other cultures, and other eras, regard(ed) it as honourable and admirable, as an index of the possession of wisdom or understanding, for instance. Thus, traditional representations of Socrates or God the

---

3 I recall Williams at a conference on literary theory in the 1980s becoming increasingly irritated at the nervous apologies offered by speakers whenever they had to use the word 'nature' – even apparently innocent phrases like 'the nature of the problem' had become taboo, or were felt to require elaborate fumigation before being used in public.

Father show elderly, grey-bearded patriarchal figures in flowing garments, rather than glossy, sharply dressed, youngish men or women, as if age and masculinity were the natural fleshly garb of the 'wisdom of the ages'. But these different, culturally determined ways of regarding the fact of ageing should not prevent us from realising that it doesn't follow that age is 'socially constructed', or that it is part of culture rather than nature. Such statements, we must be clear, are figurative and hyperbolic – they gesture towards an *element* of truth, but they must not be passed off as *literal* truth. They are like the statements sometimes made about actors in film advertisements which proclaim (for instance) that 'Marlon Brando *is* The Godfather'. In teaching literary theory we have perhaps not made this and kindred distinctions as clear as we ought to have done. One of the welcome side-effects of ecocriticism is to bring this vital issue to the fore, making us clarify our thoughts about it, even if somewhat belatedly.

A related issue, which is also thrown into relief by ecocriticism, is whether a distinction is deconstructed into self-contradiction by the fact that (like the nature/culture distinction) it is not always absolute and clear-cut. At one level this can be answered very easily: the existence of distinctions is not undermined at all by the simultaneous existence of intermediate states – grey is real, but its existence doesn't destabilise the difference between black and white. If we translate this into issues directly relevant to ecocriticism, we can say that we have nature, and culture, and states partaking of both, and that all three are real. Consider, for instance, what we can call the 'outdoor environment' as a series of adjoining and overlapping areas which move gradually from nature to culture, along the following lines:

Area one: 'the wilderness' (e.g. deserts, oceans, uninhabited continents)

Area two: 'the scenic sublime' (e.g. forests, lakes, mountains, cliffs, waterfalls)

Area three: 'the countryside' (e.g. hills, fields, woods)

Area four: 'the domestic picturesque' (e.g. parks, gardens, lanes)

As we move mentally through these areas, it is clear that we move from pretty well 'pure' nature in the first to what is predominantly 'culture' in the fourth. Of course, the wilderness is affected by global warming, which is cultural, and gardens depend on sunlight, which is a natural force, but neither concept ('nature' or 'culture') is thereby invalidated. Furthermore, the two middle areas, to varying degrees, contain large elements of *both* culture and nature, so that we might have doubts about the right positioning of some of the component elements within them (should mountains be categorised as part of area one, hills as area two?), but these uncertainties should not be seen as destabilising the fundamental distinction between nature and culture. Even if it could be shown that all four areas were actually different degrees or kinds of culture, it would still not follow that there is no such thing as nature. (In the same way, the fact that drizzle is merely a kind of rain does not mean that there is no such thing as drizzle, nor does it mean that it makes no difference whether we say 'It's raining' or 'It's drizzling'.)

If we return to the four environmental areas, it will be clear that most of what is called 'nature writing' concerns the two middle ones: eighteenth-century topographical writing, which might be exemplified by James Thomson's *The Seasons* (1730), Thomas Gray's 'Elegy in a Country Churchyard' (1751), and William Cowper's *The Task* (1785), had area three as its preferred location, while British Romantic writing, like Wordsworth's *The Prelude* (1805, in its best-known form) often centred on area two; but American transcendentalist writing of the nineteenth century was predominantly interested in area one (mountain ranges, prairies, colossal cataracts, space itself).[4] Areas three and four are often the setting for domestic fiction and lyric poetry, both of which centre upon relationships between human beings, while the first two areas are the preferred settings for epic and saga, which centre on relations between human beings and cosmic forces (fate, destiny, the deity, etc.), and for 'Promethean' narratives in which human beings test the limits of their scope and powers – such as Milton's *Paradise Lost*, Mary Shelley's *Frankenstein,* and Herman Melville's *Moby Dick*. The wilderness is entered as if instinctively by those who would 'find' themselves –

4 See, for instance, Thoreau's essay 'Walking' (extracted in Coupe, pp. 23–5), which discusses these matters: he writes 'I do not know of any poetry to quote which adequately expresses this yearning for the Wild'.

Moses ascends the mountain to receive the commandments, Christ goes into the wilderness to pray, the aboriginal initiate goes 'walk-about' in the outback, Huck Finn 'lights out for the territories', and so on. These spaces, then, seem to perform a special function for us, a function vital to our well-being, though this, of course, is to view them in anthropocentric (human-centred) fashion, as if they existed for our benefit, a point which 'deep ecology' would resist.[5] The point repeatedly made by ecocritics is that for the first time in human history, no true wilderness any longer exists on the planet, for every region is affected by global warming, and other 'anthropo-centric' problems, such as toxic waste and nuclear fallout. Our sense of these problems will vary, but we surely need to concede, at least, that issues of gender, race, and class cannot any longer exhaust the range of concerns that literature and criticism ought to have, though 'social ecologists' and 'ecofeminists' will rightly seek to blend such concerns with an ecologically driven programme and outlook. Seek-ing to contribute to rectifying injustices in the areas of gender, race, and class is a praiseworthy aim for critics and theorists to have, but it isn't sensible to ignore the fact that making a difference in these presupposes that we can manage to avoid environmental catas-trophe. Otherwise, it might seem like working flat out to secure improved working conditions for the crew as the *Titanic* speeds to-wards the iceberg.

Turning criticism inside out

An ecocritical reading of a literary text is, simply, one which in some way incorporates a consideration of the kind of issues and concerns we have just been discussing. But there is, as we have said, no

---

5 Bate distinguishes 'light Greens' and 'dark Greens' (*The Song of the Earth*, p. 37): the former are 'environmentalists' who value nature because it 'environs' hu-manity and contributes to our well-being; they believe we can 'save' the planet by more responsible forms of consumption and production: 'dark Greens', or 'deep ecologists' take a more radical stance – technology is the problem and therefore can't be the solution, so we have (in some way) to 'get back to nature': they dislike the anthropocentric term 'environment', preferring 'nature', viewed as being there for its own sake, not ours.

universally accepted model that we have merely to learn and apply. Often, it is just a matter of approaching perhaps very familiar texts with a new alertness to this dimension, a dimension which has perhaps always hovered about the text, but without ever receiving our full attention before. This is well illustrated in the opening of a short piece by Ralph W. Black entitled 'What we talk about when we talk about ecocriticism':

> Not long ago I saw *King Lear* again. Olivier's *Lear*. I marvelled as usual at Lear's deep rage and deeper sadness, and I cried as usual as he carried Cordelia's body across the stage at the end. But I was struck even more by the beginning: A map of the kingdom is unrolled. It is painted across the tanned hides of a small herd of royal deer. The old Sovereign uses his sword to symbolically divide his domain among his daughters. Even before the daughters have spoken, or refused to speak, the trajectory of their love, there is this transgression: the commodified landscape is sliced up and parcelled out to the highest rhetorical bidder. For a moment I wonder about my understanding of the tragedy, about what hubristic act instigates Lear's fall, about the significance of the natural world in the play, the moments of clarity that all seem to take place outside – in a storm, on the moors, at the seashore.[6]

These introductory remarks signal a reading of *Lear* which would have a distinctly different flavour from any other, not because the play is being reduced to ecological considerations, but, rather, because these are being added for the first time to all the other issues which more traditional approaches have always seen in the play. Such a reading would remind us that the slice of the kingdom available to Cordelia (the 'third more opulent'), provided she says what her father wants to hear, is real, peopled landscape – hills, fields, rivers, farms, communities – which are about to be randomly chopped up at the monarch's whim, as if they had no claims or integrity of their own. Likewise, the 'blasted heath' on which Lear enacts his madness is a real place located somewhere within this territory, and perhaps emblematic (in its 'blastedness') of the neglect and degradation which that territory suffers as a political consequence of

6 This is one of the items from the symposium mentioned in footnote 1.

Lear's act. The storm, too, isn't just the emblematic correlative of Lear's madness, but real weather, representing the natural processes which his unnatural behaviour refuses to come to terms with, processes such as his own ageing, and his consequent side-lining by the following generation ('All old men are King Lear', said Tolstoy, and Freud, too, saw *Lear* as an archetypal 'family drama'). Ecocritical readings of canonical texts, then, begin by adding a different perspective, and are not limited to works self-evidently about nature.

But the *Lear* reading implied here does have one other characteristic which is worth noting particularly, namely the way it tends to turn the conventional manner of reading inside out (so to speak). By this is meant that its strategy seems to be to switch critical attention from inner to outer, so that what had seemed mere 'setting' is brought in from the critical margins to the critical centre (so that, among other things, the storm *is* a storm, and not just a metaphor for the turmoil in Lear's mind). I want to illustrate this important move – this refusal to privilege the inner over the outer – at slightly greater length using another text as example, the aim being to emphasise that this need not be a reductive move, and that the complexity which is (after all) the life-blood of our literary study is thereby enriched rather than diluted. The text I am using here is Edgar Allan Poe's well-known tale 'The Fall of the House of Usher'.[7] In the tale, Roderick Usher and his sister Madeline undergo a kind of voluntary imprisonment in the ancient, crumbling, isolated House of Usher, which stands next to an evil-looking lake, 'a black and lurid tarn that lay in unruffled lustre by the dwelling'. The sister suffers from a strange wasting disease, while Usher himself, a being of 'lofty and spiritual ideality', is afflicted by 'a morbid acuteness of the senses', which makes him unable to bear any contact with the natural world – 'the odours of all flowers were oppressive; his eyes were tortured by even a faint light'. His only contact with the world beyond himself is through art, and when the narrator first encounters him, 'many books and musical instruments lay scattered about, but failed to give any vitality to the scene.'

7 If you do not have it to hand you can download the complete text from a website, such as: www.kingkong.demon.co.uk/gsr/usher.htm.

The tale is usually read with a focus on the morbid psychology of Usher, and on the strange way in which the narrator's arrival triggers Madeline's decline: the narrator's complicity in her premature entombment in the vault directly beneath his own room is described, as well as his orchestration of her reappearance (he reads aloud to Usher from a lurid novel which parallels the grotesque drama of break-out and resurgence taking place below). The shock of seeing his resurrected sister kills the neurasthenic Usher, and because the presence of the unnamed narrator triggers all these events, it is common to read Usher and Madeline as aspects of the narrator's own being, that is, as the subconscious underside of his rationality. This is a common literary-critical ploy – the *external* (whether characters, objects, situations, or events) is read as *internal* (in this case, as elements of the subconscious).

The ecocentred reading, by contrast, focuses *outside*, on the house and its environs, rather than inside, on the owner and his psychology. It uses ideas of energy, entropy (which is a kind of negative energy within systems which tends towards breakdown and disorganisation), and symbiosis ('sym-biosis', literally 'living together', denoting mutually sustaining, co-existing systems). Thus, the house exists as an isolated entropic system which has no symbiotic connections at all with the broader biosphere. The stagnant lake reflects the house's own unmoving image; the house breathes in the atmosphere of its own decay – the 'gradual yet certain condensation of an atmosphere of their own about the waters and the walls'. It has its own sealed-off microclimate, and as the climax approaches it seems to stew in its own locked-up and aborted energies, for when Usher and the narrator look out of the window 'the exceeding density of the clouds (which hung so low as to press upon the turrets of the house) did not prevent our perceiving the lifelike velocity with which they flew careering from all points against each other, without passing away into the distance'. The House of Usher, then, is not part of a living system; no new elements come in from outside to energise it and enable it to contribute to other systems; it is a light that failed, a stream that has ceased to flow, a fire with nothing to burn. Its narcissistic aloofness from the flow of the broader life-force turns it into a kind of Black Hole, which becomes a vortex into which its energies are sucked and destroyed – 'a whirlwind had apparently collected its force in our vicinity' says the narrator when he looks out of the window, and we also have the black tarn (or lake) into which the house collapses and disappears at the end. Most eerie of all is Usher's mind, 'from which darkness, as if an inherent positive quality, poured forth upon all objects of the moral and physical universe, in one unceasing radiation of gloom'. Usher, then, radiates not energy but entropy, like an imploded star rushing towards its own disintegration. Frighteningly, he is all 'culture' and no 'nature'; he is 'photophobic' (hyper-sensitive to light) and cannot bear natural light at all, and prefers the represented light in paintings; he cannot bear natural sounds either, only the 'processed sound' of music. What is imaged here, then, is an ecosystem damaged beyond repair and in its death-throes: this is life on a cooling planet, a system clogged with its own detritus and cut off from any possible sources of catharsis or renewal. On this reading, the centre of the story is not a dark night of the soul, with its accompanying ontological anxieties, but the permanent night of wilfully courted ecological disaster, nuclear winter, or solar exhaustion. This is a more frightening tale than conventional readings usually produce, for when the narrator runs from the collapsing house there will be nowhere for him to run *to*.

STOP and THINK

The offices in my college department have what I think of as 'counter-intuitive' door locks – you unlock the door by turning the key *towards* the door jamb, rather than *away* from it. The result is that you must consciously reverse the intuitively obvious procedure every time you unlock the door. Critical theory has provided us with sets of keys for unlocking doors (Yale keys, in some cases), and many of them seem to have a strongly 'counter-intuitive' base. By this I mean that they put forward positions which seem to contradict notions which in everyday life we tend instinctively to regard as right or true. In the case of ecocriticism, the intuition we have to counter is a long-standing, deeply ingrained Western cultural tradition of anthropocentric attitudes, which are both religious and humanist, and often enshrined in commonplace references and sayings:

thus, the early Greek philosopher Protagoras (fifth century BC) makes the famous statement 'Man is the measure of all things', which places *us* confidently at the centre of everything; in the Book of Genesis human beings are given 'dominion' over 'the fish of the sea and the birds of the air and every creature that moves on the ground'; likewise, Leonardo da Vinci's famous drawing 'The Vitruvian Man' (the familiar image shows a naked male figure set within a circle and a square, with arms out-stretched both horizontally, and diagonally above the head) sees the proportions of the human body as the basis of the most fundamental geometrical shapes, and hence, supposedly, of all proportions which please the eye; and in the eighteenth century Alexander Pope writes (in *An Essay on Man*) 'Know then thyself, presume not God to scan; / *The proper study of mankind is Man'* [my italics]. All these, and many more images and sayings like them, seem to give us a high cultural licence for attitudes which are anthropocentric rather than ecocentric.

In the nineteenth century the great Victorian art critic John Ruskin, in his *Modern Painters*, vol. 3 (1856), coined the term the 'pathetic fallacy' for our instinctive tendency to see our emotions reflected in our environment, which seems to be an-other form of the habit of seeing everything as centred upon ourselves: 'All violent feelings', he says, 'have the same effect. They produce in us a falseness in all our impressions of external things, which I would generally characterize as the "pathetic fallacy".' Hence, a phrase like 'the *cruel* sea' manifests the pathetic fallacy by projecting a human attribute (cruelty) on to a natural element. Ruskin was deeply eco-conscious, the first major British writer to record a sense that nature's powers of recovery might not be infinite, and that modern forms of pro-duction and consumption have the potential to inflict fatal en-vironmental damage: in his lectures on what he called 'the storm-cloud of the nineteenth century', which he also called 'the modern plague-cloud', he expressed his deep anxiety that the atmosphere was being permanently damaged by industrial pollution, which we might say was the environmental conse-quence of assuming that our 'dominion' over nature need have no limits. The 'minatory' Ruskin is convinced, after twenty years of making observations, that cloud formations, atmospheric conditions, and weather patterns had changed (had *been* changed) during that time.

Interestingly, Emerson, by contrast, had no worries about the pathetic fallacy – 'Nature always wears the colours of the spirit', he says, in the first chapter of *Nature*, and it is difficult not to sympathise with what he is saying. Is it going too far to suggest that the difference between these two figures on this point is symptomatic of that divergent tendency between US and UK ecocriticism mentioned earlier? Is it an over-simplification to label the two viewpoints as symptomatic of (respectively) environmental optimism and environmental pessimism? Are crowded islands like Britain and Japan likely to inspire the gut feeling that nature is rapidly being gobbled up by culture, while on the other hand, vast land-masses like America or Australia tend by their very surrounding presence to produce the deep-down conviction that the earth will survive, no matter what evidence there might be about global warming and the ozone layer? Whichever way we instinctively incline on this, can our own well-meant awareness of the problem make any difference? What changes in the world order will be needed to make an improvement in the situation, and will they inevitably curtail our freedoms? After all, what gave Ruskin the freedom to write about and worry about industrial pollution (while other men and women had to sweat for a living)? Wasn't it, ultimately, the family fortune, which was based on the importing of sherry, a trade which must be as intimately linked as any other to the forces which produce industrial pollution? Can our own lives, of books, and courses, and websites, and social media, be any less implicated?

The Anthropocene, and things

For nearly the past 12,000 years – the merest speck of time in relation to the age of the Earth – we have been in the geological epoch known as the Holocene (the Greek roots of the term mean 'entirely recent'), which covers the late and post-Stone Age period of human history, since the glaciers retreated at the end of the last Ice Age. During the first two decades of the new millennium it has been proposed that a new geological epoch has now dawned, and that it should be called the 'Anthropocene'. This word is roughly translatable as 'the human age', and it is chosen because substantial evidence of human activity, much of it environmentally negative, can be found in the geological record. So this still 'informal' (meaning provisional or popular) term reflects the idea that 'humans are now the main drivers of the Earth's geology'.[8] It was coined by Paul J. Crutzen at a conference in Mexico in the year 2000, Crutzen being an eminent atmospheric chemist who won the Nobel Prize in 1995 for his work on 'the mechanism of human-driven ozone destruction'. It first appeared in print in a short article by Crutzen and Eugene F. Stoermer of the University of Michigan (*Global Change Newsletter*, May 2000, pp. 17–18), and then in a related piece called 'The geology of mankind' in the journal *Nature* in the same year. The term was much debated over the following decade, quickly entering popular usage, and in 2009 a 'Working Group on the Anthropocene' (WGA) was set up, chaired by Jan Zalasiewicz, a professor of palaeobiology at the University of Leicester. The WGA reported its findings to the International Geological Congress in Cape Town in 2016, advising the official adoption of this term by the scientific community. The evidence cited is that human-made minerals are becoming 'distinctive proponents of the sedimentary strata now forming', including the 'flash-metamorphosed rock' produced in brick making ('Something like a trillion bricks are now made a year'), and the 'novel rock' concrete, which is 'distinctive geologically' – 'something like half a trillion tons has now been produced'. Other frequently mentioned features now registering stratigraphically (that is, in 'the sedimentary [rock] strata now forming') include 1) radioactive elements dispersed across the planet by nuclear-bomb tests; 2) plastic pollution; 3) soot from power stations; 4) the bones left by the global proliferation of the domestic chicken; 5) the acceleration of anthropogenic (meaning human-generated) carbon

8 This and all the remaining quotations in this paragraph are from Jan Zalasiewicz, *Rocks: A Very Short Introduction* (Oxford University Press, 2016), pp. 122–4.

dioxide emissions; 6) sea-level rise, because of the resulting shrink-age of the polar icecaps; 7) the transformation of land by deforesta-tion and development; and 8) related global mass extinction of species.

This data may turn out to be crucial to human and planetary survival, but it is also legitimate to ask how it might affect the way we read literature. In a deep psycho-layer of metaphor, rocks and stones seem to connote whatever is permanent and beyond change – we speak of (say) a decision not being 'set in stone', meaning that it could still be changed, or we imagine an eternal deity as the 'Rock of Ages'. Thus, in *Wuthering Heights* (Chapter 9) Cathy proclaims that while her love for Linton might change over the years, her love for Heathcliff won't, and to express this feeling she uses rocks metaphorically:

> My love for Linton is like the foliage in the woods: time will change it, I'm well aware, as winter changes the trees. My love for Heathcliff resembles the eternal rocks beneath: a source of little visible delight, but necessary.

In a similar way, Wordsworth, in his Lucy poem 'A slumber did my spirit seal', contrasts human transience with the 'eternal' of primal forces like rocks and stones, as the dead Lucy is 'Rolled round in earth's diurnal course,/ With rocks, and stones, and trees.' Interest-ingly, the trees seem to shift sides in the dichotomy across these two examples, but in both the rocks represent whatever is eternal, non-human, and unchanging. But learning just a little about rocks and stones shows us that they are actually always in a state of flux and transition, and that that is the only constant thing about then. They may look and feel like unfeeling permanence, but all of them bear the marks of weathering, and they pass from state to state, ani-mate to inanimate, liquid to solid, bending, moving, shifting, sifting, sinking, rising, and so on. The merest knowledge of stratigraphy has always told us that, and now we know (in the epoch of the Anthropocene) that we cannot even regard rock strata as entirely non-human, since evidence of our presence and effects is present within them.

The notion of the Anthropocene has had a strong impact on ecocriticism, and its attributes and effects are worth debating. The current consensus (in 2017) seems to be that its starting date should be about 1950, but this may seem a little arbitrary. It enables the effects of nuclear bombs, nuclear tests, and nuclear accidents to become decisive, but plays down the effects of at least a couple of hundred years of industrial, steam-powered pollution – we saw earlier in this chapter, for instance, Ruskin's conviction, as a systematic and life-long observer, that the quality of air and light had very much changed since his own childhood in the 1820s.

Another development since the previous edition of this book is the increasing prominence in anthropocentric eco-studies of Timothy Morton, a British-born scholar of the Romantic period who, at the time of writing, is a professor in the English Department at Rice University in Houston, Texas. Morton's early work, as represented by *Shelley and the Revolution of Taste* (1995) and *The Poetics of Spice* (2000), was a blended post-structuralist/postmodernist/Marxist 'take' on aspects of Romantic writing. In the decade of roughly 1995–2005 there was a shift towards 'commodification', as I called it, in literary criticism, with a spate of books being published about the depiction of objects, substances, etc., in literature. This later developed into what became more generally known as 'object studies', or studies in 'material cultures', and then became fully blown, so to speak, as 'Thing Theory'. This drew upon the theory of Jean Baudrillard, Pierre Bourdieu, Bruno Latour, and others, and this whole constellation of interests was characterised by 'an intensified concern with the "thingness" and materiality', and a switching of attention to human interactions with, and influences on or by, objects. All this represented a major 'turn' in literary study, which had previously centred mainly on humans' relationships, interactions, etc., with other humans, so that places, objects, commodities, and so on were merely the 'props' which featured in the human drama, or else provided the 'background' against which it was played out. The 'turn' represented by the 'new materialism' or 'post-humanist materiality' approach directs the spotlight elsewhere, or elsewhere as well, to be more precise, and to continue with the theatre metaphor. All this can be viewed as repeating in new ways the decentring of humanity and human agency which is seen in different forms in most of the theories discussed in this book. Thus, in Marxism, history itself becomes a force that acts above and beyond the individual human's will or intention; in structuralism and post-structuralism language speaks us, determining what we can think and say; and in narratology, 'story' itself is a force beyond the control of individual authors, with its own currents and patterns that authors have to learn to ride with.[9]

In all these 'new materialisms', the 'thing' is not a mere object but a force with a 'life', energy, and agency of its own (again, I find the river analogy helpful in trying to conceptualise these matters). Hence, the highly influential notion of the 'hyperobject', which is the dominant concept of Morton's later work, is foreshadowed by the 'new materialist' emphasis of his early work. The concept of the hyperobject is introduced in Morton's book *The Ecological Thought* (2010) and fully developed in *Hyperobjects: Philosophy and Ecology after the End of the World* (University of Minnesota Press, 2013). The term is defined and exemplified in the opening paragraph of the latter book, which reads in full:

> In *The Ecological Thought* I coined the term hyperobjects to refer to things that are massively distributed in time and space relative to humans. A hyperobject could be a black hole. A hyperobject could be the Lago Agrio oil field in Ecuador, or the Florida Everglades. A hyperobject could be the biosphere, or the Solar System. A hyperobject could be the sum total of all the nuclear materials on Earth; or just the plutonium, or the uranium. A hyperobject could be the very long-lasting product of direct human manufacture, such as Styrofoam or plastic bags, or the sum of all the whirring machinery of capitalism. Hyperobjects, then, are 'hyper' in relation to some other entity, whether they are directly manufactured by humans are not.

The list of examples presents some obvious problems: if these things are all massively distributed in time and space how can the Lago Agrio oil field be one, since it is only 'in Ecuador'? If plastic bags are hyperobjects, meaning either each of them or all of them, why aren't all physical objects hyperobjects too? In fact, later on, Morton admits that 'In a strange way, every object is a hyperobject' (p. 201), as I implied in discussing the provenance of the concept in

9 For an initial 'taster' on Thing Theory try the article 'Can the Sofa Speak? A Look at Thing Theory' by John Plotz at http://digitalcommons.wayne.edu/cgi/view-content.cgi?article=1094&context=criticism (accessed 11 April 2017).

his earlier thinking. If a definition cannot distinguish what is in the designated category from what is not, it cannot really be called a definition at all.

In a useful seven-minute YouTube video called 'Dawn of the Hyperobjects', uploaded in 2011, Morton opens with a different list of examples of hyperobjects, mentioning just 'tectonic plates, global warming, nuclear radiation, and evolution', defining the term as 'entities that are massively distributed in time and space, at least relative to the human world'.[10] Again, it's difficult to see how these make a 'set' of any kind, since the first and last are natural global phenomena, whereas the middle two are anthropogenic (Morton rejects the term 'climate change' and insists that global warming is the distinctive product of the Anthropocene). The 'distribution in time and space' doesn't seem especially 'massive' (whatever that precisely means) 'at least relative to the human world' (ditto), since all these are limited to the age and size of the Earth, and, in comparison to the inter-galactic scale of things, they are as close as your fellow students on the corridor upstairs who may be a couple of months older or younger than yourself. To a post-lecture questioner at Southern Illinois University, Carbondale, in 2011, who asked 'Is God a hyperobject?' Morton immediately replied 'Yes', while denying that he himself is either an atheist or a theist. The performance, both in print and on video (the style is off-hand, colloquial, informal, chatty, full of throw-away lines) is entertaining, in a Žižekian way, but it lacks logic and rigour, and does not seem to be based on any significant scientific knowledge or training. The book was reviewed by Ursula K. Heise, Chair in Literary Studies at the Department of English and the Institute of the Environment and Sustainability at UCLA, a former President of ASLE (the Association for the Study of Literature and the Environment), and one of the most prominent academics in the field, and I am indebted to her comments.[11] She sees Morton as engaging with the important issue of scale which underlies a great many 'contemporary discussions in the humanities' (she mentions 'big data', 'deep time', 'slow

10 https://www.youtube.com/watch?v=NS8b87jnqnw (accessed 11 April 2017).
11 In *Critical Inquiry*, June 2014, http://criticalinquiry.uchicago.edu/ursula_k._heise_reviews_timothy_morton (accessed 11 April 2017).

violence', and 'species thinking' as well as the Anthropocene), but feels that he does so without actually clarifying the issues, so that 'it is not easy to make out what Morton is actually saying about scale'. I think this is at least partly because his five characteristics of hyper-objects (viscosity, non-locality, temporal undulation, phasising [*sic*], and interobjectivity), all seem to be more or less the same thing, which may, of course, be the point; but if it is, then, like Heise, I cannot quite see what useful work the concept is capable of doing. If you are just looking for something pacy, quirky, and stimulating which might in some oblique way 'make you think', you will possibly find something in Morton's approach. But if you seek scientific or cultural understanding, or are looking for polemical concepts that might be usable in opposing scepticism about environmental crises, then I don't think you will find that in his writing.

Another prominent British figure in writing about the environment is Robert Macfarlane, of Emmanuel College, Cambridge. The backbone of his work is extensive fieldwork, footwork, and ropework (as a climber) recounting a series of loosely themed journeys. His most notable and successful books are *Mountains of the Mind: A History of a Fascination* (2003), recording the imaginative power, over himself and generations of others, of heroic narratives of the climbing of mountains and journeys to extreme latitudes; *The Wild Places* (2007), contesting the idea that there is nowhere left to escape to in small countries like Britain and Ireland; *The Old Ways: A Journey on Foot* (2012), about 'following the tracks, holloways, drove-roads and sea paths that form part of a vast ancient network of routes criss-crossing the British Isles and beyond'; and *Landmarks* (2015), which is about the power of language to shape our response to landscape and environment. The ingredients of his books are intensified forms of observer-centred, 'thick description' which are as meticulously detailed as the ethnographic field studies of classic anthropology, giving evidence of a trained eye which can 'read' terrain, interpret its past uses and significances, and predict its still unfolding future. It is writing that reverses the priorities of Morton's work, where fairly small quantities of data and observation are combined with a hugely ambitious overlay of theory. By contrast, Macfarlane provides a plenitude of data and experience combined with a theoretical component which is often disarmingly modest, and sometimes presented in articles rather than books. An example is his overview article 'Generation Anthropocene' which identifies an 'anthropocenic' form of art which is 'obsessed with loss and disappearance', citing the Australian philosopher Glenn Albrecht's term 'solastalgia', which describes the sense of '[localised] psychic distress caused by environmental change', this being the opposite of nostalgia, which is psychic distress caused by moving to another location.[12] With solastalgia the location remains the same, but the sufferer feels deracinated because of its defamiliarisation.

What ecocritics do

1. They re-read major literary works from an ecocentric perspective, with particular attention to the representation of the natural world.
2. They extend the applicability of a range of ecocentric concepts, using them of things other than the natural world – concepts such as growth and energy, balance and imbalance, symbiosis and mutuality, and sustainable or unsustainable uses of energy and resources.
3. They give special canonical emphasis to writers who foreground nature as a major part of their subject matter, such as the American transcendentalists, the British Romantics, the poetry of John Clare, the work of Thomas Hardy and the Georgian poets of the early twentieth century.
4. They extend the range of literary-critical practice by placing a new emphasis on relevant 'factual' writing, especially reflective topographical material such as essays, travel writing, memoirs, and regional literature.
5. They turn away from the 'social constructivism' and 'linguistic determinism' of dominant literary theories (with their emphasis on the linguistic and social constructedness of the external world) and instead emphasise ecocentric values of

---

12 Robert Macfarlane, 'Generation Anthropocene: How humans have altered the planet forever', *The Guardian*, 1 April 2016, accessible online at http://www.theguardian.com/books/2016/apr/01/generation-anthropocene-altered-planet-for-ever (accessed 11 April 2017).

meticulous observation, collective ethical responsibility, and the claims of the world beyond ourselves.

Ecocriticism: an example

In 1915 the ageing Thomas Hardy, overwhelmed by a sense of the collapse of civilised values as the First World War dragged on, wrote a brief poem called 'In Time of "The Breaking of Nations"':

I
Only a man harrowing clods
In a slow silent walk
With an old horse that stumbles and nods
Half asleep as they stalk.

II
Only thin smoke without flame
From the heaps of couch-grass;
Yet this will go onward the same
Though Dynasties pass.

III
Yonder a maid and her wight
Come whispering by:
War's annals will cloud into night
Ere their story die.

As 'Dynasties pass' and nations are broken in the onslaught, the poet desperately looks around him for an example of immutability, seeking to reassure himself that there is *something* permanent which will 'go onward the same' for ever, in spite of the catastrophe of world war; and the something he chooses is that most commonplace manifestation of low-tech agricultural practice – a ploughman working a field with a horse-drawn plough, 'a man harrowing clods / In a slow silent walk'.

But it's only *literally* true to say that the poem was written in 1915; it would be more accurate to say that it was *written down* in 1915, since the remembered ploughman had actually been seen by Hardy in 1870, from the garden of a rectory in Cornwall when he was courting his first wife, Emma Lavinia Gifford. Thinking of this from a broadly ecological perspective, we might say that in his now remote personal past, the seed of an idea was planted in the poet's mind, an image grew and matured over time, and was eventually re-cycled to meet a need which arose many years later. So the gestation of the poem itself mirrors the patient processes of growth and cultivation which are depicted in it. As Hardy relates in the autobiography 'ghosted' by his second wife, the courtship with Emma took place during an earlier European conflict, the Franco-Prussian War of 1870–1871, and the ploughman used in the 1915 poem was seen on 18 August 1870, the day of 'the bloody battle of Gravelotte' (a Prussian victory that cost 20,000 Prussian casualties and 13,000 French), when Hardy and Emma had been reading Tennyson together outdoors. In spite of all that had changed or passed away in the meantime – the old European order, the transformations in farming practices which his own novels had recorded, the passing of his own youth, the years of estranged bitterness between the two of them, and finally the death of Emma herself – Hardy still believed in durance and immutability, in natural forces which are timeless and inexhaustible. The 'timeless' ploughman, therefore, lives on for forty-five years in his mind without alteration, embodying the time-defying qualities Hardy seeks. The 'maid and her wight', by contrast, are not persons seen by Hardy, either in 1870 or in 1915, but a retrospective 'back projection' of himself and Emma into that 1870 scene, drawn into the artifice of eternity by their association with the ever-enduring ploughman, the figure whom the agnostic poet makes into a kind of guarantee of the future and of the indestructibility of nature and humanity.

In terms of the landscape schema given earlier, the leisured speaker/observer in the poem is poised between areas three and four, looking out from the rectory garden (gardens being the place of decorative flora intended for aesthetic and sensuous pleasure, and hence a traditional setting for relaxation and erotic dalliance – 'Come into the garden, Maud'!). He looks out into the valley of arable land, area three, locus of planting for sustenance, and scene of the labour required to bring the good life to fruition. The two regions, agriculture and horticulture, adjoin each other and Hardy implies an ideal fusion between them by projecting the courting couple out 'yonder', which is to say beyond the garden, giving them attributes in common – horse and man slow and silent and half asleep, maid and wight whispering and hence also moving slowly. The whole scene moves slowly and quietly, as if under hypnosis, but they are not quite fused into one, for the ploughman in the first stanza and the couple in the third are divided by the second stanza, with its more negative image – thin smoke without flame from the heaps of burning grass, as if the vision of united, productive harmony across the local and domestic landscape is ominously interrupted. All that destructive human activity which hovers just beyond the poem (the breaking of nations referred to in the title's quotation from Jeremiah, and the battles of the Franco-Prussian war mentioned in the autobiography) splits and dislocates the two areas, and is represented by the burning. The symbiosis between the two areas, we might say, between these different phases and aspects of life, is threatened by the entropic carnage of war.

Burdened with a sense of the disruptive waste of war, what comfort, we might ask, could the couple have found in Tennyson? What Tennyson poems might they have been reading? Was it the work of the patriotic, armchair-warrior Tennyson of 'The Charge of the Light Brigade' (according to his son, so excited by the *Times* account of that charge that he whooped about the room swishing the newspaper round above his head like a mock sabre)? Or the Tennyson of 'Locksley Hall', who celebrated technological change and the coming of the railways, with little sign of any environmental anxieties? Or the sombre Tennyson of 'In Memoriam', who seemed to have little trust in life going on forever, for he realised that the fossil record of the loss and extinction of species (then gradually being interpreted by pioneer Victorian geologists, many of whom were clergymen amateurs) carried no reassuring message of a benign, natural continuity, but told vividly of a life-force that cared nothing even for the disappearance of innumerable entire species, and of 'nature red in tooth and claw', driven by ruthless predatory instincts rather than by love? This Tennyson spoke from his agnosticism (which was similar to Hardy's – he was 'churchy', but not solidly religious) of hills and continents whose forms and identities are quite without durance and (when viewed across the vista of geological aeons) seem as fluid as cloud formations.[13] Finding words of comfort in Tennyson, then, would probably have been pretty difficult, so that the poet looks for comfort in the world around him, rather than in his reading, and so lights upon the figure of the ploughman.

From the perspective of our own present, the confidence which is restored by contemplating the 'timeless' figure of the ploughman will seem somewhat over-optimistic and self-deluding – Hardy's figure of immutability would be *our* emblem of fragility, a being redolent of a vanished era of human-scale agriculture and of a remote time when the primary associations of farming were not with subsidised over-production, diseases like BSE and Foot and Mouth, and the disappearance of songbirds and hedgerows. To react in this way is to begin to frame an ecocentred reading of the poem, centred, that is, not on the pathos of the author's personal life, but on that bizarre contrast between, on the one hand, the loving incubation of a single poetic image across a whole lifetime, as if a poet had all the time in the world, and, on the other, the actual precariousness of the ecological balance, which is what that figure must embody for us.

What, in conclusion, are some of the characteristics of this kind of ecocentric reading? The list below indicates what my ecologically inflected reading attempted, rather than what it perhaps achieved, but it is illustrative, I hope, of the traits which ecocritical readings commonly have. So, *firstly*, the commentary gives evidence of the incorporation of broadly conceived ecological thinking, showing, for instance, a keen awareness of the growth processes of the poem itself, how it builds in several layers across a lifetime, and does not come into being in a single flash of inspired imaginative insight which has no visible means of support. *Secondly*, the reading is aware that the materials which contribute to the poem's slow growth are diverse and disparate; some are actual events – some from the past, some from the present – and others are imaginative projections, so that the poem isn't 'true' in any simplistic way, but has the much more potent quality of 'truth-to-life'. *Thirdly*, of course, an explicitly ecological level of content has been identified (the mate-

13 *In Memoriam*, 123: 'The hills are shadows, and they flow / From form to form, and nothing stands; / They melt like mist, the solid lands, / Like clouds they shape themselves and go'.

rial about the 'areas' of environment again), and these too have appropriate weight in the discussion. *Fourthly*, we have read back into the poem a hard-edged, retrospective irony (that its emblem of permanence cannot function as that for us, a century after Hardy wrote the poem), this irony arising from our own acute sense of environmental crisis and danger. *Finally* (which is the sum of these), the reading is itself diverse and eclectic, not hidebound by a single issue (such as an allegorical parallel or some kind of esoteric symbolism) but having a methodological balance and openness which allows it to build from a wide range of materials, not restricting itself, in the way that most critical approaches do, to a single type of evidence (purely textual for the 'Formalist' critic, predominantly historical for the Marxist, mainly counter-intuitive linguistic elements for the deconstructor, and so on). Such eclecticism is often very marked in ecocritical readings, but not usually remarked upon, since anxieties about critical method can seem somewhat remote from this approach. A well-known remark by American ecocritic Scott Slovic comes to mind as encapsulating this attitude; Slovic quotes Walt Whitman's line in 'Song of Myself' in which the speaker proclaims 'I am large, I contain multitudes' and applies it to the community of ecocritics, adding 'There is no single, dominant world-view guiding ecocritical practice – no single strategy at work from example to example of ecocritical writing or teaching' (Coupe, p. 160). Of course, most critical and theoretical movements make the same eclectic claim about themselves, even those which are closely aligned with the insights of a single founding figure (such as Freud, Lacan, Foucault, Derrida, etc.), but it is striking that there is no single figure within ecocriticism who has that kind of dominance – ecocriticism itself is a diverse biosphere.

Selected reading

Readers

Branch, Michael P., and Slovic, Scott, eds, *The ISLE Reader: Ecocriticism: 1993-2003* (University of Georgia Press, 2003).
  An 'official' rival to Coupe, Glotfelty, and Kerridge/Sammells.
Coupe, Laurence, ed., *The Green Studies Reader: From Romanticism to Ecocriticism* (Routledge, 2000).

This is the definitive early UK collection, but it represents major contemporary American voices (Soper, Snyder, Slovic, Buell, Roszak, Glotfelty, etc.) as well as British ones (Bate, Gifford, Garrard, Kerridge, etc.), and includes earlier material from the Romantic period onwards. Fifty chapters, mostly quite short, in six well-conceived and well-introduced sections, so the book is kept to a sensible size of around 300 pages.

Garrard, Greg, ed., *The Oxford Handbook of Ecocriticism* (Oxford University Press, 2014).

In four parts, headed History (with chapters on the development of ecocriticism), Theory (with chapters on ecocriticism and science, postcolonialism, and posthumanism), Genre (covering new areas such as music, children's books, and eco-film), and The Views from Here (with chapters on ecocriticism in Japan, India, China, and Germany). A very welcome collection.

Glotfelty, Cheryll, and Fromm, Harold, eds, *The Ecocriticism Reader: Landmarks in Literary Ecology* (University of Georgia Press, 1996).

The US rival of the above – another excellent, but not mammoth, collection (brevity and concision are ecocritical virtues).

Heise, Ursula K., Christensen, Jon, and Niemann, Michelle, eds, *The Routledge Companion to the Environmental Humanities* (Routledge, 2017).

Part 1 is on anthropocenic issues concerning the human 'domestication' of the planet, Part 2 on posthumanist and 'multispecies' approaches to living on Earth, Part 3 on issues of inequality and environmental justice, Part 4 on environmental narratives of decline and resilience, Part 5 on environmental arts, media, and technology, and Part 6 contains essays on 'the state of the environmental humanities'. A demanding book of immense scope and originality.

Hiltner, Ken, ed., *Ecocriticism: The Essential Reader* (Routledge, 2014).

Divided into 'First Wave' (1960s–1990s) and 'Second Wave' (1990s onwards) ecocriticism, each with a contextualising introduction. A very good range of material.

Kerridge, Richard, and Sammells, Neil, eds, *Writing the Environment* (Zed Books, 1998).

Fifteen essays by major British and American contributors to the field, in three sections – 'Ecocritical theory', 'Ecocritical history', and 'Contemporary writing'. Still a useful and engaging book, in spite of the subsequent publication of Coupe's collection.

General

Barry, Peter, and Welstead, William, eds, *Extending Ecocriticism: Crisis, Collaboration and Challenges in the Environmental Humanities* (Manchester University Press, 2017).

Takes ecocriticism into new areas, including material on techniques for assessing the visual impact of planned wind turbines, signage and information boards in wildlife reserves and nature trails, and the environmental impact of trends in dog-mess disposal. Also has chapters on collaborative work across literary and visual arts and on public environmental projects.

Bate, Jonathan, *Romantic Ecology: Wordsworth and the Environmental Tradition* (Routledge, 1991).

Already a classic; the founding text of contemporary British ecocriticism: a brief, thought-provoking and engaging book.

Bate, Jonathan, *The Song of the Earth* (Picador, 2000).

Impressive for its overall scope and for the breadth and variety of the individual readings. The book shows that this approach can make full use of technique and learning as well as zeal.

Buell, Lawrence, *The Environmental Imagination: Thoreau, Nature Writing, and the Formation of American Culture* (Harvard University Press, 1995).

A highly significant and influential work in this field – this is the book most frequently cited by ecocritics.

Egan, Gabriel, *Green Shakespeare: From Ecopolitics to Ecocriticism* (Routledge, 'Accents on Shakespeare' series, 2006).

On a 'growth area' in ecocriticism – a lively book in an innovative series.

Garrard, Greg, *Ecocriticism* (Routledge, 'New Critical Idiom' series, 2nd edn, 2011).

A very useful and succinct guide to the field.

Gifford, Terry, *Green Voices: Understanding Contemporary Nature Poetry* (Manchester University Press, 1995).

Discusses R. S. Thomas, George Mackay Brown, John Montague, Norman Nicholson, Patrick Kavanagh, and others in what he calls the 'anti-pastoralist' tradition of Crabbe and Clare; and, in what he calls the 'post-pastoral' mode, Heaney (successor to Wordsworth) and Hughes (successor to Blake).

Gifford, Terry, *Pastoral* (Routledge, 'Critical Idiom' series, 1999).

A very useful book developing the three-layer model of pastoral, anti-pastoral, and post-pastoral used in the previous book.

Kroeber, Karl, *Ecological Literary Criticism: Romantic Imagining and the Biology of Mind* (Columbia University Press, 1994).

Another brief and engaging book, making an ideal paired read with either of Bate's (above).

Macfarlane, Robert, *Mountains of the Mind: A History of a Fascination* (Granta Books, 2003).

Macfarlane, Robert, *The Wild Places* (Granta Books, 2008).

Macfarlane, Robert, *The Old Ways: A Journey on Foot* (Penguin, 2013).

Macfarlane, Robert, *Landmarks* (Penguin, reprint edn, 2016).

Morton, Timothy, *The Ecological Thought* (Harvard University Press, 2012).

Morton, Timothy, *Hyperobjects: Philosophy and Ecology after the End of the World* (University of Minnesota Press, 2013).

Murphy, Patrick D., ed., *Literature of Nature: An International Source-book* (Fitzroy Dearborn, 1998).

'A reference work that explores the diversity of genres, modes, and orientations of literary representations of nature and of human interaction with the rest of the natural world.'

Plumwood, Val, *Feminism and the Mastery of Nature* (Routledge, 1993).

'Explores the emergence of ecofeminism or ecological feminism, explaining its relation to other feminist theories, and to radical green theories such as deep ecology.'

Schama, Simon, *Landscape and Memory* (Harper Collins, 1995).

'How does environment influence history? … This work attempts to answer these questions and gives a portrait of the world around us and how it shapes us.'

Soper, Kate, *What is Nature? Culture, Politics, and the Non-Human* (Blackwell, 1995).

Another readable and fundamental text from the mid-1990s period which laid the foundations of contemporary ecocriticism.

14

Literary theory – a history in ten events

Several of the available introductory guides to literary theory incorporate such features as glossaries of key terms, 'timelines', and potted accounts of the ideas of important theorists arranged in encyclopaedic format. I have not been tempted to include any of these features in the fourth edition of this book, because I have always preferred to integrate information into a themed narrative. But one way of presenting the story of literary theory is to centre it upon a series of key events which constitute its public history. The advantage of doing this is that many of the underlying themes are thereby brought to the fore, so that the trajectory of theory – the arc of its rise and fall – becomes strikingly apparent. Of course, I am using the term 'literary theory' here in its narrow sense, which is to say in reference to its resurgence from the mid-twentieth century onwards, and disregarding the earlier history of theory which was touched upon in Chapter 1. Within these limitations, we can tell the story of theory through ten key events.

The Indiana University 'Conference on Style', 1958

> *Reading*: for the book of the conference see *Style in Language*, ed. Thomas A. Sebeok, MIT Press, 1960.

In its early phase (as explained in Chapter 2), literary theory was the direct offspring of developments in linguistics. The interdisciplinary 'Conference on Style' at Indiana in 1958 can be seen as an important marker of the growing importance of linguistics within the Humanities. Thomas Sebeok (1920–2001), who convened the conference, was a Hungarian scholar in linguistics who had become an American citizen in 1944. His doctoral studies at the outset of his career had been supervised by the linguist Roman Jakobson, whose 'Closing Statement: (Linguistics and Poetics)' became the most lastingly influential item of the conference. But the most innovative feature of the conference itself was its interdisciplinarity: it debated the question of style (how to define it, how to describe it, how to investigate its effects) from the viewpoints of three relevant disciplines, these being linguistics, literary criticism, and psychology. However, the overall bias of the papers was very much dominated by linguistics, and of the nine sections into which the book of the conference is divided, four of them centre on phonology, metrics, grammar, and semantics, respectively, which are prime areas of investigation in linguistics, while the fifth is called 'Linguistic approaches to verbal art', and the sixth is merely the collection of opening and closing statements (one of each from the three contributing disciplines). So there is a strong sense of linguistics extending its influence into the other two spheres – but especially into literary criticism – and entering the era of its highest dominance and prestige. Hence, the conference signals a distinct shift in the balance of power within the Humanities, marking the moment when the scientific method of enquiry extends its empire, and becomes the accepted model of enquiry in general, spreading from the sciences, to the social sciences, and now into the Humanities. Indeed, the book of the conference, which reproduces papers delivered at the event, abounds with diagrams, graphs, and tables of statistical analysis: if you had taken it down from the shelf without realising what it was, you might assume on flicking through that it is a scientific treatise of some kind. Its writers aim to *demonstrate* what is or is not the case, rather than seeking merely to *persuade* us that what they assert is truly the case. They want to *prove* that certain assertions are true, rather than merely *arguing* that they are, and that is the essence of the scientific method.

The conference did not, of course, settle these matters, and there were actually three closing statements, not just Jakobson's, as is often supposed. The closing statement on behalf of literary criticism was made by the eminent critic René Wellek, and he was deeply sceptical about the claims of the linguists. All the same, the period of dominance in literary studies by the humanistic approach of the New Critics was entering its final phase, and the prestige of linguistics was rising – the American linguist Noam Chomsky, born in 1928, and about to become as dominant a force in the linguistic thinking of his generation as Saussure had been half a century earlier, had already published his first book (*Syntactic Structures*, 1957), and it was discussed by some of the speakers at the conference. Using concepts drawn from linguistics would soon become almost the default way of doing theory, partly because of the enormous success of Chomsky's work in arguing that grammar and semantics (that is, meaning) cannot be separated, and that 'deep' syntactical structures are the ultimate determinants of meaning.[1]

Jakobson's closing statement makes no attempt to sum up the arguments put forward in the course of the conference. Rather, his densely technical analyses of poetry show the linguistic method at work. The argument, if there is one, is brutal and simple: poetry is language, so poetry must now come within the sphere of linguistics; 'the linguist whose field is *any kind* of language may and must include poetry in his study' (p. 377, my italics). He moves towards his conclusion by approvingly quoting the critic John Hollander to the effect that 'there seems to be no reason for trying to separate the literary from the overall linguistic', and he ends with this resounding proclamation:

> All of us here, however, definitely realize that a linguist deaf to the poetic function of language and a literary scholar indifferent to linguistic problems and unconversant with linguistic methods are equally flagrant anachronisms. (p. 377)

Henceforth, literary criticism would strive above all to be 'scientific' and methodical, and mere intelligence, combined with literary sensibility, would no longer be enough. Welcome to the brave new post-Indiana world!

---

1 To give a clichéd example, the following two sentences have the same 'surface' syntax but different 'deep' syntax, and that is where their true meaning lies: 'The chicken was ready to eat.' 'The Chairman was ready to eat.'

The Johns Hopkins University international
symposium, 1966

Reading: *The Structuralist Controversy*, ed. Richard Macksey and
Eugenio Donato, Johns Hopkins University Press, 1970 (40th anniversary edn, 2006). This is the 'book of the conference', containing
Derrida's lecture 'Structure, Sign and Play', and the questions which
followed.

In October 1966 an international symposium was held at Johns
Hopkins University in the USA under the title 'The Languages of
Criticism and the Sciences of Man'. The sequence of elements in the
title of the symposium indicates the ongoing primacy of linguistics,
but again the aim of the gathering was to be interdisciplinary. The
symposium was a co-production, so to speak, with the '*Sciences
de l'Homme*' section of the *Ecole des Hautes Etudes*, Paris, which was
the cradle of structuralism. This term 'the sciences of man' indicated a new subject area which linked the interests of what would
more conventionally have been called the Humanities and the Social
Sciences, taking in (among other areas) anthropology, philosophy,
literature, linguistics, psychology, and history. This is the nexus of
disciplines which, so to speak, had pooled resources under the aegis
of structuralism, and this symposium celebrated the arrival and establishment of structuralism, with contributions from its major figures – René Girard, Georges Poulet, Lucien Goldmann, Tzvetan
Todorov, and Roland Barthes. This consolidation of structuralism
can be seen as a move forward and beyond the complete dominance
of linguistics, for it was now realised that linguistics could not really
deliver on its promise to provide 'a universal matrix for understanding all human phenomena' (p. xi). Hence, the ground was
shifting again, and the impact of Derrida's contribution was to
announce his scepticism about the structuralist triumph and to inaugurate a new stage of 'post-structuralism'.

The content of Derrida's talk is described in Chapter 3, and what
strikes me about it now is that – like most of the memorable and significant contributions at conferences – it takes very little notice
of the surrounding arguments or contexts and simply bangs down
its challenge with flair and conviction. But the characteristic weaknesses as well as the strengths of his approach are already apparent

in Derrida's response to questions (see 'Discussion' after his paper, pp. 265-72). He is questioned with some persistence by Jean Hyppolite, whose query comes from a structuralist perspective – can you have structures without a referent? The previous 'centres' of our thought (notions like 'Man', 'God', 'Truth', and so on) have been 'de-centred' and wiped away, and instead we are left with structures like 'difference', that is, we have neither A nor B, we have only the difference between them. Language, for instance, is a game, with a structure of rules, but we don't ask what the game is for, or what ultimate end it serves. So Hyppolite wants to know what Derrida thinks is behind the structure of language – 'One cannot think of the structure without the centre', he says (p. 266). To see what he is getting at, think, for instance, of a game of football. There is an intricate structure of rules and conventions which govern the event, but what is *behind* the rules? Is it something to do with the excitement of playing or watching the game? Is it the cup which the winning team receives? Is it the glory of victory, or the sublimated sense which winning gives of triumphing over the adversities of life? Obviously, there must be *something* behind the structures, and Hyppolite wants to know what Derrida thinks it is. But of course, Derrida doesn't tell him, and the question is deflected in ways which later became all too automatic for Derrida as his fame grew – 'I do not know where I am going,' he says (p. 267). Pressed further to say what structure is ('how will you define a structure for me? – to see where the centre is', p. 268), Derrida replies that the concept of structure 'is no longer satisfactory', so 'what I have said can be understood as a criticism of structuralism' (p. 268). He is accused of always speaking of '*non-centres*' by a questioner who says that without a notion of centres you can't explain what perception is, 'for a perception is precisely the manner in which the world appears *centred* to me' (p. 271). In response, Derrida *denies* that he has denied the existence of centres, but adds, 'I believe that the centre is a function, not a being – a reality, but a function' (p. 271). But he *does* conclude by denying the existence of perception – 'I don't believe that anything like perception exists . . . I don't believe that there is any perception' (p. 272). This would seem to close off the 'soft option' view of post-structuralism, that is, the view that it is merely a system which emphasises the constructedness of everything, in other words, the notion that *perc*eiving is always *con*-ceiving. It is striking that the questioning process seems to show Derrida almost being pushed into more extreme formulations than he intended, from which it will later be impossible to pull back. The material from the 1966 conference was written up in 1971, and the book of the conference was finally published in 1972. The change in intellectual climate between the mid-1960s and the early 1970s was very considerable. By 1972, the implications of the Derridean challenge to structuralism were sinking in, and for the major thinkers, at least, the age of post-structuralism was already in full swing.

The publication of *Deconstruction and Criticism*, 1979

Reading: the book itself, and a sample of key reviews, including S. L. Goldberg, *London Review of Books* (22 May–4 June 1980), and Denis Donoghue, *New York Review of Books* (12 June 1980), under the title 'Deconstructing Deconstruction', and Roger Scruton's talk, which was broadcast on BBC Radio 3 in 1980 and is reprinted in his book *The Politics of Culture and Other Essays* (Carcanet, 1981).

This book – by five authors – was published by Yale University Press in 1979, the five being Harold Bloom, Paul de Man, Jacques Derrida, Geoffrey Hartman, and J. Hillis Miller, a group sometimes collectively referred to as the 'Yale Mafia' of theory. The book exemplified deconstructive reading with reference to Shelley's uncompleted visionary final poem 'The Triumph of Life', presenting this approach to reading in its most uncompromising and even brutal form. It showed deconstruction (which by that time was being taken as representative of literary theory as a whole) in its pomp – brash, confident, and provocative, and, for many, a kind of Orwellian nightmare of what literary studies had become, as if they had been asked to imagine the future of literary criticism, and were being shown a picture of a boot stamping on the face of a literary text for ever. The reviewers of the book were polarised, and uncompromising in either praise or blame, as if conscious that a decisive battle was being fought for the soul of literary studies. The most notable and sustained attacks on it were S. L. Goldberg's in the *London Review of Books*, Denis Donoghue's in the *New York Review of Books*, and Roger Scruton's BBC Radio 3 talk.

Deconstruction and Criticism caused such outrage because it wasn't in fact a work of deconstructive *theory*, but (ostensibly) of deconstructive *practice*. Had it been 'mere' theory, hostile academic readers (or dippers-in) of other persuasions could have dismissed it as not really being germane to their own core business of reading and interpreting literature. It could then have been brushed aside as just one more of the increasing number of books which spoke only to other theorists and carried on a debate purely in the realm of philosophical ideas, with little evident relevance to the day-to-day business of reading and writing about literature. But this was not the situation, and the feelings of affront and outrage which the book provoked came about because it seemed to have invaded the humane space of 'letters' (to use a traditional but now antique term for literary study), threatening to transform the field from within into something alien. There was great fear that this kind of thinking, with its arcane vocabulary and its abstract formulations, was particularly appealing to young academics, so that the future of literary study would be poisoned if it caught on. For the first time (in the UK, at least) literary studies began to be discussed on radio and TV, using this book as an example of the strange events which were taking place in English departments. Word got out that a 'war' of some kind was going in English faculties across the land. The term 'the theory wars' quickly became current in discussions of the Humanities in the early 1980s, and the publication of *Deconstruction and Criticism* can be seen as the declaration of war by the newly empowered theorists on the disorganised status quo in literary studies.

The MacCabe affair, 1981

Reading: No formal academic account of this event exists, but see the newspaper reports from late 1980 and early 1981 (which you can find in most university libraries by using the *Times Full-text Database* and searching for 'Colin MacCabe' in the period 1980 and 1981), beginning with the *Times* of Saturday 24 January 1981, and the *Sunday Times* of Sunday 25 January.

The fuss about *Deconstruction and Criticism* was hardly over, when, in the autumn of 1980, it was decided at Cambridge University that a young assistant lecturer called Colin MacCabe would not be upgraded to a permanent lectureship, after holding a temporary post for five years. Students protested, and there were disagreements and divisions on the Faculty Board which had made the decision. The events were reported in the newspapers and became a running news story in the UK during the first half of 1981. The result was a public argument about how English should be taught at universities, with eminent figures from the English Faculty publicly taking sides. Raymond Williams and Frank Kermode supported MacCabe (the former liking the Marxist aspects of his work, and the latter the structuralist elements), while Christopher Ricks opposed MacCabe's appointment and favoured more traditional scholarly methods. On Saturday 24 January 1981 the *Times* had a news article and a leader on the matter, the article struggling to explain to its readers what structuralism is: 'Structuralism can be described simply as a linguistics technique which studies how language itself influences the way an author writes', it informed us, not very helpfully. The leader took a very lofty view of the whole business ('Dons dispute as children squabble, to test out and develop their muscles'), and it too saw structuralism as being primarily about linguistics: 'Structuralism is first of all about grammar – not grammar conceived in the prescriptive sense in which it was once taught in schools (and seems to be no longer), but grammar as a pattern of the subliminal forms of language, and therefore of the human mind'. This is a very anachronistic note to strike as late as 1981, for it seems to be unaware that structuralism had now long been replaced by post-structuralism, but the key names the reporters were told about were those of the structuralist founding fathers – Lévi-Strauss, Roland Barthes, and so on – rather than Lacan and Derrida, and there is no mention of the fact that the tune in literary theory was now being called by philosophy and deconstruction rather than linguistics. The comments on grammar and the subliminal patterns of the human mind seem to me more like a description of Chomsky's idea of 'deep syntax' than the state of literary theory in the 1980s. The leader was partly based on an interview with Colin MacCabe which had been hurriedly conducted by journalist Ian Jack. He met MacCabe at Heathrow Airport, on his return from a British Council lecturing trip to Europe, and interviewed him during the taxi ride into London. The interview was published in the *Sunday Times* the next day (25 January), and again the emphasis on language is very marked – MacCabe in the taxi kept 'banging on about the need of Eng. Lit. students to know grammar', and Jack tells his readers that MacCabe laments the fact that his students no longer seem to have been taught grammar at school, making it difficult to convey ideas which build upon that framework. Ian Jack was evidently puzzled to hear a lament about the decline of formal grammar teaching in schools coming from a radical left-winger like MacCabe.

The dispute dragged on at Cambridge and seemed to descend into farcical parody, like an episode in Tom Sharpe's 1974 satirical novel *Porterhouse Blue* (which is about the struggle between reactionaries and reformers at a mythical Cambridge college). The proceedings of the appointments committee had by now been leaked, and it was announced that the leak would be investigated 'by the university's ancient court the *Septem Viri*' (the Seven Men). Then the students revolted and passed a vote of no confidence in the Faculty Board, calling for an open enquiry into the state of the English Faculty. This duly took place in the Senate House, inevitably described in the newspaper reports as 'oak-panelled'. It should have been a high-level intellectual debate between structuralists, Marxists, humanists, and the rest, but of course it wasn't – it was about procedures, and administration, and committees. Higher education in those days was expanding rapidly, but funding was being rigorously curtailed by the Thatcher government – there was wet rot in buildings and a lack of cleaners, and students complained about inadequate contact time with tutors who were increasingly being pressured to get on with their research. The 'affair', in the end, fizzled out: a compromise was reached whereby MacCabe's post would be extended for a further year, but in July 1981 he left Cambridge to take up the offer of a professorship at the enterprising Strathclyde University in Glasgow. On the whole, theory benefited from all this publicity: here, it seemed, was a bright young talent with cutting-edge ideas whose career was being threatened by the forces of reaction. Theory, we might say, now had its martyr, and an increased sense of its own coherence and importance.

The publication of Eagleton's *Literary Theory: An Introduction*, 1983

> *Reading*: the book itself, and early reviews such as John Bayley's in the *Times Literary Supplement* (10 June 1983).

The spread of literary theory since the 1970s seems in retrospect to have been inevitable and relentless, but in reality it was dependent upon finding effective ways of *teaching* theory, not just ways of *studying* it at faculty and postgraduate level. The MacCabe affair highlighted some of the difficulties of doing this and showed the need for detailed exposition, exemplification, and discussion. Most of the primary texts of literary theory had been written in French, with a few in German or Russian, and by no means all of them had yet been translated. There was an acute need for 'mediating' works, that is, introductory books which could be used as course textbooks on undergraduate and MA courses. Without such books, literary theory would be doomed to remain an elitist minority interest. The need for basic secondary exposition was first supplied by the founding in 1977 of the series of books known as 'Methuen New Accents', which provided students with individual introductory books on structuralism, deconstruction, post-structuralism, and the rest. An introductory overview of literary theory was also a necessity, and the first book to meet this need was Terry Eagleton's *Literary Theory: An Introduction*, published by Blackwell in 1983. The book was an instant success because it was written in a lively and provocative manner, and resisted the temptation to produce a dense and elephantine tome – such a book might have impressed peers but would have been inappropriate for students seeking initial enlightenment. These qualities distinguished it from most of its successors, and from the course-book 'readers' in literary theory which began to appear from the late 1980s onwards. 'Readers' containing key articles and chapters by a range of major figures can be very useful if they are selective and if they try to meet the actual needs of their users, but such books succumbed long ago to competitive supersizing, with publishing firms striving with each other in a ridiculous poker game to see who can produce the biggest theory reader (Publisher N to Publisher B: 'I'll see your thirteen hundred pages and raise you by another thirteen hundred').

Eagleton, by contrast, kept it simple: his introduction is called 'What is Literature?' and the first chapter tells the history of the rise of English Studies; the next four chapters deal in turn with phenomenology, structuralism, post-structuralism, and psychoanalysis, and the Conclusion is entitled 'Political Criticism'. Eagleton makes no pretence to neutrality – he is a Marxist critic writing from a committed and identified position, not a sipper and taster of 'isms' who swills each one around for a few moments and then passes on to the next one. The omissions are striking – the index (this is in 1983) has no entry on 'feminism' or 'feminist theory', for instance, and it seems somewhat eccentric (in a book called *Literary Theory*) to begin by asking 'What is Literature?' rather than 'What is Literary Theory?' The overall argument is vigorous but taxing: the answer to the question 'What is Literature?' is that literature 'does not exist in the sense that insects do'. It might be retorted impatiently that literary theory must certainly exist, possibly even in the sense that insects do, since Eagleton has written a book about it. But literary theory's purpose, for Eagleton, seems *anti-literary*, and that distinguishes it from literary criticism, which is usually (one would presume) on literature's side. For him, theory's insect-like purpose seems to be to act as a kind of super-bug, attacking literature from within, with the aim of bringing about its death (though if literature doesn't exist, how can it die?). That is the kind of theological question which is posed by Eagleton's famous allegorical ending:

> I shall end with an allegory. *We* know that the lion is stronger than the lion-tamer, and so does the lion-tamer. The problem is that the lion does not know it. It is not out of the question that the death of literature may help the lion to awaken.

As John Bayley said in his *Times Literary Supplement* review (10 June 1983), the question is 'What is the lion?' Presumably, the lion is the proletariat, and the lion-tamer is literature. So the job of theory is to *oppose* literature and deprive it of its power to subdue and pacify the masses. Eagleton's lion, however, seems wiser than he allows, for the lion knows that the lion-tamer has a whip, and that is what makes him stronger than the lion. The metaphor must envisage literature as the whip, seeing it as part of the 'Ideological State Apparatus', which controls us by ideology rather than force (see Chapter 8 for the Althusserian notion of the 'ISA'). The power and impact of Eagleton's book lay in its overall energy, wit, and mental agility, and in its deft summaries of large bodies of thought. He is brilliantly compressed and informative, for instance, in his chapter on structuralism; in the chapter on post-structuralism he raises the issues that others only got around to more than a decade later; the psychoanalysis chapter is more routine; and his final chapter on political criticism puts his Marxist cards uncompromisingly face-up on the table, but in a way that anticipates the ethical and moral issues which would preoccupy him twenty years later – 'What it means to be a "better person",' he says, 'must be concrete and practical.' Eagleton's book, then, greatly contributed to the 'consolidation' of literary theory and helped to establish it firmly on the undergraduate curriculum, giving tutors confidence that it might be possible to teach it in a systematic way. In this ten-event history it marks the apex of the rise of theory.

J. Hillis Miller's MLA presidential address, 1986

> *Reading*: 'Presidential Address, 1986. The Triumph of Theory, the Resistance to Reading, and the Question of the Material Base', *PMLA*, 102(3) (May 1987): 281–91; response by new historicist Louis Montrose, 'Professing the Renaissance: The Poetics and Politics of Culture', reprinted in Rivkin & Ryan, pp. 777–85.

By the mid-1980s, symptoms of the coming decline of literary theory had begun to emerge. A key moment was the Modern Language Association's presidential address by J. Hillis Miller in 1986. The MLA is the main professional body for university teachers of English in the USA, and its annual conventions are major events for the discipline. The keynote address from the president is the climax, and it takes the form of a kind of 'state of the discipline' pronouncement which will often point to future lines of development. Hillis Miller, as one of the 'famous five' authors of *Deconstruction and Criticism*, had long been a proponent of deconstruction, and his address shows that he had expected that the confident momentum of the early 1980s – when deconstruction seemed to be making a clean sweep of prestigious English departments in the USA – would continue. However, what was actually happening, it seemed, was that the dominance of theory was being checked by a new contrary force. The contrary force was the rise of historicist approaches to literature, emanating from the field of early modernist studies, and begun in the USA by Stephen Greenblatt's *Renaissance Self-Fashioning* (1980) and in the UK by Jonathan Dollimore and Alan Sinfield's *Political Shakespeare* in 1985 (see Chapter 9). Historicism, as Hillis Miller realised, is the polar opposite of deconstruction, which had become the most prominent public embodiment of theory itself in the 1980s, taking over the status which structuralism had had in the 1970s. So Miller noted that (in effect) the 'Triumph of Theory' was being interrupted by regrettable outbreaks of historicism:

> Literary study in the past few years has undergone a sudden, almost universal turn away from theory in the sense of an orientation toward language as such and has made a corresponding turn toward history, culture, society, politics, institutions, class and gender conditions, the social context, the material base. (p. 283)

Historicism (as distinct from history) is what the theory-weary academic masses (in the main) moved on to, and to ever more elaborate forms of it, entailing extensive archival work, the setting up of inter-disciplinary research centres, and the pursuit of cross-institutional collaborations. As he presents the choice, it might seem rather obvious why many were choosing the side that Hillis Miller disapproved of, for 'history, culture, society, politics, institutions, class and gender conditions, the social context, the material base' sound rather more interesting as a field of study than (as Miller phrased it) 'an orientation toward language as such'. Essentially, deconstructive literary theory believed that students should study 'literariness' itself, rather than literature (that is, the process of the conceptualisation of meaning in general, rather than the specific meanings of, for example, *Middlemarch*). In practice, it has always been very difficult to translate this notion of 'literariness itself' into a viable undergraduate curriculum, and all those elephantine literary theory 'readers' merely demonstrate that this is so. Likewise, striving for 'an orientation toward language as such' is a bit like trying to look at the sun in literary studies – you can't do it for long, it can be damaging, and you very quickly want to look elsewhere. Studying history, culture, gender conditions, and the rest is much more concrete, and translating that range of interests into a syllabus which students would want to follow isn't such a difficult task. So the turning of the tide away from deconstruction and towards historicism was not really a surprising trend.

But what exactly, we need to ask at this point, is the difference between historicism and history? Well, a historian might seek through diligent research to recover the past, and enable us to walk again the streets of Shakespeare's London, making for the playhouse to see a performance of *Hamlet*. We will know how the streets looked, smell the smells, hear the sounds, and know exactly what coins we need to have in our hands in order to get into the theatre. (This is Stephen's intellectual fantasy in the 'Scylla and Charybdis' section of Joyce's *Ulysses*, of course.) These, notice, are external, material things, representative of what *historical* research uncovers. The ultimate end of such enquiry might be the Bankside Globe in London, an Elizabethan theatre as authentic as we can make it, where we can now go and have an approximation of that experience, standing in the open air as the groundlings did, and even hearing the sounds of English as the Elizabethans heard them if the performance we attend is in 'Old Pronunciation' (of course, you have to be able to ignore the constant noise of jets flying into Heathrow). But *historicists* don't really like enterprises like the Bankside Globe, because, in the end, such external, material things are not their goal. Historicists are interested in *internal* things. They are less interested in what the Elizabethans *saw* in the theatre, than in how it *felt* to *see* what Elizabethans *saw* there. They are interested, too, in what we call 'identities' – including 'early modern identities', 'gender identities' and 'national identities' – that is to say, not mere external and material things but something deeper which suffuses or transcends the material fabric of the era. 'Who cares', I can hear them say, 'what kind of shirts the Elizabethans wore, or how they pronounced English – I want to understand how it felt to *be* Elizabethan.' So historicists are primarily interested in 'discourses', 'structures of feeling', 'mind-sets', and 'identities', and they seem to me much more confident than 'real' historians usually are that such fundamental and yet intangible elements of the past are recoverable. Unlike historians, historicists want to go straight to that 'identity' level, without all the boring archeological spadework that historians spend most of their time doing. 'Historians are always materialists, historicists are always idealists', as Maurice Zapp (the literary-theorist hero of David Lodge's novels) would have said. Hillis Miller, I think, ignores the distinction between historians and historicists in his address, and sees the opposing force of historicism as representing just a kind of Gradgrindian interest in facts, and he naturally cannot understand how that could compete in interest with the fascination of 'language as such'. As I read this sixth event, then, it is symptomatic of the moment when theory's enormous and rapid success began to induce a certain complacency. Its huge impact at highly privileged institutions in the UK and the USA caused it both to under-estimate the appeal of other approaches, and over-estimate the likely intellectual shelf-life of its own ideas.

The Strathclyde University 'Linguistics of Writing' conference, 1986

> *Reading*: The 'book of the conference' is *The Linguistics of Writing: Arguments Between Language and Literature*, ed. Nigel Fabb, Derek Attridge, Alan Durant, and Colin MacCabe (Manchester University Press, 1987). A TV documentary film about the event, called *Big Words Small Worlds*, was written and presented by David Lodge and broadcast on Channel 4, on 22 November 1987.

The sense that literary theory was perhaps becoming a little complacent again seemed in evidence when a high-profile conference on literary theory took place in Glasgow in the summer of 1987, with many of the most prominent theorists as speakers. In retrospect, the conference seems both the point when theory reached the height of its glamour and success, and at the same time the beginning of the era when a certain triumphalism began to provoke dissent and resistance which wasn't just coming from diehard traditionalists. I think of that event now as being rather like the British Labour Party's infamous 'Sheffield Rally', which was a political convention mounted just before the General Election of 1992 when Labour was well ahead in the polls. Unfortunately, the rally came across on TV as a premature victory celebration before any victory had been achieved. The poll lead evaporated and the result for the Labour Party was another five years in opposition. The same air of triumphal celebration was in evidence at Strathclyde, curiously mixed with an attempt to revive the prestige of linguistics, for the conference was organised by the Programme in Literary Linguistics at Strathclyde University, and sought to repeat and recreate the impact of the legendary 'Conference on Style' at Indiana in 1958 (the first theory event discussed here). So in reference back to the Indiana conference, this one opened with a 'Closing Statement', and closed with an 'Opening Statement', as if confident that it was setting in motion a whole new era of theory. Yet the sessions were not always distinguished: several of the famous linguists seemed very monodisciplinary to me, and they were in that sense a step backwards from the evangelistic interdisciplinarity of Indiana. David Lodge, at the start of his lecture on Bakhtin, reminded us that one of the Indiana sessions had been a densely statistical and tabular paper on stylistic deviations in suicide notes, and as it went on, the Glasgow conference began to seem more and more like a lengthy suicide note for literary theory.

Derrida gave his lecture 'How to Avoid Speaking', a particularly taxing and relentless address on negative theology, which lasted, as I recall, for nearly two hours, the last half hour of which was constantly punctuated by the sound of the lecture-theatre doors opening and closing as members of the audience left the auditorium in exhaustion. This lecture is not in the book of the conference, I think because Derrida had already promised it elsewhere, but he also gave a question and answer session which is included in the book as 'Some questions and responses' (pp. 252–64). The format for this session was that questions had been written out the day before and handed to the chairperson, who passed them on to Derrida, giving him time to consider his response. At the event each question was read out by the chair and then Derrida responded, not from extensive written notes, so far as I could tell, but anyway with the benefit of prior consideration, making it similar in feel to a present-day interview conducted by e-mail. My memories of this session are firstly of Derrida's wit and charm, and secondly, of the way he startled his audience by announcing that he had never said or thought that the metaphysics of presence was evil – 'I'm inclined to think exactly the contrary, that it's good' (p. 257). It took some minutes for people to take in the implications of what had been said:

if the metaphysics of presence is good, why spend a whole career seeking to deconstruct it? That was precisely what Jonathan Culler now asked him from the floor (the session drifted away from the written questions). The answer was essentially theological: the desire for presence is natural, but to accomplish it 'would be death itself' (p. 260), so one is compelled to deconstruct it, to keep on showing that what we mistake for the full presence of something is really the shimmer of *différance*. This leads to what became in the years which followed a familiar and habitual statement of his, that 'Deconstruction is not a method', it 'doesn't consist in a set of methodological rules' (p. 262). Of course, I haven't taken this statement at face value, so I *do* seek to demonstrate and quantify deconstructive practice in Chapter 3. After all, Derrida does say that it 'has some methodological effects' (p. 262), though without explaining how exactly that is different from being a method. Overall, it was an impressive performance, but it did give a foretaste of the remaining years of his career, in which he was always happy to say what deconstruction (or anything else) was not, but never seemed able or willing to explain what it *was*. There was a growing tendency within the theory world to claim that people had misunderstood what he said, or had taken it too literally, or in a naïve or simplistic way, and this complaint was constantly echoed by his supporters. When people argued that he was wrong about something, the response was always that that wasn't what he had said, or what he had meant.

As the conference went on, frustrations built up. It had seemed a masterstroke to get a TV film made of the event (which hadn't been part of the original plan), but lights and microphones are intrusive, and even at coffee time the camera crews clustered round the big names with their giant microphone booms, and rushed up to delegates with release forms to sign if they had asked a question at a session. The 'Opening Statement' on the final morning was interrupted from the floor by people who wanted their say, not least about the highly divisive power structures which the proceedings had laid all too bare. Delegates voted for the studio lights to be turned off and for the camera crew to leave the room, and it all ended rather raggedly, with the resounding 'Opening Statement' losing its impact.

What had gone wrong? Certainly, there were too many big plenary sessions (nearly all by American and British male speakers) and the responses were dominated by the same group, leaving very little space or time for open and democratic exchange. No matter how socially progressive its message, literary theory has to be socially progressive in its methods too. Almost without realising it, and in the space of a few years, theorists had become the new establishment and the new elite of the academic world, and they seemed to be taking their position too much for granted. Like the Labour shadow-ministers arriving for the ill-starred Sheffield Rally in a cavalcade of pseudo-ministerial black limousines, the big names suddenly looked as if they were treating the triumph of theory a little too much like a *fait accompli*.

The scandal over Paul de Man's wartime writings, 1987–88

Reading: 'Yale Scholar Wrote for Pro-Nazi Newspaper', *New York Times*, 1 December 1987, p. 1; *Paul de Man: Wartime Journalism, 1939–43*, ed. Werner Hamacher, Neil Hertz, and Tom Keenan (University of Nebraska Press, 1988); Jacques Derrida, 'Like the Sound of the Sea Deep within a Shell: Paul de Man's War', *Critical Inquiry*, 14 (Spring 1988): pp. 590–652. For 'Critical Responses' to this piece, see issue 15 (Summer 1989): pp. 765–811. Derrida's reply to the responses is 'Biodegradables: Seven Diary Fragments', pp. 812–73.

We have already discussed the 'famous five' Yale University deconstructionists who were joint authors of *Deconstruction and Criticism* in 1979, one of whom was Belgian-born Paul de Man (1919–83). His trio of books – *Blindness and Insight* (1971), *Allegories of Reading* (1979), and *The Resistance to Theory* (1986) – have been highly influential, and he was much revered at the time of his death as the austere intellectual embodiment of literary deconstruction. But in 1987 an article in the *New York Times* revealed that as a young man in Nazi-occupied Belgium in the early 1940s he had written nearly two hundred articles of a markedly anti-semitic kind for the newspaper *Le Soir* – for the material itself see *Paul de Man: Wartime Journalism, 1939–43*. The original discoveries were made by Ortwin de Graef, who was a Belgian student who had been doing research on de Man's early life and work. Though the case was shocking, it was not primarily the personal guilt or otherwise of de Man which damaged the standing of deconstruction and of literary theory in general, but the grounds on which other theorists attempted to defend him. Especially counterproductive, in my view, were Derrida's lengthy articles in the journal *Critical Inquiry*, his original defence of de Man being seventy-five pages long, and his response to the responses a further sixty pages.

Derrida begins speculatively, asking whether it is possible to respond to questions, what it might mean to do so, whether that would imply taking responsibility, and what responsibility is. It is at once evident that a defence conducted in this way is going to take a very long time, and also that what is really required is what Derrida was never able to supply – clarity, concision, brevity, and strength of conviction and compassion. The problem, too, is that the defender's position is an impossible one: the best 'defence' might be to publish these writings entire so that they are on the record, saying briefly whatever can be said in mitigation – de Man's youth, his possible ignorance, at least at the start, of what was actually happening to Jews in Europe, and that there may have been threats or dangers, so that he might have been acting out of fear rather than conviction. This might not amount to much, but I think it is actually all that could have been done. It would be neither necessary nor right for former friends and colleagues to turn against him and denounce him, but nor need they feel obliged to defend him. Intellectually, theorists might feel that if de Man remained undefended then deconstruction and literary theory would sink with his reputation, but defences of him which seemed to be motivated by that self-interested professional motive would prove highly damaging. As a friend, Derrida did feel the need to defend de Man, but he seemed to be using all the subtleties of deconstruction in order to do so, so that all those convictions about the unreliability of language, and the fragility of notions of truth and the self, were brought into play. The result was inevitable – such concepts begin to seem themselves morally suspect, for questioning the very concept of responsibility seems to glide towards denying that we are responsible for what we do and say. To write in the 1940s that 'A solution to the Jewish problem that aimed at the creation of a Jewish colony isolated from Europe would entail no deplorable consequences for the literary life of the

West' gives public support for (at best) deportations, and it is especially shocking, in view of de Man's subsequent career as a literary
academic, that he endorses anti-semitism *as* a literary intellectual.
Literary theory, then, was seriously compromised by the de Man
affair, and thereafter it never quite recovered its prestige, its confidence, and its sense of moral and political rectitude.

Jean Baudrillard and 'The Gulf War never happened', 1991

> *Reading*: Jean Baudrillard, *The Gulf War Did Not Take Place* (Power
> Publications, Sydney, 1995); Christopher Norris, *Uncritical Theory:
> Postmodernism, Intellectuals, and the Gulf War* (Lawrence and Wishart,
> 1992).

As a result of three essays first published early in 1991, Jean
Baudrillard (1929–2007) became known, in the popular imagination,
as the notorious French postmodernist philosopher who professed
to believe that the (first) Gulf War of 1990–91 never happened. The
three essays were written (respectively) just before the war started,
while it was in progress, and just after it ended, and were originally
published in the French newspaper *Libération* in January, February,
and March 1991, all three then being republished together in
French as *La Guerre du Golfe n'as pas eu lieu* and in English translation as *The Gulf War Did Not Take Place*. Baudrillard was impla-
cably imposed to Western foreign policy in the Gulf, and he uses a
powerful and extreme rhetoric to make his points. The tone is savage
and offensive, like the rhetoric of Jonathan Swift in the eighteenth
century when he is attacking political corruption and social self-
deception. For Baudrillard, what happened was not a war – of the
half million Western soldiers involved, he says, more would have
died in traffic accidents had they stayed at home than became casualties (p. 69), and the estimated 100,000 casualties (p. 2) were all on
one side. This represents an 'entirely asymmetrical operation'
(p. 19), but what is notable is 'the obscene aphrodisiac function ful-
filled by the decoy of the event, by the decoy of war' (p. 75). The
sexual imagery builds up: 'the war has unfolded like a long striptease' (p. 77), billed as a 'surgical war', and typified by the footage
relayed from the nose-cameras of 'smart weapons' homing in on
their targets. The media event which the war became showed no
actual human casualties, and was typified by 'clean' technological

images of 'surgical strikes'. But the striptease of the war culminated with television images of the horrific and merciless bombing of the retreating Iraqi army on the Basra Road at the end of the war, and the irony is that perhaps the most lasting image of the event is Ken Jarecke's widely published photograph of an incinerated Iraqi soldier in a burned out vehicle after the bombardment.

From the point-of-view of literary theory, the great irony of Baudrillard's Gulf War essays is that they became victims of the very condition they diagnosed. Just as the image or 'simulacrum' (see Chapter 4) of the war, in Baudrillard's accusation, was wrongly taken to be the war itself, so the popular view of what Baudrillard was thought to have written was substituted for what he actually wrote. Hence, he became the whipping-boy of anti-theorists and the target for high-moral-ground condemnations of postmodernism, which was now, in the 1990s, being seen as representative of literary theory in general (following the sequence of linguistics in the 1960s, structuralism in the 70s, and deconstruction in the 80s). In the caricature or 'simulacrum version' of what he had said, the hyper-clever postmodernist quibbled about notions of reality and was indifferent to the suffering and death that (we were indignantly informed) had undoubtedly taken place, even if Baudrillard thought the Gulf War hadn't. If we start by doubting the reality of the Gulf War, it was now suggested, won't we end by doubting the reality of the Holocaust?

Whereas the real damage to theory in the de Man affair was caused by his defenders, the damage in the case of the Baudrillard episode was partly caused by his attackers. Christopher Norris, who had defended de Man over the wartime writings, felt differently about Baudrillard, for he had now turned decisively against 'rhetorical formalism' in general, and postmodernism in particular, seeing many aspects of theory as an abandonment of principles of rational objectivity and truth in favour of relativism, consensus, and pragmatism. The result was his angry and scathing book *Uncritical Theory: Postmodernism, Intellectuals and the Gulf War*, for in his view the Gulf War controversy brought all these issues to a head. Norris wrote in the heat of events as they were happening, responding to the *Guardian*'s January 1991 edited version of the first Gulf War essay. He took Baudrillard's words to mean literally what they said (that the Gulf War will not happen), a proposition, he says, already refuted on empirical grounds by the commencement of the bombing. As he says (and he's right), 'perhaps it would be missing the point to observe that Baudrillard's predictions were flat wrong' (p. 14). Baudrillard is then lumped in with the theorists who had now become Norris's targets – Richard Rorty, Stanley Fish, Foucault, and the rest – all those 'anticognitivists' who argue that '"truth" in any given situation can only be a matter of the values and beliefs that happen to prevail among members of some existing "interpretive" community' (p. 16). Seeing 'reality' as 'a purely discursive phenomenon' (that is, constructed by codes, conventions, language, etc.) is part of the same thing, as is '*a prevalent misreading* of Derrida's work which takes him to be arguing – in solipsist fashion – that there is, quite simply "nothing outside the text"' (p. 16, my italics). Puzzlingly, the alleged misreading of Derrida seems exactly the same as Norris's misreading of Baudrillard. Norris, in other words, reads Baudrillard as saying that there is *literally* nothing outside the media misrepresentation of the Gulf War. But why the double standard? Why is Baudrillard to be read only literally, and Derrida only figuratively, so that the former *always* literally means what he says and the latter *never* does? The 'Postscript (Baudrillard's second Gulf War article)' makes some concessions, but still ends by attacking Baudrillard's 'thoroughgoing cognitive and epistemological scepticism' (p. 196).

Fierce though his attack is, it is surely the case that Norris and Baudrillard are essentially in agreement – both deplore the unprincipled cruelty of Western policy in the Gulf. Baudrillard shows how the event was re-made as it was happening, and a replacement reality of 'smart' weapons and surgical strikes was fed to the public. In reality, which was Baudrillard's point, the vast majority of the weapons used in the war were anything but 'smart', and their effects are still being experienced today. The overall effect of theory's intervention in the Gulf War is that it became further discredited because it was seen (quite wrongly in my view) as subscribing to the erosion of absolute principles of truth and value, and as supporting tricksy blurrings of the edges between word and world, concept and percept, reality and illusion, imagination and event. The theory 'community' had wrongly defended de Man and then wrongly attacked Baudrillard.

The Sokal affair, 1996

Reading: Alan Sokal and Jean Bricmont, *Intellectual Impostures: Postmodern Philosophers' Abuse of Science* (Profile Books, 2nd edn, 2003, first published in French in 1997 and in English in 1998).

In 1996 Alan Sokal, a physics professor at New York University, wrote a hoax article entitled 'Transgressing the Boundaries: Towards a Transformative Hermeneutics of Quantum Gravity', which was largely made up of what he considered to be a skein of postmodernist clichés. He sent it to Duke University's postmodernist cultural studies journal *Social Text*, which duly accepted and published the piece. On the day it appeared he published an article in another journal revealing the hoax and arguing that the acceptance of the original piece exposed the vacuity of postmodernist theory, and, by implication, of all cultural theory, given the pre-eminent status now enjoyed by postmodernism. The hoax became a celebrated and much-debated event, but a significant element of its immediate relevance here is that Derrida is quoted in the article and later joined in the public controversy about it.

The original article is reproduced in Sokal and Bricmont's book *Intellectual Impostures: Postmodern Philosophers' Abuse of Science*, published in English in 1998. The book and the article are not a wholesale attack on postmodern theory (though they were widely taken to be that) but an exposure of the misuse of ideas derived from physics and mathematics by prominent French theorists, notably Lacan, Kristeva, Irigaray, Baudrillard, Deleuze and Guattari, and others. Broadly, the scientific and mathematical ideas borrowed by the French theorists are those which seem to validate 'constructivist' or 'relativist' notions of reality (for instance, Heisenberg's 'Uncertainty Principle', Godel's thesis regarding incompleteness, Einstein's Theory of Relativity, and so on). The implication, says Sokal, is that a good deal of postmodern 'jargon' seems to have no very concise or 'rigorous' meaning, and that consequently the editors of an important journal in the field were unable to recognise that the approved terms and formulations were being mixed and multiplied to produce an article which had no overall coherence or logic. If, when the hoax was revealed, the editors had simply acknowledged that they had made a mistake and needed to tighten up their refereeing procedures, then the whole business might have blown over very quickly. But they didn't, and a rapid escalation followed – for Sokal's comprehensive bibliography of the controversy see www. physics.nyu.edu/faculty/sokal/index.html.

Because the accuser was American and nearly all the accused French, the hoax was seen as an attack on the standing of French intellectuals, and Julia Kristeva (one of the thinkers most harshly criticised in the book) responded in the French newspaper *Le Nouvel Observateur* (25 September 1997, p. 122) with the view that after a period of Francophilia, the pendulum had swung back in the other direction, and what was now being witnessed in the USA was '*une véritable francophobie*' ('genuine francophobia'). Derrida is not one of the thinkers subjected to sustained criticism in either the original article or the book, but in the article he is the first theorist to be quoted, and the quotation is described as 'the article's first major gibberish quote' (*Intellectual Impostures*, p. 244). The quotation, rather oddly, is from Derrida's off-the-cuff response to questions from Jean Hyppolite, back in 1966 (as discussed above), and Derrida refers to this when he comments on the Sokal affair (originally in the newspaper *Le Monde*, and reprinted in his book *Paper Machine*, Stanford University Press, 2005, pp. 70–2). In contrast to his intervention in the de Man case, Derrida's comments are brief: what is usually quoted is just the remark 'poor Sokal', referring to the plight of a physicist who is better known for his hoax than his physics. But Derrida too sees the affair in nationalistic terms – the 'credit' being given in the USA to himself as a 'foreign professor' was perceived to be excessive, so he is now attacked alongside other French writers for a fault (that of using in a loose way metaphors drawn from science and mathematics) which surely cannot be confined to the French. He would like to comment further on 'the American context and the political context', he says, but he has not the space to do so.

Overall, the Sokal affair does seem to have some of the nationalistic overtones perceived by Kristeva and Derrida. Having invited literary theory into the country in 1958 and 1966, and having played host to it for some forty years, the intellectual establishment of the USA now seemed to be giving it its marching orders. The message seemed to be that the 'moment' of theory had gone on long enough, and it was now time for the theorists to pack their bags and go home.

Given that postmodernism had come to stand for theory in general, as suggested earlier, the humiliation of postmodern theory by Sokal's hoax (which is how the event was generally perceived) was now seen as marking a comprehensive defeat of 'theory'. It was undoubtedly the case that powerful forces in the USA were working to reclaim and re-Americanise the Humanities syllabus, and these would gather pace as the 1990s went on. A general counter-revolution was taking place in American universities against a cluster of targets – political correctness, relativism, postmodernism, multi-culturalism, among others – and these tendencies were hardened in the post-9/11 climate. As we approach the end of the second decade of the new millennium, pervasive anxieties about further terror attacks have made international gatherings more difficult, and to this has been added our growing concerns about global warming and carbon footprints. In some ways, too, the gatherings are less necessary (in the age of e-mail, video-conferencing, conference calling, Blackberries, 'social networking', and so on). Consequently, intellectual life has become more insular, more national than international in character, and literary theory has not been immune to these trends. Perhaps we can expect greater divergence in the coming decades between the versions of literary theory which hold sway in different parts of the world, rather than total dominance of the field by a narrow range of global brands. That, surely, is an exciting new situation, and one which already seems to be coming about, as the next chapter will illustrate.

Theory after 'Theory'

Legacies of theory

'Is there life after theory?' a major UK conference wanted to know in 2003. The book of the conference was called *Life. After. Theory* (ed. Michael Payne and John Schad, Continuum, 2003) and it contains interviews with the major participants – Jacques Derrida, Frank Kermode, Toril Moi, and Christopher Norris. Interestingly, the title of the conference itself was a question – it had been advertised as 'Is there life after theory?' – whereas the title of the book might be taken as a profession of faith in the view that there is indeed life after theory. In the introduction to the first edition of *Beginning Theory* in 1995 I mentioned the common feeling even then that the real business of literary theory was already over, citing Thomas Docherty's 1990 book *After Theory*. Terry Eagleton re-used the title *After Theory* for his own book of 2003, implying that theory was still over, so to speak, and Eagleton's book was itself 'post' Valentine Cunningham's *Reading After Theory* (Blackwell, 2001), which it doesn't mention. Cunningham was thankful, on the whole, that theory had run its course, and he saw himself as beginning the process of repairing aspects of criticism which theory had damaged, and restoring them to their proper places within literary studies, rather like someone starting to tidy up after a flood or a hurricane. There have been other 'restorative' books, some with a more localised brief, such as David Scott Kastan's *Shakespeare After Theory* (Routledge, 1999). In this book 'after theory' is understood to mean, not the period after the passing away of theory, but the period during which theory has ceased to be news. Theory is no longer news-worthy, it might be claimed, because there has been a general acceptance of many of its key ideas, so that its impact and charisma have been 'routinised' (to use the terms of the sociologist Max Weber). So it has ceased to have to assert its uniqueness, and has passed into the general stream of ideas. This air of 'non-assertiveness', indeed, may be taken as typical of the general character of theory after 'Theory', that is, theory in the period when the 'preaching' phase is over, precisely because so many of its ideas have become the common currency of the intellectual climate we now live in.

What are some of those ideas, then, which were fiercely resisted a quarter of a century ago but now seem commonplace and taken for granted? A rudimentary list would include such things as: *firstly*, our feeling that identity is as much a shifting as a fixed thing. Thus, to be British, or gay, or female, or religious is not a matter of possessing some fixed entity or outlook which has always been the same – rather, these are identities which are constantly prone to drifting, in response to various currents which operate differently on different people. We might sum this up by saying that our notion of 'being', 'after theory', is that it always has significant elements of 'becoming' within it. *Secondly*, our notion of the literary text after theory is likewise unstable, whether we are thinking of 'canonised' texts or not, for each text is subject to shifting perceptions of what it 'is', so it may have different 'identities' for different groups, and may exist in several differently edited and differently presented versions. Likewise, 'the' text is always subject to different (and possibly serial) appropriations – think of all the Shakespeares we have seen even in the recent lifetime of theory, such as the 'sexual dissidence' and 'postcolonial' Shakespeares of the cultural materialists of the 1980s, and the 'Catholic' and 'Republican' Shakespeares of the 1990s, to name but a few. *Thirdly*, we are aware of the instabilities of language itself, and its capacity for slithering beyond the net of delineation and tight definition. This isn't just our wary, post-Freudian sense that 'slips' and slippage are part of the fabric of language itself, for we are also acutely aware of language's 'dream life' of metaphor and figuration which can sometimes disrupt the most prosaic and instrumental of utterances. And *finally*, there is our sense of the pervasiveness of theory itself, our realisation that it isn't possible to opt out of the business of position-taking, because every stance is a viewpoint, so that *all* our assertions are improvisatory, contingent, and provisional, like speculative cheques drawn against the intellectual and cultural bank, so that we can never know for sure what deposits are in the account to back them up. Those four mind-sets, I would say – that is, unstable identities, unstable texts, unstable linguistic structures, and uncertain truth-banks – are what many of us have been left with 'after theory'. We don't sign up to these four as a set of beliefs – almost by definition, our convictions about the four different kinds of instability are themselves unstable, but they are there all the time and they constitute the climate, rather than just the weather, of our thinking and sensibility.

Four further general shifts or 'settlements' in the intellectual landscape of theory itself ought to be mentioned. One general shift has been that theory has become less willing than hitherto to suspend disbelief in the face of vast and speculative intellectual claims, and more committed than it used to be to engaging with its material at an empirical level. Hence, findings are now more likely to be *demonstrated*, or at least more meticulously argued than before, rather than just being magisterially asserted. Indeed, the old Gallic disdain for 'mere' empiricism now seems as dated as the assumption that French *cuisine* and French fashions are inherently superior to all others. Clarity is now expected, even of literary theorists, and the poetic licences liberally issued to Francophone theorists in the 1970s and 1980s are no longer valid (or, at least, are not valid abroad). The current 'afterlives' of theory, then, are characterised by a certain strategic 'downsizing' of the old intellectual 'mega-zones': thus, structuralism has been eclipsed by narratology, originally one of its own specialist sub-sets, and the abstractions of 'Ideology' and 'Politics', which were the subject of Marxist-materialist theory, have been replaced by minute attention to the cultural logistics of specific periods – especially Early Modernism, Romanticism, and Victorianism.

Secondly, there is evidence of a turning away from the dominant materialism epitomised by British cultural materialism and American new historicism, and even a drift towards aspects of 'the spiritual', whether conceived of as metaphorical renderings of various aspects of reading, writing, and textuality (see Julian Wolfreys, *Victorian*

Hauntings: Speciality, Gothic, the Uncanny and Literature, Palgrave, 2001), or as metonymic representations of a world more real (in the sense of deeper, more fundamental) than material reality. Indeed, the religious turn seems much in evidence in literary studies in the present millennial era, far more so than for several decades, and perhaps the ongoing widespread preoccupation with Shakespeare's religion is indicative of this 'turn' (see E. A. J. Honigmann, *Shakespeare: The Lost Years*, 1988, and Richard Wilson, *Secret Shakespeare*, 2004, both Manchester University Press).

Thirdly, there has been a marked shift away from what I call the 'linguistic sublime', which is that 'constructivist' notion of language which sees it as constructing or forming our world, so that effectively everything is language, or language is everything, depending on how you want to look at it. The theorist and philosopher Christopher Norris (b. 1947) has long been a major force in confronting and dismantling the prestige of full-on linguistic constructivism. Norris is suspicious (and more) of the view that language speaks us rather than vice versa, a notion which, he says (presumably with Heidegger and de Man in mind), too easily allows us to deny responsibility for our own pronouncements. Norris has also vehemently attacked the 'anti-realists' in philosophy (those who deny the existence of 'mind-independent' reality and tend to see everything as 'mind-determined'), and even the much-discussed 'third way' between the 'realist' and 'anti-realist' poles he has tended to see as just another form of the latter. Likewise, he has taken issue with the 'endless, playful, polysemic interpretations' offered, in his view, 'at the expense of systematic argument' in such theorists as Baudrillard, Fish, Rorty, and Lyotard, seeing that kind of thing as typical of postmodernist relativism (see his books *What's Wrong with Postmodernism?*, Johns Hopkins University Press, 1990, *Quantum Theory and the Flight from Realism*, Routledge, 2000, and *Truth Matters: Realism, Anti-Realism and Response-Dependence*, Edinburgh University Press, 2005).

Finally, a new kind of cultural critique has arisen in response to extreme events such as 9/11, and the global pessimism which is the product of apparently intractable problems such as the Arab-Israeli conflict, Iraq, Afghanistan, the spread of religious fundamentalism, and the relentless progress of environmental deterioration. A sense of a world situation which is increasingly desperate, and in the shadow of which cultural critique itself comes to seem a foolish luxury, lies behind much of the post-millennial work of Terry Eagleton (see *Sweet Violence*, Wiley-Blackwell, 2003, *After Theory*, Allen Lane, 2003, and *Holy Terror*, Oxford University Press, 2005). Eagleton provides a cultural critique increasingly pre-occupied with violence, terror, and evil, a form of writing which might be called 'crisis critique' (of which ecocriticism could plausibly be seen as a sub-branch). This work is much burdened by a sense of catastrophe as both pervasive and impending, and the more usual concerns of literary and cultural criticism are made to seem darkly complicit with the forces poised to destroy us. Eagleton's increasing preoccupation with moral, religious, and ethical issues, and his shift away from Marxism, can also be seen as symptomatic of the 'religious turn' mentioned earlier.

So theory in recent years has tended to become more empiricist, less exclusively materialist, less susceptible to versions of the 'linguistic sublime', and more suffused with an awareness of ever-impending global crisis. But it hasn't shut up the shop and gone out of business. In fact, it has continued trading, and it has even developed several new lines. So we can now ask, in what precise ways has theory been *added to* and *developed* since, say, 1995, when it started to become common to say that theory was over? Without trying to be comprehensive, I will look at five areas of development which beginning-theorists might usefully be aware of.

Presentism

Presentism is an approach to literature which is 'oriented towards the text's meaning in the present, as opposed to "historicist" approaches oriented to meanings in the past' (Hugh Grady). It was initially concerned with the literature of the early modern period, especially Shakespeare, but has more recently emerged in the field of Romanticism, under the designation 'critical presentism'. Among others, the practioners of presentism are Terence Hawkes, Hugh Grady, and Ewan Fernie.

The recent trend of critical presentism can be seen as a reaction against the history-centred approaches to literature (such as new historicism and cultural materialism, see Chapter 9) which have been dominant since the 1980s. That emphasis on history built upon the work of Michel Foucault, who had stipulated, in the first chapter of *The Archaeology of Knowledge* (1972), that in the analysis of the discursive field 'we must grasp the statement in *the exact specificity of its occurrence*' (my italics). So it is not enough merely to analyse 'the statement' (and one kind of 'statement' is the literary text); rather, we must seek to 'place' it within its laboriously rebuilt historical specificity: so we must 'determine its conditions of existence, fix at least its limits, establish its correlations with other statements that may be connected with it, and show what other forms of statement it excludes'. That was the method of enquiry which Foucault advocated, and the implications for literary study are potentially devastating. Indeed, Foucault's own 'statement' is, if you like, a Historicist Charter, and if we sign up to these rhetorical pronouncements – as so many did – we will be committed to a lifetime of never-ending historical archeology. Historicism also built upon Raymond Williams's emphasis (in *Marxism and Literature*, Oxford University Press, 1977) on understanding *'the whole* lived social process, as practically organized by specific and dominant meanings' (my italics again). The intimidatory use of words like 'specific', 'exact', and 'the whole' in such proclamations drove many towards exhaustive historicist study, so that literary scholars became pre-occupied by historical method. By the late 1990s it seemed to be taken for granted that only an amateur reader of literature would deny that literature can best be understood through history.

That is the situation which presentism reacts against. 'Presentism' is a term which goes back to the early twentieth century; it originally denoted the naïve tendency to read the past exclusively in terms of the present, taking the present day as the summit and culmination towards which the past has been striving. For a 'presentist' in this naïve sense, the past is only of interest when its concerns are seen as directly relevant to our own, so that we scan history for what is 'germane' to ourselves and discard the rest. Clearly, 'presentism' would be a grievous fault in a historian, but what of the literary scholar? It could be argued that a literary scholar who *isn't* a presentist isn't really a literary scholar at all, since there could be no point in reading literature if it did not address our concerns today. Hence, since around the year 2000, we have seen the development of a group of literary scholars who *call themselves* 'presentists', partly to indicate that they see their position as opposed to that of the historicists. Terence Hawkes is the leading practitioner of presentism, and his Routledge series 'Accents on Shakespeare' has been one of its major publishing outlets. Hawkes was also a major figure in the promulgation of literary theory back in the 1970s, when he was the General Editor of Methuen's 'New Accents' series which did the essential work of popularising and mediating the writing of the major figures of the theory movement. His new series continues the mission of the original 'New Accents', and the brief is to 'either "apply" theory, or broaden and adapt it in order to connect with concrete teaching concerns' (General Editor's series statement). Some of the defining positions of presentism are set out in Hawkes's own book in the series, *Shakespeare in the Present* (2002), beginning with the point that it is 'fundamentally impossible' (p. 2) 'genuinely to capture, or repeat, the past'. So we start from the position that the past is past, and that we can never reconstruct or recapture its 'identity' (as seems to me the essential aim of most historicist approaches to literature). Hence, it is impossible for historians or literary scholars to 'make contact with a past unshaped by their own concerns' (p. 3), for (Hawkes here quotes the view of the Italian critic and philosopher Benedetto Croce, 1866–1952) 'all history is contemporary history'. So the 'presentist' literary scholar will actively seek out 'the present in the past', as we might call it, with the explicit aim of speaking with, or negotiating with, the living. By contrast, historians and historicists seek to 'speak with the dead' (p. 4), which is often said to be one of the main aims and satisfactions of the historian. Indeed, you may remember that the pioneer new historicist Stephen Greenblatt began his influential book *Shakespearian Negotiations* (1988) with the words 'I began with the desire to speak with the dead . . . It was true that I could only hear my own voice, but my own voice was the voice of the dead' (p. 1). So a basic distinction between presentists and historicists would be that the former aim to speak primarily to the living and the latter to the dead, though both will realise that they are often in fact negotiating with themselves (as Greenblatt's opening statement seems to acknowledge).

The historicist aim is essentially to study literature in the 'embeddedness' of its time and place (Foucault's 'the exact specificity of its occurrence' again), and this seems at first a logical and obvious way to approach literature. Presentism merely asks what the 'time and place' of (say) a Shakespeare play actually is, for as Ewan Fernie says, 'Shakespeare, in particular, is primarily a contemporary dramatist and writer, because he is currently taught, read and performed on a global scale unmatched by any other author . . . he is more embedded in our modern world than he ever was in the Renaissance' (in his article 'Shakespeare and the prospect of presentism', p. 175). It could be argued, too, that historicism is founded on a logical contradiction, for if identity really is historically constructed, then we can never step out of our own historically constructed identities to identify that of any other epoch. Hawkes also mentions two particular areas of presentist emphasis in Shakespeare studies: firstly the recent development of devolution in British politics – the establishment of separate parliaments or assemblies in Scotland, Wales, and Northern Ireland in the late 1990s, and the consequent re-definition of what is meant by the 'United Kingdom'. Hawkes's sense of the tensions and ambiguities within the British 'Union', especially since the devolution movement of the 1990s, informs his reading of Shakespeare's *Cymbeline* in Chapter 4. It is entitled '*Aberdaugleddyf*', which is the Welsh name (literally 'the mouth of two streams') for the port of Milford Haven, an 'English' port in Wales, long of great strategic importance to the defence of 'the realm' (a suitably vague term), and featuring strongly in the play. In British history the Welsh Tudors and the Scottish Stuarts accede in turn to the 'British' throne, but with the national status of Ireland, Scotland, and Wales left somewhat ambiguous (are they nations in their own right, or not?). The project was to fuse Englishness, Welshness, Scottishness, and Irishness into a single 'Britishness', but not by adopting a federal model. Hawkes reads Shakespeare's play in the knowledge that the two streams of Welshness and Englishness were never fused into one, and that present-day processes of devolution are increasingly causing them to diverge.

The second area of presentist emphasis in Shakespeare studies concerns a series of strategic reversals of established priorities or preferences, including 'apparently immutable conceptual hierarchies such as primary/secondary, past/present' (p. 4). For instance, the influence of Shakespeare on Marx and Freud will be seen as being just as interesting and important as Marxist and Freudian readings of Shakespeare, and the 'performance' of a Shakespeare play will be taken to be as important as its 'reference' – that is, what it *does* is as important as what it *says*. A slightly fuller definition of presentism is given a little later: it is, says Hawkes, a criticism 'whose roots in and connections with the here and now are fully and actively sought, deliberately foregrounded, exploited as a first principle … A presentist criticism's engagement with the text takes place precisely in terms of those dimensions of the modern world that most ringingly chime – perhaps as ends to its beginnings – with the events of the past' (pp. 21–2). So presentism sees itself as 'reversing, to some degree, the stratagems of new historicism' (p. 22), beginning with 'the material present' and allowing that 'to set its interrogative agenda'.

Presentism in practice

The nub of the theoretical position represented by presentism is perhaps contained in the statement 'All ends, when they arrive, shape the beginnings that precede them' (p. 62). Though its premises are so different, the *methods* of presentism, on the evidence of Hawkes's *Shakespeare in the Present*, can seem quite closely analogous to those of new historicism. The essays tend to begin with a vivid 'cultural snapshot', rather like the new historical 'anecdote' (see Chapter 9), but the 'snapshot' is taken from the present, or the near-present. Thus, Hawkes's *Hamlet* essay, 'The Old Bill', sees *Hamlet* as a play about policing, investigating, 'gleaning', for many of the characters in the play are constantly both under surveillance and on the watch ('the Old Bill' is British slang for the police). The 'snapshot' at the start concerns the fact that in Berlin in 1945 the American occupation forces imposed a list of approved and non-approved drama, with *Hamlet* on the former list because of its treatment of 'corruption and justice', while *Julius Caesar* and *Coriolanus* were on the latter because they allegedly 'glorified dictatorship'. Thus the play itself becomes an element in the process of surveillance in the specific circumstances of the immediate aftermath of the Second World War. Hawkes then goes into the use of stages and acting within the play, and then weaves in the true-life story of the Jewish actor Mauriz Leon Reiss, who in 1930s Nazi Germany constructed a whole new non-Jewish identity for himself which he 'acted' in real life, culminating in his move to the USA and Hollywood in the 1940s, where, by a cruel irony, he ended up playing the part of Nazis in propaganda films. These elements are woven in the essay into what I would want to call a 'critical plot', and it is that element of 'plotting', with its more familiar suggestion of creative rather than critical writing, which I would see as a characteristic element of presentist writing. There *is* close-up textual work in the 'presentist' essay, but it is highly 'themed', drawing out from the text innumerable aspects of the key themes of surveillance, acting, and so on. Those, in short, are the key elements of the presentist 'plot' or 'performance' of the play – the vivid initial 'snapshots', the highly plotted discursive structure in which key motifs keep reappearing, the intensely 'themed' engagements with the text, and the driving force of a present-day overriding concern which is usually political in nature.

In the last analysis, the contest between historicism and presentism is an argument about choice of contexts – we can read *Hamlet* either in the context of the past (as Stephen Greenblatt does in *Hamlet in Purgatory*, seeing the play in terms of the religious beliefs and conflicts of the early modern period), or in the context of the present (or, at least, of the more recent past, as Hawkes does). Ewan Fernie too, in the *Hamlet* essay listed above, makes a 'presentist' reading when he reads the randomised violence of much of the play in the context of the present-day threat of terrorism. But as Fernie says, this could be seen as a kind of agreement, for both historicists and presentists seem to be saying 'anything but the text' (p. 176), since both see the choice of context as the decisive act in their strategy of reading – it's as if Hamlet had said 'The context's the thing' rather than 'The play's the thing'. We will come back to this issue in considering new aestheticism.

What to read on presentism

Fernie, Ewan, 'The last act: presentism, spirituality and the politics of *Hamlet*', pp. 186–211 in *Spiritual Shakespeares*, ed. Ewan Fernie (Routledge 'Accents on Shakespeare' series, 2005).

Fernie, Ewan, 'Shakespeare and the prospect of presentism', in *Shakespeare Survey*, 58 (2005).

Grady, Hugh, and Hawkes, Terence, eds, *Presentist Shakespeares* (Routledge 'Accents on Shakespeare' series, 2006).

Hawkes, Terence, *Shakespeare in the Present* (Routledge 'Accents on Shakespeare' series, 2002).

Headlam Wells, Robin, 'Historicism and "Presentism" in Early Modern Studies', *The Cambridge Quarterly*, 29(1) (2000): 37–60.

For an internet discussion of presentism visit: http://www.shaksper. net/archives/2007/0091.html.

New aestheticism

New aestheticism is an emergent movement in literary criticism and theory which arose from philosophical debates about the status of aesthetics in the 1990s and started to become a distinct literary practice around the time of the millennium. It emphasises the 'specificity' and 'particularity' of the literary text, seeking dialogue with it rather than mastery over it, and seeing the text as part of an ongoing debate, within itself and with its readers, rather than viewing it as representative of a fixed position, or as the pre-determined expression of socially conservative views. Among the practitioners of new aestheticism are Isobel Armstrong, Emeritus Professor of English at Birkbeck College, London; John Joughin, currently Vice-chancellor of the University of East London; and Simon Malpas, currently of Edinburgh University.

New aestheticism runs contrary to the major varieties of literary theory as they came to prominence from the 1970s onwards, for nearly all of these increasingly challenged and increasingly denied the autonomy of literature. Thus, the Marxist critic saw literature as the expression of social forces, the psychoanalytic critic saw it as the voicing of psychic drives and instinctual conflicts, and the post-structuralist saw every act of literature as a demonstration of the instabilities of language itself. The theoretical consensus was that whatever writers thought they were doing or saying, they were always doing or saying something else – in fact, literature couldn't ever speak, it could only *be spoken* by various combinations of social, psychic, or linguistic forces, and the critic/theorist always knew better than the writer what these forces were. Literature, then, lost its autonomy, its strangeness, its specificity, and was always being stopped and cautioned by critics and theorists, even when it seemed to be behaving perfectly well – championing the underdog, standing up for self-determination and equality, or calling for tolerance and understanding of the claims of others. Jane Austen, for instance, might have thought she was doing all those things in her novels, but the critical-theoretical thought-police always knew better. They could see that she was really occluding the French Revolution, condoning the brutality prevalent in the British Navy, laundering knowledge of the links between the gentry and slavery, or recommending sexual repression – and all that in a single novel – *Mansfield Park*! This instinctive distrust of writers is part of what the French philosopher Paul Ricoeur (1913–2005) called the 'hermeneutics of suspicion' (in *Freud and Philosophy*), which he defined as 'a method of interpretation which assumes that the literal or surface-level meaning of a text is an effort to conceal the political interests which are served by the text. The purpose of interpretation is to strip off the concealment, unmasking those interests'.[1]

Theorists and critics, then, for around a quarter of a century had been the strippers-off and unmaskers of literature, and they had gone largely unchallenged since the defeat of the liberal humanists back in the early 1980s. The unique qualities of each text were pretty well disregarded, for whatever its specific qualities, a literary work would be found guilty of the broad generic crimes which each of the theoretical approaches specialised in investigating – sexism and phallocentrism in the case of the feminist critics, orientalism for the postcolonialists, logocentricism for the deconstructionists, and so on. After a few decades of this relentless onslaught, it was inevitable that literature must eventually reassert itself. The counter-argument of the literary text (if it were allowed to speak) would be simple, and it would go something like this: all literary texts are different, and they shouldn't be typecast as all sharing socially conservative tendencies. The postcolonialist quite rightly says that all Arabs or 'Asiatics' or Muslims are different and particular and shouldn't be represented in collective negative stereotypes, as

1 For a lively and sustained counter-interrogation of the hermeneutics of suspicion see Rita Felski's *The Limits of Critique* (University of Chicago Press, 2015).

happens in the pernicious 'orientalist' thinking that lumps them all together. But this resistance to thoughtless homogenisation is not carried through to the way we regard works of literature. It is a gross anomaly that literary theory should champion difference, alterity, agency, and particularity in every sphere except its own professional sphere of literature, and should view literature *as a whole*, as a socially regressive intellectual formation. New aestheticism, then, emerging since 2000, can be seen as one element in the inevitable fight-back of literature after its thirty-year interrogation by the hermeneutics of suspicion.

But is this reassertion of the power of the literary text, which is a key element in new aestheticism, simply a return to the old 'close reading' which theory long ago displaced? I don't think so, for it goes back for its rationale, not to I. A. Richards's *Practical Criticism* of 1929 and William Empson's *Seven Types of Ambiguity* of 1930 (the founding texts of close reading), but to the philosophy of Kant and Hegel, which it *re*-re-reads after they had been re-read by Derrida and others. The theorists of the 1970s and 1980s always seemed to imagine their own 're-readings' to be permanent and decisive, whereas they are in fact merely moments in an ongoing cycle, so that their re-readings are just as open as any other to being themselves re-read. In other words, new aestheticism is not seeking to reverse the reversal whereby *Practical Criticism* of 1929 became *Critical Practice* (the title of Catherine Belsey's influential book of 1980), but is making a series of interventions which seek to alter the very trajectory of theory itself. In addition, the 'new' aestheticism represents a revival of the interests and attitudes towards the aesthetic which were expressed in the late nineteenth century by the 'aesthetic movement', as seen in the work of the poet Algernon Charles Swinburne (1837–1909), the poet and painter Dante Gabriel Rossetti (1828–82), the Irish writer Oscar Wilde (1854–1900), and the essayist and critic Walter Pater (1839–94), attitudes often summed up in the slogan 'Art for Art's sake', which asserted the autonomy of art and literature, and its freedom from considerations of moral correctness or social utility. The desire to reinstate the literary text at the centre of literary studies – but in a newly 'totalised' form – is of great interest, and, as I see it, is a welcome reaction against both historicism and the tradition of the hermeneutical suspicion of the literary text.[2]

New aestheticism, then, can be considered in various ways – one is to see it as a revival of interest in the aestheticism of the late nineteenth century; another regards it as re-opening debates about aesthetics which stem from the philosophy of Kant and Hegel; a third is to see it (through the notion of the ongoing 'dialogue' between the reader and the text) as a new kind of ethical criticism; and a fourth, finally, is to see it as a 'new formalism' which foregrounds the formal features of the text and the effects of those features on readers. New aestheticism often confronts the dominant critical and theoretical consensus with a sense of exasperated impatience, asserting the importance of some long-excluded and reviled aspect of literary study. As if suddenly fed up with being constantly on the back foot, it snaps out the un-askable question – 'What's wrong with the aesthetic?' 'What's wrong with Kant?' 'How close is close?' All these questions are section or chapter headings from Isobel Armstrong's book, which is discussed next.

New aestheticism in practice

The book which marks the beginning of the new aestheticism is Isobel Armstrong's *The Radical Aesthetic* (Oxford University Press, 2000). The introduction discusses the rejection of notions of the aesthetic by all recent schools of literary theory, and Armstrong writes that 'Evolving another poetics means challenging the politics of the anti-aesthetic by re-making its theoretical base and changing the terms of the argument' (p. 2). This, she says, means reinstating the 'foundational philosophers Kant and Hegel' (p. 1), from whom the most viable notions of the aesthetic derive. Armstrong identifies Terry Eagleton's book *The Ideology of the Aesthetic* (1990) as a widely

2 I put forward roughly this view in a lecture and article entitled 'An academic discipline foresees its death', *PN Review*, 173 (vol. 33, no. 3) (Jan.–Feb. 2007), pp. 16–20 (text of plenary lecture at the 'European Society for the Study of English' Conference, 2006). It advocates a notion of 'total textuality' which is further explained in Chapter 4 of my *English in Practice* (Bloomsbury, 2nd edn, 2014).

influential statement of the 'politics of the anti-aesthetic', and her own book *The Radical Aesthetic*, appearing ten years later, can be seen as a direct challenge to it. She sees Eagleton's book, too, as a kind of highpoint of the hermeneutics of suspicion – we might character-ise the new aestheticism as the approach to literature which begins with suspicion of the hermeneutics of suspicion. Armstrong's first chapter argues closely against Eagleton. For him, all the text-specific effects of a sonnet, for instance, would 'always already' have been accounted for. This would include such things as: the rhyme pattern; the 'turning' of the thought between the octet and the sestet; the compressing of a long sweep of thought into a couple of images and a fourteen-line frame; the use of words and phrases which finesse two different senses into one paradoxical formulation; the way 'heavy' topics (love, death, religion, and so on) are 'lightened' by verbal dexterity; and the characteristic 'drama' of the sonnet form itself, which requires writers to work themselves into a conceptual or metaphorical cul-de-sac, and then escape with a deft phrase in the final lines. All these things give aesthetic and intellectual pleasure to the reader, and are both the fuel and the engine of the sonnet form. But 'suspicious' theorists see them as 'mere' devices whose pri-mary effect is ideological – for them, the verbal skill on display in the sonnet is class-linked and elitist; it is a redundant luxury, decorating thought in intricate, filigree patterns. The skills and techniques re-quired to produce these effects can only be acquired by those priv-ileged enough to have vast amounts of free time to devote to their acquisition, so that each time these skills are displayed, there is a reinforcement of class boundaries. Further, when *apparent* contra-dictions or opposites are 'staged' in the sonnet and then reconciled with a verbal sleight of hand in the concluding lines, the literary form itself conveys the implicit message or ideology that *all* conflicts are like this. Conflicts, says the literary form, are apparent only, im-plying that social differences can always be solved by sitting down together and agreeing on a little evolutionary tinkering, and that no contradiction is ever so fundamental as to require the complete revo-lution of the system that contains it. Something like the above points would constitute a 'hermeneutically suspicious' view of literary form. How exactly would a new aestheticist version of the matter be different?

Isobel Armstrong gives an excellent demonstration of the newer practice towards the end of the third chapter of *The Radical Aesthetic*, which is entitled 'Textual Harassment: The Ideology of Close Reading, or How Close is Close?' The chapter is about Wordsworth's 'Tintern Abbey', a poem which has long been a critical and theoretical battleground, a 'site of struggle' if ever there was one. Her answer to the question in her title ('How close is close?') is 'not close enough': conventional close reading has actually maintained a distance between the reader and the poem by entertaining sexual/textual fantasies of 'mastery', as the (usually male) critic performs the usual dissective erotics on the text – 'laying bare' its physics, 'uncovering' its pyrotechnics, 'savouring' the physical taste of its language – all these phrases come from an unfortunate quotation, placed at the start of her chapter, from critic and theorist Stanley Fish, who is describing how he feels in the act of textual analysis. This 'mastery' approach, says Armstrong, is an evasion of the 'affect' of the text, by which is meant the *emotional* effect it has on the reader, something much feared and constantly exorcised by male critics down the ages - I. A. Richards, for instance, condemns such things as 'stock responses' and 'prior doctrinal adhesions' – which sound very messy indeed; Wimsatt and Beardsley condemned the 'affective fallacy'; and William Empson, writing about this same poem as a vehicle for carefully separating and defining his several different varieties of verbal ambiguity in poetry, gets very worked up about the reprehensible vagueness of Wordsworth's 'something' in the line 'a sense of something far more deeply interfused'. Armstrong's point is that when we are describing feelings and sensations, a certain degree of vagueness is inescapable, and may even be the only way of saying anything at all.

Armstrong's response to the dilemma is to go 'closer than close' – for instance, she spends two of her seven pages on Wordsworth's poem writing about the word 'of'. One aspect of the new aesthetic technique, then, is the 'ultra close-up', the attention to a 'form word' like 'of', when more traditional versions of close-textual scrutiny tend to be centred on 'content words' – that is, nouns and adjectives, verbs and adverbs. Secondly, Armstrong uses the twin concepts of 'bifurcation' and 'erasure', taken, via the philosopher Emmanuel Levinas (1906–95), from the French writer and ethnographer Michel Leiris (1901–90): in 'bifurcation', the choice of one path rather than another brings both into play, while 'erasure' connotes 'over-writing', as in the palimpsest, where the erasing is done by rewriting, that is, by writing a new word over an old one. Both words ('bifurcation' and 'erasure') suggest that poems contain an unsettled element, that they are arguing within themselves, and inviting us to join in the argument; perhaps they have something to *ask* us, rather than something to *tell* us – quite possibly, Wordsworth himself doesn't quite know what the 'something' is, and as he isn't a philosopher, he doesn't have to decide before he puts pen to paper. As Armstrong shows, there is plenty of both bifurcation and erasure in 'Tintern Abbey': Wordsworth writes of 'hedge-rows', for instance, and immediately self-corrects and rewrites it as 'hardly hedge-rows, little lines/ Of sportive woods run wild'. Likewise, the smoke seen rising above the trees gives 'some uncertain notice, as might seem,/ Of vagrant dwellers in the houseless woods'. Here 'as might seem' might make the reader ask impatiently, 'Well does it seem that way or not?' Similarly, the oxymoronic phrase 'vagrant dwellers' seems to make the people concerned (who may or may not be there, as Wordsworth has not seen them) appear both settled and nomadic at the same time. Also relevant is the fact that the poem constantly repeats and rewrites itself on a larger scale – the visit described in the 'now' of the poem repeats one of five years earlier, and the poem Wordsworth is engaged in writing echoes and challenges another (unmentioned) one of a very similar type, 'Frost at Midnight', written by his friend-rival Coleridge. So the poem, says Armstrong, is fraught with anxieties on many levels, and its nervousness of tone and structure reflects that. The reader shouldn't be attempting to 'master' it, evading its anxious-making 'affect', but should enter the turmoil of the emotions it presents, getting closer, in other words, not just to the words, but to the feelings of the poem. That too, that element of closeness to the affect, is a major component of new aesthetic practice. So Armstrong's reading draws attention to the 'protean' qualities of the text, emphasising that it presents, not so much a static target for critical attention, as a dynamic vortex of thoughts and emotions, the two hardly distinguishable from each other, and possibly describable as a unique intensity of affect. The text, so to speak, calls out its need to 'enter into a relationship with someone' (p. 102). Readers are 'likely to find in the "body" of the text what they fear, hate and desire'; a ' "narcissistic" moment of identification may be an essential response . . . because it escapes from the master/slave model of reading which is the dominant model in our culture'. We need to face the 'terrors of closeness', Armstrong says, rather than retreating to the safe territory of masterly dissection of the textual corpse. Indeed, as 'theory after Theory' knows, the text isn't a corpse and isn't dead at all – it was up and dancing even as Theory was conducting its wake.

The introduction to another key book in this area, *The New Aestheticism* (edited by John Joughin and Simon Malpas, Manchester University Press, 2003), agrees with Armstrong's emphasis in suggesting that the survival of certain literary texts from remote eras is not due to their having 'timeless' significance, but lies in their capacity to 'sustain interpretations which are often either contestable or politically opposed' (p. 8). This suggests that the crucial quality which literary texts need to possess if they are to outlive the era of their own production is that they should leave space for readers to 'join in', to talk back with and to them, and 'enter into a relationship with them', to pick up the term used by Armstrong. By contrast, a literary work which is merely pious, or propagandistic, or 'right on' doesn't allow this space: it tells us what it thinks we ought to think, in a take it or leave it way. So the mark of the work that survives is that it has the quality of still being in progress, so to speak, of still being engaged in the business of working things out. That is the aspect of the work that the new aestheticist responds to and seeks engagement with, that quality of keeping questions open and never quite concluding. The new aestheticist, in other words, seeks to keep the conversation with the work going on, rather than looking for capping, or closure, or end-stopping, as other critical approaches seem to do when they take it as their main aim to show how orientalist, or phallocentric, or auto-deconstructive the work is. It is true in one sense that this 'keeping talking' approach 'privileges' the literary work itself, but then other approaches privilege the critic or theorist, and the un-ending dialogue with the work envisaged by the new aestheticist seems fundamentally 'democratic' in character, for it is a conversation which can never be finally rounded off and concluded. So there is an acceptance that the aim of the critical enquiry

can never be to reach conclusive scientific truth (in this it is quite
different from the premises of cognitivism; see later) – it can never be
finally established, for instance, that Conrad's *Heart of Darkness* is or
is not a 'racist' book written by a racist author (this text is the subject of Robert Eaglestone's chapter in Joughin and Malpas), or that
Hamlet is or is not 'mad', for there isn't that kind of 'isness' (of either the positive or negative sort) in either text. Rather, it is only
possible to discuss the *issue* of racism in *Heart of Darkness* and the
issue of madness in *Hamlet*. In any case, it would be extremely difficult to imagine any possible benefit arising from *settling* either of
these questions, while on the other hand, it is certainly possible to
imagine plenty of benefits coming from *discussing* them. That emphasis on our open-ended readerly dialogue with the literary text is
as close as I can get to explaining what the new aestheticism is ultimately about.

What to read on new aestheticism

Armstrong, Isobel, *The Radical Aesthetic* (Oxford University Press,
    2000).
Joughin, John, and Malpas, Simon, eds, *The New Aestheticism*
    (Manchester University Press, 2003).
Shrimpton, Nicholas, 'The Old Aestheticism and the New',
    Literature Compass, 2(1) (January 2005).

Cognitive poetics

Cognitive poetics is a method of reading literature which combines
linguistics and psychology, with the aim of better understanding
basic cognitive processes. Some of its important practitioners are:
Reuven Tsur, Professor Emeritus of Hebrew Literature at Tel Aviv
University; Peter Stockwell, currently of Nottingham University;
Alan Richardson, currently of Boston College, USA; Joseph Tabbi,
currently of the University of Illinois at Chicago, and Ellen Spolsky,
Professor Emeritus of English at Bar-Ilan University, Israel.

The Latin verb *cognoscere* means to get to know, and from it
comes the English term 'cognition', which means (says the *Concise
OED*) 'the mental action or process of acquiring knowledge through
thought, experience, and the senses'; the adjective is 'cognitive',

meaning 'relating to cognition'. The 'cognitive sciences' study the way the mind is organised, the processes of thought itself, and the mind as the interface between inner and outer worlds. A 'revolution' in this field took place from the 1950s onwards, closely connected to the cross-disciplinary currents looked at in the previous chapter, whereby the disciplines of anthropology, psychology, and linguistics began to talk to each other. It was also partly the product of the growth in computer technology, which began to offer possible models for the mechanisms of mental processing. Another signifi-cant factor was the challenge offered by the American linguist Noam Chomsky (born 1928) to the 'behaviourist' approaches to the mind associated with the psychologist B. F. Skinner (1904–90). Chomsky's famous review of Skinner's book *Verbal Behavior* (in *Language*, 35(1) (1959), pp. 26–58) challenged the view that language acquisi-tion can be accounted for in terms of cumulative responses to ex-ternal cues and stimuli. Chomsky took the opposite view, seeing language acquisition as a creative, internalising process for which the human mind is uniquely equipped. It is natural to suppose that studying language will help to explain how the mind works, since language use seems the most intricate and characteristic of human cognition processes. For instance, basic language tropes like meta-phor and metonymy seem to correspond to fundamental methods of apprehension and understanding, since the first fuses two or more concepts into a single new whole, while the latter lets part of some-thing stand for the whole something. But, say the cognitivists, if we are talking about mental processes and relating them to metaphor and other rhetorical devices, then we have entered the territory of literary criticism, so the idea of a combined form of critique which blends literary criticism, philosophy of mind, and even evolutionary biology and neuroscience begins to seem less bizarre.

During the early 1990s the basis for this combination of fields was being laid, in the work of Israeli critics Reuven Tsur (*Toward a Theory of Cognitive Poetics*, Sussex Academic Press, 2nd edn, 2008) and Ellen Spolsky (*Gaps in Nature: Literary Interpretation and the Modular Mind*, SUNY Press, 1993). At that time, literary theory was dominated partly by post-structuralism, which brooked no counter to its view of language as nothing but 'instabilities' and 'relativities', and partly by the historicism whose bottom line is that 'everything is socially and historically constructed'. Any notion of 'nature' was regarded with extreme suspicion – the very word was taboo, and as we saw in Chapter 13, this was the intellectual taboo that ecocriticism had to challenge. In a way, Chomsky's theories of language bring 'nature' back into play: language acquisition can't be entirely accounted for 'in terms of such notions as stimulus, reinforcement, deprivation', as Chomsky says in the Skinner review. That is, 'social' factors (such as encouragement, rewards and approval, demonstrations and coaching) cannot entirely account for the child's acquisition of language, and the capacity to learn language must in some way be 'wired in' or innate. And while Lacan had, it is true, argued that the unconscious is structured like a language (see Chapter 5), his ideas about how a language is structured were not very precise, since they were not based on any systematic empirical investigation. Indeed, the disregard of empiricism (by which we mean detailed practical investigation, rather than conceptual theorising) was another of the great weaknesses of the dominant theoretical paradigm of the 1980s which now met its inevitable challenge.

These are the factors, then, which came together in the 1990s and resulted in the growth of 'cognitive poetics'. A key moment in its emergence was the 1998 annual convention of the Modern Language Association in the USA when a forum was set up by Francis Steen and Lisa Zunshine on 'Literature and the Cognitive Revolution', and a discussion group on 'Cognitive Approaches to Literature' was started at the same event – see 'Literature and the Cognitive Revolution: an Introduction', the first item in the *Poetics Today* special issue on Cognitivism, which is itself an important landmark in the establishment of the field of cognitive poetics, and makes an excellent starting point on this topic.

Alan Richardson's essay in that special issue ('Of heartache and head injury: reading minds in *Persuasion*') gives a sense of the characteristic interests of cognitivist critics. The essay reads the character of Anne Elliot in Jane Austen's *Persuasion* in relation to the cognitive science of the day: the broadly accepted view of the mind in Austen's day was 'socially constructivist', which is to say that it saw the mind as formed by 'circumstances and events'. A classic literary example illustrating this consensus would be Mary Shelley's *Frankenstein*, where the monster's character is formed by the treatment it receives. Generally the mind was seen as passively imprinted, a *tabula rasa* (that is, a blank slate) shaped by the imprint of circumstance, following the views of British 'empiricist' philosophers John Locke (1632–1704) and David Hartley (1705–57), both of whom saw the mind as a kind of 'empty' potentiality which is shaped by the impress of experience, so that the crucial factors are education and social conditioning. Those forces make us what we 'are', or rather what we become. From Mary Wollstonecraft's *The Wrongs of Woman* through to Simone de Beauvoir and beyond ('One is not born a woman, one becomes a woman'), this view has been essential to feminism, and it is essential too to modern notions of social justice, where we believe that merely punishing the criminal (with prison, etc.) will not eradicate crime, because we also need to eradicate the social conditions which breed criminal patterns of behaviour ('One is not born a criminal, one becomes a criminal', de Beauvoir might also have said). Likewise, we might believe (following the Ancient Greek philosopher Heraclitus and the German Romantic poet Novalis) that 'character is destiny', which sounds like a form of fatalism indeed, though less so if we also agree with George Eliot that 'circumstances make character'. The first of these statements about character essentially means 'everything is given', while the second means 'everything is made'. A third view would be 'everything is partly given and partly made', and this seems closest to the view that Jane Austen puts forward in *Persuasion*, embodied in her character Anne Elliot, who, at twenty-seven, is pretty well middle-aged by the standards of heroines in novels, for whom the going rate was then about eighteen. The word 'embodied' is deliberately chosen, for the novel, in Richardson's reading, insistently shows mind and character as embedded and embodied in brain and body. Anne Elliot, says Richardson, is paired with the 'false heroine' Louisa Musgrove, whose 'mistimed leap towards Frederick's arms' (p. 145) results in her 'headfirst fall onto the paving stones of the Seawall known as The Cobb at Lyme Regis'. The blow to the head alters her character for life, just as Anne's character has been altered by her life's disappointments (her mother's death when Anne is fourteen, and the break-up of her romance with Frederick Wentworth five years later). One suffers from a broken heart, the other from a broken head, says Richardson (p. 148). The fall changes Louisa's 'nerves' and her 'fate', says Austen, for mind is 'embodied', not free-floating in soul-like independence. Likewise, her descriptions of Anne's reactions show mind and body, cognition and corporality, in close alignment: when Anne thinks of Captain Wentworth 'unshackled and free', Richardson says, it makes 'her heart beat in spite of itself and brought the colour into her cheeks' (p. 151). In Richardson's reading, then, the subject matter of the novel shows a concern with 'cognitivism'. In *Persuasion*, Austen is in dialogue with the thinking of her period about thinking, somewhat distancing herself from the extreme social constructivism seen in contemporaries such as Mary Wollstonecraft, William Godwin, and Mary Shelley. The cognitivist reading of the novel brings these issues to the fore, concentrating on how the novel centres on these notions of the construction of subjectivity.

Cognitive poetics in practice

More frequently, however, cognitive readings focus, not on the content as such of the work, as in the example just discussed, but on the cognitive processes which are made evident in the reader's decoding of the content. Two essays from *Cognitive Processes in Practice* (edited by Joanna Gavins and Gerard Steen, Routledge, 2003) are closer to this cognitive norm: Peter Stockwell's chapter 'Surreal Figures' reads surreal poetry, while Craig Hamilton's 'A Cognitive Grammar of "Hospital Barge" by Wilfred Owen' reads a seldom-discussed piece by Owen. Stockwell takes the key cognitive distinction between 'figure' and 'ground' as his basis, and I will use his terminology, but my own example, to give a sense of the kind of procedures used in cognitivist essays. Here are the opening sentences of a short story:

> The liner began to move away from the quayside. On the boat-deck stood a woman in a purple evening dress. In her hand was a crumpled telegram bearing the postmark *Paris, 14h.15, 30 Juin 1958*. Staring ahead, her arm resting on the ship's rail, she let her fingers loosen – as if unconsciously – their grip on the crumpled paper, and it fluttered down into the waters of the harbour.

In a literary text, a common kind of 'attractor' (that is, a way of drawing the mind's attention) takes the form of presenting a (smaller, or moving) *figure* against a (larger, or static) (back)*ground*, as in the opening sentence 'The liner began to move away from the quayside'. The 'ground' (whatever in the mental picture isn't the ship) suffers 'neglect' (the opposite of 'attraction'), while the liner attracts attention. The original 'figure' can then be 'grounded' (made into background, or 'occluded') by a second figure/ground pairing: 'On the boat-deck stood a woman in a purple evening dress': now the ship (or, rather, a specific part of it) is the 'ground' for the 'figure' of the woman, and the process can be repeated: 'In her hand was a crumpled telegram bearing the postmark *Paris, 14h.15, 30 Juin 1958*'. In this sentence there are three more figure/ground 'profilings' in rapid succession: the woman becomes 'ground' to the 'figure' of the hand, then the hand becomes 'ground' to the 'figure' of the telegram, and finally the telegram itself becomes 'ground' to the 'figure' of the postmark. The term 'to profile' is used because it is the 'outline' of the figure *against* the ground – that is, figure and ground working together or intersecting – to which, or by which, the attention is drawn. Here, then, I am taking the technical terms (figure, ground, profile, attraction/attractor, neglect, and occlusion), and illustrating how they work with a simple example. It will be clear that I am focusing on how the mind is 'directed' by the words and images of the text, and I haven't commented at all on *aesthetic matters* – for example, how effective is this opening? Is it too fast, or too stark, or too melodramatic? Nor has there been comment on matters of *literary history* – for example, issues such as: how typical is this of the author's usual opening ploy? How familiar is it, as technique and subject matter, of the short stories of its day? Nor has there been comment on matters of *interpretation* – for example, questions such as: who is the woman? What's in the telegram? Is this a story about loss and separation? As even this brief example implies, cognitivists tend to be less interested in such questions than in the mapping of the mechanisms of the cognitive processes involved.

The next sentence reads:

Staring ahead, her arm resting on the ship's rail, she let her fingers loosen – as if unconsciously – their grip on the crumpled paper, and it fluttered down into the waters of the harbour.

In this sentence, the loosening fingers are the figure and everything else is the ground. But there is also another foregrounded element which is designed to attract our attention to a particular detail, for as Stockwell says, 'Attractors can be formed by stylistic features in the text that display linguistic *deviance*' (p. 16, his italics). The detail of the loosening fingers is led up to by a series of 'participial' verbs (those ending in 'ing', like 'staring' and 'resting') which are passed over rapidly, and the focal detail is indicated by the finite verb 'she let'. But here we have an 'interrupting construction' which interrupts the expected word order, and thereby draws attention to the adverbial phrase 'as if unconsciously'. This happens because the phrase is unexpectedly positioned, for it breaks up the usual English word order of subject ('her fingers'), verb ('loosen'), object ('their grip'). Normally we would expect the adverbial phrase 'as if unconsciously' to follow its verb, as in a sentence like 'He (subject) lifted (verb) the dog (object) with great care (adverbial phrase)'. Moved from its expected position, the adverbial phrase 'as if unconsciously' is 'defamiliarised', losing its cloak of familiarity and suddenly seeming very prominent. So the notion is conveyed that the action may not actually be unconscious at all, but deliberated performed so as to *look* unconscious. Hence, the notions of 'acting' and 'looking' introduce the idea that somebody is watching, at whom this performance is directed, possibly someone unseen, maybe in the distance (with binoculars?) and yet sensed, as somebody whom she is pretty sure must be there. Perhaps, too, another person is to retrieve the paper from the harbour, someone of whose presence, for the benefit of the unseen watcher, she feigns unawareness. Little of this is explicitly *stated* in the text, but drawing attention to the words 'as if' nudges the reader's thought processes in that direction. The scenario, then, is open to development in these ways, and this is subtly conveyed to the reader through the disposition of the language, and the perceptions I have been tracing, which instigate the cognitive processes of the reader in response to the verbal cues and clues which are on the page.

One further verbal element which is worth commenting on is the phrase 'she let her fingers loosen', which also contains a peculiarity, one which can be seen if we ask how that phrase differs in effect from 'her fingers loosened'. We can begin to answer that question by comparing it with a variation such as 'She forced her fingers to loosen', a version which would indicate that she performed the action with reluctance, as if under duress of some kind, and not wishing to be a party to the consequences which will follow that action. So the added word 'forced' would indicate an inner conflict of some kind: what effect, by contrast, does the word 'let' have? But this question is hard to answer precisely. It may imply that she gives in to an urge or a necessity, without being entirely in assent with the action – she goes along with it, but without being entirely happy with herself for doing so, perhaps. This is speculative, but it does seem clear that the phrase gives the first glimpse of complexities of motive or psychology within the character, which begins to move our attention from the scene without to the scene within.

The foregoing gives an impression of the aims, style, and emphasis of the cognitive approach, and perhaps some of its potential drawbacks will be apparent. For instance, while it is interesting to show cognitive processes at work on a key segment like the opening of a text, it is not necessary to go all the way through the story in this manner if the primary aim is merely to demonstrate or explicate those cognitive processes. If the reader's main interest is the story itself, however, some more complete analysis will be needed, though this kind of analysis will soon begin to seem tedious, surely, to most readers, even for a fairly short short story. The problems are similar to those of stylistics, with which the cognitive approach shares a good deal, procedurally and intellectually.

One solution to such problems is to look for very short texts to operate on, but the disadvantages are obvious: Craig Hamilton uses Wilfred Owen's sonnet-length poem 'Hospital Barge', but the literary merit of that poem seems slight to me. Another is to find items which are marked by a high degree of linguistic or procedural eccentricity, such as Hemingway's 'A Very Short Story' in Elena Semino's piece, or the experimental fiction of Donald Barthelme in the chapter by Joanna Gavin. In most cases, the reader learns in each essay something about some aspect of cognitive science (Cognitive Grammar in the Wilfred Owen essay, Possible Worlds Theory and Text Worlds Theory in the two chapters just mentioned, and Contextual Frame Theory in Catherine Emmott's chapter on plot twists in popular fiction). Since about half of each essay is devoted to explicating the theory in question, this shifts the centre of literary study a long way towards the study of cognition itself, and there would need to be very solid and convincing grounds for doing that. The cognitivists themselves keep saying that cognitivist poetics is exciting, but that, of course, must remain a matter of opinion, and as Hans Adler and Sabine Gross say in their answering essay to the special issue of *Poetics Today* on cognitive poetics, 'cognitive analyses ... quite often seem unexciting and didactic to non-cognitivists' (p. 19). The given grounds for shifting the orientation of literary study are of a surprisingly moralistic kind – that it makes the study of literature 'much less elitist' (p. 1), because cognitivist poetics 'sees literature not just as a matter for the happy few' (p. 1). Also, the cognitivists seem – surprisingly – to go along with the 'functionalist' challenge to the study of literature and the arts – 'the practice of producing yet another interpretation of a text from the canon', they say, 'has been challenged by the taxpayer' (p. 2). Cognitive poetics offers 'justification' for the spending of taxpayers' money, because the cognitivists show that literature 'is grounded in some of the most fundamental and general structures and processes of human cognition and experience' (p. 2). Ultimately, they are aiming to give 'a psychological account of the whole problem of aesthetic and artistic experience, or, another hot issue, literary invention'. You may wonder whether this double agenda is really sensible, and you do have to decide which you most want to spend your time studying, great literature, or the cognitive processes of the human mind. 'It's the same thing,' the cognitivists would say, 'and you can't study one without the other.' But in reality, we surely can, and (as Adler and Gross say) the rest of us have the option on cognitive poetics of either 'adopting it or [merely] paying heed to what its practitioners have to offer'. Inevitably, most will choose the latter. But to see even the second as necessary, 'cognitivism will have to make itself relevant for the analysis of specific texts to appeal to "mainstream" literary studies'. Richardson's discussion of *Persuasion* from a cognitive angle certainly seems to me to add a new dimension to our understanding of that text, so it passes the test, but I am not entirely convinced that the more technically cognitivist readings always tell me a great deal about the text that I couldn't have reached by a simpler route. However, there is something intriguing about the immense optimism of the cognitivists – they always seem to see themselves as being on the threshold of a great breakthrough, so I am keeping an open mind on this, as on other varieties of 'theory after Theory'.

What to read on cognitive poetics

Adler, Hans, and Gross, Sabine, 'Adjusting the Frame: Comments on Cognitivism and Literature', *Poetics Today*, 23(2) (summer 2002), pp. 1–26 (which is a response to the previous issue of the journal; see Richardson below).

Gavins, Joanna, and Steen, Gerard, eds, *Cognitive Poetics in Practice* (Routledge, 2003).

Richardson, Alan, and Steen, Francis F., eds, *Literature and the Cognitive Revolution*, which is a special issue of the journal *Poetics Today*, 23(1) (spring 2002).

Stockwell, Peter, *Cognitive Poetics: An Introduction* (Routledge, 2002).

Tsur, Reuven, *Toward a Theory of Cognitive Poetics* (Sussex Academic Press, 2nd edn, 2008).

Zunshine, Lisa, ed., *The Oxford Handbook of Cognitive Literary Studies* (Oxford University Press, USA, 2015).

An excellent and important collection, representing the generous 'open-borders' approach to cognitivism, and a rejection of scientific fundamentalism.

Consilience and 'conciliatory' approaches to literary studies

The term 'consilience' designates the ambitious attempt, beginning around the time of the millennium, not just to *bridge* the two cultures of science and the humanities – few would deny that it would be a good thing to do that – but to *fuse* them. The adherents of consilience wish to replace what they regard as a failed grand fusion project with one that might succeed. The failed project, in their eyes, is the thirty-year period from the 1980s during which literary and cultural studies seemed fused with speculative theory, particularly that of the post-structuralist and postmodernist kind. The one they believe might succeed involves ditching theory and replacing it with science, that is, with empirical knowledge gleaned by specialists in relevant scientific fields. Important, too, as part of this project is the supporting idea that this new alliance between literary and scientific study should proceed systematically and collaboratively, developing and evolving its fitness for purpose by a shift 'towards a more integrated knowledge base for academic pursuits', in this case English studies (see Erica Moore, 'Conciliatory approaches in English Studies', p. 2).

The consilience ideal is a broader version of the approach known as 'literary Darwinism', or, occasionally, as 'evocriticism', the aim of which is to apply insights derived from the study of evolution to the study of literature. For example, the origin and development of narrative can be studied in this way, as in *The Literary Animal: Evolution and the Nature of Narrative*, co-edited by Jonathan Gottschal and David Sloan Wilson, with a foreword by Edward Wilson, or Gottschal's own *The Storytelling Animal: How Stories Make Us Human*, or Brian Boyd's *On the Origin of Stories*. Such titles are in themselves indicative of the fact that this 'unified' approach to literary study clearly involves a big shift in what literary students and scholars have long assumed is the point and purpose of literary study.

The E. O. Wilson who wrote a foreword to the first Gottschal book mentioned above is the distinguished American biologist who reintroduced the term consilience into cultural practice and debate with the publication of his book *Consilience: The Unity of Knowledge* in 1999. At the start of the second chapter Wilson notes that the word was coined by the nineteenth-century polymath and Master of Trinity College, Cambridge, William Whewell (whose surname is pronounced 'you-ull') in his 1840 book *The Philosophy of the Human Sciences*. The word denotes, says Wilson, 'literally a "jumping together" [or synthesis] of knowledge by the linking of facts and fact-based theory across disciplines to create a common groundwork of explanation' (p. 6). Whewell also coined the words 'scientist', 'physicist', and 'linguistics', which gives some indication of his range of intellectual interests.[3]

Advocating a shift to 'a more integrated knowledge base' for literary studies seems an attractive enterprise, and the same aspiration lay behind the turn to theory in literary studies from the 1980s onwards. Theory too sought to incorporate scientific concepts into

3 I have drawn in this paragraph on discussion in William Welstead's doctoral thesis '"Braided Narratives": An Ecocritical Reading of Contemporary Welsh Poetry in English', Aberystwyth University, 2012, pp. 111–13.

the range of its thinking, but without negotiating the prior assent, tutelage, or imprimatur of the scientific and mathematical scholars whose ideas they made use of. This led, ultimately, to allegations that the appropriated ideas had been misunderstood or misapplied, culminating in the debacle of the Sokal affair (see Chapter 14). As Wilson explains in his book, consilience is firstly a belief in the potential union of the sciences which he then sought to extend so as to include the social sciences and the humanities. But such a programme, once entered into by the humanities with the agreed aim of integration, would inevitably have to be monitored in some way by scientists – 'consilience', says Wilson, at the start of his second chapter, 'is the key to unification' – and unification (of literary and scientific study) is exactly what the literary Darwinists are putting into practice. As Erica Moore (a firm literary believer in consilience) writes in her article, 'Wilson presupposes that science will be the definitive determiner', and she quotes his justification for this, which is that 'Science offers the boldest metaphysics of the age' (p. 7).

Whewellian/Wilsonian consilience recognises that inventiveness in all significant intellectual and creative activity does not, in practice, proceed in a linear or programmatic fashion, and that as Einstein (one of Wilson's scientist heroes) said, 'No worthy problem is ever solved within the plane of its original conception'. But affirmations of the same kind are found in Coleridge too, so the imperative to accept science as the 'definitive determiner' and seek compatibility, compliance, and conciliation with contemporary systems of scientific knowledge seems (paradoxically) to limit the very 'jumping together' of ideas and ways of knowing which the consilience movement itself advocates.

Perhaps scepticism about consilience is to be expected from traditional humanist scholars and from many who have made their names as oppositional theorists in recent years. Hence, the views of academics who were engaged in forms of literary scholarship which draw upon science-based disciplines such as linguistics and stylistics (see Chapter 11), narratology (Chapter 12), and cognitive literary studies (Chapter 15) would be of particular interest, since their fields were established and thriving long before the term consilience became current. Professor Lisa Zunshine (University of Kentucky, Lexington), a leading figure in cognitive literary studies,

and editor of the *Oxford Handbook of Cognitive Literary Studies*
(Oxford University Press, USA, 2015), writes about consilience
with a strong sense of urgency in her four-page introduction to that
volume, presenting a very different intellectual ideal, and insisting
that 'striving towards a grand unified theory … is to engage in
mythmaking'. Zunshine describes cognitive approaches as 'dialogic
and decentralized' rather than 'unified', so that 'because they don't
see themselves as working on a puzzle whose pieces must fit neatly
together, they feel no need to iron out differences' (p. 1). We should
work, she says, 'not towards a consilience with science but towards a
richer engagement with a variety of theoretical paradigms in literary
and cultural studies'. She goes on:

> The division between the sciences and the humanities … reflects
> meaningful differences in ways of thinking about the world. Consil-
> ience with science, moreover, though an attractive ideal theoretically,
> in practice often comes down, as Nancy Easterlin has observed, to
> 'assimilating literature to [the] epistemic prerogatives' of science.
> (p. 2, and see Easterlin's article listed below)

The vitality of the combined field of literary and cognitive studies
lies not in consilience but in its decentralisation, for '[w]hen one
draws on two fields that are already heavily interdisciplinary (i.e.,
literary criticism and cognitive science), the outcome will be inevitably represented by a broad variety of paradigms and approaches'.
It seems to come down to this –that subscribing to consilience in
theory seems likely to result, in practice, in a discouragement of the
intellectual vitality that consilience itself stands for. This is not to
say, of course, that 'combined field' literary work, in which the other
field is hard science, cannot or should not take place. On the contrary, it can and does, as is shown by the existence and practice of
cognitive literary studies. For an excellent example, which uses another kind of science, see the article listed below by two literary
critics, Jayne Archer and Richard Marggraf Turley, and Howard
Thomas, who is a professor of biology.

What to read on consilience and 'conciliatory' approaches to
literary studies

Archer, Jayne Elisabeth, Turley, Richard Marggraf, and Thomas, Howard,
    'The Autumn King: Remembering the Land in *King Lear*', in *Literary
    Theory: An Anthology*, ed. Julie Rivkin and Michael Ryan (Wiley-

Blackwell, 3rd rev. edn, 2017), pp. 1547–66, originally published in *Shakespeare Quarterly*, 63(4) (2012), pp. 518–43.

An excellent literary article, which is 'consilient' in its practice without professing any explicit allegiance to consilience.

Boyd, Brian, *On the Origin of Stories* (Harvard University Press, 2010).

The title is a deliberate echo of the title of Darwin's ground-breaking *Origin of Species* – the writing is lively and relentlessly committed to replacing literary theory with evo-centred 'biocultural' theory. Part II of the book applies his ideas on narrative to *The Odyssey* and the 2008 computer-animated cartoon film *Horton Hears a Who!*

Easterlin, Nancy, 'Voyages in the Verbal Universe: The Role of Speculation in Darwinian Literary Criticism', *Interdisciplinary Literary Studies*, 2(2) (2001), pp. 59–73.

A powerful challenge to the incorporation of a single-level scientific preoccupation (with evolution) into literary study: she concludes 'The history of literary criticism demonstrates that narrowly-conceived models of critical activity do not last very long.'

Evans, E. O., *Consilience: The Unity of Knowledge* (Abacus, 1999).

This is the central work for 'consilience', the work of a powerful writer and thinker who makes a compelling case and sets out the factors in his own life and professional experience which led him in this direction.

Gottschal, Jonathan, and Wilson, David Sloan, eds, *The Literary Animal: Evolution and the Nature of Narrative* (Northwestern University Press, 2006).

Aims to study the origin and development of narrative by applying insights derived from the study of evolution.

Gottschal, Jonathan, *The Storytelling Animal: How Stories Make Us Human* (Mariner Books, 2013).

Aims to tells us how 'storytelling has evolved, like other behaviors, to ensure our survival'.

Moore, Erica, 'Conciliatory approaches in English Studies', *Postgraduate English*, 23 (September 2011), available at http://community.dur.ac.uk/ postgraduate.english/ojs/index.php/pgenglish/article/view/91 (accessed 11 April 2017).

Though I have come to different conclusions, I found this article very helpful and informative, and it would make an excellent introduction to the scope of this topic.

Posthumanism

I remember a conversation I had one coffee time in the early 1980s with a colleague from the Computer Science Department. He was telling me that computers are thinking machines, and I replied, no doubt naively, that he was only using the word 'thinking' as a metaphor, since computers have no consciousness and without that there cannot be thinking. The only thing computers can do, I went on, is mechanically carry out the tasks which humans have programmed them to perform. He insisted that computers really can think, and perhaps we were both glad when the bell went and we could get back to our respective domains, in different buildings and different mental worlds. If I were to get involved in the same discussion today, the person putting views like those of my Comp-Sci colleague would probably be a posthumanist from the English Department, quoting Hans Moravec (of the Robotics Institute at Carnegie Mellon University), and telling me that one day soon it will be possible to download human consciousness on to a computer.

In some ways, posthumanism in its current form as a well-established field of both theory and practice was anticipated by thinkers in the 1960s and 70s, a period that might be labelled first-wave posthumanism. Marshall McLuhan's *The Medium is the Massage: An Inventory of Effects* (1967) conveyed a similar message in the same computer-based vocabulary: 'All media are extensions of some human faculty – psychic or physical' (p. 26). His pronouncements were set on the page like the free-verse poetry of that era: 'the wheel is an extension of the foot/ the book/ is an extension of the eye/ clothing, an extension of the skin,/ electric circuitry,/ an extension of/ the/ central/ nervous/ system' (pp. 31–40). In all these, the point is that the border line between the human body and an ever-increasing accumulation of techno–electronic prostheses is becoming increasingly blurred, so much so that we will have to rethink and redefine who and how we are:

> The medium, or process, of our time – electric technology – is reshaping and restructuring patterns of social interdependence and every aspect of our personal life. It is forcing us to reconsider and re-evaluate practically every thought, every action, and every institution formerly taken for granted.

A prosthesis – which has become a key term and concept in posthumanism – is an external or implanted synthetic device which supplements, replaces, or enhances a body part. By its very 'nature' (or non-nature) its existence and use deconstructs boundaries between self and other.

Another major predecessor of today's posthumanism was the American scientist, philosopher, and MIT professor Norbert Weiner (1894–1964), who coined the term 'cybernetics' in 1948. He defined it as 'the scientific study of control and communication in the animal and the machine' (it derives from the Greek word meaning governor or steersman), and it can be more loosely defined as the science of control and automation, crucially based on what are known as feedback loops (definable as a 'system structure that causes output from one node to eventually influence input to that same node'). Weiner's interest in cybernetics partly arose from work on auto-aiming systems for anti-aircraft guns in the Second World War, and he became the pioneer of robotics, computerised control systems, Artificial Intelligence (AI), cognitive science, and neuropsychology. He explains in his 1950 book *The Human Use of Human Beings* that if automation is further developed and extended by the findings of the science of cybernetics, it will be possible to release human beings from menial repetitive tasks or jobs so that they can fulfil their potential in the leisure time thereby gained; so he maintained a clear demarcation and hierarchy between humanity and technology, while at the same time paving the way for posthumanists who would later deconstruct precisely that demarcation.

According to Jay David Bolter, in a very useful overview article on posthumanism, the theorist Ihab Hassan coined the term posthuman (or re-circulated it, some would say) in his article 'Prometheus as Performer: Towards a Posthumanist Culture?' of 1977.[4] The pioneering and highly influential book on the topic is *How We Became Posthuman*, published in 1999 by Katherine Hayles, now a Duke University professor, who has degrees in chemistry and English. In her preface, Hayles describes a version of the 'Imitation Game' proposed by Alan Turing (1912–54, the founder of theoretical computer science) in a 1950 paper entitled 'Computer Machinery and Intelligence':

4 Bolter's article is 'Posthumanism' © 2016 John Wiley & Sons, Inc. Published 2016 by John Wiley & Sons, Inc. DOI: 10.1002/9781118766804.wbiect220

> You are alone in the room, except for two computer terminals flick-
> ering in the dim light. You use the terminals to communicate with
> two entities in another room, whom you cannot see. Relying solely on
> their responses to your questions, you must decide ... which is the
> human, which the machine. (p. 1)

She explains that the 'erasure of embodiment' means that you can
only see the on-screen responses, not the body which is or isn't
there producing them, with the consequence that ' "intelligence"
becomes a property of the formal manipulation of symbols rather
than enaction in the human lifeworld'. Then, 'If you cannot tell the
intelligent machine from the intelligent human, your failure proves,
Turing argued, that machines can think.' Because thinking has long
been regarded as the definitive human attribute ('I think, therefore
I am'), it follows that once the human exclusivity of this attribute
has been compromised we have entered the realm of the posthuman, in which we will have to accept that there can be 'no *essential*
differences or *absolute* demarcations between bodily existence and
computer simulation, cybernetic mechanism and biological or-
ganism, robot teleology and human goals' (Hayles, p. 3, my italics).

    This kind of thinking (or perhaps we should designate it by a
more neutral, less anthropocentric term like 'awareness') is
prompted by accelerated developments in technology, including
Artificial Intelligence (AI), Artificial Life (AL), robotics, pros-
thetics, genetic manipulation, and bioengineering. It is also stimu-
lated by an increased awareness of the importance and prevalence of
non-human agency, as we recognise when we jokingly refer to
'gremlins' which interfere with the smooth workings of machines,
or artefacts that 'seem to have a will of their own'. In broader terms,
posthumanism involves a rejection of what is sometimes called
'human exceptionalism', which is the conviction that our own
species is special, and uniquely gifted and privileged, as the pinnacle of evolution. It recognises that evolution itself is a force which
has 'non-human agency', and will surely proceed beyond us into a
posthuman, post-anthropocentric future that we may be part of, but
could *only be part of.*

    The most obvious application of this material and outlook in
literary studies is to works of science fiction, cyberpunk, and

steampunk fiction, which are, of course, genres defined by their pre-occupation with this kind of material and outlook. It is also directly relevant to other genres, such as ghost stories, where consciousness, awareness, aversions, and desires (both malevolent and benevolent) are attributed to places, to the dead, and to a range of 'transhuman' entities such as vampires, zombies, and revenants. Likewise, myth-ological texts attribute consciousness to animals, gods, and hybrid beings, creating a realm of transhuman entities, often caught in cross-over states between human, animal, arboreal, or divine, the one grafted uneasily, tragically, or temporarily on to the other, thereby producing the story.

A final word on posthumanism? Well, no, I'm not quite as naive as I was in the 1980s. But just a comment. One pattern which post-humanists don't usually discuss is the one of which they themselves are components, that is, the patterns of academia, with its publica-tions, promotions, conferences, and so on. Their books make no clean break with academic styles of discourse, or at most, do no more than follow the well-established loosening of academic style and manners which has been evident for some thirty years. By con-trast, McLuhan's *The Medium is the Massage* was brilliantly innova-tive in design and presentation – bizarre, provocative and artistic, and self-consciously part of a 'counter-culture' that went well be-yond the boundaries of the academic world. The books listed below are all very good, but they are unmistakably academic books which will advance academic careers. I have often noticed that the more intellectually adventurous the theorist, the more conservative the pedagogy, and no aspect of posthumanist academic practice looks as radical as the experimentation in refashioning learning and teaching that went on in universities in the 1960s, though of course, the man-agerial demands and restraints on academic practice today are con-siderable. So I am not quite converted. But the posthumanists are most welcome as the latest group to join the conversation of theory. Undoubtedly that conversation is made richer, and given additional potential and insight, by their contributions to it.

What to read on posthumanism
Badmington, Neil, *Posthumanism* (Readers in Cultural Criticism series, Palgrave Macmillan, 2000).

'This reader offers an introduction to the ways in which humanism's be-lief in the natural supremacy of the Family of Man has been called into question at different moments and from different theoretical positions.'

Badmington, Neil, *Alien Chic: Posthumanism and the Other Within* (Routledge, 2004).

'*Alien Chic* examines the concept of posthumanism in an age when the lines between what is human and what is non-human are increasingly blurred by advances in science and technology, for example, genetic clon-ing and engineering, and the development of AI and cyborgs.'

Braidotti, Rosi, *The Posthuman* (Polity Press, 2013).

Contains four chapters on 'Posthumanism: Life Beyond the Self', 'Post-Anthropocentrism: Life Beyond the Species', 'The Inhuman: Life Beyond Death', and 'Posthuman Humanities: Life Beyond Theory'. Clear, direct, challenging, and informative writing throughout.

Braidotti, Rosi, *Posthuman Glossary* (Bloomsbury, 2018).

Will include material on 'the neoliberal economics of global capitalism, the perpetual war on terror, environmental destruction on a mass scale, and extensive security systems'.

Hayles, Katherine N., *How We Became Posthuman: Virtual Bodies in Cyber-netics, Literature and Informatics* (University of Chicago Press, 1988).

A ground-breaking book, richly informative and speculative: chapter 1 is entitled 'Towards Embodied Virtuality', chapter 4 is on Weiner and 'cybernetic anxiety': second-wave cybernetics is dated from 1960 in chapter 5; chapter 7 is on the novels of Philip K. Dick; and the final chapter asks 'What Does it Mean to Be Posthuman?'

Herbrechter, Stephan, *Posthumanism* (Bloomsbury, 2013)

First published in German in 2009 and translated by the author; chapter 2, 'A genealogy of posthumanism', traces the development of a field which has 'only in the past ten years established itself … within the so-called "theoretical humanities"'. Chapter 4 is 'Posthumanism and sci-ence fiction'.

Herbrechter, Stephan, Callus, Ivan, and Rossini, Manuela, eds, *European Posthumanism* (Routledge, 2016).

'In literary studies and beyond, "theory" and its aftermaths have argu-ably been over-influenced by US- and UK-based institutions, publishers, journals, and academics. Yet the influence of theory in its Anglo-Ameri-can forms has remained reliant on Continental European ideas. Similar patterns can be discerned within the latest theoretical paradigm – post-humanism.' This book seeks to redress the balance – the editors are from Germany, Malta, and Switzerland.

Mahon, Peter, *Posthumanism: A Guide for the Perplexed* (Bloomsbury, 2017).

Another very good introduction to the topic from an excellent writer – it opens with a dialogue between two posthumanists in a bookshop. Chapter 5, 'Philosophical Posthumanism', is especially useful.

Malpas, Simon, and Wake, Paul, eds, *The Routledge Companion to Critical and Cultural Theory* (Routledge, 2nd edn, 2013).

Chapter 13, pp. 144–53, is 'Posthumanism', by Ivan Callus and Stephan Herbrechter.

Nayar, Pramod K., *Posthumanism* (Polity Themes in 20th and 21st Century Literature, Polity Press, 2014).

Another excellent brief introduction to the field: Chapter 4 is 'Absolute Monstrosities: "The Question of the Animal" ', with sub-sections on 'The Humanimal [*sic*]' and 'Speciesism'.

Wolfe, Cary, *What is Posthumanism?* (University of Minnesota Press, 2009).

This is number 8 in the 'Posthumanities' series which includes titles from Michel Serres, Donna Harraway, and Roberto Esposito. The opening chapters in Wolfe are on the legacy of deconstruction within posthumanism, and this is a running theme throughout. This is a distinct second or third step, rather than a first introduction to the topic.

Appendices

Appendix 1 Edgar Allan Poe, 'The Oval Portrait'

The chateau into which my valet had ventured to make forcible entrance, rather than permit me, in my desperately wounded condition, to pass a night in the open air, was one of those piles of commingled gloom and grandeur which have so long frowned among the Apennines, not less in fact than in the fancy of Mrs Radcliffe. To all appearance it had been temporarily and very lately abandoned. We established ourselves in one of the smallest and least sumptuously furnished apartments. It lay in a remote turret of the building. Its decorations were rich, yet tattered and antique. Its walls were hung with tapestry and bedecked with manifold and multiform armorial trophies, together with an unusually great number of very spirited modern paintings in frames of rich golden arabesque. In these paintings, which depended from the walls not only in their main surfaces, but in very many nooks which the bizarre architecture of the chateau rendered necessary – in these paintings my incipient delerium, perhaps, had caused me to take deep interest; so that I bade Pedro to close the heavy shutters of the room – since it was already night – to light the tongues of a tall candelabrum which stood by the head of my bed – and to throw open far and wide the fringed curtains of black velvet which enveloped the bed itself. I wished all this done that I might resign myself, if not to sleep, at least alternately to the contemplation of these pictures, and the perusal of a small volume which had been found upon the pillow, and which purported to criticise and describe them.

Long – long I read – and devoutly, devotedly I gazed. Rapidly and gloriously the hours flew by, and the deep midnight came. The position of the candelabrum displeased me, and outreaching my hand with difficulty, rather than disturb my slumbering valet, I placed it so as to throw its rays more fully upon the book.

But the action produced an effect altogether unanticipated. The rays of the numerous candles (for there were many) now fell within a niche of the room which had hitherto been thrown into deep shade by one of the bed-posts. I thus saw in vivid light a picture all unnoticed before. It was the portrait of a young girl just ripening into womanhood. I glanced at the painting hurriedly, and then closed my eyes. Why I did this was not at first apparent even to my own perception. But while my lids remained thus shut, I ran over in my mind my reason for so shutting them. It was an impulsive movement to gain time for thought – to make sure that my vision had not deceived me – to calm and subdue my fancy for a more sober and more certain gaze. In a very few moments I again looked fixedly at the painting.

That I now saw aright I could not and would not doubt; for the first flashing of the candles upon that canvas had seemed to dissipate the dreamy stupor which was stealing over my senses, and to startle me at once into waking life.

The portrait, I have already said, was that of a young girl. It was a mere head and shoulders, done in what is technically termed a *vignette* manner; much in the style of the favorite heads of Sully. The arms, the bosom and even the ends of the radiant hair, melted imperceptibly into the vague yet deep shadow which formed the back-ground of the whole. The frame was oval, richly gilded and filagreed in *Moresque*. As a thing of art nothing could be more admirable than the painting itself. But it could have been neither the execution of the work, nor the immortal beauty of the countenance, which had so suddenly and so vehemently moved me. Least of all, could it have been that my fancy, shaken from its half slumber, had mistaken the head for that of a living person. I saw at once that the peculiarities of the design, of the *vignetting*, and of the frame, must have instantly dispelled such an idea – must have prevented even its momentary entertainment. Thinking earnestly upon these points, I remained, for an hour perhaps, half sitting, half reclining, with my vision riveted upon the portrait. At length, satisfied with the true secret of its effect, I fell back within the bed. I had found the spell of the picture in an absolute *life-likeliness* of expression, which at first startling, finally confounded, subdued and appalled me. With deep and reverent awe I replaced the candelabrum in its former position. The cause of my deep agitation being thus shut from view, I sought eagerly the volume which discussed the paintings and their histories. Turning to the number which designated the oval portrait, I there read the vague and quaint words which follow:

'She was a maiden of rarest beauty, and not more lovely than full of glee. And evil was the hour when she saw, and loved, and wedded the painter. He, passionate, studious, austere, and having already a bride in his Art; she a maiden of rarest beauty, and not more lovely than full of glee: all light and smiles, and frolicsome as the young fawn: loving and cherishing all things: hating only the Art which was her rival: dreading only the pallet and brushes and other untoward instruments which deprived her of the countenance of her lover. It was thus a terrible thing for this lady to hear the painter speak of his desire to portray even his young bride. But she was humble and obedient, and sat meekly for many weeks in the dark high turret-chamber where the light dripped upon the pale canvas only from overhead. But he, the painter, took glory in his work, which went on from hour to hour and from day to day. And he was a passionate, and wild and moody man, who became lost in reveries; so that he *would* not see that the light which fell so ghastily in that lone turret withered the health and the spirits of his bride, who pined visibly to all but him. Yet she smiled on and still on, uncomplainingly, because she saw that the painter, (who had high renown,) took a fervid and burning pleasure in his task, and wrought day and night to depict her who so loved him, yet who grew daily more dispirited and weak. And in sooth some who beheld the portrait spoke of its resemblance in low words, as of a mighty marvel, and a proof not less of the power of the painter than of his deep love for her whom he depicted so surpassingly well. But at length, as the labor drew nearer to its conclusion, there were admitted none into the turret; for the painter had grown wild with the ardor of his work, and turned his eyes from the canvas rarely, even to regard the countenance of his wife. And he *would* not see that the tints which he spread upon the canvas were drawn from the cheeks of her who sat beside him. And when many weeks had passed, and but little remained to do, save one brush upon the mouth and one tint upon the eye, the spirit of the lady again flickered up as the flame within the socket of the lamp. And then the brush was given, and then the tint was placed; and, for one moment, the painter stood entranced before the work which he had wrought; but in the next, while he yet gazed, he grew tremulous and very pallid, and aghast, and crying with a loud voice, "This is indeed Life itself!" turned suddenly to regard his beloved: – *She was dead!*'

(Source: Edgar Allan Poe: *Selected Writings*, Penguin, 1970)

Appendix 2 Dylan Thomas, 'A Refusal to Mourn the Death, by Fire, of a Child in London'

Never until the mankind making
Bird beast and flower
Fathering and all humbling darkness
Tells with silence the last light breaking
And the still hour
Is come of the sea tumbling in harness

And I must enter again the round
Zion of the water bead
And the synagogue of the ear of corn
Shall I let pray the shadow of a sound
Or sow my salt seed
In the least valley of sackcloth to mourn

The majesty and burning of the child's death.
I shall not murder
The mankind of her going with a grave truth
Nor blaspheme down the stations of the breath
With any further
Elegy of innocence and youth.

Deep with the first dead lies London's daughter,
Robed in the long friends,

The grains beyond age, the dark veins of her mother,
Secret by the unmourning water
Of the riding Thames.
After the first death, there is no other.

(Source: *Collected Poems 1934–52*, Dent, 1977)

Appendix 3 William Cowper, 'The Castaway'

Obscurest night involv'd the sky,
    Th' Atlantic billows roar'd,
When such a destin'd wretch as I,
    Wash'd headlong from on board,
Of friends, of hope, of all bereft,
His floating home for ever left.

No braver chief could Albion boast
    Than he with whom he went,
Nor ever ship left Albion's coast,
    With warmer wishes sent.
He lov'd them both, but both in vain,
Nor him beheld, nor her again.

Not long beneath the whelming brine,
    Expert to swim, he lay;
Nor soon he felt his strength decline,
    Or courage die away;
But wag'd with death a lasting strife,
Supported by despair of life.

He shouted: nor his friends had fail'd
    To check the vessel's course,
But so the furious blast prevail'd,
    That, pitiless perforce,
They left their outcast mate behind,
And scudded still before the wind.

Some succour yet they could afford;
    And, such as storms allow,
The cask, the coop, the floated cord,
    Delay'd not to bestow.

But he (they knew) nor ship, nor shore,
Whate'er they gave should visit more.

Nor, cruel as it seem'd, could he
    Their haste himself condemn,
Aware that flight, in such a sea,
    Alone could rescue them;
Yet bitter felt it still to die
Deserted, and his friends so nigh.

He long survives, who lives an hour
    In ocean, self-upheld;
And so long he, with unspent pow'r,
    His destiny repell'd;
And ever, as the minutes flew,
Entreated help, or cried – Adieu!

At length, his transient respite past,
    His comrades, who before
Had heard his voice in ev'ry blast,
    Could catch the sound no more.
For then, by toil subdued, he drank
The stifling wave, and then he sank.

No poet wept him: but the page
    Of narrative sincere,
That tells his name, his worth, his age
    Is wet with Anson's tear.
And tears by bards or heroes shed
Alike immortalize the dead.

I therefore purpose not, or dream,
    Descanting on his fate,
To give the melancholy theme
    A more enduring date:
But misery still delights to trace
Its 'semblance in another's case.

No voice divine the storm allay'd,
    No light propitious shone;

When, snatch'd from all effectual aid,
   We perish'd, each alone:
But I beneath a rougher sea,
And whelm'd in deeper gulphs than he.

(Source: *The Penguin Book of English Romantic Verse*, ed. David
Wright, Penguin, 1973)

Where do we go from here? Further reading

General guides

Bennett, Andrew, and Royle, Nicholas, *An Introduction to Literature, Criticism and Theory* (Routledge, 5th edn, 2016).
Lively and interesting.

Bertens, Hans, *Literary Theory: The Basics* (Routledge, 3rd edn, 2014).
New addition to an interesting series.

Castle, Gregory, *The Literary Theory Handbook* (Wiley-Blackwell, 2013).
Methodical and broad in scope, but more a reference work than a read-through book, as its name implies.

Culler, Jonathan, *Literary Theory: A Very Short Introduction* (Oxford University Press, new edn, 2011).
Useful and lively.

Culler, Jonathan, *The Literary in Theory* (Stanford University Press, 2006).
Discusses the neglect of literature by literary theory – a welcome book from one of the pioneer presenters of theory.

Durant, Alan, and Fabb, Nigel, *Literary Studies in Action* (Routledge, 1990).
Ambitious and innovative, but not always successful. A linguistics approach to literature.

Eagleton, Terry, *Literary Theory: An Introduction* (Blackwell, anniversary edn, 2008).
A re-issue of this pioneering book. The first comprehensive guide to be published. Sometimes entertaining, sometimes difficult, and now in need of updating.

Leitch, Vincent B., *Literary Criticism in the 21st Century* (Bloomsbury, 2014).
A richly informative book which illustrates and asserts the vigorous ongoing health of theory.

Lynn, Steven, *Texts and Contexts: Writing about Literature with Critical Theory* (Longman, 7th edn, 2016).

Very user-friendly and with a strong emphasis on theory as critical practice, but the emphasis on step-by-step help with writing seems excessive to me, since the writing tasks exemplified are so very specific.

Selden, Raman, Widdowson, Peter, and Brooker, Peter, *A Reader's Guide to Contemporary Literary Theory* (Harvester, 6th edn, 2017).

Even-handed, detailed coverage: originally published soon after Eagleton's, and though it lacks his wit, it has the advantage of recent updating.

Tyson, Lois, *Critical Theory Today: A User-Friendly Guide* (Routledge, 3rd edn, 2014).

A good book, though the ploy of applying all the theories to a single text (*The Great Gatsby*) risks set-book fatigue.

Webster, Roger, *Studying Literary Theory: An Introduction* (Arnold, 2nd edn, 1995).

Very brief, but quite often clear where others are not.

Wolfreys, Julian, ed., *Introducing Literary Theories: A Guide and Glossary* (Edinburgh University Press, 2001).

A new and distinctive format: the various contributors use a small 'reservoir' of literary texts for their literary applications – a better idea than using just one text.

Wolfreys, Julian, ed., *New Critical Thinking: Criticism to Come* (Edinburgh University Press, 2017).

A collection which goes 'beyond the standard "isms" ' to 'Thing Theory', Animal Studies, 'Affect Theory', etc.

Reference books

Brooker, Peter, *A Glossary of Literary and Cultural Theory* (3rd edn, Routledge, 2017).

Extremely helpful.

Coyle, Martin, *et al.*, eds, *Encyclopedia of Literature and Criticism* (Routledge, 1990).

A wealth of helpful material.

Cuddon, J. A., and Habib, M. A. R., *The Penguin Dictionary of Literary Terms and Literary Theory* (Penguin, 5th edn, 2014).

Much improved, and the long entries on major critical approaches are well-researched.

Hawthorn, Jeremy, *A Glossary of Contemporary Literary Theory* (Edward Arnold, 4th edn, 2000).

I have found most of these entries very helpful.

Sim, Stuart, and Parker, Noel, *The A to Z Guide to Modern Literary and Cultural Theorists* (Prentice Hall, 1997).

An alphabetical listing of all the major theorists, with a brief essay and a bibliography on each. Consistently useful.

Wales, Katie, *A Dictionary of Stylistics* (Routledge, 3rd edn, 2011).

Impressive in every way and always enlightening.

Wolfreys, Julian, ed., *The Edinburgh Encyclopedia of Modern Criticism and Theory* (Edinburgh University Press, 2002).

A well-organised resource of substantial essays to consult in your library.

General readers

Leitch, Vincent, B., ed., *The Norton Anthology of Theory and Criticism* (Norton, 2nd edn, 2011).

Coverage is from earliest times to the present, but this volume is eight times the length of the pioneer theory readers of the 1980s.

Lodge, David, and Wood Nigel, eds, *Modern Criticism and Theory: A Reader* (Longman, 3rd edn, 2008).

An excellent source of material. Will give initial 'hands-on' experience of the writings of many of the major figures. Sensible length.

Newton, K. M., ed., *Theory into Practice* (Macmillan, 1992).

A strong collection of pieces on applied theory.

Newton, K. M., ed., *Twentieth Century Literary Theory: A Reader* (Palgrave, 2nd edn, 1997).

Useful and wide-ranging. A valuable non-elephantine reader.

Rice, Philip, and Waugh, Patricia, eds, *Modern Literary Theory: A Reader* (Arnold, 4th edn, 2001).

Another excellent source. Still a sensible length.

Rivkin, Julie, and Ryan, Michael, eds, *Literary Theory: An Anthology* (Wiley-Blackwell, 3rd edn, 2017).

Popular, but too big for its purpose, and not enough of the theory it contains is literary. But two 'Theory in Practice' essays have now been added to each of the ten sections – a very big improvement.

Selden, Raman, *The Theory of Criticism from Plato to the Present: A Reader* (Longman, 1988).

Comprehensive time-span, but the brevity of some of the extracts is irritating, and the groupings are sometimes eccentric.

Walder, Dennis, *Literature in the Modern World: Critical Essays and Documents* (Oxford University Press, 2nd edn, 2004).

A very useful collection of important documents and statements, with excellent editorial linking.

Waugh, Patricia, ed., *Literary Theory and Criticism: An Oxford Guide* (Oxford University Press, 2006).

A collection of essays written especially for a student readership, so this is a reader with a difference. Four sections, of which the last, 'Futures and retrospects', is particularly interesting.

Applying critical theory: twelve early examples

Dollimore, Jonathan, and Sinfield, Alan, eds, *Political Shakespeare: New Essays in Cultural Materialism* (Manchester University Press, 2nd edn, 1994).

Much useful material. See, for example, chapter two 'Invisible bullets: Renaissance authority and its subversion, *Henry IV* and *Henry V*', Stephen Greenblatt. This is the classic new historicist essay, much reprinted. Also chapter five 'The patriarchal bard: feminist criticism and Shakespeare: *King Lear* and *Measure for Measure*'.

Easthope, Antony, ed., *Contemporary Poetry Meets Modern Theory* (Harvester, 1991).

Chapter five: 'Tony Harrison's languages' by Rick Rylance. Another example of a 'theoreticised' form of practical criticism. The approach is, roughly, 'culturalist' – it places the poetry within its contemporary setting using relevant documents, social data, etc. ('Culturalist' readings would be called 'new historicist' if the material were not contemporary.)

Gilbert, Sandra, and Gubar, Susan, *The Madwoman in the Attic: The Woman Writer and the Nineteenth Century Literary Imagination* (Yale University Press, 1979).

Chapters on Austen, the Brontës, George Eliot, etc.

Jacobus, Mary, *Reading Woman: Essays in Feminist Criticism* (Methuen, 1986).

Chapters on *Villette*, *The Mill on the Floss* and Freud's case studies (see 'Dora and the Pregnant Madonna').

Kurzweil, Edith, *Literature and Psychoanalysis* (Columbia University Press, 1983).

Chapter fifteen is a psychoanalytic reading of Henry James's extraordinary tale 'The Jolly Corner'. Chapter twenty is by William Empson, 'Alice in Wonderland – The Child as Swain', from his 1935 book *Some Versions of Pastoral*.

Lodge, David, *After Bakhtin: Essays on Fiction and Criticism* (Routledge, 1990).

Chapter two, 'Mimesis and diegesis in modern fiction', examines different ways of presenting material in a novel, using Fay Weldon, George Eliot, James Joyce, etc., as examples (structuralism). Chapter five, 'Dialogue in the modern novel', examines different ways of presenting dialogue, using Evelyn Waugh as the main example (linguistics).

Machin, Richard, and Norris, Christopher, eds, *Post-structuralist Readings of English Poetry* (Cambridge University Press, 1987).

Chapters on Donne, Milton's 'Blindness' sonnet, Gray's 'Elegy', Coleridge's 'Ancient Mariner', and so on. Not always easy reading, but some good things here. Catherine Belsey's essay on Marvell's 'To his Coy Mistress' is actually a good example of the new historicist approach to literature.

Muller, John P., and Richardson, William J., eds, *The Purloined Poe: Lacan, Derrida, and Psychoanalytic Reading* (Johns Hopkins University Press, 1988).

This collection of essays is about Poe's tale 'The Purloined Letter', which excited much attention in the late 1980s from critical theorists. But see also chapter six (pp. 101–32) extracted from Marie Bonaparte's 1930s book on Poe, which subjects him to a 'straight' Freudian psychoanalytic approach.

Murray, David, ed., *Literary Theory and Poetry: Extending the Canon* (Batsford, 1989).

Chapter three: 'The imperfect librarian: text and discourse in *The Waste Land* and *Four Quartets*'. Chapter four: 'Frames of reference: the reception of, and response to, three women poets' (Dickinson, Plath, Moore). These two chapters are good examples of 'theoreticised' practical criticism. They make use of techniques derived from feminism, deconstruction, and (in the latter case) psychoanalysis.

Selden, Raman, *Practising Theory and Reading Literature: An Introduction* (Harvester, 1989).

Twenty-four short chapters give examples of all the main theories in practice – structuralism, post-structuralism, Marxism, feminism, and so on. Useful items but often excessively brief.

Stubbs, Patricia, *Women and Fiction: Feminism and the Novel, 1880–1920* (Harvester, 1979).

Essays on Hardy, Forster, Lawrence, Woolf, etc.

Tallack, Douglas, ed., *Literary Theory at Work: Three Texts* (Batsford, 1987).

Structuralism, Marxism, feminism, psychoanalysis, and deconstruction applied to three stories: Conrad's *Heart of Darkness*, Henry James's 'In the Cage', and D. H. Lawrence's 'St Mawr'.

Against theory

Burgess, Catherine, *Challenging Theory: Discipline after Deconstruction* (Ashgate, 1999)

A thoughtful book about the effects of theory on the teaching of the Humanities.

Ellis, John M., *Against Deconstruction* (Princeton University Press, 1989).

A well-argued book, temperate rather than belligerent in tone, and with a firm focus throughout on the effects of literary theory on the practice of reading literature.

Jackson, Leonard, *The Poverty of Structuralism: Literature and Structuralist Theory* (Longman, 1991).

Mainly on foundational errors in the underlying linguistics and philosophy of structuralism; has rather less on the consequences of structuralist theory for literary-critical practice.

Lerner, Laurence, ed., *Reconstructing Literature* (Blackwell, 1983).

See chapters one and five by Cedric Watts. A brusque attack on theory, but mainly about its philosophical shortcomings.

Patai, Daphne, and Corral, Will H., *Theory's Empire: An Anthology of Dissent* (Columbia University Press, 2005).

An anti-theory reader consisting of around fifty essays, mainly from the 1980s and 1990s: some lively and classic pieces from eminent writers, but like most readers, it is counter-productively over-sized.

Paulin, Tom, *Ireland and the English Crisis* (Bloodaxe, 1984).

See pp. 148–54, 'English Now', which was originally a hostile review in the *London Review of Books* of *Re-Reading English*, ed. Peter Widdowson, an influential 'theory' book. The piece provoked a year of angry correspondence in the journal under the heading 'Critics at War'.

Tallis, Raymond, *Not Saussure: A Critique of Post-Saussurean Literary Theory* (Macmillan, 1988).

A vigorous critique of the use of Saussure's ideas by structuralists and post-structuralists.

Tallis, Raymond, *Enemies of Hope* (Palgrave, 1999).

A general denbunking of 'Kulturkritik' and 'hysterical humanism' by this always lively writer.

Washington, Peter, *Fraud: Literary Theory and the End of English* (Fontana, 1989).

Mainly concerned with attacking the linking of radical critical theory and radical politics.

Index